Pivot of China

Harvard East Asian Monograph Series 466

Pivot of China

Spatial Politics and Inequality in Modern Zhengzhou

Mark Baker

Published by the Harvard University Asia Center
Distributed by Harvard University Press
Cambridge (Massachusetts) and London 2024

Published by the Harvard University Asia Center, Cambridge, MA 02138

The Harvard University Asia Center publishes a monograph series and, in coordination with the Fairbank Center for Chinese Studies, the Korea Institute, the Reischauer Institute of Japanese Studies, and other faculties and institutes, administers research projects designed to further scholarly understanding of China, Japan, Vietnam, Korea, and other Asian countries. The Center also sponsors projects addressing multidisciplinary and regional issues in Asia.

Publication of this book was partially underwritten by the Mr. and Mrs. Stephen C. M. King Publishing and Communications Fund, established by Stephen C. M. King to further the cause of international understanding and cooperation, especially between China and the United States, by enhancing cross-cultural education and the exchange of ideas across national boundaries through publications of the Harvard University Asia Center.

Library of Congress Cataloging-in-Publication Data

Names: Baker, Mark, 1986- author.
Title: Pivot of China : spatial politics and inequality in modern Zhengzhou
    / Mark Baker.
Other titles: Spatial politics and inequality in modern Zhengzhou |
    Harvard East Asian monographs ; 466.
Description: Cambridge (Massachusetts) : Harvard University Asia Center,
    2024. | Series: Harvard East Asian Monograph series ; 466 | Includes
    bibliographical references and index.
Identifiers: LCCN 2023044124 | ISBN 9780674293816 (hardcover)
Subjects: LCSH: Railroads--China--Henan Sheng--History--20th century. |
    Urbanization--China--Henan Sheng--History--20th century. | Regional
    disparities--China--History--20th century. | Regional
    disparities--China--History--21st century. | Zhengzhou
    (China)--History--20th century. | Zhengzhou (China)--History--21st
    century. | Zhengzhou (China)--Historical geography. | Zhengzhou
    (China)--Economic conditions--20th century. | Zhengzhou
    (China)--Economic conditions--21st century.
Classification: LCC DS797.44.Z444 B35 2024 | DDC 951/.18--dc23/eng/20240130
LC record available at https://lccn.loc.gov/2023044124

Index by Roger C. Bennett

♾ Printed on acid-free paper
Printed in the United States of America

For my family,
especially in memory of
Charles and Stuart

CONTENTS

Contents

MAPS, FIGURES, AND TABLE

Maps

Figures

Table

ACKNOWLEDGMENTS

It is a pleasure to acknowledge some of the debts sustained in the writing of this book. My apologies for any omissions. I would like to start by thanking my doctoral advisor, Peter Perdue, who was willing to let me off the leash to veer off in an unexpected direction and whose depth and breadth of knowledge allowed him to offer both precise suggestions and ways to think bigger. I was extremely lucky to have a supportive and rigorous dissertation committee in the shape of Daniel Botsman, Valerie Hansen, and Denise Ho. Their suggestions made me a much better historian and writer. The project would not have been possible without the financial support of the American Council of Learned Societies, the Henry Luce Foundation, the MacMillan Center for International and Area Studies, the Yale University Council on East Asian Studies, and Balliol College, Oxford.

My time as a visiting scholar in Zhengzhou and Kaifeng was hugely productive and enjoyable. I owe many thanks to the College of History at Zhengzhou University for their support, both formal and informal. Special thanks are due to Bo Hou, Xingguang Wang, Xiaopeng Xie, and, in Kaifeng, Zhixing Ge. Professor Hou is the finest friend and colleague one could hope to find in a strange city, and Professor Wang went above and beyond to secure archival access. Many thanks to the staff at Henan Provincial Archives, Zhengzhou Municipal Archives, Henan Provincial Library, Zhengzhou University Library, Kaifeng Municipal Library, Henan University Library Ancient Books and Republican Reading Room, and the National Library of China, who were as helpful as possible within the limits of source survival and what overseas researchers are permitted to see. I also owe a debt to the many local historians of Zhengzhou, both academic and nonacademic, who have made possible the study of the city's past. I have not met them in person, but the contributions of Zhu Junxian and Zhao Fuhai in particular will be clear in the chapters that follow. The COVID-19 pandemic stymied my plans to return to Zhengzhou to conduct further research, so special thanks are due to all the staff at CNEbuys (especially Alice Li) for their assistance in sending over materials.

I have been very fortunate to have wonderful colleagues in New Haven, Zhengzhou, Lincoln, Oxford, and the community of scholars beyond who have shaped this book in all sorts of ways, from giving writing advice and answering factual queries to tracking down sources and making sure I was not too swamped to write. Many thanks to Jennifer Altehenger, Avital Avina, James Belich, Tom Bishop, Jennifer Bond, Thomas Burnham, Aoife Cantrill, Cheow Thia Chan, Yuan Chen, Jim Cheshire, Annping Chin, Minh Chung, Martin Conway, Chris Courtenay, Edmund Downie, Fabian Drixler, Kathryn Edgerton-Tarpley, Joseph Esherick, Laura Fernández-González, Kevin Fogg, John-Paul Ghobrial, Helen Gittos, Aaron Glasserman, Randy Green, James Greenhalgh, Matthew Grimley, Steven Gunn, Pak Hei Hao, Henrietta Harrison, Fei Huang, Faisal Husain, Takako Inada, Marc Jaffré, Koh Choon Hwee, Emmett Kaplan, Simon Lam, Joseph Lawson, Ji Li, Tang Li, Wankun Li, Yiwen Li, Toby Lincoln, Amy Livingstone, Tommy Yui Chim Lo, Helena Lopes, Xiqi Lu, Alex Lui, Kathi Matsuura, Michael Meng, Tommaso Milani, William Minter, Rana Mitter, Giustina Monti, Micah Muscolino, Chinami Oka, Adam Page, Diane Ranyard, Leon Rocha, Peter Rowe, Leah Russell, Qin Shao, Simon Skinner, the late Jonathan Spence, Kristin Stapleton, Weihan Sun, Mamtimyn Sunuodula, Mitchell Tan, Ying Jia Tan, Michael Taylor, Lucas Tse, Brian Turner, Natalya Vince, Mengxiao Wang, Shenshen Wang, Luke Waring, Kristy Warren, the late Ann Waswo, Róisín Watson, Emily Whewell, Andrew Womack, Beau Woodbury, Pengfei Wu, Woody Wu, Michael Wuk, Youli Xu, Yongle Xue, Faizah Zakaria, Huasha Zhang, and Jiushun Zhang. Many thanks to Toby, Faizah, Yiwen, and Chris for commenting on my dissertation. I would like to offer special thanks to two people: first, to Nicholas Santascoy, who is a wonderful friend and writing partner; and second, to Gordon Barrett, who has provided encouragement, advice, and support in huge quantities.

I wrote this book in Birmingham, England, which sometimes reminds me of Zhengzhou: both are somewhat maligned provincial cities; both are shaped by layers of migration for industrial work; and both are core regional centers but culturally distant from nationally dominant global cities. This is not a comparison I sustain in this book (readers of Richard Vinen's *Second City* can make up their own mind), but Birmingham and Zhengzhou have both been fascinating places to think about urban history. In Birmingham, special thanks to Mel Abraham and Jerry Orne for all their excellent company and intellectual stimulation.

I have also been very fortunate to have two wonderful peer reviewers at the Harvard University Asia Center. Their careful reading and precise interventions have improved this book immeasurably, especially in conceptual clarity and accessibility to a wider audience. The errors and imprecisions that remain are mine alone. The role of the peer reviewers was especially important because I had not given any of the manuscript to colleagues to read. I hope any early career colleagues reading this are more successful than I was in overcoming imposter syndrome and early career crises of confidence to distribute materials more widely. Extra thanks to Martin Conway for reading the book proposal and to John-Paul Ghobrial for prising an early draft of the introduction from my reticent clutches. Their incisive comments were extremely helpful.

Our daughter Felicity never really believed that I was writing a book. She told me several times, "Daddy, a book can't just be on a laptop." Whether Felicity was right is up for debate, but the Microsoft Word documents only became a book with the help of numerous individuals. At Harvard University Asia Center, many thanks are due to Bob Graham for his support for the project and for tirelessly answering endless queries. Kristen Wanner and especially Qin Higley did a terrific job seeing the manuscript through to publication. Susan Stone's copy-edits were efficient, thorough, and much appreciated. Jogu Gopinath did a wonderful job with the maps, patiently accommodating my many amendments. For the sourcing and use of photographs, thank you to Bo Hou, Leonardo Ramondetti, Caroline McMahon and the Murray-McMahon family, the Z. Smith Reynolds Library at Wake Forest University (especially Rebecca Petersen May), and the American Geographical Society Library at the University of Wisconsin-Milwaukee (especially Susan Peschel).

This book is dedicated to my family, in memory of my father and grandfather and in thanks for our two new(ish) arrivals. Thank you to my sister Helen and my mother Elizabeth for their extraordinary love and support. And most of all thank you to Ruth. "Acknowledgment" is inadequate to convey eternal gratitude, but I would like to acknowledge everything you have given to me and this project, in time, mental load, and emotional labor.

WEIGHTS, MEASURES, AND CONVENTIONS

jin: a weight equivalent to either 500 grams (in official post-1930 weights) or almost 600 grams (in older and customary usage).

li: a measure of distance equivalent to about one-third of a mile or half a kilometer.

mu: a measure of area approximately equivalent to one-sixth of an acre or 600 square meters.

shidan: a weight equivalent to 50 kilograms. *Shidan* as a measure of volume is not used in this book.

"tons" refers to metric tons throughout.

Pinyin is used throughout the book, apart from in a very few direct quotations and the familiar exceptions of Sun Yat-sen and Chiang Kai-shek. Chinese characters for proper nouns can be found in the index of the book.

Simplified Chinese or traditional Chinese is used in the bibliography, depending on the language each reference was originally published in. Traditional Chinese is used in the index.

Several terms are used anachronistically to avoid confusion: for example, "Beijing" rather than "Beiping" even during 1928–1949. I therefore refer to the Beijing–Hankou railway as the "Jing–Han Railroad" throughout. The east–west line running through Zhengzhou was known by various names, but I refer to it consistently as the "Long–Hai Railroad."

Introduction

Spatial Politics in Modern China

Catching the slow train eastwards out of Zhengzhou is an extraordinary visual lesson in China's changing society and economy. From the bustling, narrow streets around the old railroad station, the train snakes around the urban core of Zhengzhou before picking up speed through the towering apartments of the southeastern suburbs. From the left-hand window, the passenger looks out toward Zhengzhou's new eastern district (Zhengdong xinqu), complete with eye-catching financial district and vast high-speed rail station. To the right lies the 1990s Economic and Technological Development District; beyond that is the Airport Economy Zone of the 2010s, flagship of China's wave of inland manufacturing and production site for around half of the world's iPhones. The landscape changes again as the train enters neighboring Zhongmu County, into a setting that defies neat categories of rural or urban. Surviving pockets of agriculture and polytunnels of intensive fruit and vegetable production jostle for space with industrial estates, warehouses, theme parks, exhibition centers, and new housing developments. The rubble of former villages lies under netting. This fast-changing landscape is part of the Central Plains City Cluster (Zhongyuan chengshiqun), the beating economic heart of China's north-central Henan Province. What is perhaps most remarkable is that this vast city conglomeration is only a small part of China's twenty-first-century urban transformation.

Almost a century ago, the journalist Wu Shixun made the same journey but saw a very different world. Zhengzhou in the 1920s was already an important railroad junction and commercial city, boasting a growing population of almost one hundred thousand (map 0.1). Wu's account of the busy lanes around the railroad station suggests that he would recognize

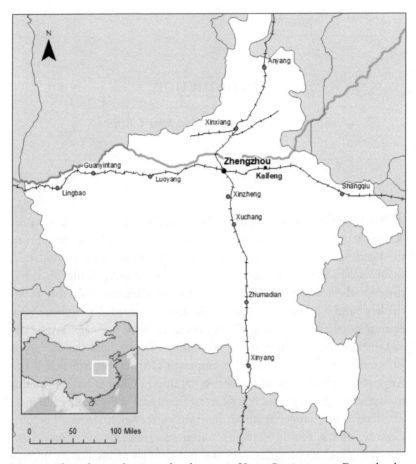

MAP 0.1. Zhengzhou and major railroad towns in Henan Province, 1934. Drawn by the author using OpenStreetMap data, adapting "Henan jingnei tielu gaikuang shiyitu" [Sketch map of the railroads within Henan's border] from Henan sheng difang shizhi bianzuan weiyuanhui, ed., *Henan sheng zhi*, vol. 37: *Tielu jiaotong zhi* [Henan provincial gazetteer, vol. 37: Rail transport gazetteer], unpaginated front maps.

something of the atmosphere in those same streets today. But in Wu's day the largest city and provincial capital of Henan was not Zhengzhou but Kaifeng, 60 kilometers to the east; today Zhengzhou is in every respect the dominant regional powerhouse, and its population of almost eight million in the city proper is five times that of urban Kaifeng. Pulling out of Zhengzhou by train, Wu passed almost immediately into a rural landscape of walled villages, grain fields, and fruit orchards. This was a world conditioned by local ecology, as Wu saw in the areas of marginal land just east of Zhengzhou: "Every time the wind blows, the sand forms into undulating lumps, and hollows form. . . . There is so little vegetation that there is no protection against drifting sand, and it remains a wasteland. Production is low, and villages are few."[1]

Much has changed, but, whether in the 1920s or in the 2020s, spatial questions are key to understanding Zhengzhou and its surroundings: What is the city, and where are its boundaries? How easy is it for people to cross those boundaries? How does urban growth affect nearby rural areas? What is the role of the city in the region? Why has Zhengzhou boomed while other nearby cities have stagnated? These would be profoundly political questions anywhere in the world. But they are perhaps especially significant in China, where since the late nineteenth century the state has practiced a distinct form of spatial politics.

By "spatial politics" I refer to the role of the state in exacerbating or diminishing spatial inequality. "Spatial inequality" refers to the unequal distribution of resources across space, especially income, wealth, social capital, opportunities, and access to services. These inequalities operate at multiple scales, including between neighborhoods, cities, and regions, as well as between rural and urban areas. They are in part a reflection of other inequalities, particularly of class and, in many parts of the world, race and ethnicity. But, following Doreen Massey, spatial difference is not simply the outcome of other social processes and inequalities but "has causal effectivity"—in other words, that space itself "makes a difference to how society works."[2] This insight may have liberatory implications for Massey—"the spatial is integral to the production of history, and thus to the possibility of politics"[3]—but is also key to understanding inequality. For Massey, spatial difference both intersects with and exacerbates other differences, including of class, ethnicity, gender, age, and disability, to produce inequalities. To put it most simply, the fate of individuals depends on *where* they are as well as who they are.

It is, of course, difficult to disentangle the extent to which space is an independent variable in producing inequality as opposed to a reflection of other social differences. But, as Edward Soja points out, inequality is

1. Wu Shixun, *Henan*, 71–72.
2. Massey, "Politics and Space/Time," 70–71.
3. Massey, "Politics and Space/Time," 84.

most damaging when spatial and social differences reinforce each other, which can produce negative spirals concentrating poverty in particular places.[4] A global study by economists Ravi Kanbur and Anthony Venables estimates that, depending on the scale and society under investigation, up to a quarter or a third of income inequality is accounted for by location alone, that is, without taking into account any other household characteristics. Strikingly, Kanbur and Venables attribute most of this power of space to inequalities of infrastructure and public services rather than the direct influence of physical geography.[5] This means that spatial strategies of the state can markedly worsen or improve these inequalities, either deliberately or as a byproduct of other policies. This is spatial politics.

In China, the effects of spatial politics are most obvious in the period of "high Maoism," when collectivization and a strict household registration (*hukou*) system enshrined rural-urban difference, forcibly extracting agricultural surpluses for the industrial sector. Chapter 5 of this book discusses this process in detail, including China's most devastating episode of spatial inequality, the Great Leap Forward famine (1959–1961). However, this book argues that this disaster was not simply an anomaly but that China's entire twentieth century was shaped by a politics that exacerbated spatial inequality, backing "winners" for economic growth and concentrating rather than dispersing resources. This pattern runs from the patchy modernization schemes of the late Qing and Republican periods, through the inequalities of wartime strategy against Japan (1937–1945) and China's socialist period, down to Deng Xiaoping's "let some people *and some regions* get rich first" (*keyi xian fu qilai*) doctrine of China's reform decades.

Zhengzhou: Pivot of China

China's spatial politics can be studied in various settings, from the great cities of the coast to the ethnospatial questions of frontier regions. This book instead examines how space and power have intersected in and around an "ordinary" inland city. A 2010 pop song by Li Zhi (b. 1978) captures something of Zhengzhou's place in the national imagination:

4. Soja, "Socio-Spatial Dialectic."
5. Kanbur and Venables, "Spatial Inequality and Development," 5–10. Note that this study does not assign a quantitative causality to space.

an anonymous city that one might pass through on the train but that only the most whimsical would want to visit:

> I don't know much about Zhengzhou, but I did go there for
>   love,
> How many times have I been through this city on the train,
>   alone and quietly thinking of her?
> She said she liked Zhengzhou's sunlight in winter and the
>   smell of coal stoves that floats in its alleyways.[6]

Li's lyrics point to the first reason why Zhengzhou can be understood as the "pivot of China": its very ordinariness. There was the same sense of a nondescript inland city in the journalism of the 1940s as in the pop music of the 2000s, with one visitor remarking that "if you brought the scenery of Guilin, the imperial palace of Beijing, and even the modern girls of Shanghai to Zhengzhou, it still couldn't make people like it (*ye bujiande shi ren ke'ai*)."[7] Although Jennifer Robinson rightly clarifies that "all cities are best understood as 'ordinary,'" Zhengzhou for most of its modern history was the kind of medium-sized, inland city that is still underexamined in global and Chinese urban studies, a city nationally peripheral but at a regional core.[8] Zhengzhou is now the capital and largest city of Henan Province, which for one historian of the Ming dynasty "can serve, better than any other province, as a microcosm of all of China."[9] This statement may not quite apply in the modern period—Henan's twentieth-century history is a little too bleak to be typical—but Zhengzhou brings a new focus to the cities of what might be called "Middle China," the band of inland provinces running from Shanxi through Henan, inland Shandong, most of Anhui and Hubei to lowland Jiangxi and Hunan. "Middle China" has mostly been overlooked by historians in recent decades at the expense of China's coastal and western regions. This is especially true of its cities, which, with

6. Li Zhi, "Guanyu Zhengzhou de jiyi" [Memories of Zhengzhou], track 3 on album *Nihao, Zhengzhou*, September 2010, Quanqiu changpian studio, lyrics at https://mojim.com/cny110257x18x7.htm.

7. Fan Shiqin, "Mantan Zhengzhou," 15.

8. Robinson, *Ordinary Cities*, 1. The term "modern" is used here to refer to the period after Zhengzhou was connected by railroad, that is, it began the shift from connections based on human and animal power to a transport system partly based on the burning of fossil fuels.

9. Des Forges, *Cultural Centrality and Political Change*, xiv.

the exception of the atypical river port of Wuhan, have hardly been examined in English since David Buck's 1978 study of Jinan.[10] Yet this area is the very heart of China, where the grand projects of its modern history have faced their sternest tests—and sometimes failed: Western economic penetration, Nationalist Party (Guomindang/Kuomintang, GMD/KMT) modernization, Japanese occupation, the socialist planned economy, market reform, and twenty-first-century globalization. The regional cities of "Middle China" were pivotal to these projects. In the early twentieth century, they were the key pivots connecting inland agricultural China and the semicolonial urban China of the treaty ports. Under the People's Republic, many of these cities became flagships of the planned economy and efforts to industrialize inland China. In recent decades, China's central government has used these regional cities as pivots to attract investment and kickstart economic takeoff in sluggish provincial economies.

In parallel to its ordinariness as an inland regional city, Zhengzhou is also the "pivot of China" in a second, more specific, sense. In 1906–1907, Zhengzhou became a major railroad junction, almost by chance, when China's new north–south and east–west lines crossed here (see map 0.1). Zhengzhou became the hub of inland China's economic networks, the key link between north and south, and a gateway to the northwest. This book examines the short- and long-term consequences of this small town becoming the focal point of China's railroads. A walled town of a few thousand inhabitants was transformed into a bustling commercial city. In the mid-twentieth century, Zhengzhou's residents suffered grievously from the city's strategic importance during the Second World War in China (1937–1945) and the Chinese Civil War (1946–1949). After the establishment of the People's Republic of China (PRC) in 1949, Zhengzhou became something of a success story within the planned economy and in 1954 replaced Kaifeng as capital of Henan Province. Yet the Mao era did not bring an end to spatial inequalities, and, although Zhengzhou boomed, rural Henan Province was one of the epicenters of famine during the Great Leap Forward. The retreat from the Great Leap Forward

10. David Buck, *Urban Change*; for an exception on Changsha, see Hudson, "River Sands/Urban Spaces." Note also Luman Wang's recent work on an earlier period, which conceptualizes Shanxi Province as both heartland and hinterland. See Luman Wang, *Chinese Hinterland Capitalism*.

FIGURE O.I. Zhengdong xinqu CBD (Central Business District), 2022. Photograph by Hou Bo, reproduced with permission.

was also Zhengzhou's slide into late Mao-era obscurity. The reform era after 1978 saw Zhengzhou reemerge as a commercial center but against a backdrop of complex and unequal spatial politics, including industrial decline, ongoing rural-urban inequality, and infrastructural growing pains. In the present century, the city has undergone an economic takeoff dramatic even by Chinese standards and been catapulted into the first rank as one of China's nine "National Central Cities" (Guojia zhongxin chengshi) (fig. O.I).

Three Histories: Edge, Hinterland, Region

The physical and social fabric of Zhengzhou has therefore been transformed, destroyed, and rebuilt several times in its modern history. Yet these urban displacements cannot simply be understood from within the city; they are also the product of Zhengzhou's multiple spatial relationships. Rather than writing a history of the city's core, this book takes the "outward-facing" approach to urban history identified by Dai Yifeng.[11] It focuses on three sites: Zhengzhou's urban edge, its nearby villages, and its role in the wider region of north-central China.

Zhengzhou's urban edge is understood here as the zone where the commerce, industry, housing, and leisure of the city gave way to or overlapped with agriculture. Contemporary Chinese has similar terms, such

11. Dai Yifeng, "Chengshi shi yanjiu de liangzhong shiye."

as the rather academic-sounding *chengshi bianyuan* (city fringe) and *chengxiang jiehebu* (urban-rural interface), though older sources on Zhengzhou usually refer to *jinjiao*, "near suburbs."[12] As anthropologist Erik Harms shows, the fringes of cities are important social spaces in their own right as well as a useful way to escape idealized categories of rural and urban.[13] They are also important sites for investigating social and political change, as in Daniel Abramson's definition of the periurban as "an edge or zone between city and countryside where disorder expresses society's rapid transformation."[14] In the twenty-first century, China's urban edges have become some of the fastest changing and most contested spaces in the world, with urban expansion and land speculation becoming drivers of economic growth and vital sources of local state revenue, in Zhengzhou as elsewhere. What You-tien Hsing calls this "deterritorialization" of the rural has brought multisided struggles over land rights, compensation packages, and the proceeds of growth.[15] This is high-stakes spatial politics, but as the example of Zhengzhou shows, it is only the latest manifestation of a larger pattern: although it has received little specific attention from historians, the urban edge has been a site of exclusion and conflict as well as opportunity throughout China's modern history.[16]

At the dawn of the twentieth century, Zhengzhou was sharply bounded by a defensive wall, but with the coming of the railroad a few years later, the city burst beyond that boundary. Over the coming decades, the residents and rulers of Zhengzhou used the urban edge for a wide range of purposes: for activities relating to agriculture such as vegetable gardens and livestock grazing; as a site for things deemed unsuitable for the city proper, including rubbish dumps, graveyards, power plants, and the informal housing of migrants; for the political display of war memorials, military training sites, and "model" neighborhoods; for

---

12. On terminology for the urban periphery in Chinese, see Ren, "Lost in Translation."

13. Harms, *Saigon's Edge*, esp. 5–11.

14. Abramson, "Periurbanization," 157.

15. Hsing, *Great Urban Transformation*, esp. 14–18 and 181–207.

16. For an exception, see Stapleton, "Outside the Gates." Beyond China, the urban edge in modernity has received recent attention from historians. See Labbé, *Land Politics and Livelihoods*; Logan, *In the Suburbs of History*; Poling, *Germany's Urban Frontiers*. For a now-classic study, see Merriman, *Margins of City Life*.

the rural-urban exchange of wholesale markets and abattoirs; as well as for real estate speculation, railroad marshaling yards, warehouses, and successive generations of factories.

But is there any pattern among these sundry uses of Zhengzhou's peripheral land? And do they reveal anything about China's spatial politics? First, in the twentieth century, Zhengzhou's urban edge moved from the sharp boundary of the city wall to a much more blurred zone of transition—although at times of crisis, such as China's midcentury wars and the Great Leap Forward, there was still potential for a hard, militarized urban boundary to emerge. Second, the urban edge underlines the importance of connectivity for the city. This zone was where many rural-urban exchanges occurred and where the physical sinews of transport connections were located, from cart yards and railway depots to the airport infrastructure of today. Third, the chapters of this book show that the urban edge has been the site for many of Zhengzhou's most ambitious *and* most marginal activities. It is where successive governments have conducted flagship projects of urban planning, but it is also where systems of removal and exclusion have consigned the city's unwanted objects and people.

If Zhengzhou's edge throws up issues of who or what belongs in the city, moving outwards into nearby villages raises important questions of rural-urban relations across modern history: How did urban growth affect Zhengzhou's hinterland? Did the proximity of the city benefit or damage this zone? How and when did urban infrastructures extend into rural areas? And what happened to villages swallowed up by Zhengzhou's successive waves of expansion?

This book focuses on Zhengzhou's nearby hinterland, the zone of 15 to 25 kilometer radius from the downtown that was always administered from the city. In the Republican period, this zone was under the jurisdiction of Zheng County (see map 1.3) and was usually called the *sixiang* (surrounding countryside). In 1953 Zheng County was abolished and absorbed into the Zhengzhou's municipal government as the Jiaoqu, "Suburban District." For most of the twentieth century—before the widespread use of mechanized transport in the 1980s and 1990s—this nearby hinterland is best understood as two distinct zones. The very closest villages made up what I call Zhengzhou's "diurnal hinterland," the area within an easy journey for daily marketing or labor, sometimes called *jiaowai* (the outskirts, outside the urban suburbs) in older sources. This diurnal hinterland broadly corresponds with Eugene Van Cleef's use of the German borrowing "Umland": the zone where economic activities are "essentially one with those of the primary center," since there were no markets closer than the city itself.[17] Farther out, villages had less daily exchange with the city but were still closely tied to its economic and political orbit.

This book uses Zhengzhou's nearby hinterland to explore rural-urban relations in action across the twentieth century.[18] It finds a deeply ambivalent relationship, with the impulse to disperse urban resources and connect city and nearby countryside contrasted with countervailing forces of disconnection and the concentration of resources in the city.

On the one hand, Zhengzhou's nearby hinterland usually benefited from proximity to the city, at least relative to rural areas elsewhere in impoverished Henan Province. Laborers, animals, and rural products (especially fruit and vegetables) crossed into the city on a daily basis. Except where disrupted by war or collectivized agriculture, the quickening pace of trade brought consumer goods from the city to the nearby hinterland. Since the 1920s, local governments have tried to tackle problems of rural poverty, and villages around Zhengzhou have been important testing grounds for these efforts and investments. Under the collective rural economy, Zhengzhou's suburban communes enjoyed a higher standard of living than most rural communes and escaped relatively lightly during the Great Leap Forward famine. In the reform era, township and village enterprises (TVEs) close to Zhengzhou used connections with urban factories to develop production facilities, while villagers also benefited from the rental opportunities and compensation payments of urban expansion.

On the other hand, these positive connections cannot hide the

17. Van Cleef, "Hinterland and Umland." The best early twentieth-century map of Zheng County shows twenty-four villages within 3 kilometers of the city. See Liu Ruilin, *Zheng xian zhi*, front maps, unpaginated.

18. Studies of rural-urban relations in modern China include economic, political, and discursive discussions. Key historical studies include Cohen, "Cultural and Political Inventions"; essays in Faure and Liu, *Town and Country*; Wei Yingtao, *Jindai Changjiang shangyou chengxiang guanxi*; Jeremy Brown, *City Versus Countryside*; Day, *Peasant in Postsocialist China*; Lincoln, *Urbanizing China*.

countervailing moments of disconnection and inequality between Zhengzhou and its nearby villages. This zone around the city may have benefited relative to other rural areas, but it was also on the front line of rural-urban difference. There is little sign that rural Zheng County was socially or economically transformed during the Republican period by its proximity to a major railroad junction. Indeed, until the spread of motor transport in the last decades of the twentieth century, much of the county—nearby as the crow flies—was rather remote from the city. Rapid rail connection to more distant points left the rural hinterland relatively farther from the city in terms of journey time. During times of war, proximity to a strategic junction city brought heavy burdens of extraction and militarization to Zhengzhou's nearby villages. Rural areas could also be politically and socially cut off from the city. At times, urban authorities have limited the right of rural people to enter the city for trade, an issue that was still a flashpoint of protest in the twenty-first century. In both the Republican era and the People's Republic, underlying visions of urban-first modernization weakened efforts to bring infrastructure, capital, and expertise to rural areas. Zhengzhou's hinterland has been given little place in the imagining of the urban future, with several iterations of city planning from the 1920s onwards ignoring the rural surroundings of the city. As this book explores, during Henan's periods of famine in 1928–1930, 1942–1943, and 1959–1961, various state, market, and charitable mechanisms to shift grain from the city to the nearby countryside did not prevent rural starvation. Indeed, by the time of the 1959–1961 Great Leap famine, land and people had been strictly divided into rural and urban categories, leaving villagers close to Zhengzhou frozen out of the nearby city.

The Chinese state in the twenty-first century has been grappling with this legacy, with a new spatial politics placing great emphasis on closing rural-urban divisions. Zhengzhou's municipal government has granted stronger rights to rural migrants in the city, and the rural-urban income gap around Zhengzhou municipality has fallen. But, for the nearby rural hinterland discussed in this book, these issues have been superseded by the rapid growth of the city. By the beginning of the 2020s, almost all of pre-1949 Zheng County had been absorbed by the city, with the municipal authorities overseeing the appropriation of its agricultural land and the demolition of its villages. The demolition of Zhengzhou's "villages in the city" (*chengzhongcun*) during the 2010s wiped out almost all physical traces of this former rural hinterland.

But urbanization of the former hinterland does not mean an end to spatial politics around Zhengzhou. Questions of spatial inequality in modern China are more complex than just rural-urban relations. This book therefore examines a third key aspect of Zhengzhou's spatial relationships: the city's regional role.[19] Over the course of the twentieth century, Zhengzhou rose from obscurity to become the dominant city not just of Henan Province but of all inland north-central China, the wider region of the Central Plains (Zhongyuan).[20] As with Zhengzhou's urban edge and rural hinterland, the key questions here concern the production of difference over space: What kind of connections did Zhengzhou have with nearby cities? How and why did Zhengzhou become the dominant regional center? What were the effects of its rise on other cities in the region? How have inequalities between cities—in wealth, prestige, political authority—changed over time?

Zhengzhou's most important intercity relationship was with neighboring Kaifeng. At the beginning of the second millennium, Kaifeng was China's capital and probably the largest city in the world. Even at the end of the nineteenth century, Kaifeng was still the cultural, commercial, and political hub of the Central Plains. Yet over the next hundred years the city suffered a steep decline relative to Zhengzhou, which displaced it as the commercial and industrial center of Henan during the 1910s and 1920s and as provincial capital in 1954. By the early 1990s, Kaifeng's economic growth rate was rock bottom among all seventeen cities in Henan, and a decade later it was one of the poorest cities in the province.[21] This book explores this upending of regional urban hierarchy,

19. In the tradition of G. William Skinner, there is a rich scholarship on the place of Chinese cities in wider regional networks, but this has tended to focus on the nineteenth century and the first half of the twentieth century, rather than across the modern period. For examples from different perspectives, see Guan Wenbin, "Qingmo minchu Tianjin yu Huabeide chengshihua"; Meng Yue, *Shanghai and the Edges of Empire*; Xin Zhang, *Global in the Local*.

20. This is taking a broad definition of "Central Plains" to include lowland areas of neighboring provinces as well as Henan itself. Historians have investigated the question of Zhengzhou's regional shifts for the period up to the mid-1950s. See especially Zhu Junxian, *Yin ge zhi bian*; Liu Hui, *Tielu yu Zhengzhou chengshihua*.

21. Wu Pengfei, "Kaifeng chengshi shengming zhouqi tanxi," 123. For measures of decline, see Liang Liuke, *Kaifeng shi kechixu fazhan*, 41–45.

arguing that environmental and economic factors alone are insufficient to explain the rise of Zhengzhou and the decline of Kaifeng; instead, it should be understood as a product of spatial politics, of a series of specific choices to concentrate resources in Zhengzhou.

These intercity ties are of much more than local interest. Zhengzhou's rise to dominance across the twentieth century shows how political choices have constructed the urban hierarchy of China today. It also underlines the tension of spatial politics, between impulses to concentrate or to redistribute resources. On the one hand, Zhengzhou's rise has been at the expense of Kaifeng, and its concentration of wealth, power, and prestige was a deliberate creation of inequality over space; on the other hand, more recently regional planners have been trying to spread Zhengzhou's economic growth across the region. Since 2005, the provincial government has promoted "Zhengzhou and Kaifeng integration" (*Zheng-Bian yitihua*), promising to share Zhengzhou's wealth with its poorer neighbor. Almost two decades on, it remains to be seen whether this plan will be sufficient in the long term to overcome entrenched urban hierarchies and bring convergence between the two adjacent cities.

The Making of Spatial Inequality

This book examines modern China's spatial politics through Zhengzhou's urban fringes, nearby villages, and intercity relationships. It argues that forces of division and inequality have concentrated power, capital, and prestige in a single dominant regional city. This argument does not deny countervailing moments of connection and state efforts at greater equality across space. Nor does it claim that Zhengzhou's modern history has been smooth or without very serious human suffering for those in the city. At times, such as under Nationalist Party control (1930–1948) and in the late Mao era, Zhengzhou has been neglected relative to other cities. But across the twentieth century, Zhengzhou's successive urban transformations brought only limited benefits to surrounding rural areas and nearby cities.

How can this long-term pattern be explained? Part of the explanation is environmental: compared with most of inland North China, regions with greater fertility and a stronger rural economy sometimes show a more positive, more equalizing picture of spatial relations.[22] Zhengzhou's

22. See, for instance, Lincoln, *Urbanizing China*.

long-distance rail connections meant that the city was able to escape some of the ecological and infrastructural constraints of the struggling Central Plains region. Another part of the explanation lies in market forces. Rural-urban price scissors usually—if not always—left city residents better off in relative terms than their rural counterparts. At moments of rapid economic growth, whether the 1910s or the 2000s, investment from both inside and outside the province concentrated in Zhengzhou. Access to capital was more limited for rural residents.

But the most important strand for understanding spatial inequality is the role of the modern Chinese state. Successive Chinese states have played a stronger role in constructing the distribution of resources than in many nation-states. As discussed above, spatial politics in modern China have been marked by two opposing impulses. China's central and local authorities have sometimes sought to connect and equalize across space, connecting rural and urban and sharing the benefits of growth between cities and regions; conversely, this book also finds patterns of disconnection and inequality, cutting off city from countryside and institutionalizing systems of inequality across space. The tension between these two impulses has run through different iterations of Chinese political economy and continues today in the policies of regional development and rural urbanization in the Xi Jinping era.[23]

For most of the twentieth century, the impulse toward concentration and inequality was the dominant mode of spatial politics. Earlier iterations of the Chinese state had spatial strategies, but these were usually driven by logics of administrative and environmental control rather than efforts at socioeconomic transformation.[24] Although the central authorities did oversee a spatial distribution of resources (such as by interprovincial revenue transfer), the small and diminishing place of the state in the late imperial economy limited its effects. The spatial role of the Chinese state was transformed in two stages in the second half of the nineteenth century. First, growing governance and military challenges led to a shift in territorial thinking and a more active role for the state in

---

23. See, most recently, Jaros, *China's Urban Champions*.

24. On the spatial politics of administration, see, for example, Mostern, *"Dividing the Realm"*; on environment, see, for example, Ling Zhang, *The River, the Plain, and the State*.

the distribution of resources, especially from the 1870s onwards.[25] With a concentration on first continental, then maritime defense, inland central China tended to be overlooked until the second stage of transformation, the Xinzheng (New Policies) era of the first decade of the twentieth century. The Xinzheng era saw the completion of railroads in inland China, the creation of new open cities for foreign trade (*zikai shangbu*, including Zhengzhou in 1908), and, by quadrupling government spending, heralded the ambition of the central state to lead a wider social and economic transformation on the model of Meiji Japan.[26]

From the Xinzheng era onwards, then, successive Chinese states had ambitious schemes for economic development, technological transformation, political state building, and the spreading of such changes across space. However, crucially, although the Chinese state in the twentieth century was sometimes powerful enough to oversee these transformations at certain sites, the ambition of dispersing them across space usually fell by the wayside owing to lack of resources and, often, political will. This meant that local and national authorities combined ambition and weakness, sometimes in toxic ways. With limited resources, they tended to back "winners" and pursue uneven development strategies, whether a bias for urban over rural development, backing certain cities over others, or support for particular regions. Zhengzhou was usually, although not always, one of the "winners" of this strategy of concentrated development, but it brought costs and inequalities across each generation. The late Qing state was able to construct an impressive railroad system centered on Zhengzhou but did very little for local infrastructure; governments during the Republic promoted projects of urban modernization but reduced the rural hinterland to an afterthought; the wartime Nationalist state was strong enough to fight a decade of war but at the cost of virtually abandoning the frontline region around Zhengzhou; the Mao-era state made Zhengzhou an industrial flagship but only at the expense of extraction from the rural sector; reform-era political economy promoted rapid growth in some places and in some sectors

25. See, for instance, Hsü, "Great Policy Debate"; Pomeranz, *Making of a Hinterland*; Shellen Xiao Wu, *Empires of Coal*; for a recent example of the 1870s spatial shift, see Giersch, *Corporate Conquests*, 14–15, 123–43.

26. Huaiyin Li, *Making of the Modern Chinese State*, 112–31; Reynolds, *China, 1898–1912*.

but by the end of the twentieth century had generated a crisis in spatial inequality in Henan Province.

In the twenty-first century, the Hu Jintao/Wen Jiabao and Xi Jinping leaderships have, in their different ways, tried to break this pattern of spatial politics. New wealth and technologies of control have enabled the state to combine ambition and strength for the first time. The People's Republic promised to use this power to spread the benefits and produce a "moderately well-off society" (*xiaokang shehui*) for all. In absolute terms, huge strides have been made toward that goal, even if one might be wary of Xi Jinping's official 2021 declaration that it had been fully achieved. But, as chapter 7 shows, uneven wealth, an entrenched urban hierarchy, and ongoing difficulties for those of rural origin mean that life experiences and chances still deeply depend on where a citizen is. The legacies of China's twentieth-century spatial politics will not be easily unpicked.

This stress on the state is not to deny the importance of nonstate actors or individual agency, and where sources permit, this book uncovers the human responses to the state's spatial politics.[27] This argument is also not intended to pathologize the developmental patterns of modern China. Spatial politics is a global phenomenon, and inequality—whether between or within countries—has haunted the world in the industrial age. In the twenty-first century, developed economies are struggling to balance the sometimes very different needs and political impulses of cores and peripheries. I wrote this book in a Britain wracked by the aftermath of a spatially divided Brexit vote and haunted by the disappointments of a much-heralded policy to "level up" poorer regions. Many developing nations are struggling to escape the legacies of a political economy that concentrated wealth in certain urban areas. Although capital has—at least until very recently—been more footloose than ever before, spatial inequality and clustering by class and education on local, national, and global scales have perhaps become more entrenched. As James Meek puts it, global economic integration has linked people and places but "without doing anything to bring them together."[28] This presents new problems at a time when global challenges such as climate change bring a moral challenge to share burdens across space.

27. On the importance of human-level urban history beyond the state, see Zhao Ma, "Individual Agency and Social Networking."
28. Meek, "Somerdale to Skabimierz," 3.

Seven Ages of Modern Zhengzhou

Zhengzhou's modern history begins with the coming of the railroad in the first years of the twentieth century. From 1907, China's new north–south and east–west trunk railroads crossed at Zhengzhou. Chapter 1 shows how the railroad reconfigured Zhengzhou's spatial relationships, from rapid changes at the urban edge to the first of many flows of migrant labor into the city. Zhengzhou became a key logistical and wholesaling link between China's commercializing, primary product-producing agricultural hinterland and the treaty port and global economies that sucked in those cash crops: tobacco, opium, tea, wool, leather, peanuts, and especially cotton. However, this chapter also argues that although the railroad transformed Zhengzhou's long-distance links in and beyond the Central Plains region, these changes tended to exclude the city's nearby rural hinterland, where the lucrative cash crops being traded through the city did not take hold.

This disconnect did not escape the notice of local authorities, and chapter 2 explores the more ambitious spatial policies that emerged in Zhengzhou under the warlord Feng Yuxiang (1927–1930) and then the Nationalist authorities (1930–1937). These measures included efforts to bring new infrastructure and village improvement to Zhengzhou's nearby rural areas. Yet the dominant tone of the decade was one of urban-first modernization and ambitious city planning. The fringe of the city became a zone for experimentation, including sites of political commemoration and new projects to house and control Zhengzhou's urban poor. However, neither urban nor rural projects saw much success before full-scale Japanese invasion in 1937. Village improvement was stymied by low agricultural prices, while Zhengzhou's growth was checked by the rise of rival railroad towns and the political dominance of the provincial capital at Kaifeng.

Zhengzhou was close to the front line throughout the Second World War in China (1937–1945). Chapter 3 argues that this brought new spatial inequalities on several different levels. The neglect and mistreatment of frontline Henan was a deliberate spatial policy of the Nationalist government, which in 1938 broke the Yellow River dikes north of Zhengzhou to flood the rural plain and in 1942–1943 was deeply culpable in the devastating famine in the region. The combined death toll of flood and famine was around two million. For Zhengzhou, Nationalist sabotage of railroads removed its regional and interregional economic roles, throwing residents back on the resources of its nearby hinterland. The city's civilians—both existing residents and refugees—used the urban edge and nearby villages as part of their survival strategy, as bomb shelters and black markets, informal settlements, and sites to scavenge for food. These spatial adaptations ended in April 1944 with the Japanese occupation of the city, followed by strict militarization of the urban fringe and prohibitions on rural-urban movement.

Zhengzhou had two postwar periods in the second half of the 1940s. Chapter 4 begins by showing the similar spatial concerns of Nationalist authorities after Japanese defeat in August 1945 and of the new Communist rulers after the takeover of October 1948. In both cases, the local state sought to reestablish Zhengzhou's regional role and rural-urban connections. This "double postwar" period of reconstruction ended in 1953–1954 in the form of two distinct revolutions. In 1953, the First Five-Year Plan brought industrial revolution to Zhengzhou, with the western suburbs of the city becoming a new textile manufacturing zone. The following year, the central government moved Henan's provincial capital from Kaifeng to Zhengzhou. The city's population tripled in just five years, reaching half a million by 1957. Zhengzhou's regional economic role, its urban edge, and its relations with nearby villages were transformed, primarily to the benefit of those in Zhengzhou and at the expense of Kaifeng and the rural hinterland.

Chapter 5 reveals the paradoxes of Zhengzhou's spatial politics under the planned economy. On the one hand, Communist rule offered the promise of spatial equalization. Zhengzhou was a model for Maoist rural-urban relations, and in the Great Leap Forward it became the first city in China to establish urban communes, combining industry, services, and suburban agriculture in collective units. A similar impulse to integrate city and countryside was at work in the Cultural Revolution, when Zhengzhou's young people were sent to agricultural communes, mostly in the suburbs of the city. Yet this rhetoric cannot hide the spatial inequalities of the Maoist system. Zhengzhou may have been a model for rural-urban relations, but the city's industry was built on ruthless extraction from the rural economy, a strict household registration system, and the expulsion of migrants. At its height in the Great Leap Forward, the utopia of equal development was left hollow by rural famine, with an unusually brutal provincial government in Zhengzhou isolating the city from the violence and suffering across the region.

In absolute terms, China's reform era after 1978 brought infrastructural and income benefits across space. Yet chapter 6 uses three issues to show that the spatial politics of market reform brought new challenges. First, rural migrants to Zhengzhou faced systematic inequalities because of where they had come from. This "floating population" of migrants had already reached four hundred thousand by 1993, accounting for over a quarter of Zhengzhou's inhabitants.[29] Two decades later it was over three million, at a density higher than any other inland city.[30] By preserving much of the *hukou* system from the Mao period, the urban state was enshrining spatial inequality to maintain a low-wage labor force. The second-class status of migrants in the city manifested itself in discourse as well as limited access to state benefits. Second, reform did little to equalize China's urban hierarchies. While Zhengzhou boomed, by the 1990s Kaifeng had fallen into a steep decline relative to its neighbor, and the "Kaifeng phenomenon" became a byword for stagnation in the market economy. Third, Zhengzhou's urban edge became a site for struggles over space. As municipal government planned grand housing estates and high-tech industrial parks, nearby villagers grappled with the mixed consequences of being swallowed up in the booming city.

Since the mid-2000s, fast-growing Zhengzhou has grown from a provincial center to the most important city in north-central China. Chapter 7 explores the spatial consequences of this shift. As part of government efforts to spread growth across space, provincial planners aimed to reverse Zhengzhou's earlier spatial politics: rather than simply pulling in resources, capital, and labor from the wider region, Zhengzhou's growth promised both to pull along its large, mostly poor hinterland of Henan Province and to spill over into the ring of nearby medium-sized cities—especially struggling Kaifeng. This twenty-first-century transformation has had mixed results. Spatial inequality has declined by many metrics, the status of rural migrants in the city has improved, and Kaifeng has been pulled out of the doldrums. Yet spatial inequality did not go away in the 2010s, amid overheated

29. Hao Pengzhan, "Lun jindai yilai Zhengzhou de chengshi guihua," 64.
30. "Zhengzhou shiqu liudong renkou 340 wan," *Dahebao*, February 28, 2013.

high property prices, clear urban hierarchies, ongoing marginality for poorer migrants, and the risks of overconcentration in Zhengzhou. With a rocky start to the 2020s, Zhengzhou's authorities and residents continue to grapple with the legacy of its twentieth-century spatial politics even as they face the new infrastructural and environmental challenges of a twenty-first-century megacity.

CHAPTER ONE

Zhengzhou and the Railroads to 1927

Steam-powered railroads and ships were the most important tech-nologies in the global reach of industrial capitalism in the decades before 1914. They changed perceptions of space by lowering the cost and raising the speed of transporting bulk goods. Railroads facilitated the penetration of this new economy into continental interiors, away from ports and navigable rivers. However, even as steam-powered trans-port increased global wealth and production, it also produced, as Tony Ballantyne and Antoinette Burton put it, "differential outcomes and new inequalities."[1] As well as new links, railroads created peripher-ies and brought decline to older systems; in much of the world, they also enabled new structures of extraction, inequality, and dependency. Historians have shown that China was no exception to these uneven effects of railroads. In the first decades of the twentieth century, China's new railroad network transformed overland movement and stimulated commercial cash cropping. Yet it exposed China's rural economy to the hazards of global price movements and did not bring major long-run improvements in living standards for most cultivators. It also marginal-ized those parts of the country that did not have access to railroads or easily navigable waterways.[2]

In many ways, Zhengzhou was one of the great success stories of rail-road China. In 1906, this small walled town became China's first major railroad junction and an overnight commercial boomtown. Zhengzhou became the key node connecting the agricultural sector of the Central Plains and Northwest China to the treaty ports and the global economy beyond. Its population grew almost twenty times over within a couple

1. Ballantyne and Burton, "Empires and the Reach of the Global," 352.
2. Pomeranz, *Making of a Hinterland*; Huenemann, *Dragon and the Iron Horse*.

of decades, from around five thousand inhabitants before the railroad to nearly one hundred thousand in the early 1920s—a similar rate to Denver, the fastest-growing city of the railway age in the United States.[3]

Yet this chapter argues that even here, at the heart of the railroad system, its effects around Zhengzhou were deeply uneven. It begins with a brief survey of Zhengzhou's prerailroad history—always intertwined with the vicissitudes of transport politics—before showing how Zhengzhou's regional economic role was transformed by its railroad links. It then demonstrates the mixed local effects of the railroad in two ways. First, Zhengzhou's rapid expansion brought new spatial inequalities within the city. Second, outside the city, for reasons of both ecology and limited infrastructure, rural areas around Zhengzhou did not see major economic benefits in the first decades of the railway age.

Railroad Zhengzhou: "Number 1 Thoroughfare for the Inland North"

Some of the world's great railroad towns emerged almost completely from scratch, even where they were close to existing villages. Examples include Atlanta, Georgia; Atbara in Sudan; and, in China, the junction city of Shijiazhuang south of Beijing. In other cases, as at Changchun, Chicago, and Zhengzhou, railroad cities grew rapidly from an existing urban form.[4] In the case of Zhengzhou, the city had a much older history, with waves of rise and decline intricately tied to its place in administrative and transport networks.

The Central Plains of what is now Henan Province were the heartland of one of the world's great agricultural and state systems. In the mid-second millennium BCE Zhengzhou was the site of the area's first major city, the capital of what Brian Lander calls the "first indisputable state in East Asian history," usually associated with the Shang dynasty of the textual tradition.[5] The walled city was home to around one hundred thousand residents,

---

3. Population estimates for prerailroad Zhengzhou range from as low as 3,300 to as high as 20,000. For the figure of around five thousand, I follow Zhu Junxian's calculations, *Yin ge zhi bian*, 6; Zhengzhou shi gongshangye lianhehui, *Zhengzhou gongshangye xingshuai shi gaikuang*, 16; Xie Xiaopeng, *Jindai Zhengzhou*, 123–24. Denver's population growth in the first twenty years of the railroad was strikingly similar to Zhengzhou's: around 5,000 in 1870, 35,000 by 1880, and 106,000 in 1890. See Barth, *Instant Cities*, 136.

4. See, for instance, Sikainga, *"City of Steel and Fire,"* 31–35; Sewell, *Constructing Empire*, 28–32; Cronon, *Nature's Metropolis*, 55–63.

5. Lander, *King's Harvest*, 7.

one of the biggest settlements in the Bronze Age world and the largest urban population at Zhengzhou until the twentieth century.[6] Yet in the mid-Shang period the capital was moved away from Zhengzhou, and the city was abandoned as a political center. Although there are signs of subsequent settlement, it was another two thousand years before urban life once again flourished at Zhengzhou. This was in the seventh century CE, when Zhengzhou emerged as an important transshipment node on the canal and river networks linking China's imperial capitals—Xi'an, Luoyang, and later Kaifeng—with the emerging economic core of the Lower Yangzi region.

This politically driven transport network declined from the twelfth century onwards. China's imperial capital moved away from the region, never to return, and the deterioration of water control along the Yellow River brought floods, damaged soils, and silted up waterways across the Central Plains.[7] This cycle of economic, environmental and political decline reduced Henan Province from civilizational core to much-disparaged periphery by the twentieth century—what the American journalist Agnes Smedley (1892–1950) called a "wide, wheat plain where famine, flood, drought, banditry, and poverty are the constant companions of the people."[8] Zhengzhou's urban life was hard hit by this decline. Although still an administrative center at the lowest (county) level, it was left commercially isolated by the silting up of watercourses and the growing difficulty of using the tightly channeled, fast-flowing Yellow River for bulk transport.[9] Silt from the 1887 Yellow River flood devastated farmland and local rivers to the east of Zhengzhou and left the city 150 kilometers from the nearest reliably navigable river at Zhoukou. "All the way from Zhengzhou to Kaifeng," ran one report of the 1920s, "east and south of Zheng County . . . is blocked with silt and sand, and the

---

6. For population estimates, see Liu and Chen, *Archaeology of China*, 282.

7. For a summary, see Pietz, *Yellow River*, 48–50; for the buildup to the twelfth-century collapse of this system, see Ling Zhang, *The River, the Plain, and the State*. On the challenge of river management in the nineteenth century, see Dodgen, *Controlling the Dragon*; on the long-term peripheralization of the area between the Yellow and Huai Rivers, see Ma Junya, *Bei xisheng de "jubu."*

8. Smedley, *Battle Hymn of China*, 374.

9. After 1734 Zhengzhou was a *zhou* (department) at the county level, that is, without subordinate counties. In 1903 it was raised to the status of "autonomous department" (*zhilizhou*) with three subordinate counties.

rivers are cut off (*duanjue*) for hundreds of *li*."[10] Given the poor condition of roads and the expense of overland transport compared to waterborne cargo, Zhengzhou was not facing a bright future. At the end of the nineteenth century, the city had only a few thousand inhabitants, and large areas within the city walls had been given over to agriculture.[11]

Such was the unprepossessing site of China's first great railroad boomtown. It is not surprising, then, that Zhengzhou's status as railroad hub owed more to ecological and geographical circumstances than to its political clout. In spring 1889, Zhang Zhidong (1837–1909), the reformist governor-general of Guangdong and Guangxi, proposed building a north–south railroad between the imperial capital Beijing and the important Yangzi riverport of Hankou. Zhang mooted two possible routes, the first a direct line through the Henan provincial capital at Kaifeng. As Zhang noted, this route would make Kaifeng the key commercial center on the middle part of the route: "when the line is finished, traveling merchants will soon converge there."[12] But Zhang and his associate Sheng Xuanhuai (1844–1916) rightly suspected that the Yellow River due north of Kaifeng would be too unstable for a railroad bridge and that the river crossing would have to take place farther upstream.

It proved difficult for Zhang to raise the necessary finances, and the idea was shelved, but, following defeat to Japan in the war of 1894–1895, the Qing court backed railroad construction. In May 1897, a Belgian-led syndicate won the contract to build a line between Beijing and Hankou, and its survey engineers endorsed Zhang's views on the Yellow River bridge. The route therefore kinked some 70 kilometers to the west and crossed the river northwest of Zhengzhou. After the delay of the Boxer Uprising (1899–1901), the Beijing–Hankou Railroad (hereafter Jing–Han Railroad) opened for full traffic at the beginning of 1906, running through Zhengzhou and bypassing Kaifeng altogether.[13] Instead, follow-

10. Chen Shantong, *Yu he xu zhi* (Kaifeng, 1926), quoted in Zhu Junxian, *Yin ge zhi bian*, 78.

11. Tōa dōbunkai, *Kanan-shō*, 21–22; 162–64. By one estimate, land haulage in Henan could be up to forty times the cost of water transport depending on the season. See Guinness, "Province of Honan," 150. The Buck/Jinling University study of 1929–1933 suggests that a factor of five was more typical. See John L. Buck, *Land Utilization in China*, vol. 3: *Statistics*, 346–47.

12. Quoted in Zhu Junxian, *Yin ge zhi bian*, 92.

13. On this process, see Kent, *Railway Enterprise*, 34–35; Zhang Ruide, *Ping–Han tielu*, 6–7.

ing an earlier suggestion of Sheng Xuanhuai, an east–west railroad was constructed through Zhengzhou to Kaifeng to its east and Luoyang to the west. The section between Zhengzhou and Kaifeng was completed in 1907 and that to Luoyang at the end of 1908. With further extensions at either end, this Long–Hai Railroad evolved into China's first—and, for many decades, only—east–west trunk line south of the Great Wall. Zhengzhou therefore became the meeting point of two of China's most important railroads (see map 0.1). For one foreign resident, Zhengzhou would now be of transcontinental significance: "Chengchow [Zheng-zhou] will be the crossing of the two lines to Europe—the old Siberian northward, and the new Tibetan westward, and the Shanghai people when they pass here en route to Europe will be fast asleep."[14]

Such hyperbole was premature, and it is only in the twenty-first century that Zhengzhou's railroad connections have reached across Eurasia. But the coming of the railroad did transform Zhengzhou's economic geography. Given the continuing price competitiveness of water transport, the greatest impact of China's railroads came in areas with few navigable waterways. This was certainly the case for Zheng-zhou, cut off from canal and river networks but made central by its rail-road junction. As historian Liu Hui shows, the meeting of railroads at Zhengzhou connected several distinct economic systems—a key "pivot" of inland China. Long-distance trade in Henan had previously been divided into three different riverine hinterlands: the Huai River to the southeast, the Hai River system northwards toward Tianjin, and the Han River running south to Hankou.[15] The north–south Jing–Han line connected all three watersheds, with Zhengzhou as the meeting point. In addition, Zhengzhou was connected by the east–west Long–Hai line both to the railhead for trade with Northwest China and to the Lower Yangzi region (via Xuzhou and the Tianjin–Pukou railroad). In terms of G. William Skinner's division of China into "macroregions," Zhengzhou became the meeting point of four regional economies, connecting the North, Middle Yangzi, Lower Yangzi, and Northwest regions.[16]

With prices buoyant and transport costs reduced, many areas close to North China's railroads saw a boom in cash cropping during the 1910s

14. *North China Herald*, February 27, 1909.
15. Liu Hui, *Tielu yu Zhengzhou chengshihua*, 41–42.
16. Skinner, "Introduction," 3–31.

and early 1920s.[17] Zhengzhou linked this commercializing rural economy to the treaty ports of Shanghai, Tianjin, and Hankou, just one of the many railroad and riverine entrepôts of the colonial and semi-colonial world connecting inland primary products to the global economy.[18] One report of 1919 called Zhengzhou the "number 1 thoroughfare (*yaodao diyi*) for the inland north": "around the middle of each day, when the trains from three directions all pass each other, the goods are passed up and down from the trains, and traveling merchants go to and fro in a never-ending stream, too many to keep track of."[19] A huge variety and volume of goods passed through Zhengzhou: wool and hides from the northwest; tea, kerosene, and sugar from the south; tobacco from central Henan; coal from the mountains to the north; and foodstuffs from all directions. Opium—whether legal and taxed or illegal and smuggled— was ubiquitous. But the greatest change to Zhengzhou's regional role came from perhaps the most transformative product of the modern world economy: cotton.

Cotton accounted for over a third of the value of the goods being traded through Zhengzhou.[20] Cotton had been produced in north-central China for centuries, but as had occurred in India and Russian Central Asia, it was railroad construction that enabled large-scale production in continental interiors for industrial needs.[21] Nor was Zhengzhou the only cotton entrepôt in inland North China— Anyang, Shijiazhuang, and Luoyang all saw substantial volumes— but it was by far the most important during the 1910s and 1920s. Merchants shipped cotton to Zhengzhou from grassroots markets in the cotton-producing regions of western Henan and the southern parts of Shanxi and Shaanxi. In Zhengzhou it was stored, resold, and sometimes baled before being transported by rail to Hankou, Tianjin, Qingdao, and especially Shanghai. At the beginning of the Republic, Zhengzhou had three cotton trading houses; by 1919 it boasted thirty

17. He Hanwei, *Jing–HanJing–Han tielu chuqi*; Liu Haiyan, "Jindai Huabei jiaotong."

18. For a nineteenth-century example of a brokerage entrepôt build on north-south connections and links to the treaty port and global economy, see Xin Zhang, *Global in the Local*.

19. "Zuijin Zhengzhou jinrong," 23b.

20. Liu Hui, *Tielu yu Zhengzhou chengshihua*, 80.

21. Beckert, *Empire of Cotton*, 294–98.

such dealers.[22] The same year, the Henan provincial government began offering cash incentives for cultivators to switch to cotton production. The sown area of cotton in the province duly doubled by 1922, and traders in Zhengzhou were handling between 20,000 and 30,000 tons of cotton each year.[23]

The example of cotton underlines an important facet of Zhengzhou's spatial relationships: that the city's role depended not so much on the seamless delivery of goods but on the difficulties of transport. The arrival of the railroad made movement of goods cheaper and faster, but the importance of an entrepôt like Zhengzhou was boosted by intermediate hurdles and processes between origin and destination. The movement of goods was full of this kind of stickiness, due in part to the difficulties of organizing through shipments on China's fragmented railroad system. Through-traffic arrangements for goods switching railroads began in China in 1920, but the Long–Hai line did not join until summer 1925. It was only then that goods wagons could move between Zhengzhou's two railroads without the cargo being unloaded.[24] By then, Zhengzhou had become a center for "sticky" logistical processes: unloading and repacking, direct wholesale marketing, middleman brokers, and shipping insurance. In the cotton sector, because the rural primary marketing centers had few facilities for storage or processing, Zhengzhou also became a key center for the carding, baling, and warehousing of cotton. Although there were complaints about the quality of these intermediate services in Zhengzhou, as the hub of the rail network in north-central China, it was hard to avoid the city altogether.[25]

22. On Zhengzhou's changing cotton geography, see Di Fuyu, "Zhengzhou mianye zhi diaocha," 1–4. Zhu Junxian estimates that in 1922, 60 percent of cotton handled through Zhengzhou was bound for Shanghai. Zhu, *Yin ge zhi bian*, 126–31. On the number of cotton dealers, see "Zuijin Zhengzhou jinrong shang kuang diaocha," 23.

23. Estimates for the first half of the 1920s range from 400,000 to 600,000 *dan* per year, here converted to tons. Compare Di Fuyu, "Zhengzhou mianye zhi diaocha," 1–2; Liu Hui, *Tielu yu Zhengzhou chengshihua*, 80. Not all cotton in Zhengzhou was from Henan, but for reference this amounted to around a quarter of Henan's total cotton output—a very high figure, given that most (around 60 percent) of cotton was still being used for local hand spinning and padding of winter clothes. See Kraus, *Cotton and Cotton Goods*, 23–25 (on Henan production) and 86 (for uses of raw cotton).

24. See Liu Hui, *Tielu yu Zhengzhou chengshihua*, 113. For more on the transshipment issue, see Köll, *Railroads and the Transformation of China*, 102–11.

25. On complaints, see "Zhengzhou shangye jinrong diaocha," *Xinwenbao*, April 14,

This stickiness in the cotton trade helped Zhengzhou become the most prominent of the emerging railroad towns—Shijiazhuang, Bengbu, Zhuzhou, and Xuzhou are others—that benefited from the growth of China's economy during the First World War and into the 1920s. Foreign commentators began to note the city's growth and the potential of its connections. "Chengchow is a typical boom city," noted Zhengzhou's YMCA secretary, "and not an Interior city as it is supposed to be."[26] A Japanese report of 1922 envisaged Zhengzhou as the "Chicago of China."[27] This was a little wide of the mark: Hankou was a more accurate comparison for Chicago, especially given the intersection of water and overland transport at the Yangzi port. Nonetheless, looking at Zhengzhou's central transport role in north-central inland China, a more modest 1907 prediction in an overseas Chinese newspaper of the city becoming a "second Hankou" seemed to be coming to fruition.[28]

The impact of railroad construction on Zhengzhou's spatial relationships is underlined by a comparison with neighboring Kaifeng. Like Zhengzhou, Kaifeng was distant from navigable waterways, and the coming of the railroad ended its logistical isolation and brought commercial growth. The population rose by 70 percent, from 160,000 in 1910 to 227,000 in 1925.[29] But compared to the breakneck growth of Zhengzhou, this seemed slow. Already by 1910 Zhengzhou had ten transshipment and warehousing firms to Kaifeng's six and, according to the income figures of the Long–Hai railroad, was bringing in about three times the cargo revenue of Kaifeng.[30] A decade later, Zhengzhou was already being touted as a possible provincial capital to replace its neighbor.[31]

1922. Xiong Yaping identifies 1921–25 as the heyday of cotton transshipment brokers. From the mid-1920s, more cotton buyers were arranging purchases and shipment directly rather than going through middlemen. See Xiong, *Tielu yu Huabei xiangcun shehui*, 131.

26. B. Ward Smith, "Questions for the Annual Administration Report for 1922," January 1, 1923. University of Minnesota Libraries, Kautz Family YMCA Archives, digitized version at https://umedia.lib.umn.edu/item/p16022coll358:1798.

27. Cited in Xu Youli, "Zhengzhou jian 'shi' de lishi kaolü," 23.

28. "Zhengzhou shangbu zhi fada," 3.

29. Cheng Ziliang and Li Qingyin, *Kaifeng chengshi shi*, 214.

30. "Bian–Luo tielu chengbao benbu gezhan shangwu," comparing no. 22, 33b–35a (Zhengzhou figures) and no. 23, 38b–40a (Kaifeng).

31. Lin Chuanjia, *Da Zhonghua Henan sheng*, 71. Also quoted in Zhu Junxian, "Bianyuan yu zhongxin de huhuan," 105–6.

Some observers offered cultural reasons for Kaifeng's relatively slow growth. One report in the first years of the railroad insisted that "the customs of the people are closed off, and they are not knowledgeable about trade (*buzhi maoyi*)."[32] But a spatial explanation is sufficient: as Kaifeng historian Si Changyu puts it, unlike for Zhengzhou, the railroad "did not fundamentally alter the position of Kaifeng within the Chinese transport system."[33] Kaifeng had been bypassed by the crucial north–south Jing–Han railroad, which was more important than the east–west Long–Hai line that did run through the city. In contrast to Zhengzhou, Kaifeng played little role in Henan's most lucrative cash crops of cotton and tobacco; instead, its commercial growth was largely confined to the peanut and wheat trades of its existing hinterland to the south and east.[34]

This does not mean that Zhengzhou's growth was straightforward. After the city's boom during the uneasy peace of the 1910s, the turbulent North China of the 1920s brought political and economic uncertainty. In 1923 Zhengzhou was a focal point of the Jing–Han railroad workers strike, later mythologized in Communist Party history, and conflicts between warlord factions demonstrated the dangers of Zhengzhou's strategic centrality. The city became, in the words of journalist Sun Xiaoquan, "a point between north and south that must be struggled over, and every time there is a war everyone takes Zhengzhou as a hub (*shuniu*) to fight for control of."[35] Occupation of Zhengzhou gave control in all directions—as well as of the railroad revenues that were so vital for funding warlord armies. The recurrent wars between Zhili and Fengtian factions were most serious, but historian Hao Pengzhan counts no fewer than thirteen separate conflicts around Zhengzhou during the 1920s.[36] At one point in 1926, each of the four railroads connecting Zhengzhou was controlled by a different faction.[37] In part because of this disruption, Zhengzhou's trade and population grew more slowly in the 1920s. Zhengzhou's spatial connections that had brought commercial growth

32. "Bian-Luo tielu chengbao benbu gezhan shangwu," 39b.

33. Si Changyu, "Minguo shiqi Kaifeng chengshi," 9.

34. By one 1924 estimate, Kaifeng's peanut trade was worth only a quarter or a third of Zhengzhou's cotton business. See "Zhengzhou ji qi linjing zhi diaocha," 59–61.

35. Sun Xiaoquan, "Zhengzhou xunri," 61.

36. Hao Pengzhan, "Lun jindai yilai Zhengzhou," 38.

37. *China Press*, December 7, 1926.

were proving to be a double-edged sword in time of conflict—as would be demonstrated with even more devastating effect during Japanese invasion a decade later.

From Suburban Fringe to City Center:
Zhengzhou's Changing Urban Edge

The coming of the railroad transformed Zhengzhou's regional economic role. But how did this shift affect the spatial configuration of the city itself? Although historians have examined the effects of the railroad on Chinese cities, this section focuses on the changing fringes of Zhengzhou, those crucial spaces into which the city grew and where it intersected with its rural surroundings.[38] In Zhengzhou, a city previously bounded by its walls expanded into agricultural land between the West Gate and the railroad station. During the 1910s the core of this new railroad suburb evolved from urban edge into the commercial center of the city; on its northern and southern edges, mixed rural-urban zones formed a blurred boundary between city and countryside. Local authorities struggle to assert control over these patchwork districts. Like most of the nineteenth-century French cities explored by John Merriman— another setting of early industrialism and rapid urban growth—these urban edges became sites for many of Zhengzhou's most marginal and most innovative activities, from mechanized industry and Christian mission to sex work and informal squatter settlements.[39] This established a recurring pattern through the twentieth century: Zhengzhou's urban edge would remain a contested space, a site of struggle for political control, and a zone of innovation and opportunity as well as poverty and exclusion.

The city of Zhengzhou was defined by its walls up to the end of the nineteenth century. This was not the case in many Chinese cities. Although cities in late imperial China were usually referred to as simply *cheng*, meaning both "city" and "wall," Frederick Mote argued that walls could be "meaningless" in demarcating urban space: walls "dignified

---

38. See, for instance, David Buck, *Urban Change*, 44–60; David Buck, "Railway City and National Capital," 67–75.

39. Merriman, *Margins of City Life*. On the peripheralization of China's urban poor, in this case on the fringes of Tianjin's foreign concessions, see Liu Haiyan, "Formation of the Marginal Area of Modern Tianjin."

cities; they did not bound them."[40] In some cities, commercial extramural suburbs were more densely built up than the walled city. Yet apart from a few houses outside the south gate, prerailroad Zhengzhou had no such built-up suburbs. The commercial activities of this small administrative city were inside the walls, mostly on the main western street (*xidajie*) or around the mosque in the northern part of the city. The 5.5-kilometer line of Zhengzhou's city wall had remained unchanged since the 620s, but the brick wall itself had been renovated by officials in the 1860s and 1890s following the disorders of the mid-nineteenth century across Central China.[41] Each of the corners was topped by a watchtower, and a single gate along each side gave access, at least during the day: Zhengzhou's city gates were locked at night until well into the 1920s.[42]

Yet the presence of the wall as a stark spatial boundary does not mean that Zhengzhou was marked by serious division between city and countryside. There were moments of rural-urban conflict—particularly when officials in the city curtailed farmers' irrigation rights by diverting the nearby Jinshui River to form a city moat—but little sign of major social or economic cleavage. Although historians have argued about the presence or absence of rural-urban division around China's larger cities, pre-1900 Zhengzhou was in any case too small for such a gulf to develop.[43] Much of the sparsely populated eastern side of the walled area was given over to agriculture, while poorer residents in the northern part of the city scratched a living from salt production.[44] Meanwhile, outside the wall, there were at least fifteen temples, altars, and shrines at the beginning of the twentieth century, almost all closely associated with the city. At these sites and others slightly farther afield, temple fairs ensured regular interaction between those living inside and outside the walls.[45] Zhengzhou's inhabitants also left the city for leisure: from the late nineteenth century, there was a teahouse with popular opera performances

40. Mote, "Transformation of Nanking," 138.

41. Liu Ruilin, *Zheng xian zhi, juan* 3, 2b–3a.

42. Tōa dōbunkai, *Kanan-shō*, 46–50; Zhu Junxian, "Wuxu shengcheng yu jindai Zhengzhou," 84–90.

43. For the classic statement of underlying rural-urban unity, see Mote, "Transformation of Nanking." For Si-yen Fei's revision of the Mote thesis, see Fei, "Ming Qing de chengshi kongjian yu chengshihua."

44. Zhao Fuhai, *Lao Zhengzhou: Shangdu yimeng*, 172–83.

45. Liu Ruilin, *Zheng xian zhi, juan* 3, 24b–27b.

just outside the west gate, close to the grave site of a celebrated imam of the Ming dynasty.[46]

It was this "western suburb" (called in contemporary sources *xiguan*; sometimes, referring to a wider area, *xijiao*) that became the center of railroad Zhengzhou in the early twentieth century. As if to emphasize the scale of change, later sources describe it pejoratively—usually as "bleak and desolate" (*huangliang lengluo*)—but this seems rather unfair.[47] The topsoil was somewhat less sandy than that outside other city gates, and the diverted Jinshui River flowed from the southwest toward the city before snaking around the western and northern side of the walls (see map 1.1). In the late nineteenth century, local poet Si Xingqu (1846–1901) described an idyllic scene:

> The Jinshui River wraps itself around Guancheng
> [Zhengzhou],
> The rays of sunshine spread out on the green ripples,
> On both banks the view is open and clear, and the clouds cast
> a thin shadow,
> And, when the full stream sways, the rays of the sun seem to
> grow and grow.[48]

At the time of Si's death, Zhengzhou's western suburb was just beginning to be transformed by railroad construction. The north–south Jing–Han line was routed west of the existing walled city, with the railroad station about 1 kilometer from the west gate. The east–west Long–Hai railroad met the Jing–Han line south of the railway station. Both lines ran together west of the walled city before the Long–Hai route peeled off westwards toward Luoyang. The area around Zhengzhou was therefore split into four quadrants divided by the two V-shaped railroad junctions. Until the early 1950s, almost all the built-up area of Zhengzhou—both the old walled area and the new commercial district around the railroad station—lay in just one of those quadrants, north of the Long–Hai railroad and east of the Jing–Han line (map 1.1).

Xiong Yaping has discussed how railroads brought major changes to

---

46. Tōa dōbunkai, *Kanan-shō*, 46–47.

47. See, for example, Zhang Yanqing, "Zhengzhou mianhang jiuwen," 15.

48. Reproduced in Zhuang Xiao, *Dangdai shiren song Zhengzhou*, 394. Guancheng is a former name for Zhengzhou, used poetically here and revived in 1958 as the name of one of Zhengzhou's administrative districts (*qu*).

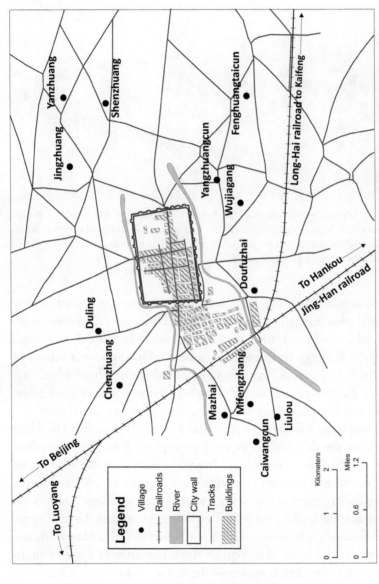

MAP 1.1. Zhengzhou and nearby villages, 1916. Adapted from Liu Ruilin, *Zheng xian zhi*, unpaginated front maps. Map by Jogu Gopinath.

FIGURE 1.1. Zhengzhou railroad station, 1920s. Photograph by the Southern Baptist missionary Katie Murray (in Zhengzhou from 1923 to 1948). Reproduced with permission from Caroline McMahon and the Murray family. Original photograph held by Z. Smith Reynolds Library Special Collections, Wake Forest University.

Chinese urban form. Since railways usually ran outside city walls, they generated what Xiong describes as a "boundary region . . . an area with mixed urban and rural land use characteristics."[49] In most cities, including nearby Kaifeng, this district became a railroad-oriented suburb of the main walled city; in Zhengzhou, it became the new heart of the city. But how did this process occur? How was the west side of Zhengzhou transformed from suburban farmland and temples into city center?

The first stage was the change in land use caused by railroad building itself. After the delay of the Boxer Uprising, work on the Zhengzhou section of the Jing–Han railroad began in earnest in the summer of 1902. The railroad construction office took over the Lü ancestral shrine (Lüzumiao) just outside the western wall of the city. Large houses were built outside the wall for both the Belgian engineers and the senior railroad contractors, who were mostly from Fujian in China's far southeast. By contrast, and in the first sign of the urban edge as a site of sharp inequalities, construction workers—the majority of whom were also not from Zhengzhou—lived in cramped improvised dormitories or make-

49. See Xiong Yaping, *Tielu yu Huabei*, 297.

shift shack housing nearby. The railroad itself was built across farmland from Mazhai and Liuloucun Villages, and it transformed the flat local landscape. Laborers dug and raised an 800-meter-long strip of land as a rail embankment, then built the railroad station (completed in March 1904) and adjacent sidings (fig. 1.1).[50]

Zhengzhou's western urban edge began to be used in new ways during and soon after railroad construction. The open space on the east side of the railway station became an informal market, with farmers and small traders coming from the surrounding countryside to sell raw cotton to larger dealers. With the full opening of the Jing–Han line in 1906, transshipment and warehousing firms began to set up operations, especially just north of the railroad station.[51] Already in 1907, the missionary Walter Sellew (1844–1929) could report that "since the advent of the railroad, a large native city has been built up in the vicinity of the station, which is constantly and rapidly growing."[52] By the time the Long–Hai line opened to Luoyang in 1908, Zhengzhou's railroad suburb was a tessellation of warehouses, railway yards, scattered agricultural plots, cheap guesthouses, Christian mission compounds, grazing land, and pools of stagnant water. Apart from rough pathways, no clear street pattern had been laid out by either the county or railroad authorities. In 1905 and again in 1907, the Jinshui River had flooded, inundating the land east of the railroad station. Drainage of the damp soil was a constant problem.[53]

Yet over the next few years, the area of land in front of Zhengzhou's station evolved from a mixed zone of rural and urban land use to the fully urbanized downtown of a railroad city. There was no master plan for this process, and in its narrow lanes and twisting streets it was hardly more ordered than the fringe zone it replaced. It is tempting to call it "organic," but as urban morphologist Spiro Kostof points out, there is little spontaneous about the land transactions and local power structures that produce such apparently natural urban patterns.[54] The transformation of Zhengzhou's urban edge into built-up center was caused by a

50. Zhengxie Zhengzhou shi Erqiqu weiyuanhui, *Yuanqu zhi jiyi*, 58 (Liuloucun), 317 (on early railroad buildings at the urban edge). On the construction process, see *North China Herald*, November 25, 1904; *North China Herald*, December 21, 1904.
51. Liu Hui, "Tielu yu jindai Zhengzhou," 104.
52. Sellew, *Clara Leffingwell*, 257.
53. Wang Junzhi, "Huashuo Jinshuihe," 98.
54. Kostof, *City Shaped*, 10, see also 43–69.

mixture of land speculation and efforts by the local authorities to regularize the neighborhood as urban space. In 1908 prefectural magistrate Ye Ji (also called Ye Gong, in office from 1905 to 1913) oversaw a project to lay a loose surface on the road leading out from the west gate and line it with willow trees.[55] Running perpendicular, the authorities also laid out the first north–south road in front of the railroad station (Yimalu, "No. 1 Road"). In the same year, the Qing authorities designated Zhengzhou's western suburb an open commercial zone (*shangbu*) for foreign trade. This was the first such designation in Henan Province and catalyzed further private land speculation.[56] Map 1.2 shows the rapid growth of Zhengzhou's extramural area by the mid-1910s.

Some streets and lanes had their origin in collaborative ventures, most notably Dunmulu, laid out by the traders of an informal market that had sprung up between the railroad station and the walled city.[57] But the majority seem to have been individual investments, usually not by natives of Zhengzhou. Hubei native Xie Baochang had worked as a foreman on Jing–Han railroad construction and invested his earnings on a patch of land in front of the station that became Baochang Alley. On a larger scale, Dehuajie, today as in the Republican period Zhengzhou's busiest shopping street, had its origin in land speculation even before the railroad was complete. Liu Bangji (1868–1930) was a military educator in Hubei and—perhaps not coincidentally—a former subordinate of Zhang Zhidong, who had planned the railroad route through Zhengzhou. Liu was traveling between Beijing and Hankou during the period of railroad construction when he decided to buy up land near the Zhengzhou railroad station. Liu joined with his former student Lu Shuqing to buy a 300-meter strip of land, later divided into rental plots for shops.[58]

Although some of Zhengzhou's early real estate investors can be identified, it is harder to retrace the details of their purchases. Provincial official Wang Youqiao (1888–1951) later reported that land sales had not been handled fairly in this commercial zone—"some bad elements (*buxiao fenzi*) colluded with outside businesses, stealthily selling land for

55. Zhengzhou shi difang shizhi bianzuan weiyuanhui, *Zhengzhou shizhi*, 1:65; On Ye, see Zeng Qiji, "Ye Gong zhu Zheng banian," 23–28.

56. On this designation, see Xu Youli, "Zhengzhou jian 'shi,'" 20–21.

57. Zhengxie Zhengzhou shi Erqiqu weiyuanhui, *Yuanqu zhi jiyi*, 320.

58. Zhengxie Zhengzhou shi Erqiqu weiyuanhui, *Yuanqu zhi jiyi*, 321.

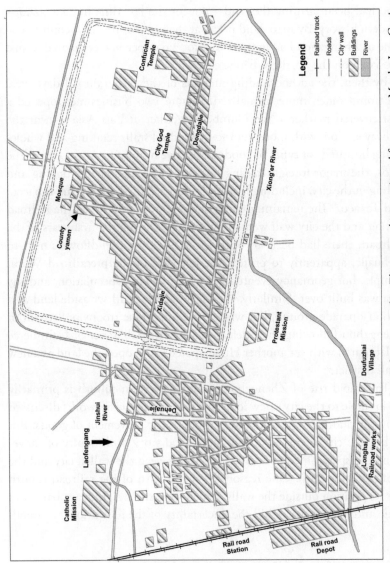

MAP 1.2. Urban Zhengzhou, 1916. Adapted from Liu Ruilin, *Zheng xian zhi*, unpaginated front maps. Map by Jogu Gopinath.

building"—but without giving precise details.[59] Even where there was no trickery in the purchase, early investors got a much better deal than those who had been farming the land—not for the last time in Zhengzhou's modern history. By 1920, land prices at the heart of this new commercial zone of Zhengzhou had jumped to 2,500 yuan per *mu*, compared to just 300 yuan on the northern fringe of town.[60]

By then, the ad hoc trading markets of the early railroad days were becoming much more formalized. In 1916 two businessmen opened a vast covered market—"the Number 1 Market of East Asia"—near the railway station, with more than four hundred stalls retailing and wholesaling hundreds of types of goods across five buildings. At the end of the 1910s, the major foreign trading houses already had agents buying and selling in the city, including Mitsui, Jardine's, British American Tobacco, and Texaco.[61] The remaining areas of open ground between the railroad station and the city wall were disappearing. During the first years of the railroad, there had been an open space filled with wildflowers next to Dehuajie, apparently to protect the fengshui of the prerailroad Wuhu Temple, but geomancy eventually lost out to land speculation, and the area was built over. Similarly, the local garrison had set aside land as a military parade ground, but when the Zhili clique troops pulled out of Zhengzhou following their defeat in 1924, the Chamber of Commerce collaborated with yet another Hubei merchant to open the land as a new retail district.[62]

This rapid rise of Zhengzhou's railroad western suburb is primarily attributable to the city's new long-distance economic networks discussed above, including some of the difficulties in the movement of goods. But within the city there was also a more local story of difficulty of movement and spatial inequality, in this case between the walled city and the commercial suburb. One reason for the growth of the railroad suburb was its position outside the walls, which were still a significant barrier to trade and movement. Amid the uncertainty of the revolutionary period,

59. Wang Youqiao, *Henan fang yu renwen zhilüe*, 139.
60. Liu Hui, "Tielu yu jindai Zhengzhou," 7.
61. Wang Ruiming, "Zhengzhou zuizao de baihuo shangchang"; Zhengzhou shi gongshangye lianhehui *Zhengzhou gongshangye*, 27.
62. Zhengxie Zhengzhou shi Erqiqu weiyuanhui, *Yuanqu zhi jiyi*, 300 (on Wuhu Temple) and 324 (on the former parade ground).

in 1912 the county authorities added four battery towers and forty guns to the fortifications.[63] Guards continued to lock the city gates between 9:00 p.m. and 6:00 a.m. This practice had been normal for centuries, but once trains began running overnight and arriving at Zhengzhou at unpredictable hours, it was hardly conducive to business within the walls—and, if the surviving accounts of a firm inside the walls are anything to go by, guards at the city gates expected a small transit payment even in the daytime.[64] Zhengzhou's walled city was therefore marginalized by the transformation of the western suburb. One report of 1918 noted that "if you go into the [walled] county city, you are entering a declining town," and by the early 1930s the geographer Zhang Qiyun (1901–1985) felt that the whole sense of what was "urban" in Zhengzhou had changed: "it might be said that inside the wall is like the countryside," he suggested, "and the area around the railway station is the city."[65]

By the end of the 1910s, then, Zhengzhou's railroad district had become the new city center, and the term "western suburb" fell out of use. Instead, a mixed rural-urban fringe emerged on the edges of this new commercial core, on the far side of the Jinshui River (to the north) and the Xiong'er River (to the south). These urban edges were sites for a variety of activities, particularly those that required large areas of land or were otherwise excluded from the urban center. Railroad infrastructure and industry are good examples in the first category. On the southern edge of the city, close to the junction of the two railroads, lay the Long–Hai office and maintenance workshops and a railroad machine tools factory. On the west side of the railway station, the large depot for the Jing–Han line backed onto open fields of Mifengzhang and Mazhai Villages (see maps 1.1 and 1.2).[66] Zhengzhou's nascent mechanized industry required both open space and proximity to the railway yards and duly clustered on the edges of the new commercial zone. Zhengzhou's only large factory during the Republican period was not in the new urban core but at the suburban village of Doufuzhai, beyond the Xiong'er River on the southern fringe of the commercial district (see map 1.2). This was

63. Liu Ruilin, *Zheng xian zhi, juan* 3, 3b.

64. Huang Mingyuan, "Zhengzhou de dangpu 'gonghedian,'" 191–92.

65. Tōa dōbunkai, *Kanan-shō*, 730; Zhang Qiyun, *Benguo dili* (1932), cited in Zhu Junxian, "Zhengzhou chengshi guihua yu kongjian jiegou," 46.

66. Tōa dōbunkai, *Kanan-shō*, 513–14.

the Yufeng (Abundant Henan) Spinning Mill, established in May 1920 by the Shanghai industrialist Mu Ouchu (1876–1943). The Yufeng mill dwarfed any other industrial facility within several hundred kilometers, employing 4,500 mostly female workers to operate some 10,000 spindles.[67] Its opening brought Doufuzhai Village firmly into the orbit of the city, with alleyways of snack stalls, restaurants, and small shops springing up around the mill.[68]

If the south side of Zhengzhou was dominated by railway infrastructure and the Yufeng works, the northern fringe was a more eclectic zone. North of the main commercial streets, formal brick buildings gave way to informal mud-and-straw housing, small workshops, and the North Market (Beicaishi), a large open-air retail space set up in 1923. Looking back on 1920s Zhengzhou from the vantage point of 1931, one report remembered that it was "full of straw shacks and stalls, crisscrossed (*zongheng jiaocuo*) with foul open sewers, and there were no roads to speak of."[69] Zhengzhou's northern edge was rapidly becoming the least desirable part of the new town, with land prices falling to 700 yuan per *mu* and only 300 yuan on the far side of the Jinshui River.[70] Many railroad cities have had a "wrong side" of the tracks, but Zhengzhou's marginal residents and activities tended to be pushed out not beyond the rail lines but to the far side of the Jinshui River. Small handicraft workshops were strung along the river, and just to the north lay the Laofengang neighborhood. In the 1910s and 1920s, this urban fringe district emerged as the center for Zhengzhou's growing population of beggars, sex workers, and the community of drifting street entertainers (*jianghu*).[71]

It was also this northern fringe of the city that was site of the first— but by no means the last—twentieth-century effort to repurpose the urban fringe for political ritual. In 1922 the first Zhili-Fengtian War saw skirmishes around Zhengzhou and the deaths of several senior officers of the victorious Zhili faction. To commemorate their deaths, the Zhengzhou Chamber of Commerce bought 20 *mu* of land at West Chen

---

67. "Henan Zhengzhou zhi Yufeng shachang," 88–89.

68. Zhao Fuhai, *Lao Zhengzhou: Shangdu yimeng*, 257.

69. *Dagongbao*, July 7, 1931, also quoted in Zhu Junxian, "Wuxu shengcheng," 86.

70. Liu Hui, *Tielu yu Zhengzhou chengshihua*, 7.

71. Laofengang is discussed in more detail in chapter 2; for a history of the district, see Zhao Fuhai, *Lao Zhengzhou: minsu shengdi Laofengang*.

Village (Xichenzhuang) and laid out a memorial garden.[72] This politically symbolic act—perhaps an attempt to curry favor with the dominant
Zhili clique warlord Wu Peifu (1874–1939)—had the secondary effect of
extending Zhengzhou to the north. The two hamlets of East and West
Chen were just 500 meters north of the Jinshui River but, as map 1.1
shows, had hitherto been separated from the city by open fields. The new
road from the city to the memorial garden catalyzed the transformation
of the Chen villages into a mixed zone and site for rural-urban exchange.
Nearby farmers and traders brought pigs to a new market here, which
quickly became Zhengzhou's largest, and the coal depot in West Chen
Village was a key point of supply for the city.[73] Even as villagers still
farmed fields to the east and north, in 1925 the south side of West Chen
Village was bought up by the Yuzhong (Central Henan) Baling Factory.
Backed by British capital, Yuzhong was the largest cotton baling works
in the city—but also a reminder that Zhengzhou's urban take-off came
with heavy human costs. This baling factory employed hundreds of
temporary workers on a brutal labor gang system, carding and packing
cotton in appalling conditions of cotton dust and fire risk. In 1933 sixty-
six mostly female workers died in a blaze at the Yuzhong works.[74]

Doufuzhai to the south and the Chen villages in the north were therefore the first of many villages to be incorporated into the growing city
of Zhengzhou during the twentieth century. Yet, although Zhengzhou
was growing across the narrow rivers to its north and south during the
1920s, it did not spread to the west side of the Jing–Han railroad—
indeed, despite the ongoing growth of the city, the railroad station would
mark its western edge into the 1950s. This is not to say that Zhengzhou's
growth had no impact west of the Jing–Han railroad. Some railroad
workers rented rooms in nearby Mazhai and Mifengzhang, and in 1924
Wu Peifu requisitioned land between the two villages for a makeshift
airstrip.[75] But the main uses of Zhengzhou's urban edge—warehouses,

72. Zhengxie Zhengzhou shi Erqiqu weiyuanhui, *Yuanqu zhi jiyi*, 36.
73. Zhengxie Zhengzhou shi Erqiqu weiyuanhui, *Yuanqu zhi jiyi*, 40.
74. Ma Zimin, "Zhengzhou yiri youji," 10–12; Shanghai media reported that the
"deaths [were] attributed to negligence on the part of the firm's management." *China
Press*, April 4, 1933.
75. Zhengxie Zhengzhou shi Erqiqu weiyuanhui, *Yuanqu zhi jiyi*, 53; on the airstrip,
see Henan sheng difang shizhi bianzuan weiyuanhui, *Henan sheng zhi*, 37, part 61,
Minyong hangkong zhi, 1.

workshops, shack housing—were confined to the east side of the Jing–Han railroad and the north side of the Long–Hai (see map 1.1). This is an important reminder that railroads could be barriers at the local level as well as regional-level connectors. As the next section explores, though the coming of the railroad caused an urban boom in Zhengzhou and brought benefits to Henan's wider rural economy, its effects in Zhengzhou's rural hinterland were more muted.

A Left-Behind Hinterland: Rural Zheng County

Zhengzhou's closest rural hinterland was in Zheng County, which before the establishment of municipal government in 1928 included both the city and the surrounding countryside. The county was almost wholly flat, densely dotted with over six hundred villages, many with defensive walls built or rebuilt during the mid-nineteenth-century social upheavals in the region. The rural population in the mid-1910s was a little over 160,000, or about twice the city's population.[76] Apart from a pocket of rice production just southeast of the city at Fenghuangtai, most farmers concentrated on wheat for the spring harvest and grew other grains such as sorghum and millet as fall crops. There were some landlords, but the vast majority of households owned some or all of their own farms.[77]

In other words, Zheng County was in most respects an unremarkable grain-producing county of the North China Plain. What was unusual from the first decade of the twentieth century was the dense railroad presence in the county. Most rural counties in China did not have any rail connection; of those that did, almost all had only a single line, with large parts of the county some distance from the railway. Yet with Zhengzhou serving as a rail junction, Zheng County had railroads running in all directions. Nor was rural Zheng County remote from railroad stations. As well as the main station in the city, the county had three rail stations, and there were a further four just beyond its borders (map 1.3).[78]

---

76. County population calculated in Zheng Fazhan, "Jindai Henan renkou," 61.

77. One survey conducted in 1929–1933 found that 81 percent of farmers around Zhengzhou owned their plots, with a further 16 percent part owning, part renting. See John L. Buck, *Land Utilization in China,* vol. 3: *Statistics,* 57. A slightly later study (1935) gives corresponding figures of 70 percent and 18 percent. See "Henan ge xian shehui diaocha: Zheng xian," *Henan tongji yuebao* 1, no. 1 (1935): 102.

78. Zhengzhou tielu fenju shizhi bianzuan weiyuanhui, *Zhengzhou tielu fenju zhi,* 856–57.

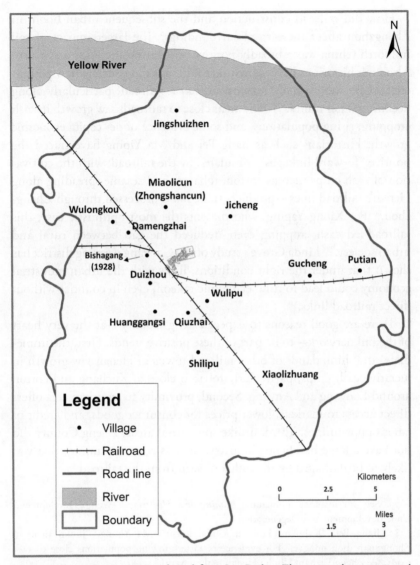

Yellow River

Jingshuizhen

Miaolicun
(Zhongshancun)

Jicheng

Wulongkou

Damengzhai

Bishagang
(1928)

Duizhou

Gucheng

Putian

Wulipu

Huanggangsi   Qiuzhai

Shilipu

Xiaolizhuang

N

Legend

•   Village

┼┼┼┼ Railroad

──── Road line

    River

    Boundary

Kilometers

0   2.5   5

Miles

0   1.5   3

MAP 1.3. Zheng County, 1916. Adapted from Liu Ruilin, *Zheng xian zhi*, unpaginated front maps. Map by Jogu Gopinath.

How did railroad construction and the subsequent urban boom in Zhengzhou affect these rural surroundings? The larger impact of rail in North China was a broadly positive one during the 1910s and 1920s. Although historians have shown that railroads did generate new peripheries, these were usually regions *without* a railroad, particularly along declining water routes.[79] Many areas close to railroads saw growth in cash cropping, rising populations, and some evidence of per capita economic growth. Historians such as Jiang Pei and Ma Yiping have traced the positive "forward linkages" stimulated by the railroad, with the cultivation of cash crops such as cotton, tobacco, and sesame spreading along Henan's railroad lines—products traded and processed through Zhengzhou.[80] For Xiong Yaping, who presents the most optimistic case, this railroad-led cash cropping even "reduced the gap between rural and urban society."[81] Linda Grove's study of the Gaoyang weaving district has shown that under the right conditions, links with the urban industrial economy could lead to rural economic takeoff, even in counties without direct railroad links.[82]

There are good reasons to expect Zheng County—at the very heart of the rail network—to be part of these positive trends. First, the immediate rural hinterlands of other railroad towns in Henan saw growth in lucrative cash crops, particularly tobacco close to Xuchang and cotton around Luoyang and Anyang. Second, proximity to an urban area offers direct access to markets, lower prices for consumer goods, and credit or labor opportunities. Third, unlike some rural areas, Zheng County did not have a large handicraft industry, such as cotton spinning, that was likely to be damaged by the influx of yarn from the railroad.[83]

79. See, for instance, Pomeranz, *Making of a Hinterland*; Wou, "Development, Underdevelopment and Degeneration."

80. Jiang Pei, "Kahoku ni okeru kindai kōtsū"; Ma Yiping, "Jindai tielu yu Zhongyuan diqu nongye." For evidence of faster-growing populations close to railroads, see Zheng Fazhan, "Jindai Henan renkou wenti," 53–85.

81. Xiong Yaping, *Tielu yu Huabei*, 242. This is not to suggest that cash cropping was a panacea for all rural problems, particularly given structural inequalities in the global economies for commodities such as cotton. For a more negative view of cash cropping, see Shen Songqiao, "Jingji zuowu yu jindai Henan nongcun jingji," esp. 330–39.

82. Grove, *Chinese Economic Revolution*.

83. One study of 1933 found that in Zheng County "there is really not much handicrafts, just some home weaving." See Long–Hai tielu chewuchu shangwuke, "Long–Hai quanxian diaocha," 160; the closest large handicraft sector to Zhengzhou was the

The data on rural Zheng County are patchy, but there are some signs of a positive trajectory, particularly in areas close to the city. Unlike around some larger cities, such as David Buck's Jinan, the countryside closest to Zhengzhou does not seem to have been very different from the wider county before the twentieth century, but this began to change after 1900.[84] Prices were buoyed by urban demand during Zhengzhou's early boom period, with the going rate for eggs and chicken reckoned to have doubled within a year of the coming of the railroad.[85] A kilometer and a half southeast of the city, the rice-growing pocket around Feng-huangtai also benefited from proximity to urban markets. By producing rice for new residents of Zhengzhou of southern origin, Fenghuangtai villagers were said to "all live in comfortable circumstances."[86] In other areas close to the city with good, silty-glutinous soil, vegetables were the key cash crop for the urban market and benefited from easy availability of nightsoil fertilizer from the growing city.[87] Although only a fifth of farmers in the county were growing vegetables commercially, those who did so seem to have specialized intensively, giving Zheng County vegetable cultivation rates over four times the regional average.[88]

Yet even as some Zheng County farmers benefited from urban growth, especially those closest to the city, across the wider county there is little evidence of large-scale commercial cash cropping or economic growth in the first twenty years of the railroad. Without denying an overall positive picture along Henan's railroads, focusing on Zheng County—at the heart of the province's railroads—the rate of rural economic and social

---

straw basket- and hat-weaving industry of Xushui, 12 kilometers west of the city and just outside the county boundary in Xingyang. Tang Hao, historian of North China market towns, describes it as in slow decline in the twentieth century, although the Long–Hai line survey attributes this to the economic crisis of the early 1930s rather than the presence of the railroad. See Tang, "Tieqi maoyi," 182; Long–Hai tielu chewuchu shangwuke, "Long–Hai quanxian diaocha," 176.

84. David Buck, *Urban Change*, 35–36.

85. *North China Herald*, January 12, 1906.

86. Zhang Zhenzhi, "Bian Zheng Luo shengyou ji," 105.

87. On vegetable production, see Sun Wenyu et al., *Yu E Wan Gan sisheng tudi fenlei*, 60, 467 (and map after page 50).

88. A sample of Zheng County farmers found that they devoted an average of 3.4 percent of cultivated land to vegetable production. This does not sound like much, but the average in this grain-dominated winter wheat/sorghum region of North China was only 0.8 percent. See John L. Buck, *Land Utilization in China*, vol. 3: *Statistics*, 172, 190.

change looks surprisingly lackluster. Most cultivators near Zhengzhou did produce some commercial crops that were shipped out by rail but usually as a sideline on marginal land rather than as their core activity. Contemporary observers noted the weakness of Zheng County's commercial production relative to its transport advantages. "Zhengzhou is the meeting point of north, south, east, and west, but what it actually produces is nothing more than jujube [*hongzao*, also called Chinese dates] and melon seeds (*guazi*)."[89] Some peanuts were also grown on poor quality land, although Henan's most important peanut belt was on the sandier soils some distance east of Zhengzhou. Farms producing such crops were probably slightly better off than those that did not, but these were distinctly low-price cash crops compared with cotton, tobacco, or even sesame.[90] Even including grains, the total value of all commercial products being shipped out from rural Zheng County in the early 1920s was only around 1 million yuan per year, less than 6 yuan per head of the county's rural population and only a twentieth of the value of the cotton trade through the city.[91] Henan's most lucrative crops of cotton and tobacco were hardly grown around Zhengzhou. An experimental cotton farm 7 kilometers outside the city at Miaolicun was established in 1920, but its improved varieties did not catch on—indeed, the Buck/Jinling University survey of 1929–1933 found no cotton at all being grown in their ninety-nine-farm Zheng County sample.[92]

A key sign of rural economic growth is the development of towns with permanent shops and regular markets. Such towns (usually *zhen*) are key to rural-urban relations, described by urban historian Wei Yingtao as

89. "Fu Bian–Luo luju daohui qianshen youchuanbu wen," no date, but must predate 1913 (when the Bian–Luo line became the Long–Hai line). Quoted in Zhu Junxian, *Yin ge zhi bian*, 145.

90. "Zhengzhou ji qi linjing zhi diaocha," 59–61. In the 1920s Wu Shixun calculated that the profit from melons in Zheng County was higher than that from commercial grain production—though they had had less to offer for food security. See Wu, *Henan*, 75.

91. "Zhengzhou shangye jinrong diaocha," *Xinwenbao*, April 14, 1922. Six yuan was roughly equivalent to the monthly wage of a rural worker in the 1920s. See John L. Buck, *Land Utilization in China*, vol. 2: *Atlas*, 125.

92. John L. Buck, *Land Utilization in China*, vol. 3: *Statistics*, 176; on the experimental farm, see Wang Enxi, "Kaocha Dongnan daxue Zhengzhou mianzuo fenchang," 229–31.

the "heads of the villages and the tails of the cities."[93] Although scholars going back to Fernand Braudel have shown that the growth of a city can stimulate the development of surrounding market centers, Braudel points out that such a trend is most likely in a rural hinterland with distinct specializations.[94] In the Lower Yangzi region, for example, Toby Lincoln has found that rapid growth of Wuxi and its mechanized silk sector stimulated the development of towns in the surrounding county, with some taking on a more urban character in the 1910s and 1920s. This growth re-created in Wuxi an urban-centered version of the continuum of city and countryside posited by Frederick Mote for earlier centuries.[95]

Zheng County was different. Some fourteen villages in the county were the sites for periodic markets (usually called *ji*) every few days, but even by the early 1930s, one survey noted that "Zhengzhou's countryside (*sixiang*) does not have any large market towns. Thirty *li* [15 kilometers] north of the city, near the Yellow River, Jingshuizhen has quite a few shops, but the rest of the county is just countryside (*qiyu duo xi xiangcun*)."[96] Even the railroad stations of rural Zheng County saw little commercial activity. Only small quantities of peanuts were traded through Xiaolizhuang station in the south of the county, and Gucheng station to the east remained a small village: "few people live nearby, and there's very little passenger or goods traffic."[97] If anything, the presence of the nearby city may have inhibited the development of local towns. Northwest of Gucheng station it was reported that "though there are some periodic markets on alternate days in some villages, for many of the ordinary things that the people need, they go to Zhengzhou to buy them (*minjian riyong duo you fu Zheng gou*)."[98]

Many rural residents were evidently used to walking to and from the city, but there is little sign of improved transport connections within Zheng County during this period. Railroad-led commercialization in China did sometimes lead to improvements in other modes of transport,

93. Wei Yingtao, *Jindai Changjiang shangyou chengxiang guanxi*, 3.

94. Braudel, *Civilization and Capitalism*, 504.

95. Lincoln, *Urbanizing China*, 4–5, 38–45.

96. Long–Hai tielu chewuchu shangwuke, "Long–Hai quanxian diaocha," 162. For a list of markets, see Liu Ruilin, *Zheng xian zhi, juan* 3, 29–30.

97. Long–Hai tielu chewuchu shangwuke, "Long–Hai quanxian diaocha," 162. On the poor performance of Zheng County's rural stations, see 174–75, 379–84.

98. Long–Hai tielu chewuchu shangwuke, "Long–Hai quanxian diaocha," 363.

particularly roads connecting rural areas to markets and railroads.[99] But Zheng County saw little change in its local transport links. The gradual spread of rubber-tired carts did improve overland haulage, but their efficacy was limited by the absence of any graveled roads in the county. The first surfaced route, to Kaifeng via the Yellow River, opened only in 1928. Overland travel was on the rough tracks described by one survey: "the roads are everywhere dusty and uneven to an extent that you cannot imagine, with deep wheel ruts everywhere and deep mud following the slightest rain."[100] The Qing era postroads, now superseded by the railroad, seem to have been getting worse, and the small towns clustered at post stations and road bridges fell into decline, with the relay stations abandoned entirely around Zhengzhou in 1913.[101] The result was that Zheng County saw little change in economic geography—neither the flourishing towns that Lincoln finds near Wuxi nor the pattern of better communication and the pull of urban centers killing off rural markets that G. William Skinner identified in the hinterland of Qingdao.[102] By the 1940s, the number of periodic markets in Zheng County had risen but without driving the development of significant rural towns with permanent shops and marketing.[103] This lack of development seems to have had secondary effects in holding back wider social change in rural Zheng County. Surprisingly, male literacy rates in Zheng County were slightly below the provincial average in the 1930s, despite its proximity to Zhengzhou.[104]

This slow pace of change in Zheng County during the 1910s and 1920s underlines the piecemeal nature of the impact of north China's railroads. Elsewhere, in the cotton belts around Luoyang and Anyang, and the tobacco zone of south-central Henan, railroad-led commercialization

99. See, for instance, Huenemann, *Dragon and the Iron Horse*, 38–39.

100. Tōa dōbunkai, *Kanan-shō*, 163.

101. Long–Hai tielu chewuchu shangwuke, "Long–Hai quanxian diaocha," 177. For an example, note the local memory of a declining bridge and market hub on the Zhengzhou–Luoyang postroad: "Zhengzhou Xiliuhu xia cang Qingdai shiqiao," *Zhengzhou jiyi*, October 25, 2013.

102. Skinner, "Marketing and Social Structure," part 2, 219–20.

103. Zheng County had twenty-one periodic markets in the period just before the Communist takeover in 1948. See Zhengzhou shi jiaoqu liangshiju, *Zhengzhou shi jiaoqu zhi: liangshi zhi*, 104.

104. Henan sheng tongji xuehui, *Minguo shiqi Henan sheng tongji ziliao*, 1:12–14.

transformed agricultural practice and, for better or for worse, tied rural areas more closely into the world economy. But Zheng County, despite its location in the provincial core and at the heart of the rail network, shows that economic transformation was by no means automatic. As well as the large regional peripheries in inland China explored by Kenneth Pomeranz and Odoric Wou, there were powerful local variations and smaller peripheries even close to railroads.

How can we explain the economic underperformance of Zhengzhou's Zheng County hinterland? The answer is primarily ecological. Soils in Zheng County had been damaged by centuries of intensive cultivation and repeated Yellow River floods. The situation was worst in the east and northeast of the county, where the 1887 flood had left large areas of sand.[105] A poem by Zhu Yanzhao (1832–1919), who served as an education official in Zhengzhou in the 1890s, describes ecological degradation around the village of Putian, which had been an imperial hunting ground during the Western Zhou (eleventh to eighth centuries BCE):

> From the Eastern Capital [Luoyang], people came hunting for
>   thousands of years; this was the emperor's former Putian
>   Park.
> Underneath the birds, it was like a sea of luxuriant green
>   spring weeds in the spring,
> And the horses neighed at the green-blue pastures, which were
>   like the mist.
> Today the open fields of Zheng are strewn with windblown
>   dust into the distance,
> And, since the former days of Zhou, the rain and dew have
>   fallen unevenly.[106]

According to one survey, less than half of the land in Zheng County was suitable for arable farming, with much of it a sandy wasteland that could at best be used for hardy crops such as peanuts.[107] Soils were better for farming close to the city and in the west of the county, where a silty-glutinous soil was rated "third grade" and suitable for grain production. But even where grain could be grown, one 1918 report noted that

105. Feng Zhongli, "Cong fengshacheng dao lüman Zhengzhou," 1–2.

106. This poem along with other poetry concerning Zhengzhou have been reproduced online with explanatory notes by local poet Li Gangtai. See http://blog.sina.com.cn/ligangtai.

107. Long–Hai tielu chewuchu shangwuke, "Long–Hai quanxian diaocha," 157.

"although there is a lot of dry spacious soil, it cannot be said to produce a lot of crops."[108] One 1930s study calculated that in a typical year spring wheat yields in Zheng County were 89 *jin* per *mu*—well below the (perhaps optimistic) provincial average of 143 *jin.*[109] Taking production of all grains into account, J. L. Buck's "crop index" estimated that yields in Zheng County were 27 percent below the China-wide average and 21 percent below the average for the winter wheat/sorghum zone that covered Zheng County and most of the North China Plain.[110]

Low yields do not on their own explain rural stagnation; indeed, with farm sizes slightly larger than average farm size, actual standards of living in rural Zheng County were typical for the region despite the poor soils.[111] But soil conditions around Zhengzhou did limit the development of cash cropping. In the mid-1930s, the frustrated provincial Cotton Production Improvement Bureau (Henan sheng mianchan gaojinsuo) suggested that cultivators close to Zhengzhou eschewed cotton as a cultural choice in favor of edible crops. There may be some truth in this—with poor soils and little irrigation, security of access to grain may have trumped the temptations of higher income from cotton—but much of the county was simply unsuitable for cotton production without major irrigation works.[112] The Nationalist Party local government did push new varieties during the 1930s (see chapter 2), but large-scale cotton production around Zhengzhou began only under Communist rule in the 1950s.

Agricultural limitations help explain the slow impact of railroads on Zhengzhou's immediate rural surroundings, but it is also important to remember that a city and its hinterland do not necessarily rise together. This is particularly true where transport technology can help a city become less dependent on its nearby countryside, as was already the case for some prerailroad transport hubs such as Yangzhou, where Anto-

---

108. Tōa dōbunkai, *Kanan-shō*, 46. For Zheng County soils, see Sun Wenyu et al., *Yu E Wan Gan sisheng tudi*, map after p. 50.

109. Sun Wenyu et al., *Yu E Wan Gan sisheng tudi*, 479. Provincial average is for 1931–35, from Bennō, "Chūka minkoku zenki," 85.

110. John L. Buck, *Land Utilization in China*, vol. 2: *Atlas*, 49.

111. Zheng County reported a 412-yuan average for rural household wealth, slightly above the average (397) for wheat areas in the Buck/Jinling study. See Sun Wenyu et al., *Yu E Wan Gan sisheng tudi*, 60, 467.

112. Henan sheng mianchan gaijinsuo, *Henan mianye*, 56.

nia Finnane shows that the city was more dependent on long-distance waterborne trade than on its rather poor hinterland.[113] But this possibility was exacerbated by faster railroad transport, with connections becoming more spatially diffuse. Although there was growing demand for eggs, chickens, and vegetables from the "diurnal hinterland" of villages near Zhengzhou, most of the core economic activity in the city—the transportation sector and the wholesale processing and shipment of cotton—had little essential connection to the county's rural economy.

Railroads provide what Frederick Cooper calls in the colonial context "arterial" links between points rather than "capillary" territorial coverage.[114] This was particularly true in the early decades of the Chinese network, made up of a small number of trunk routes and with few branch lines outside Manchuria. In Zhengzhou's case, the cotton-growing counties of distant western Henan or the grain belt of eastern Henan were brought closer in time/space, while the rural hinterland, accessed only at walking pace with human or animal labor, became relatively farther away. At the most local level, Zhengzhou's railroads even disconnected across space, cutting off paths and habitual patterns of movement. In the early days, several rural residents and livestock were killed trying to follow their old routes across the railroad tracks. Eventually train whistles and manned crossing points helped limit such collisions, but patterns of movement had been disrupted.[115] One local history of the lineside village of Mazhai complains of being cut off by the railway: "Zhengzhou is a city made by railways, but the people who lived by the rail line from the very beginning have constantly been kept at a distance from that city (*baochi zhe juli*)."[116]

What about the pull of the city in Zhengzhou's rural hinterland? Even if the rapid transformation of Zhengzhou was somewhat disconnected from its nearby hinterland, one might expect rural residents to migrate to nearby cities for economic opportunities. But this is not necessarily the case. As Gunther Barth points out from North America, fast-growing

113. Finnane, *Speaking of Yangzhou*, 161–71.

114. Cooper, "Conflict and Connection," 1533. As Judd Kinzley has shown, highways as well as railroads could have a similar arterial pattern. Kinzley, *Natural Resources and the New Frontier*, 11.

115. This is a local journalist's report based on oral interviews with elderly residents. See *Zhengzhou ribao*, April 12, 2007.

116. Zhengxie Zhengzhou shi Erqiqu weiyuanhui, *Yuanqu zhi jiyi*, 61.

cities tend to attract a long-distance influx, meaning that "the inhabitants of these instant cities were likewise strangers to the people from the surrounding countryside."[117] This observation was probably less true for Zhengzhou than for Barth's gold rush towns, but those benefiting most from the city's rapid growth were arrivals from far afield, a migration both driven and enabled by the railroads. One survey of the early 1930s commented that Zhengzhou's urbanization was a long-distance phenomenon: "lots of businesspeople in particular are coming from all over. In addition to that, the police, the officials, the military, the workers—a great number of them have also come from outside."[118] Zhengzhou's merchant class was dominated by long-distance arrivals: at first from Tianjin, later from Shaanxi and Hankou. Higher managerial and technical grades in the railroad and cotton sectors were disproportionately staffed by those from the Lower Yangzi region. Only seven of eighty-one Chinese railroad senior staff hailed from Henan Province, let alone the city's rural hinterland.[119]

At a level lower down, the limited documentation available shows that Zhengzhou's workforce was more Henanese, but with the immediate region around the city underrepresented. In the 1920s, a small majority of police staff was from Henan but only 15 percent from Zhengzhou or neighboring counties. In the 1940s, almost four-fifths of workers in the Long–Hai depot were from Henan, but still only 11 percent hailed from Zheng County itself (including those originally from Zhengzhou City) and a further 11 percent from nearby counties.[120] Much of Zhengzhou's manual labor force was drawn from the wider region of central and northern Henan, especially areas with railroad connections. It seems certain that some Zheng County residents were spending time in the

117. Barth, *Instant Cities*, 18.

118. Long–Hai tielu chewuchu shangwuke, "Long–Hai quanxian diaocha," 164.

119. Wu Shixun, *Henan*, 71–72. Liu Yongli, "Minguo shiqi Zhengzhou chengshi," 20. On Henanese complaints about high-ranking jobs for southerners on the railroads, see *Henan ribao*, October 21, 1912.

120. On police staffing, see "Zhengzhou shi gong'anju zhiyuan biao," *Zhengzhou shizheng yuekan*, no. 1 (1928): 97–103; on railroad workers, "Zheng xian chewuduan shiyou yuangong mingce," September 1948, Henan Provincial Archive, M74-01-0114. With little archival material surviving from before the Japanese invasion of 1937, this is the earliest statistical information I have found on the origin place of Zhengzhou's railway workers.

city for casual labor—unskilled urban wages were substantially higher than those in the nearby countryside—but surveys of the county do not mention widespread rural dependence on urban labor opportunities.[121] Similarly, if Zhengzhou were attracting a great deal of local rural labor, one would expect agricultural wages in Zheng County to rise, but from the limited evidence available they look typical for the region.[122]

Zhengzhou's urban boom in the first two decades of the railroad had not been accompanied by wholesale rural commercialization, let alone a deeper transition to long-run per capita economic growth. Although there is some evidence of positive spillover effects in nearby villages for things like eggs, rice, and vegetables, Zheng County largely missed out on railroad Henan's cash crop boom and even by the 1930s does not seem to have seen large-scale rural dependence on urban work. Xiong Yaping's picture of rail-led commercialization closing rural-urban divides does not seem to hold here—if anything, the reverse is true. As Steven Topik and Allen Wells point out, the gulf between city and village is more easily closed in the world's "affluent areas," where capital, communications, and technology can more easily spread from the city to nearby villages.[123] Zheng County was not by any measure an "affluent area," and whatever the growth of Zhengzhou and the transformation of its regional economic role, spreading the benefits across rural space was a much more difficult affair. Factors of environment and economic geography limited the positive effects of the railroad in its first twenty years in Zheng County. Compared with later periods, this spatial disconnection was not yet directly political, in the sense of being caused by state policy. But it was political in a negative sense: in the fast-changing, militarized politics of the 1910s and 1920s, there is little sign that Henan's warlord

121. There are scarce wage data from before the 1930s in Zhengzhou, but in 1935 monthly wages in the city were reckoned to be 6 to 12 yuan per month for unskilled work. "Henan ge xian shehui diaocha: Zheng xian," *Henan tongji yuebao* 1, no. 1 (1935): 103. Agricultural wages in surrounding Zheng County varied seasonally between 3 and 6 yuan per month, 4.5 being typical. "Henan nonglin tongji," *Henan tongji yuebao*, 2, no. 8 (1936), 20.

122. Rural wages for Zheng County were at the provincial average for yearlong contracts or day labor and a little higher for monthlong hire. "Henan nonglin tongji," *Henan tongji yuebao*, 2, no. 8 (1936): 20.

123. Topik and Wells, "Commodity Chains," 602.

powerholders were interested in or capable of redistributing infrastructure and other resources across space.

This situation changed in the second half of the 1920s, when local and provincial authorities and commentators were beginning to express two distinct anxieties about Zhengzhou's rapid growth. The first of these was Zhengzhou's chaotic urban environment, particularly at the fast-changing edge of the city. The second was the question of the rural-urban divides and endemic poverty in surrounding Zheng County. After the tumult of the Nationalist Revolution of 1927, Zhengzhou's powerholders launched experiments to tackle these two problems, asserting political control at the urban edge and beginning programs of rural uplift in the nearby countryside. The next chapter explores these efforts and their consequences for spatial politics in and around Zhengzhou.

CHAPTER TWO

City Dreams and Rural Reach, 1927–1937

Zhengzhou fell to the forces of the Nationalist Revolution at the end of May 1927. The troops of the warlord Wu Peifu, who had dominated Henan Province for most of the 1920s, retreated from the city. Yet this was not the famous "Northern Expedition" of Chiang Kai-shek and the Nationalist Party. Instead, local power was seized by another of the northern warlords, Feng Yuxiang (1882–1948), who in 1922 had briefly held power in this part of Henan as Wu's subordinate. By 1927 Marshall Feng was a self-styled modernizing reformer, and he marched into Henan from Northwest China as part of the revolutionary coalition. Recognizing the strategic importance of Zhengzhou, Feng set up his headquarters in the city, at the Protestant mission hospital just outside the walls.[1] Using Zhengzhou as a base, Feng was able to consolidate his control over much of the province by playing off the competing Nationalist power centers of Wuhan (the Left, under Wang Jingwei) and Nanjing (the Right, under Chiang Kai-Shek) against one another. But Feng's independent power in Henan did not last. After a series of clashes in late 1929, full-scale war broke out in May 1930 between Chiang's Nationalist Party central government and a coalition of anti-Chiang warlords. Feng's defeat in this "Central Plains War" brought Henan under Nationalist Party control.[2]

Feng Yuxiang's power in Zhengzhou was short-lived, yet this chapter shows that his brief dominance precipitated the most important shift in the spatial politics of the city since the coming of the railroad two decades before. Feng established Zhengzhou's first municipal government in March 1928, with a program owing something to his 1926 visit to the Soviet Union as well as his Christian moralism and earlier efforts at urban

---

1. "Feng Yuxiang liangci zhu Yu," 96.
2. For more details, see Sheridan, *Chinese Warlord*, 203–67.

reform in China. In Michael Tsin's terms, Feng's rule in Zhengzhou was the turning point from a piecemeal urban reformism to a more wholesale modernist program built on mass mobilization.[3] This much more ambitious local state tried to tackle Zhengzhou's twin issues of urban governance and poverty in the surrounding countryside. Via small-scale experiments and large-scale planning, Feng's moral and environmental improvements aimed simultaneously to transform city and countryside.

Feng's projects in and around Zhengzhou were underfunded and for the most part did not survive his fall from power. In 1931 the Nanjing central government even abolished Zhengzhou's municipal government and returned the city to ordinary county administration. Yet this chapter argues that, although Feng's specific policies did not last, they established a pattern of spatial politics in Zhengzhou that recurred throughout the twentieth century. Feng's government promised to reconnect city and countryside, to use its control of urban people and environments as a springboard for village uplift and rural state building. But in practice, his administration in Zhengzhou was too weak and too focused on other priorities to bring infrastructural or economic change even within the limited confines of nearby Zheng County. Instead, this was a distinctly urban-first modernization, imagining a future for the city very separate from the surrounding countryside. Despite some efforts to spread resources from Zhengzhou to its rural hinterland in Zheng County, the more ambitious local state in these years if anything aided the powerful economic, discursive, and political forces pushing in the opposite direction, toward spatial divisions. Indeed, across the wider region of his control, Feng's policy of rural extraction and control of grain sparked rebellion and exacerbated famine. This would not be the last time a state with other priorities was complicit in Henan's twentieth-century famines—nor the last time that promises to rebuild rural-urban connections were swallowed up by the countervailing forces of inequality and disconnection between city and countryside.

This chapter begins by exploring Feng Yuxiang's municipal rule and its effects on Zhengzhou and those villages within the municipal boundaries. Although historians have examined urban reform in several Chinese cities, there has been little discussion of cities on Zhengzhou's smaller scale, city governance under Feng Yuxiang, or rural areas under munic-

3. Tsin, *Nation, Governance, and Modernity*.

ipal governments.[4] The first part of this chapter argues that in a municipality as small and fiscally weak as Zhengzhou, city government was as much about discourse and performance as real policy shifts. This was especially true at the urban edge, which Feng used as a site for political display, small-scale experiments in social control, and the performance of grandiose and unrealized urban planning. I go on to examine the spatial politics of Zhengzhou under Nationalist Party control after 1930, arguing that with its economic functions spreading elsewhere and a lack of political patronage, the city's role in the regional economy was under threat. The last part of this chapter argues that although discourses of agricultural crisis brought more attention to the problems facing Zhengzhou's rural surroundings, neither Feng Yuxiang nor his Nationalist successors were able to tackle underlying rural-urban divisions in Zheng County.

Zhengzhou under Feng Yuxiang

MAKING MUNICIPAL GOVERNMENT

The emergence of distinct urban government—what Luca Gabbiani calls the "municipal city"—was a shared feature of global modernity in the interwar period.[5] Across the industrialized, colonial, and semicolonial worlds, political reformers in different ways promoted something more ambitious than previous urban regimes, including citywide solutions to public services, housing, and urban planning. In Zhengzhou the new municipal government of 1928 separated urban administration from rural Zheng County for the first time. This is not to say that there had been no earlier urban institutions. The city had its own police force, founded in 1904 in preparation for the opening of the Jing–Han railroad. Amid the experiments in self-government in the early Republican period, Zhengzhou had had a short-lived Board for the City and Suburbs (Chengxiang dongshihui) under the County Assembly.[6] And in 1922 the central government in Beijing restored Zhengzhou's status as an open trading port, which had lapsed after the revolution of 1911. The superintendent's office

---

4. For a short discussion of Feng Yuxiang's urban rule in Xi'an, see Tai, "Opening Up the Northwest," 120–23.

5. On the "municipal city," see Gabbiani, "Connecting Urban Histories," 15–18.

6. Liu Ruilin, *Zheng xian zhi, juan* 3, 47a on police; *juan* 8, 3 on *chengxiang dongshihui*.

(Shangbu duban gongshu) controlled trading matters independently of the county government.[7]

Despite its rapid growth, Zhengzhou was still part of Zheng County, governed from the old county yamen in the walled city. Municipalities began to be established across China during the 1920s, and even where there was no municipal authority, regional powerholders and/ or local elites had been leading major urban reform projects in many cities.[8] Zhengzhou, by contrast, still had the chaotic quality of a sudden boomtown. Like many fast-growing cities, it was faced with challenges of crime, a transient population, skewed sex ratios, and weak urban governance. One commentator of 1929 looked back on the city in the mid-1920s: "Zhengzhou was very dirty indeed, the air smelled terrible, and there were beggars all over the streets; all in all it made a person want to run a mile (*tuibi sanshe*). . . . The household registers were vague, land issues were unclear, policing was ineffective, production was not increasing, buildings were inelegant, industry had no vigor, education was poor, [and] public health was disregarded."[9]

The transitional years of 1927–1930 were a key period for both Zhengzhou and the wider story of China's urban history. With the Nationalist Revolution, city government across China was moving away from regional or local initiatives toward being an administrative layer mandated by the central government.[10] Within a few weeks of takeover, Feng Yuxiang established a municipal government preparation office (Shizheng choubeichu) in Zhengzhou, which in March 1928 was converted to a full city administration under mayor Zhao Shouyu (1881–1960). This was the first municipal government in Henan, more than eighteen months in advance of the provincial capital of Kaifeng.[11]

7. Xu Youli, "Zhengzhou jian 'shi,'" 21–22.

8. Stapleton, "Rise of Municipal Government." On urban reform, see Liping Wang, "Tourism and Spatial Change"; Stapleton, *Civilizing Chengdu*; Shao, *Culturing Modernity*; Carroll, *Between Heaven and Modernity*, 23–70; Lincoln, *Urbanizing China*, 55–71.

9. "Wo ye lai tantan Zhengzhou shi de 'bu,'" *Zhengzhou shizheng yuekan*, no. 5 (1929), *yanlun* section, 21–22. Page numbers in this municipal government journal restart with each new section.

10. The Nationalist government's City Organization Law came into effect in July 1928. For a useful discussion, see Lincoln, *Urbanizing China*, 74–76.

11. Xu Youli, "Zhengzhou jian 'shi,'" 22.

Municipal life under Feng was a crash course in the structures of time discipline, mass mobilization, and the remaking of local space that came to order residents' lives during the second and third quarters of China's twentieth century. The "Fourteen Points for a New Zhengzhou" offered by Mayor Zhao—himself a military officer—offer a glimpse into the ambitious municipal agenda of control over space and people. Zhao promised education and physical training for the whole population alongside stricter policing, new building regulations, and improved roads.[12] Zhengzhou's new government asserted its control over local space, institutions, and people, closing temples, conducting a new household registration survey, daubing slogans on buildings, and ordering the blue and red of the new Nationalist flag to be painted on shop fronts.[13]

But if municipal administration was concerned with control over space, what was the space it controlled? In theory, a municipal boundary is a precise line marking the edge of the city. Things in Zhengzhou were not so straightforward, owing to the ongoing distinction, discussed in chapter 1, between the old walled city and the new commercial center around the railroad station. The ambivalence of this relationship underlines the competing impulses for local authorities to connect and disconnect across space. On the one hand, Feng Yuxiang tried to connect the two districts of Zhengzhou by ordering the removal of the city wall. This decision was made in the face of opposition from the local elite families of the walled city, but as with many cities across China, Zhengzhou's new authorities took the view that the wall was impeding transport flows. Zhengzhou's brick walls were duly knocked down in late February 1928, although the corner gun batteries and some sections of earth mound were left in place— the latter being used as dugouts for refugees during the wars of the 1940s.[14] As part of the same drive to improve connections within the city, some of the bricks were crushed and reused for new road surfaces.[15]

12. "Jianshe xin Zhengzhou shi jihua dagang shisi tiao," *Zhengzhou shizheng yuekan*, no. 2 (1928), unpaginated front matter.

13. *Zhengzhou shizheng yuekan*, no. 1 (1928), *gongdu* section, 13; *North China Herald*, March 10, 1928.

14. Eight refugees were killed in 1947, when the earth mound along the south side of the former city wall collapsed after heavy rain, crushing the holes in which they had been living. *Zhengzhou ribao*, November 4, 1947.

15. Zhao Fuhai, *Lao Zhengzhou: Shangdu yimeng*, 8–9. On opposition to demolition, see *North China Herald*, March 17, 1928.

On the other hand, when the municipal government was established the following month, it did not include the former walled city. Instead, the boundaries of Zhengzhou's municipal government were inherited from the 10 square kilometers of the *shangbu* trading zone reestablished in 1922. This area covered the extramural parts of the city that had developed after the coming of the railroad plus a few villages to the north. Even more confusingly, the city police did include the walled city in its jurisdiction but was itself only loosely under the control of the municipal government.[16] Despite a petition to incorporate the old walled city into the municipality and move the Zheng County seat to a "strategically important place in the countryside," the situation does not seem to have changed before abolition of the municipality in 1931.[17] Unsurprisingly, this administrative confusion caused a series of jurisdictional disputes, of which education funding proved the most intractable. Most of Zhengzhou's schools were inside the old walled city and hence outside municipal jurisdiction. The municipal government tried to assert control over the schools and their budgets, accusing the county government of failing to divide the funds correctly. A joint committee to oversee the revenue distribution between county and municipality does not seem to have eliminated these conflicts.[18]

This anomaly of the municipal boundary exacerbated the division between the old walled city and the new commercial district. Even after the removal of the wall, the former was usually referred to as the "walled district" (*chengqu*), as opposed to the "urban district" (*shiqu*) of the municipality beyond. This difference maintained in Zhengzhou the distinction between *cheng* (wall) and *shi* (market)—in other words, the different origins of cities in either defensive or commercial functions—which urban theorist Zhang Weici (1890–1976) suggested in the 1920s

16. Zhao Shouyu was for a time simultaneously head of the municipal government and the city police, but they remained separate bodies. See *Zhengzhou shizheng yuekan*, no. 1 (1928), *gongdu* section, 1–2. It appears that municipal control of the police occurred only in late 1929 and even then only as an interim arrangement. See *Henan minbao*, December 1, 1929.

17. *Zhengzhou shizheng yuekan*, no. 4 (1929), *chengwen* section, 6.

18. For ongoing conflict, see *Zhengzhou shizheng yuekan*, no. 4 (1929), *chengwen* section, 15–16; no. 7 (1929), *chengwen*, 1–2. The joint committee on revenue was the "Municipality-County Division of Revenue Implementation Committee" (Shi xian huafen caizheng zhixing weiyuanhui).

had already been overcome.[19] Even in the 1930s, there was still a marked difference between the bustling commercial city and the former walled area, which was still a mixed zone, with continued market gardening and even a rural-style periodic market. Ignoring the removal of the brick wall, one commentator noted that "inside Zhengzhou's city walls, there is quite a strong rural atmosphere, with thatch and mud huts everywhere and very few brick and tile buildings. . . . Those women who live inside the walls regard coming out of the walled city as entering the city (*ba chucheng kanzuo jincheng*)."[20]

POWER AND IMPROVEMENT AT THE URBAN EDGE

Although the old walled city was left out of the municipality, the fringes of Zhengzhou's new commercial city were within its boundaries—and became a focus of attention for the nascent government. These urban edges provided the biggest headache for municipal authority but were also the sites of experiment for control over space and populations. By the 1920s the northern and southern edges of the city were a patchwork of mixed land use, home to warehouses, industry, and open ground as well as informal shack housing (see chapter 1). Xu Xiangyun (1893–1965), a senior military official under Feng, felt that the authorities had little control here and called for more police posts: "most idlers and unemployed people wander around with nowhere to go, drifting around hungry and cold, and out of desperation they are willing to take risks (*ting er zouxian*), such as petty thieving; therefore, in districts away from the main downtown, we often hear that all kinds of immoral activity (*yuyuan zuanxue*) is going on."[21] Other municipal schemes included the removal of undesirable people and objects from the city proper, including the removal of vagrants and the relocation of nightsoil depots.[22] It was therefore this urban edge more than the commercial downtown that became a site for social and political experimentation under Feng,

19. Zhang Weici, *Shizheng zhidu*, 3.

20. Zi Gang, "Zhengzhou de funü," *Shenbao zhoukan* 1, no. 24 (1936): 572–73, quoted in Liu Hui, *Tielu yu Zhengzhou chengshihua*, 253.

21. Xu Xiangyun, "Duiyu Zhengzhou shizheng zhi guanjian," *Zhengzhou shizheng yukan*, no. 3 (1928), *yanlun* section, 6–7.

22. On plans for the relocation of nightsoil, see "Zhengzhou shi gong'anju qudi fenchang banfa," *Shizheng yuekan*, no. 1 (1928): 78–79.

including the mobilizing and disciplinary aspects of urban reform that had begun in the last years of the Qing era and which were deepening across China in the 1920s and 1930s.[23]

The most prominent target was Laofengang on the north side of the town, Zhengzhou's largest area of periurban informal settlement. By the late 1920s, Laofengang hosted one of the largest *jianghu* communities— drifting street entertainers, martial artists, beggars—north of the Yangzi River, rivaling Beijing's Tianqiao and Sanbuguan in Tianjin.[24] As well as hosting *jianghu*, Laofengang also attracted casual laborers, sex workers, hawkers, and small-scale traders in textiles and metal goods. Feng personally issued a blanket ban on prostitution and in February 1928 set up an office at Laofengang to enforce the order. His officials processed the cases of more than four hundred women, sending about half to work at the Yufeng spinning mill and giving the rest travel expenses to return to their home villages. Feng was sufficiently pleased with his moral improvements to Laofengang (including a major effort to tackle opium addiction in the neighborhood) that, when Chiang Kai-shek visited for negotiations, he treated the Generalissimo to a personal tour.[25] Later that year, the attention of the municipal government turned to the physical environment on this north side of the city, issuing an ordinance banning informal housing: "Look at these straw shacks (*xipeng*). At this time of new construction of municipal government, they not only make the appearance of the city very ugly; they are also very dangerous [in the event of fire]."[26] In October, in one of the first of many struggles for street trading rights over the course of the twentieth century, the city police tried to force small traders to demolish their stalls for road widening. This decree attracted opprobrium even in the opinion pages of the municipal government's own journal: "people are no longer permitted to trade on the street; because of this, the multitude of poor among Han

23. See, for instance, Lipkin, *Useless to the State*; Janet Chen, *Guilty of Indigence*; Wang, *The Teahouse*.

24. Local historian Zhao Fuhai attributes the growth of Laofengang to Zhengzhou's status as a railroad junction attracting drifting populations. See Zhao, *Lao Zhengzhou: minsu shengdi Laofengang*, 150.

25. On the fate of sex workers, see Zhao Fuhai, *Lao Zhengzhou: Shangdu yimeng*, 254–55; on Chiang's visit, see Zhao Fuhai, *Lao Zhengzhou: minsu shengdi Laofengang*, 172–74.

26. *Zhengzhou shizheng yuekan*, no. 1 (1928), *bugao* (notifications) section, 2–3.

and Hui [Muslim] alike are thrown into unemployment and grave difficulty, crying out with hunger and cold (*tiji haohan*)."[27]

In tandem with this knocking down of shacks and stalls, the municipal authorities under Feng also began a program of experimental "commoners' villages" (*pingmincun*) for the urban poor. According to the memoirs of city official Li Rongjia, three such villages were built around the edge of Zhengzhou: on the northern edge of the city, outside the south gate, and on the west side of the railroad station at the nearby village of Wulibao. Li had responsibility for the first of these. Its residents were migrant laborers and trash collectors whose shacks had been torn down in urban improvement works. This urban edge village was small—around thirty households—but offered a glimpse of Feng's vision for improved material conditions accompanied by tight moral and political control. Residents enjoyed rent-free brick-built housing in return for close administrative supervision and a strict hygiene regime.[28]

As part of the same agenda of social improvement, Zhengzhou's new authorities tried to provide green space around the city. The Long–Hai Railroad Bureau had set up a small garden in the southwest corner of the city as early as 1918. But it was only under Feng Yuxiang that public parks became part of a wider strategy to improve the morals and political consciousness of Zhengzhou's residents. Feng Yuxiang's largest and most politicized park was the Bishagang memorial gardens, dedicated to his troops who had been killed in battle. This was a much more ambitious effort—twenty times larger—than the small memorial garden set up to Zhili clique martyrs on the north side of the city in 1922 (see chapter 1). Feng bought up 60 acres of land 2 kilometers west of the city, in an area of poor, sandy soil (see map 1.3). He set aside 200,000 yuan—ten times the monthly budget of the Zhengzhou municipal government—and commissioned Xu Xiangyun, the officer mentioned above calling for more city policemen, to design the gardens. The memorial park duly opened in April 1928 and included a public graveyard as well as a park,

27. "Zhengzhou shizheng zhi yueyan," *Zhengzhou shizheng yuekan*, no. 2 (1928), *yanlun* section, 2–4. Ironically, after Feng's fall from power, he took up the cause of Nanjing residents whose homes were being demolished in the Nationalist capital. See Musgrove, *China's Contested Capital*, 84.

28. Li Rongjia, "Feng Yuxiang di'erci zhu Yu," 63–71.

woodlands, and a martyrs' monument.[29] The visiting novelist Zhang Henshui (1895–1967) was impressed by the seriousness of the graves and calmed by Bishagang's pools, paths, and trees: "to have such a place in Zhengzhou, a busy commercial and industrial city, where everything seems noisy and clamorous (*xuanxiao*), is really something entirely new."[30]

There are several ways of interpreting the Bishagang park. In the ambitious modernizing politics of 1928, it points to a new expansion of political display, territorial power, and urban leisure over the fringes of the city. As a suburban site of collective memory and ritual, Bishagang can be compared with the Sun Yat-sen mausoleum being constructed at Zijinshan outside Nanjing at the same time.[31] For Feng, the single most enthusiastic closer of shrines and temples in Zhengzhou's history, Bishagang and its military-nationalist memory offered a ritual alternative to old "superstitions." And for the historian, the next half-century of Bishagang—as experimental farm in the 1930s, military garrison during the Second World War, black market during the Mao period, nuclear bomb shelter following the Sino-Soviet split, and early reform era shopping mall—underlines the multiple reimaginings of Zhengzhou's urban fringe.

CITY PLANNING AND URBAN PERFORMANCE

As well as being the site for the Bishagang project, the west side of the Jing–Han railroad was the focus for the most ambitious urban vision in pre-Communist Zhengzhou. As part of the 1920s golden age of city planning in twentieth-century China, Feng's administration soon generated ambitious blueprints for the Zhengzhou of the future. The first urban plan, of 1927, proposed extending the built-up area to the north, filling in the remaining rural areas within the municipal boundary.[32] But this plan was still insufficient for the ambitions of the nascent municipality, which over five issues of its inhouse journal put forward a scheme for an entirely new city.[33] Leaving behind the existing city—

---

29. Liao Yongmin, "Feng Yuxiang yingjian Bishagang lingyuan," 1–8.
30. Zhang Henshui, "Xiyou xiaoji," 8b.
31. On Zijinshan, see Liping Wang, "Creating a National Symbol."
32. Hao Pengzhan, "Jijin yu baoshou," 45–48.
33. "Zhengzhou shi xin shiqu jianshe jihua cao'an," *Zhengzhou shizheng yuekan*, across five issues, no. 3 (1928) to no. 7 (1929), *yanlun* sections.

though most of it was less than twenty years old—the "New Zheng-zhou" was to be built west of the Jing–Han railway and south of the Long–Hai line. In the absence of archival documents, it is hard to know anything about the anonymous planner—or planners, for the differing styles and levels of detail in the text suggest multiple authors—but the design reveals a range of European, American, and Japanese influence, including Hausmann's Paris, Ottawa's Parliament Hill, and the Hobrecht Plan for Berlin, as well as the influence of the cities of coastal China. "New Zhengzhou" was to hold an initial population of 250,000 and cover a rectangular area of 35 square kilometers (about the size of the inner walled city of late imperial Beijing or just over half the size of Manhattan).[34]

The design of this "new planned city" (*guihua xinshi*) was governed by concerns about hygiene, green space, waste, and public order: "the buildings and facilities must all have an orderly and planned development, not obeying natural tendencies that are disorderly and chaotic (*zaluan wuzhang*)."[35] The new Zhengzhou was to be strictly divided into functional zones for administrative, commercial, residential, and industrial use (map 2.1). But with its roads alone budgeted at ten times the municipal government's annual expenditure, the cost rendered the plan fantastical, even with a vague proposal to raise city bonds.[36] In 1928 the municipality asked the provincial government for additional funds to conduct initial surveys, and in 1929 there was some discussion of laying out roads to the proposed site, but there is no suggestion that construction ever began.[37]

But to dismiss the "New Zhengzhou" plan as unfeasible is to misunderstand its purpose. More than a real blueprint for construction, this was about the municipal government condemning the messy land use, informal buildings, and chaotic street life of real, existing Zhengzhou and making a statement about the kind of order, space, and control that it imagined for the future. For the impecunious city government,

34. "Zhengzhou shi xin shiqu jianshe jihua cao'an," *Zhengzhou shizheng yuekan*, no. 3 (1928), *yanlun*, 4–6.

35. "Zhengzhou shi xin shiqu jianshe jihua cao'an," *Zhengzhou shizheng yuekan*, no. 3 (1928), *yanlun*, 2.

36. *Zhengzhou shizheng yuekan*, no. 1 (1928), *gongdu* section, 10.

37. *Zhengzhou shizheng yuekan*, no. 1 (1928), *gongdu* section, 5; *Zhengzhou shizheng yuekan*, no. 6 (1929), *yanlun* section, 19.

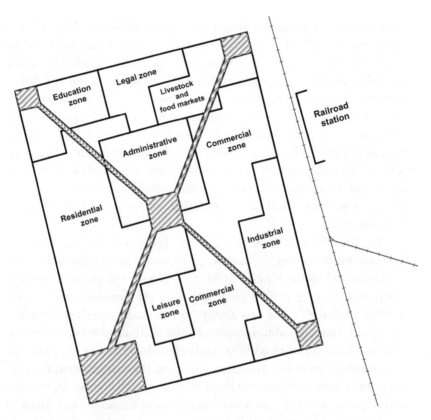

MAP 2.1. "New Zhengzhou" urban plan, 1928–1929. Adapted from *Zhengzhou shizheng yuekan*, no. 4, *yanlun section*, 5. Map by Jogu Gopinath.

it was much easier to parade these credentials by urban planning than by incurring the costs and antagonisms associated with physically transforming the existing urban environment.[38] Like the practice of social surveys investigated by Tong Lam, the actual results mattered rather less than the creation and presentation of expertise and the legitimation of new kinds of governing text.[39] The plan of 1928, then, is best seen as a political performance to claim a modern urban identity for this maligned, "chaotic" railroad town. Although its effects were fleeting,

38. On the costs in enacting urban planning, note the difficulties the authorities encountered in widening roads in other cities. See Guannan Li, "Reviving China," 119–26; Musgrove, *China's Contested Capital*, 80–86.

39. Lam, *Passion for Facts*, 16.

this was a performance that would have important echoes in urban plans for Zhengzhou under Communist rule in the 1950s and beyond.

Part of the modernist performance of the "New Zhengzhou" blueprint was the eradication of the rural context of the city. At first glance this seems unfair, given some aspects of the design. Based on the latest advice from the United States, the planners designated a precise 12.5 percent of the city's area for green space. Rather than the large square for public ritual that one might have expected, the center of the city was to be given over to parkland. Four "green avenues" connected this central park to further green space in the four corners of the city. Future residents were also promised a "rural flavor" (*nongcun fengwei*) in this "ruralizing new city" (*nongcunhua zhi xinshiqu*).[40] Yet rural reality—as opposed to an idealized version of the rural as simply green space—was excised from the plan. The stark rural-urban boundaries were promised in policy as well as cartographic exclusion, with the plan seeking to avoid the problem of informal settlements for migrant workers that worried Zhengzhou's administrators in the 1920s and created a blurred rural-urban fringe: "in the area around the city, in the belt of land surrounding it, people should not be allowed wantonly to build things."[41] As for rural-urban movement, the plan suggested that rural people and animals would not have free rein to move across the urban area, confined instead to specific sites to discharge their goods.[42] There is also no mention in the city plan of what would happen to the people already living and farming in the designated space. Judging by detailed subcounty maps of 1916, some twenty-eight villages lay within the proposed city limits, but the planners preferred to imagine a tabula rasa, calling the site a "wilderness" (*kuangye*).[43]

40. "Zhengzhou shi xin shiqu jianshe jihua cao'an," *Zhengzhou shizheng yuekan*, no. 5 (1929): 3–5.

41. "Zhengzhou shi xin shiqu jianshe jihua cao'an," *Zhengzhou shizheng yuekan*, no. 5 (1929): 12. It is hard to imagine that such a policy could have been sustained. Planned cities around the world in the twentieth century were often surrounded by unplanned settlements, housing lower-paid service workers who had little place in the planned city. Brasília is perhaps the most famous example. See Holston, *Modernist City*, chap. 7.

42. "Zhengzhou shi xin shiqu jianshe jihua cao'an," *Zhengzhou shizheng yuekan*, no. 5 (1929): 2.

43. "Zhengzhou shi xin shiqu jianshe jihua cao'an," *Zhengzhou shizheng yuekan*, no. 5 (1929): 5. See Liu Ruilin, *Zheng xian zhi*, front matter maps and lists of villages in *juan* 3, 29–31.

For all the rural language in the design, this was a plan to deterritorialize the countryside and reterritorialize it as tamed, urbanized green space in the new city. Rural people were excluded from the vision, a pattern in Zhengzhou's urban planning that persisted across the twentieth century. This pattern extended beyond urban planning. For all the homespun style of Feng Yuxiang himself, the city government promoted a distinctly urban-centered view of progress. Readers of the Zhengzhou municipality's journal could learn that "the city is where culture becomes developed, and it is the source of the progress of humanity. . . . In science and in the arts, all the engines of human progress, there has not been one that was not developed by an urban inhabitant."[44] This view was accompanied by suspicion of rural migrants drifting into the city. From 1928, anyone begging in Zhengzhou could be taken by the city police to the new "Relief Shelter" (Jiujisuo). Those found to be from rural households were forced to remain for a minimum of three months to discourage begging during the agricultural slack season.[45]

In the year this system was launched, Zhengzhou's new rulers faced a stark reminder that poverty in the surrounding countryside could not be imagined away by dreams of urban utopia or by antimigrant policies. Most of North and Northwest China was hit by severe drought in 1928 and 1929. Coupled with spiraling prices, poor transportation, and growing political conflict, subsistence crises emerged in summer 1928. Much of Henan faced famine through to 1930, while Shaanxi and Gansu were even worse hit. There are few reliable statistics, but the death toll for the 1928–1930 famine may have run into the millions, with tens of millions affected overall.[46] Although the crisis was worst in the west and southwest of Henan, conditions were also poor around Zhengzhou, with drought and locusts affecting crops in Zheng County.[47] In Yangzhai, 13 kilometers southwest of the city, locals rose up against the township government, destroyed orders for grain requisitioning, and distributed government

44. Ge Cheng, "Shizheng guanli zhi wojian," *Zhengzhou shizheng yuekan*, no. 4 (1929), *yanlun* section, 10.

45. *Zhengzhou shizheng yuekan*, no. 2 (1928), *zhangze* section, 3–5.

46. On the 1928–1930 famine in Henan, see Su Xinliu, *Minguo shiqi Henan shui han zaihai*, esp. 35–37. See also Janku, "From Natural to National Disaster."

47. Su Xinliu, *Minguo shiqi Henan shui han zaihai*, 3; Liu Jingxiang, *Henan xinzhi*, 603.

food stocks.[48] Famine refugees poured into the city from across the province, and the antibegging system of forced indoor relief was soon overwhelmed. Instead of a brand-new modern city, Zhengzhou became a point of embarkation for famine victims fleeing by rail, with some thirty-five thousand people processed in the city en route to Manchuria in the summer of 1929 alone.[49] The response of Feng Yuxiang's administration was woefully inadequate. Heavy surtaxes were imposed on relief grain traveling by railroad. Local authorities seem to have done little to divert resources to the needy, although in a rare moment of cooperation municipal and county governments jointly sold grain at below-market prices in Zhengzhou. Feng himself embezzled—or, at least, forcibly borrowed—some 120,000 yuan from the China International Famine Relief Commission (Hua-Yang yizhenhui).[50]

With his modernizing policies, down-to-earth style, and nationalist credentials, Feng Yuxiang has enjoyed a positive reputation in the People's Republic. His short tenure in Zhengzhou is an important part of local stories of progress in urban governance. But Feng has been better remembered in official histories than among those who lived under his rule, particularly in rural areas. This is perhaps not so much a paradox as a reminder that ambitious schemes for transformation in modern China have resulted in inequalities and sacrifices. Under Feng's rule, as in later periods, the combination of modernizing ambition and limited resources of the state was a damaging and unequal cocktail. As discussed below, the famine of 1928–1930 was not the last occasion that famine victims walked and died in the streets of Zhengzhou. Nor was it the final time the city's authorities faced a disjunction between modernizing dreams and the poverty of many in the surrounding countryside. At fifteen-year intervals, in 1942–1943 and 1958–1961 as well as 1928–1930, the people of Henan faced subsistence crises and a lackluster, even pitiless, response from rulers whose priorities lay elsewhere.

48. Zhengzhou shi jiaoqu minzheng zhi bianxie zu, "Zhengzhou shi jiaoqu minzheng zhi," 6:40.

49. Su Xinliu, *Minguo shiqi Henan shui han zaihai*, 126–27.

50. *North China Herald*, August 3, 1929. For criticisms of Feng's response, see Sheridan, *Chinese Warlord*, 248–52; Janku, "From Natural to National Disaster," 253. On aid in Zhengzhou, see "Zhengzhou shi zai kuang diaochabiao," *Zhengzhou shizheng yuekan*, no. 6 (1929), *diaocha* section, no page.

Zhengzhou under Nationalist Rule

Zhengzhou in the 1930s was a bustling commercial city. The city's economy was beginning to diversify beyond its base in railroads and cotton, including in retail and banking sectors. In the downtown around the railroad station, the commercial zone of Dehuajie and Datonglu (see map 1.2) was regarded by the travel writer Sun Xiaoqian as "the very best (*jinghua*) of Henan Province," with "rather wide streets and four- and five-story shop buildings."[51] These streets were typical of new-style commercial zones across provincial China in the 1930s, multistory brick buildings built in the "vernacular modern" style with some additional Chinese decorations on the façade (see figures 3.1 and 3.2). Railroad travelers and commercial sojourners meant that Zhengzhou was filled with accents from all over North China and, particularly in the most prestigious shops, voices from Shanghai.[52] The urban edge neighborhoods of Laofengang and Doufuzhai were poorer and grittier than downtown Zhengzhou but were still lively centers of leisure, trade, and production. Only the four thousand or so households in the former walled city were removed from the bustle of commercial Zhengzhou.[53]

But Zhengzhou's upward trajectory was under threat in the 1930s. The three reasons for this were all connected to the city's place in local and global hierarchies. First, after the focus of Feng Yuxiang on Zhengzhou, state investment and political patronage shifted to the provincial capital of Kaifeng. Second, the Chinese economy began to suffer the consequences of global depression, especially from 1931. The agricultural sector in particular was hit by falling prices and the declining competitiveness of exports. Third, the westward extension of the Long–Hai railroad reduced Zhengzhou's importance in the transport sector and enabled other towns to replicate its cotton processing functions. Taken together, these shifts weakened Zhengzhou's urban governance and regional role. Zhengzhou's twentieth-century story, the long-run pattern of this book, is of the city's rise from obscurity to become the dominant center of Henan Province, with people, wealth, and other resources concentrating

51. Sun Xiaoquan, "Zhengzhou xunri," 61.
52. Chen Gengya, "Xibei shicha ji," 474.
53. For more see Sun Xiaoquan, "Zhengzhou xunri," 61.

in the city, sometimes at the expense of its rural hinterland and other urban centers. But the city's difficult 1930s, with weakened logistical advantages and little political support, illustrates that this was not a smooth or inevitable trajectory.

ZHENGZHOU AND KAIFENG IN THE THIRTIES

A few months after Feng's fall from power in Henan, the Nanjing central government abolished the Zhengzhou municipality and returned the city to county government. The even more short-lived Kaifeng municipal government was abolished at the same time.[54] These measures do not seem to have been punitive or to represent a desire to undo the work of Feng Yuxiang: several municipalities that had always been under central government control were abolished around the same time. Under nationally mandated criteria, neither city qualified for municipal status. Zhengzhou did not reach the required threshold of 200,000 inhabitants, and, when that requirement was raised again in 1930 to 300,000, Kaifeng also fell short.[55]

The fate of the municipalities may have been the same, but the trajectories of Kaifeng and Zhengzhou diverged in the 1930s. Feng had made Zhengzhou an important power base and paid close attention to affairs in the city. That patronage dwindled after 1930 under Nationalist rule, which concentrated its urban governance efforts at the provincial capital of Kaifeng. This emphasis is an important reminder that differences between cities are about political resources as well as economic functions; in other words, although Zhengzhou had become a key logistical center, it did not yet have the political clout of its neighbor. In Kaifeng, the provincial government took direct control of urban affairs, with the Construction Department setting up a committee to continue projects begun under Feng Yuxiang. By contrast, Zhengzhou was neglected by the new authorities. The provincial government's own report of 1934 admitted that with no unit separate from the county administration, efforts to oversee urban work in Zhengzhou had foundered owing to

---

54. "Kaifeng Zhengzhou liangshi caiche," *Henan caizheng huikan*, no. 1 (1931): 511–13.
55. These included Suzhou, Jiujiang, and Anqing. On Suzhou, see Carroll, *Between Heaven and Modernity*, 237, 255; for an example of an abortive municipal government at Wuxi, see Lincoln, *Urbanizing China*, 87–88.

lack of funds.[56] The following year, journalist Chen Gengya (1905–1995) reported that road surfaces, drainage, and buildings were all deteriorating in the absence of a municipal authority.[57] The provincial government had established a committee to oversee urban services in Zhengzhou, but the bureau it set up to work on road and drainage improvements was tiny, with an operating budget of just 600 yuan per month.[58] Feng Yuxiang's ambitious projects at the urban edge also fell into abeyance. Despite Feng's strict control of Laofengang, by 1931 the district was once again a "refuge for gangsters and bandits" (*feitu zhi butaosou*). The authorities estimated that there were around five hundred prostitutes working in the district, though others put the number at over one thousand.[59] It was a similar story on the south side of the city. Wu Shixun in 1927 had described the Long–Hai Gardens as a suitable place for a summer stroll, but four years later Sun Xiaoquan took a different view: "even in the daytime there are kidnappings and robberies happening there, even though it is only about 1 *li* from the railway station and about 2 *li* from the downtown."[60]

Liu Hui argues that during the Republican period administrative rank became less important in determining the trajectory of cities than under the Qing, but this view may no longer hold under Nationalist rule. John Fitzgerald has shown from the case of Guangzhou that provincial capitals acquired renewed importance during the Nanjing Decade (1927–1937).[61] A similar pattern was at play in Henan Province. After Zhengzhou's rapid growth of the 1910s and 1920s, it was Kaifeng that surged ahead in the 1930s—as well as Luoyang during its period as Nationalist China's "temporary capital" during the 1932 Sino-Japanese

56. Henan sheng jiansheting, *Henan jianshe gaikuang*, section 4, *shizheng*, no page.

57. Chen Gengya, "Xibei shicha ji," 474–75. This is not to suggest that there was a popular clamor for municipal government: Wang Youqiao's report of 1932 claimed that the former Zhengzhou city government "had no plans whatsoever, apart from for increasing demands for taxes and levies." See Wang Youqiao, *Henan fang yu renwen zhilüe*, 137–38.

58. Liu Hui, "Tielu yu jindai Zhengzhou," 9. In theory, the bureau was able to raise extra money through licenses. See "Choubei Zhengzhou shizheng gongchengchu," *Henan jianshe*, no. 2 (1934): 12.

59. Sun Xiaoquan, "Zhengzhou xunri," 62b–64a; "Riqu fanrong de Zheng xian," 8b.

60. Sun Xiaoquan, "Zhengzhou xunri," 64a; compare Wu Shixun, *Henan*, 72.

61. Liu Hui, *Tielu yu Zhengzhou chengshihua*, 73; Fitzgerald, "Provincializing the City."

conflict around Shanghai. By 1936 Kaifeng's population was approaching three hundred thousand, two to three times that of Zhengzhou.[62] Kaifeng urban planner Hu Puqing (1908–1973) attributed this increase to the "political pulling power" (*zhengzhi de xiyinli*) of the city.[63] With the 1928 abolition of subprovincial *dao* units and the growth of provincial bureaucracies, Kaifeng was home to more than eleven thousand state employees—three times as many as Zhengzhou—and the site of ambitious government building projects throughout the 1930s.[64] Of the sixty-four schools and colleges funded by the provincial government, almost half (twenty-nine) were in Kaifeng and only one in Zhengzhou.[65] These spatial differences underline an important point about Nationalist rule in cities. Although the Nanjing Decade was in many ways a period of ambitious urban rule—if not always fulfilled in practice—this effort was concentrated in certain political centers. The Nationalist regime had neither the fiscal capacity nor the political reach to spread the goals to inland, subprovincial cities like Zhengzhou, where the urban ambitions of local militarists such as Feng Yuxiang may have been stronger.

GLOBAL DEPRESSION AND REGIONAL RIVALS

Zhengzhou's relative downturn of the 1930s was about more than political neglect. As with other twentieth-century conflicts, this strategic city was hard hit during the Central Plains War. From October 1929 to September 1930, the amount of cotton being distributed through Zhengzhou was only a quarter of the previous two years.[66] Business did bounce back quickly after the central government's victory. The transient, fast-changing nature of Zhengzhou meant that it was, as had been noted by its planners in 1928, "a city that is easy to destroy but one that

---

62. In 1936 Chen Shixing gave a population figure of 302,000 for Kaifeng, but this figure included almost one hundred villages inside the flood dike encircling the city (*huchengdi*). See Chen, "Kaifeng shi jianshe jihua," 77b. In 1931 this rural area was estimated to have a population of 27,000. *Henan minbao*, October 25, 1931. For Zhengzhou, the provincial government survey of October 1934 gives a city population of 125,000, though this number may also include some nearby villages. "Henan ge xian shehui diaocha: Zheng xian," *Henan tongji yuebao* 1, no. 1 (1935): 101–6.
63. Hu Puqing, "Kaifeng shi mofanqu jihua," 1.
64. "Zhiye fenlei," *Henan tongji yuebao*, 2, no. 7 (1936): 15.
65. *Henan jiaoyu ribao*, June 16, 1934.
66. Chen Junren, "Zhengzhou mianhua shichang," 15.

is also easy to construct (*yiyu pohuai, er you yiyu jianshe*)."[67] But two interrelated economic issues constrained Zhengzhou's 1930s recovery. The first was the position of the city in the world economy. Zhengzhou's boom of the 1910s and 1920s had been dependent on linkages between rural China and the industrial economy of the treaty ports and export markets. Just as Zhengzhou was beginning to rebound from war, this trade was hit by global economic depression. The silver-standard Chinese economy had previously been shielded from the worst of the crisis by falling silver prices (and hence competitive exports), but from 1931 other states abandoned the gold standard and began to buy silver. Deflation, debt crisis, and the collapse in international trade dealt the Chinese economy a serious blow.[68] As an entrepôt linking China's agricultural sector to the world economy, Zhengzhou was more exposed to the crisis than Kaifeng. By the second half of 1932, the provincial press reported that things were going "from bad to worse" (*jianghe ri xia*), with ninety shops having closed in Zhengzhou, compared to around fifty in the much larger city of Kaifeng.[69] Having risen in the relative peace since 1930, Zhengzhou's population suffered a slight decline in 1934–1935. Zhengzhou "has been suffering the impact of the world depression," noted one observer: "although there are still some large businesses, they tend to be strong in appearance but hollow on the inside (*wai qiang zhong gan*), not able to do more than try to keep going."[70] Zhengzhou's largest enterprise, the Yufeng textile works, was no exception, scaling back production and even closing down for a time before being rescued by a bank takeover in 1934.[71]

In addition to world depression, changes in the transport sector threatened Zhengzhou's position in interregional economic networks. As shown in chapter 1, the city's growth was aided by inefficiencies in the railroad system. This pattern was especially marked in the cotton sector,

67. "Zhengzhou shi xin shiqu jianshe jihua cao'an," *Zhengzhou shizheng yuekan*, no. 3 (1928), *yanlun* section, 3.

68. See Shiroyama, *China during the Great Depression*.

69. *Henan minbao*, July 22, 1932; the closure of ninety firms is reported in *Henan minbao*, December 22, 1932; on Kaifeng figures, see *Henan minbao*, January 23, 1933.

70. You He, "Zhengzhou Huijiao gaikuang," 31–33. On the population drop, see Liu Yongli, "Minguo shiqi Zhengzhou chengshi renkou," 11.

71. On the crisis, see "Yufeng jian ding," 938; on the takeover, see Zhu Junxian, *Yin ge zhi bian*, 197.

where the activities performed in Zhengzhou—processing, wholesaling, storing—depended on friction in the journey from the cotton fields of western Henan and Shaanxi to ports and textile mills on China's east coast. The ironing out of such inefficiencies in the 1930s reduced the demand for shipment and loading services in Zhengzhou. From April 1932, whole trains could be sent from the Long–Hai to the Jing–Han line (or vice versa) without being unloaded or even uncoupled in Zhengzhou. Railroad companies began offering the auxiliary transshipment services that had provided work for independent operators in Zhengzhou.[72] It is not that cotton processes and transportation became a seamless undertaking in the 1930s, but inefficiencies now began to hurt Zhengzhou's economy. Most strikingly, the city hosted a new inspection unit investigating the adulteration of cotton. Traders alleged that inspections at Zhengzhou were both too slow and too strict, and began to regard it as a place to avoid (*weitu*, literally "a dangerous road").[73]

Crucially, Zhengzhou *could* be avoided in the 1930s. The city's near-monopoly as a bottleneck in the cotton trade was dealt a blow by the long-delayed westward extension of the Long–Hai line, which inched over the border into Shaanxi in 1931 and reached Xi'an in 1934. It might be expected that Zhengzhou's economic links with Northwest China would benefit from railroad extension. The city's financial sector does seem to have been given a boost, with many banks using Zhengzhou as a jumping-off point for their northwest operations. As Zhu Junxian points out, it was a different story in the city's crucial cotton trade. Given the efficiencies gained by processing cotton closer to the point of production, Zhengzhou's functions began to be replicated in towns to its west. Some merchants moved away from Zhengzhou to these growing trading centers, especially Tongguan and Weinan in eastern Shaanxi.[74] In 1934 Weinan was reckoned the most lucrative goods station on the entire Long–Hai railroad.[75] The city's cotton trade, Chen Gengya lamented in 1935, had "lost the grand scale of its former days," with the industry

72. Liu Hui, *Tielu yu Zhengzhou chengshihua*, 103 (on transshipment services), 113 (through-traffic arrangements).
73. "Ershisan nian Zhengzhou yinhangye mianye gaikuang," *Henan tongji yuebao* 1, nos. 2–3 (combined issue, 1935): 170.
74. Zhu Junxian, *Yin ge zhi bian*, 121–26; Ma Zimin, "Zhengzhou yiri youji," 11.
75. Liu Fenghan, *Minguo jingji*, 135–36.

newspaper reporting that volumes traded through Zhengzhou had fallen by two-thirds since their peak.[76] Most cotton in Zhengzhou now came only from north of the Yellow River and production centers in Henan such as Taikang that did not have a railroad link. Even as China's cotton business recovered from depression, many cotton dealers and shipment firms in Zhengzhou were forced to close or change their line of business.[77] The neighborhood of cotton dealers, north of the railroad station at Zhengxingjie and Xinglongjie, was the "complete opposite" (*tianrang zhi bie*) of its 1920s heyday.[78]

As well as cyclical issues in the global commodity economy, then, Zhengzhou's spatial role was under threat. It was not that the entire city was facing an existential crisis. The local retail sector was recovering, and some wholesale trade such as livestock and medicinal products continued to flourish.[79] In 1936 the population of the city seems to have recovered after the reduction of the previous year.[80] But it is clear that Zhengzhou of the 1930s was settling down as a medium-sized commercial town, with little sign of the booming long-distance trade that had brought breakneck growth in the 1910s and 1920s—a pivot of China's railroads but not an economic powerhouse. Elisabeth Köll argues that outside Manchuria, China's railroads "led to the creation of very few new hub cities."[81] Although this is true on the Tianjin–Pukou line discussed most closely by Köll, where the key centers of Jinan and Xuzhou were important cities before the railroad, the Jing–Han line tells a slightly different story, with Shijiazhuang and Zhengzhou both rising to prominence as railroad hubs. But Köll's wider point still stands: these railroad towns may have been commercially important but were not major industrial or political centers during the Republican period. For all the early predictions,

76. Chen Gengya, "Xibei shicha ji," 475; "Zuijin Zhengzhou mianhua yingye dajian," *Fangzhi shibao*, no. 1222 (1935), quoted in Liu Hui, *Tielu yu Zhengzhou chengshihua*, 100.

77. "Ershisan nian Zhengzhou yinhangye mianye gaikuang," *Henan tongji yuebao* 1, nos. 2–3 (combined issue, 1935), 170; on closure of firms, see Zhengzhou shi gongshangye lianhehui, *Zhengzhou gongshangye xingshuai*, 45.

78. "Riqu fanrong de Zheng xian," 8b.

79. Liu Hui, *Tielu yu Zhengzhou chengshihua*, 232–33; on the medicine trade, in which Zhengzhou replaced Yuzhou as the dominant regional center, see Zhao Fuhai, *Lao Zhengzhou: Shangdu yimeng*, 25–31.

80. Zhengzhou shi gongshangye lianhehui, *Zhengzhou gongshangye xingshuai*, 31.

81. Köll, *Railroads and the Transformation of China*, 117.

Zhengzhou was not becoming a "second Hankou," still less "China's Chicago" or the "fulcrum of Eurasia." It was only twenty years later, during the political and economic patronage of the First Five-Year Plan, that a new kind of spatial politics brought a major shift in Zhengzhou's functions, scale, and regional role (see chapter 4).

Beyond the Fringe: Rural Uplift in Zheng County

If the vicissitudes of the 1930s threatened Zhengzhou's interregional role, what of the local spatial politics of rural-urban relations? Chapter 1 showed that although some of the closest villages to the city benefited from urban demand, Zhengzhou's growth during the 1910s and 1920s had only a limited impact on its nearby hinterland in Zheng County. As Liang Xin shows, such issues were reflected across China in the growing concern with divisions and inequalities between urban and rural areas during the 1920s, especially after the rural-urban "price scissors" worsened toward the end of the decade.[82] A range of actors began projects of rural uplift, from state bodies and overseas development agencies to individual intellectuals and technical experts. Historians have examined the best-known of these schemes, but in the mid-1930s there were rural improvements operating at more than a thousand sites across China.[83]

Zheng County provides a good example of how these local schemes operated in practice. From 1927 onwards, local authorities under both Feng Yuxiang and Nationalist control promoted village uplift in the county, aiming to spread resources of capital, technology, and expertise from the city to rural areas. But this work did little to benefit the cultivators of rural Zheng County. First, these efforts were simply too small in the face of agricultural crisis and did not extend much beyond a cluster of villages northwest of the city. Second, the rural agenda in Zheng County was also driven by modernizing politics rather than the needs of villagers, tied to what Kate Merkel-Hess calls the "authoritarian agenda" of productivity

82. Liang Xin, "Xiandai Zhongguo de 'dushi yanguang,'" 342–44. Wu Chengming estimated that the agricultural-industrial terms of trade worsened sharply for rural producers from 1926 onwards, several years before the worst effects of global depression hit. For discussion, see Gong Yusong, "Zhongguo jindai chengxiang guanxi," 35–36.

83. Merkel-Hess, "New People," 1, citing figures from James Yen (Yan Yangchu). For more studies in English, see Hayford, *To the People*; Merkel-Hess, *Rural Modern*; Yu Zhang, *Going to the Countryside*, 44–76.

and control in rural areas.[84] With rare exceptions, the rural reform agenda in the late 1920s and 1930s was driven by the extension of urban infrastructures and state power, as part of the processes by which, as Toby Lincoln puts it, "society became firmly oriented around the city."[85] Third, there was also a damaging discursive shift. In surviving newspapers and government documents of the Feng Yuxiang period, there is a sense of rural life as different, problematic, and inferior that is hard to find in earlier sources. Almost as soon as Feng Yuxiang took control of Zhengzhou in 1927, he declared his ambition to solve the "peasant problem" (*nongmin wenti*).[86] As Liang Minling points out for China as a whole, whereas in earlier periods the authorities identified specific difficulties in the countryside, the idea that rural people and society might themselves be a "problem" was new.[87] This language of "rural bankruptcy" and "rural construction" may have had its own damaging effects, reinforcing the sense of villagers as backward and problematic, and tending to isolate rural issues as a discrete ancillary problem rather than what it should have been: the central challenge of governance.

FENG YUXIANG AND RURAL STATE BUILDING

The concern for rural issues in Henan during the late 1920s was partly a response to Communist activity in the province between 1925 and 1927. After his role in its suppression in 1927, Feng Yuxiang turned to the issue of rural improvement. Feng is known for his support of the Confucian reformer Liang Shuming (1893–1988) in the north of Henan, but he also oversaw a series of lesser-known experiments around his personal power base at Zhengzhou.[88] Feng's flagship rural institution was the Henan-Shaanxi-Gansu Rural Training Center (Yu-Shaan-Gan sansheng nongcun xunlianchu), established in the fall of 1927 5 kilometers northwest of Zhengzhou at the village of Wulongkou (see map 1.3). The training center was a distinctly top-down political project, training a new class

84. Merkel-Hess, *Rural Modern*, 12.

85. Lincoln, *Urbanizing China*, 2; for a similar point about rural reform across Asia, see Stapleton, *The Modern City in Asia*, 40.

86. "Feng zongsiling tong ling kaiban nongcun zuzhi xunlian chu wen," *Henan xingzheng yuekan*, no. 2 (1927): 20–21.

87. See Liang Minling, "Jindai chengxiang guanxi," 36.

88. On Liang in Hui County, see Alitto, *The Last Confucian*, 170–76.

of cadres to organize and mobilize village society across Feng's zone of control in Henan and Northwest China. In his order for the establishment of the center, Feng insisted that rural reconstruction would have to "start from the very root, namely, making peasants completely transform their consciousness (*chedi juewu*)." The institute trained more than a thousand students in its first two cohorts.[89]

The cluster of villages on the north side of Zhengzhou became something of a model countryside under Feng. Student cadres from the training institute opened a free rural middle school, began a variety of experimental programs in rural organization, and offered propaganda performances for villagers.[90] For Feng there was a personal, even romantic identification with his rural projects. Meng Ziming, a native of Damengzhai (renamed Sanmincun—"Three People's Principles Village"—after Sun Yat-sen's political formula), remembered that Feng often stayed in the area and ordered his troops to share their food with the inhabitants, while stories circulated locally of the marshall stopping to help older villagers hoe their vegetable fields.[91] Feng was also heavily invested in the moral authenticity of the countryside. Trainee cadres had to be "pure peasants" (*chuncui nongmin*), and, in a speech to graduates of the institute, Feng invoked the importance of rural order as the foundation for political power in the ancient texts—Mencius, Mozi, and the Confucian *Daxue*: "in the future, out of good villages will grow good cities and counties, and good provinces, and a good state."[92]

There are two paradoxes at play here. The first is the dual vision of rural society as both a repository of authenticity and a social problem to be transformed. The second is the rhetorical construction of the countryside as the basis of politics, when Feng's rule in practice tried to use his

---

89. "Feng zongsiling tong ling kaiban nongcun zuzhi xunlian chu wen," *Henan xingzheng yuekan*, no. 2 (1927): 20–21. This quote contains one of the first uses of "peasant" (*nongmin*) that I have seen in a non-Communist source from Henan. For the importance of this neologism, see Cohen, "Cultural and Political Inventions." I have avoided the term "peasant" apart from in direct quotations or when referring to formal Communist Party labels.

90. Zung, "Marshall Feng and Rural Reconstruction," 523–25.

91. Meng Ziming, "Feng Yuxiang zai wo cun."

92. "Gailiang nongcun zuzhi di yiyi ji nongcun zuzhi xunlianchu xuesheng suo fu zhi shiming," speech by Feng Yuxiang, January 10, 1930, reproduced in *Zhengzhou wenshi ziliao*, no. 4 (1988): 122–24.

urban power base as a springboard for rural control against a backdrop of famine and destitution—while keeping rural migrants away from the city. Away from the model district north of the city, Feng's rural governance in Zheng County was remembered as top-down campaigns for grain requisitioning and queue cutting, and against footbinding.[93] Feng's policy brought to the fore in Zheng County several patterns that would recur across the rest of the century: the discursive and institutional separation of rural and urban, ambiguity toward and efforts to control rural populations, and suspicion of people moving across rural-urban boundaries.

City to County: Capital, Cotton, and Coops

Discussions of rural poverty and governance in Henan have focused on the regional peripheries and semiperipheries that were centers of Communist Party activity.[94] Yet around Zhengzhou, in the regional core, Nationalist rule after 1930 was haunted by the spatial politics of rural-urban division. Zhengzhou was still only a medium-sized city, and the incoming Nationalist authorities had scaled back urban ambitions, but differences between the city and surrounding countryside were still a source of anxiety for both local government and local commentators.

Some of these differences were social and cultural, and the very real changes in the city were also reinforced by a growing discourse of an essentializing rural-urban gap. In a 1932 discussion of Zhengzhou, the editor of *Henan Politics* journal reported that "before the Republic, the city and countryside were still reckoned identical (*chengxiang shang cheng yizhi*)." But especially over the previous decade, he judged, "the customs and sensibilities of city and countryside have tended to become different. . . . It is a common occurrence in the city to see young men with their Western clothes and leather shoes, and girls with short hair and wearing *qipao* all over the city. In recent years talking about love, staying in hotels, and renting rooms for sex have also become more common. The corruption of society in the future may well be as bad as in Shanghai (*yu Shanghai bingjia*)." Meanwhile, rural people around Zheng-

---

93. See, for instance, Zhengzhou shi jiaoqu zhi bianzuan weiyuanhui, "Zhengzhou shi jiaoqu zhi, Baizhuang zhi," 10–11.

94. Wou, *Mobilizing the Masses*; see also Xin Zhang, *Social Transformation*.

zhou were—perhaps predictably—described as "unhygienic" (*bujiang weisheng*) and "honest, with a very low level of knowledge, and extremely superstitious."[95]

As well as social distinction, concern about the rural-urban divide was also focused on economic inequalities, with worsening rural terms of trade from 1926 exacerbated by the effects of world depression after 1931. "Pick up any newspaper or magazine, and you will see discussion of rural crisis," noted left-leaning He Yiping (1899–1963) of Henan University Agricultural College in 1936: "there's no denying the crisis of collapse (*bengkui guocheng zhi weiji*) in China's rural economy."[96] Wheat prices in Zhengzhou crashed by some 30 percent in 1933 alone, and rural land prices in Zheng County fell by over 15 percent between 1931 and 1935.[97] By late 1934, one survey of the county concluded, "most peasants' income does not cover expenditure, and, with the increase of bandit molestations and droughts, life is rather difficult."[98]

Chapter 1 suggested that it was primarily those rural areas closest to Zhengzhou that benefited from the city's boom during the 1910s and 1920s. Conversely, this "diurnal hinterland" became a focus of concern during the 1930s. One journalist from the government's own *Henan minbao* described encountering a desperate situation as he cycled out west of the city in the wake of a hailstorm in 1932. Just beyond Bishagang, he came across farmers already on the verge of starvation. Proximity to the city may even have made things worse. The unnamed journalist describes the plight of the Zhang family: "Because of unceasing civil war in Henan over the last years, a great many soldiers were always passing through Zhengzhou, as the center of the rail lines, so the crops that they planted were pretty much all taken by soldiers [using the pejorative *qiuba*]. . . . The fierce storm has come and destroyed the entire autumn harvest, and they don't have any cash or food left over. They are facing

95. "Riqu fanrong de Zheng xian," 7b–8a. For a detailed discussion of emerging rural-urban cultural difference in South China, see Ho, *Understanding Canton*, 9–48.

96. He Yiping, "Zhongguo nongye jingji," 177.

97. For Zhengzhou wheat prices, see "Quanguo ge xian xiangcun wujia zhishubiao," 265–78; on land prices in 1931 and 1935, Sun Wenyu et al., *Yu E Wan Gan sisheng tudi fenlei*, 60 and 73.

98. "Henan ge xian shehui diaocha: Zheng xian," *Henan tongji yuebao* 1, no. 1 (1935): 103. For another example of difficulties in agriculture in a peripheralized zone close to a city, see Harrison, *Man Awakened from Dreams*, 136–58.

having to sell their three-year-old son for about 5 yuan, and they are sitting waiting for death."[99] "In the last three years things have become more difficult," admitted the provincial government's official journal in 1932, "and therefore, in the 5 *li* around the city, the men have taken to robbery and the women, to prostitution."[100] During the early Republic, proximity to the city had helped avoid most of the rural banditry that plagued much of Henan; after 1930 if anything the reverse may have been true. According to local press reports, "urban gangsters and rural bandits" were colluding to ambush and kidnap travelers on roads just outside Zhengzhou: "these kinds of crimes are ubiquitous, and people in the surrounding countryside have suffered from them many times."[101] Martial law was declared in and around Zhengzhou in April 1933 to tackle the bandit threat.[102]

With land reform shelved from the Nationalist political agenda, the effort to improve the Zheng County rural economy in the 1930s had three strands: building infrastructure, spreading capital from city to countryside, and promoting the valuable cash crops that had not previously been widely grown. All three were deeply intertwined with rural state building and the National Economic Council's agenda to increase agricultural production.[103] The connection to state power does not invalidate these efforts—with the exception of a few anarchist schemes, almost all rural improvement work in modern China has been in some way connected with state building—but their limitations throw into stark relief the scale of the rural challenge, even close to urban areas.

In Zheng County the weakest of the three strands was the building of rural infrastructure, probably owing to its high cost at a time of fiscal fragility and competing priorities. In some parts of China, the 1930s saw the spread of road networks, new schools, and even, occasionally, electricity to villages and market towns around cities.[104] There is little sign of such developments in Zheng County, where much of this infrastructure did not exist until the Mao period or even the post-Mao reform era.

99. *Henan minbao*, August 2, 1932.
100. "Riqu fanrong de Zheng xian," 7b.
101. *Henan minbao*, January 15, 1933.
102. *North China Herald*, April 19, 1933.
103. Zanasi, *Saving the Nation*, 133–42.
104. See, for instance, Lincoln, *Urbanizing China*, 89–107.

In education, the official county survey of 1935 diagnosed an "excessive focus (*guoyu zhuzhong*) on improving education in the city and neglect of rural education. The gap between the two is too wide, to the extent that it is almost impossible to speak of rural education at all."[105] Although the Henan provincial government was developing long-distance networks of motor roads and telephones during the 1930s, such infrastructure was an intercity phenomenon with little impact away from the major arterial routes. Most connections within the county were still rudimentary tracks that could only be covered at walking pace. The southwest of the county was reckoned to be especially poorly connected even by the mid-1930s.[106] The best road in rural Zheng County ran only as far as the airfield at Qiuzhai, 3 kilometers south of the city. Indeed, the Qiuzhai airstrip itself serves to underline the disjunction between new hyperfast connections of a small elite and the very different world of Zhengzhou's rural surroundings. In 1932 local authorities laid out the new airstrip, mobilizing villagers to prepare the surface using draft animals and stone rollers. After the airstrip was finished, locals—who had lost arable land in the making of the airstrip—were allowed to graze animals and cut the grass for fuel, but on wet days faced being commandeered to help pull out planes that had become stuck in the muddy ground.[107]

Compared with high-cost infrastructure building, the supply of capital seemed to offer an easier route to village development. In the 1930s, the Nationalist authorities developed agricultural cooperatives in Zheng County as a response to two related problems: the perceived flow of capital from rural to urban areas and the high cost of credit for villagers. Although the city had become an important financial center, its modern banks focused on large-scale investments farther afield. Zhengzhou's older banking houses (*qianzhuang* or *yinhao*) had more local ties but were struggling in the face of economic crisis and competition from new banks.[108] Villagers coming to the city to borrow money were charged much higher interest rates than urban business owners (up to 5 percent

105. "Henan ge xian shehui diaocha: Zheng xian," *Henan tongji yuebao* 1, no. 1 (1935): 104–5.

106. Sun Wenyu et al., *Yu E Wan Gan sisheng tudi fenlei*, 62.

107. Ji Fu, "Zhengzhou de zaoqi jichang."

108. Zhao Fuhai, *Lao Zhengzhou: Shangdu laozihao*, 19.

per month, compared with 1.2 percent for larger business loans).[109] One study published in 1931 found that over 80 percent of loans in Zheng County involved mortgaging land. Only 13 percent were on cash credit. Remarkably, given the presence of nearby banks in Zhengzhou City, the cash credit figure was less than half the average of ten surveyed counties.[110] There are no precise figures from Zhengzhou, but in 1934 the rural reformer Zhang Xichang (1902–1980) reported that across Henan "in recent years the land that peasants owned . . . has very quickly been flowing into the grasp of landlords and high-interest commercial lenders in cities."[111] By the 1930s, 60 percent of Zheng County's rural landlords lived in the city rather than in villages.[112]

In 1934 the Henan Rural Cooperative Committee, which included representatives from the major state-backed banks, established the Zheng County Rural Cooperative Instructors' Office (Zheng xian nongcun hezuo zhidaoyuan banshichu) to tackle these issues.[113] That May, the very first credit cooperative in the province was established 7 kilometers north of the city in one of Feng Yuxiang's former model villages, Miaolicun (renamed "Sun Yat-sen Village" under Feng).[114] By 1936, Zheng County claimed eighty-four cooperatives containing 3,700 members, a little under 10 percent of the rural households in the county.[115] It is easy to be cynical about the Nationalist cooperative movement, which turned existing ideas of rural collectivity in a more state-led direction, using credit as a lever for outside political penetration. In Henan, the cooperative movement of the mid-1930s was a deeply politicized, anti-Communist measure—indeed, the provincial cooperative committee was established on the orders of the Military Affairs Commission.[116] Nor do the cooperatives of the 1930s seem to have aided poorer cultivators.

109. "Henan ge xian shehui diaocha: Zheng xian," *Henan tongji yuebao* 1, no. 1 (1935): 103–4.

110. Su Xinliu, *Minguo shiqi Henan shui han zaihai*, 99.

111. Zhang Xichang, "Henan sheng nongcun diaocha," 53.

112. Sun Wenyu et al., *Yu E Wan Gan sisheng tudi fenlei*, 60–61.

113. "Zhengzhou nongcun zuoheshe," 24–26.

114. Wang Tianjiang et al., *Henan jindai dashiji*, 322.

115. "Henan sheng ge xian hezuoshe jindu ji she wu gaiyao tongji biao," *Henan tongji yuebao*, 2, no. 3 (1936): 91.

116. On the role of Chiang Kai-shek's Nanchang Field Headquarters in the cooperative movement, see "Henan hezuo shiye," undated report, Henan Provincial Archive, folder M53-01-0033, starting at p. 16 of folder.

Of sixteen cooperatives from the Zheng County sample who reported the status of their members, all declared that they consisted entirely of owner-cultivators, with an average landholding about 50 percent above the county average.[117]

Whatever the political backdrop, surviving documents from the Zhengzhou branch of the Bank of China point to a real effort to provide productive loans to ordinary villagers in Zheng County. The bank's local cooperative expert was one Li Xiaomin, whose reports form part of the small corpus of archival documents on Zheng County from before 1937. Li was not immune from disparaging rural residents—"peasants are not good at planning and preparing things in advance, and their habits are hard to change"—but was punctilious about ensuring that cooperative members themselves had oversight of local schemes. Li seems to have worked hard to provide credit wherever possible. In one report of 1935, he admits to having "bent the rules" (*tongrong*) to make a Zheng County cooperative loan that had not quite met the specifications.[118] His work was not on a large scale, but in a surviving sample of eighteen Bank of China loans to Zheng County cooperatives, sixteen were at the unusually low interest rate of 8 percent per annum. These loans were—at least on paper—used for productive investment: twelve involved the purchase of fertilizer and five, the sinking of new wells.[119]

The provision of capital was closely connected to the third strand of Nationalist rural improvement in Zheng County: the promotion of cash crops.[120] As mentioned in chapter 1, cotton production around

117. Of ten cooperatives' loans where landholdings are clear, average farm size was 36 *mu* (compared with 24 *mu* for the county). "Zhongguo yinhang Zhengzhou zhihang: guanyu Zheng xian, Luoyang nong fang jicha bao," August 1936–December 1937, Henan Provincial Archive, folder M53-01-0003. County average (median) farm size from John L. Buck, *Land Utilization in China*, vol. 3: *Statistics*, 286.

118. "Zhongguo yinhang Zhengzhou zhihang," Henan Provincial Archive, folder M53-01-0032, esp. Li Xiaomin report no. 17, April 10, 1935.

119. "Zhongguo yinhang Zhengzhou zhihang: guanyu Zheng xian, Luoyang nong fang jicha bao," August 1936–December 1937, Henan Provincial Archive, folder M53-01-0003.

120. Zheng County coop members were involved in cotton production in at least half the surviving sample. See "Zhongguo yinhang Zhengzhou zhihang: guanyu Zheng xian, Luoyang nong fang jicha bao," August 1936–December 1937, Henan Provincial Archive, folder M53-01-003. On the connection between rural coops and cotton, see Zanasi, *Saving the Nation*, 133–74.

Zhengzhou was negligible before 1930. The key shift was the promotion of higher-yield American varieties, which took off rapidly in much of Henan during 1930–1931. These imported varieties were more suitable both for mechanized spinning and cultivation on Zhengzhou's poorer soils, and in the early 1930s the Yufeng spinning works in Zhengzhou began giving out free seeds to farmers in Zheng County.[121] The focus of attention was the same cluster of villages just northwest of Zhengzhou that had been the site of Feng Yuxiang's rural experiments and the first village cooperatives. In 1933 the National Central University in Nanjing reestablished an abortive experimental cotton farm in Miaolicun (first founded in 1920). In 1935 the provincial Cotton Commission established a Guidance Institute (Mianhua zhidaosuo) nearby, and the following year it took over the experimental farm.[122] The promotion of cotton was a marked success in this cluster northwest of the city, encouraged by the new varieties, free seeds, and credit cooperatives, but it also spread into other parts of Zheng County. The sown area of cotton in the county rose from a negligible 5,000 *mu* in 1929 to an average of 36,000 *mu* in the 1930–1936 period, and per *mu* yields were above the provincial average.[123]

There is some reason, then, to follow Huang Zhenglin in his cautiously optimistic view of Henan's rural economy in the mid-1930s. Huang emphasizes that technical improvements and financial support from the state was helping the agricultural sector emerge from the crisis of the first part of the decade.[124] However, looking at the hinterland of Zhengzhou, it is important to note the patchy and limited impact of efforts to spread infrastructure, capital, and cash crops prior to the outbreak of war in 1937. Even after several years of a top-down push, cotton accounted for only 1.5 percent of the better land in the county; trade in melon seeds from more marginal land remained by far the most lucrative cash crop.[125]

121. On seeds, see Di Fuyu, "Zhengzhou mianye zhi diaocha," 4. By the mid-1930s, over 99 percent of cotton grown in Zheng County was the new US variety. See Henan sheng mianchan gaijinsuo, *Henan sheng mianye*, 56.

122. "Zhongda Zheng nongchang she hezuo mianchang," *Mianxun*, no. 1 (1934): 4–5; Henan sheng mianchan gaijinsuo, ed., *Henan sheng mianchan gaijinsuo gailan*, 14–15 and 18.

123. Henan sheng mianchan gaijinsuo, *Henan sheng mianye*, 6–7 on sown area; 22–25 on yields.

124. Huang Zhenglin, "Zhidu chuangxin," 28–44.

125. On the uses of crop land in Zheng County across harvests, see Kimura et al.,

How can the limitations of rural policy under both Feng Yuxiang and direct Nationalist Party rule be explained? Some observers in Henan saw a damaging rural-urban relationship, with "reconstructionists"—to use Susan Mann's term—working for more positive rural-urban relations facing powerful countervailing forces concentrating capital, infrastructure, expertise, and prestige in the city.[126] With the pull of the cities, noted one local advocate for rural education, "the more the cities become developed, the more the countryside becomes desolate (*huangliang*)."[127] The philosopher Feng Youlan (1895–1990), Henan native and sometime dean of humanities at Henan University, used even stronger terms: "we can indeed say that the countryside is the colony (*zhimindi*) of the cities."[128]

Although earlier iterations of the Chinese state had also struggled with rural governance, what was new in this period was the construction of rural people and society as a problem rather than the very heart of statecraft.[129] This marginalization and essentialization of rural people in the nation-state was a global issue, shared by diverse movements across the political spectrum.[130] But it was perhaps especially damaging in China's twentieth century, with its large rural population, weak fiscal capacity, and intense modernizing ambitions. It was not that the Nationalist authorities were simply indifferent to the plight of the agricultural economy, and Nanjing's response to depression did pay some attention to rural problems.[131] But this very problematizing of rural governance in the 1920s and 1930s tended to wall off the rural as a separate issue, secondary to the prioritization of military spending and urban modernization at the core of the Nationalist project and shared by factions across the

Kiwai chitai no nōsakubutsu chousa, 37–44. On the value of cotton, see "Henan ge xian wuchan zhuangkuang diaocha: Zheng xian." This survey reports that cotton production in the county was worth 226,000 yuan, versus 377,000 for melon seeds.

126. Mann, "Urbanization and Historical Change," 100–105. For a classic discussion of this issue, see Hsiao-t'ung Fei, *China's Gentry*, 119–26.

127. Cai Hengxi, "Lun Zhongguo nongcun jiaoyu gaizao zhi lu," *Henan jiaoyu ribao*, article serialized from January 12 to January 22, 1932. Quote is taken from January 13, 1932.

128. Feng Youlan, "Bian chengxiang," 41. For a more recent discussion of colonialism as an analogy for China's rural-urban relations, see Day, *Peasant in Postsocialist China*, 92–127.

129. Liang Minling, "Jindai chengxiang guanxi," 28–40, esp. 36.

130. See Kearney, *Reconceptualizing the Peasantry*, 42–72.

131. See, for instance, Shiroyama, *China during the Great Depression*, 200–228.

Party.[132] This imbalance was ultimately a question of fiscal allocation as well as discursive weight. In mid-1930s Henan, an estimated 84 percent of households were primarily engaged in farming, but in surviving monthly provincial budgets just 1.6 percent of ordinary expenditure was allocated for rural improvement. Including all government expenditure and taking a broad definition of "rural," only 8.16 percent was spent directly on rural areas—though the tax burden for provincial budgets was still largely in the countryside.[133]

There is much to be said for this reading of rural-urban divisions in the Republican period. But the struggles of urban Zhengzhou discussed in this chapter point to a second, more multilayered, reading of spatial inequalities. In this view, rural-urban relations were not inherently antagonistic or a zero-sum game, but weaknesses in both the Zhengzhou urban economy and the rural hinterland created a negative feedback loop. Although, as chapter 1 shows, Zhengzhou's transport and commercial roles had enabled it to develop beyond the constraints of its immediate hinterland in Zheng County, those functions and any further commercial growth were still dependent on the health of the agrarian economy of its wider hinterland in Henan Province. This dynamic was diagnosed by He Yiping, agronomist at Henan University, who argued that low rural incomes were holding back urban development. Instead, "we must focus on the joint progress of agriculture and industry, without leaning toward one or the other at all, because the two cannot shake off their mutual connections."[134] One visiting Nationalist official took a similar view: "Business here should be well developed, but trade in Zhengzhou is not advanced and instead is declining. This is undoubtedly due to the poverty of the countryside. . . . The people's purchasing power (*goumaili*) is extremely weak. Although transport here is convenient, that

---

132. On the marginalization of village industrialization and the subordination of rural production to urban interests, see Zanasi, *Saving the Nation*, 133–73.

133. This figure of 8.16 percent includes all disaster relief and reconstruction, hydraulic work, and pensions for demobilized soldiers but does not include spending on the coercive apparatus of the state. On the question of tax, the land tax and its supplements accounted for the majority (62.2 percent) of provincial government tax income, not to mention the (unknown) rural share of salt taxes, transaction levies, and so on. All data from the January to June 1935 provincial budgets, reproduced in Henan sheng tongji xuehui, *Minguo shiqi Henan sheng tongji ziliao*, 1:488–512.

134. He Yiping, "Zhongguo nongye jingji," 187–88.

just makes it easy to ship things; if the market for selling things is sluggish, that is something that convenient transportation cannot solve."[135]

At the same time, the struggling Zhengzhou of the 1930s was a poor springboard for rural transformation—for the spread of capital, infrastructure, and technology. David Strand points to a similar reading: of the "republican city [that] lacked the power by itself to sustain and complete a nationwide revolution or to stop one from erupting. . . . What can be said, however, is that cities at several levels and in many places were powerful enough to reset the terms of debate."[136] In other words, as in Zhengzhou, the economic power of cities was insufficient to effect the transformation of the rural hinterland but was powerful enough to generate an urban-centered political economy and discourse, not necessarily innately antagonistic in rural-urban relations but ill-equipped to spread the proceeds of growth.

To come to grips with this two-way weakness, it is necessary to move beyond simply rural-urban relations to the wider picture of spatial inequalities at all levels, from the local to the global. Against a backdrop of global depression, the potential for more positive rural-urban relations was held back by the weakening place of 1930s Zhengzhou in urban hierarchies as well as the rural challenges of inland North China as a whole, a struggling region in a country itself peripheral in the world economy. Some more positive signs were beginning to emerge in the mid-1930s, but such trends were cut off in their infancy by the outbreak of full-scale war between China and Japan in July 1937. By the beginning of 1938, the Japanese invasion had reached Henan Province. Wartime society and economy around Zhengzhou would be very different from during the prewar global depression—though still marked by arbitrary inequalities across space.

---

135. Chen Liusheng, "Dao Ningxia qu," 36a; for a similar view in Sichuan, see Wei Yingtao, *Jindai Changjiang shangyou chengxiang*, 14–17.

136. Strand, "New Chinese Cities," 223. For a more negative view of the consequences of tighter rural-urban connections, see He Yimin, *Cong nongye shidai dao gongye shidai*, 627–30.

CHAPTER THREE

Zhengzhou at War

Spaces and Strategies, 1937–1945

In July 1937 Japanese forces orchestrated a series of skirmishes with Chinese troops around Beijing. Stiffening Chinese resistance provided the pretext for a full-scale invasion of North and Central China. Just as in the warlord conflicts of the 1920s, the railroads that had brought growth to Zhengzhou made the city a key military target. During eight brutal years of war, Zhengzhou's inhabitants suffered flood, frontline fighting, famine, aerial bombardment (by the United States as well as Japan), and two periods of Japanese occupation.

After decades of neglect, historians have now put the War of Resistance at the heart of China's twentieth-century story. For Henan Province, Micah Muscolino has shown how the energy demands of competing militaries broke the region's fragile environmental infrastructure.[1] In terms of the urban experience of war, although there are now excellent studies of both Japanese-occupied eastern cities and those in the Nationalist-held rear areas, there is very little on the swathe of cities in "Middle China" that bore the brunt of frontline fighting during the long war, cities such as Changsha, Hengyang, Yichang, and Zhengzhou.[2] Cities at the front line rightly fascinate and appall historians, not least because of the contrast between, as Marcus Funck and Roger Chickering put it, "urban civility" and cities as "pivots of military violence."[3]

1. Muscolino, *Ecology of War*.
2. See, for instance, Danke Li, *Echoes of Chongqing*; Lincoln, "Rural and Urban at War"; Zhao Ma, *Runaway Wives*; Pingchao Zhu, *Wartime Culture*; Sheehan and Yeh, *Living and Working in Wartime China*. For an exception on early wartime Changsha, note Hudson, "River Sands/Urban Spaces," 294–318.
3. Funck and Chickering, "Introduction," 2–3.

Bringing the frontline city experience into China's wartime story brings renewed focus on civilian adaptation, urban resilience, and the operations of the war economy. These phenomena also link to the spatial strategies of both individuals and state actors: How can residents of a frontline city adapt in a war economy? What connections can survive between a frontline city and its divided hinterland? What happens when even the "new normal" of wartime adaptation breaks down?

The wartime period in China was one of deep spatial differences. As in other parts of the war-torn world, location was a major factor in determining the wartime experiences, opportunities, and survival chances of individuals. In particular, Zhengzhou's wartime story underlines three spatial features of the War of Resistance: First, the Nationalist war effort systematically neglected and isolated the frontline regions of "Middle China." Second, mobility was vital to civilian adaptation and survival—and the nature of movement varied sharply at different phases of the war. Although at times Zhengzhou's urban area was a refuge from violence or a site of economic opportunity, at other moments its rural hinterland fulfilled those functions. Third, although Zhengzhou lost its prewar economic role, those trading in the city reconfigured its spatial networks in new ways, particularly through local handicrafts and the smuggling of goods from Japanese-occupied territory. By 1942, though, the pressures of military requisitioning, geographical isolation, and a monthlong Japanese occupation had weakened these adaptations. Those in Zhengzhou could not escape the wider regional economic and environmental collapse described by Muscolino, and the city was overwhelmed by the inflation, refugees, and starvation of the 1942–1943 famine. It was a shrunken and isolated city that was reoccupied by Japanese forces in the Ichigo advance of April 1944.

Summer 1938: Nation and Sacrifice

Zhengzhou's wartime isolation and diminution did not begin immediately. In the first months of the Sino-Japanese War, Zhengzhou's importance was boosted by the military and civilian retreat from the coast. In December 1937 the city became the command headquarters of the Nationalist First War Area.[4] Refugees arrived by railroad and filled the

4. Xu Lianshan and Wang Zongmin, *Zhengzhou kangzhan*, 86.

city, some staying for a few days and others more permanently. With the loss of factories in eastern China, the Yufeng cotton mill on Zhengzhou's southern edge enjoyed unprecedented demand.[5]

But in February 1938 Zhengzhou became a military target for the first time, with Japanese forces moving inland as a prelude to the assault on the Nationalist headquarters at Wuhan. Zhengzhou's first major air raid was on February 14, 1938, targeting the railroad station and commercial center. One firsthand account comes from the agronomist Cui Yanshou, who was strolling into Zhengzhou from the experimental farm at Bishagang and arrived at just the wrong moment: "There was the deafening sound of falling bombs, and we lay in our hollow not daring to come out. Only when the all-clear was sounded and we saw people walking about in the street did we emerge. . . . We saw that the Huayang Hotel [on Ermalu] had been reduced to rubble. There was blood all over the entrance, and some people were buried alive under the collapsed building, giving blood-curdling screams (*canjiao*)."[6] Hundreds of people were killed, perhaps more than a thousand.[7] British writer Christopher Isherwood saw the damage a few weeks later: "in the station square, moonlight heightened the drama of the shattered buildings; this might have been Ypres in 1915."[8]

Following this first, devastating raid, Zhengzhou's residents used rural-urban mobility as an adaptation to aerial attack. Like inhabitants of other Chinese cities under bombing threat, they spent much of the day in the nearby countryside. Villagers in Zhengzhou's "diurnal hinterland" were the economic beneficiaries, letting out rooms to urban residents, and, with teahouses springing up and peddlers and entertainers plying their trade, rural areas around the city were said to be "humming with life" in daylight hours.[9] Thus, although the journalist Li Hua felt that Zhengzhou was a "dead city" (*sicheng*) when he first

5. *Zhengzhou ribao*, December 27, 1937.

6. Cui Yanshou, "Liushi nian yuanlin suiyue," 41–42.

7. Xu Lianshan and Wang Zongmin, *Zhengzhou kangzhan*, report eight hundred fatalities (p. 87). Robert McClure, a Canadian missionary-surgeon in Zhengzhou, estimated that up to 1,200 civilians had been killed. See Scott, *McClure*, 229.

8. Isherwood and Auden, *Journey to a War*, 74.

9. *China Press*, April 19, 1938. Nearby villages were not wholly safe, especially those close to railroads. Mifengzhang, just west of the railroad station, was badly bombed. See Zhengxie Zhengzhou shi Erqiqu weiyuanhui, *Yuanqu zhi jiyi*, 53.

arrived in May 1938, this was because many residents were in nearby villages as well as farther afield: "large and small shops alike were all closed, and those whose notice did not say, 'This shop has moved to Hankou [Wuhan] and ceased trading,' said, 'Business hours are from 6:00 p.m. to 10:00 p.m.'"[10]

With these adaptations, urban life in Zhengzhou survived the attack of February 14 and subsequent raids. Indeed, Zhengzhou in spring 1938 resembled a smaller version of the vibrancy of Wuhan during the same period, with its influx of refugees, open Communist activity, student mobilization, relatively free press (especially the *Tongsu ribao* [Popular daily] newspaper), and lively nocturnal life between daytime bombing raids. Without being quite the same focus of world media attention as Wuhan, among other correspondents the city briefly hosted Jack Belden and Robert Capa as well as Isherwood and W. H. Auden.[11]

On April 17, 1938, more than five thousand residents of Zhengzhou gathered at the Long–Hai Gardens for a rally against Japanese invasion.[12] In the 1920s the gardens had been a pleasant park, but by the 1930s they were a site for the "urban gangsters and rural bandits" who operated on the fringes of Zhengzhou (chapter 2). Now they were repurposed for patriotic mobilization. Journalists tried to burnish the city's reputation as a frontline resistance center: "Zhengzhou has not a trace of fear. . . . This ancient county capital has been invigorated, and everyone here has a strong will to resist. Zhengzhou is waiting, waiting calmly, and eventually the day will come when it will roar like a lion (*xiang shi yiban nuhou*)."[13] By June, it looked as if that day was approaching. Following the failure of the hundred-thousand-strong Chinese counterattack at Lanfeng, Japanese forces pushed west along the Long–Hai railroad. On the night of June 5, Nationalist troops pulled out of the provincial capital of Kaifeng. "Chengchow's Fall Expected Soon," reported Hallett Abend for the *New York Times* a few days later.[14]

But Zhengzhou did not fall, and by the time Abend's story was printed, everything on the North China front had changed. A week

10. Li Hua, "Jintian de Zhengzhou yu Kaifeng," 87b.
11. See MacKinnon, *Wuhan*.
12. Xu Lianshan and Wang Zongmin, *Zhengzhou kangzhan*, 88.
13. Lu Yinquan, "Anjing de Zhengzhou," 10c.
14. *New York Times*, June 8, 1938.

earlier Chiang Kai-shek had decided to break the dikes along the Yellow River to stem the Japanese advance. On June 7, Nationalist troops cut a gap in the levee at Huayuankou, 16 kilometers due north of Zhengzhou. With the dikes 8 meters above the floodplain, water poured through the break, triggering further breaches and collapses in the hydraulic infrastructure across southeast Henan, much of Anhui, and parts of Jiangsu (map 3.1). In the eastern portion of Zheng County, around 4,800 people lost their lives, while in neighboring Zhongmu more than 20,000 people died and 40,000 were made homeless. In Henan as a whole, more than 300,000 died across the twenty affected counties, and nearly 1.2 million people were forced to flee their homes.[15]

If the bald facts of the Huayuankou flood are now well known, its interpretations are more contested. Some historians have stressed its strategic importance. Micah Muscolino suggests that before the flood Japanese forces were "poised to capture Wuhan," and Rana Mitter agrees that the Nationalist headquarters could have been taken "within days."[16] These assessments go too far. Wuhan is over 450 kilometers from Zhengzhou, and a spur of the Dabie Mountains lies between the two cities. Japanese supply lines were stretched, and Nationalist forces had sabotaged the Jing–Han railroad. On the Yangzi front, the Japanese Eleventh Army was still hundreds of kilometers from Wuhan. Conversely, Diana Lary argues that the strategic advantages of the flood were "minimal."[17] This view underestimates its long-term significance. Shifting floodwaters made Japanese operations in north-central China difficult for the duration of the war. As well as slowing the advance into Hubei, the floodwaters also prevented a drive toward Luoyang and even Xi'an. Had western Henan fallen in 1938, the long-term safety of Sichuan, so essential to Nationalist prosecution of the war, would have looked very different.

What of the political meanings of the Huayuankou flood? Given the importance of rural-urban inequalities to China's twentieth century, it is tempting to read Huayuankou as an urban-centric act of violence against the countryside. After all, the strategic aim was to save Wuhan,

---

15. See Lary, "Drowned Earth," 201; Muscolino, *Ecology of War*, esp. 30–31. For the local impact in Zheng County, see Zhonggong Henan shengwei dangshi yanjiushi, ed. *Henan sheng kangzhan sunshi diaocha*, 2:105–15.

16. Muscolino, *Ecology of War*, 25; Mitter, *Forgotten Ally*, 160.

17. Lary, "Drowned Earth," 201.

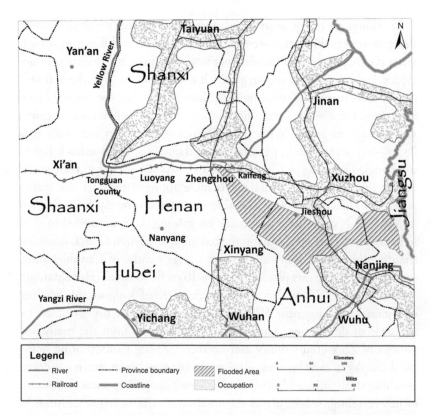

MAP 3.1. Zhengzhou and the Yellow River flood, 1939. Adapted from George Taylor, *The Struggle for North China*, 7. Map by Jogu Gopinath.

China's largest inland city, while Henan's major cities and even most of its smaller county seats avoided the worst. As Kathryn Edgerton-Tarpley shows, flood victims were overwhelmingly farmers in some of the poorest parts of Henan and Anhui Provinces. Large swathes of this rural area were devastated for the next decade.[18] Zhengzhou's eastern hinterland was badly hit, but the floodwaters saved the city from Japanese occupation. A hastily assembled dike northeast of the city protected Zhengzhou from the inundations that plagued the flood zone for the rest of the war.[19]

18. Edgerton-Tarpley, "Between War and Water."

19. On wartime flood defense for the city, see "Zheng Xian xianzhengfu gequ xingshi tu," Zhengzhou Municipal Archive, folder *jiu* (old), 03-017.

Yet things are not quite so straightforward. The idea that there is something newly cruel or urban-centric at Huayuankou is difficult to sustain given the long history of the destructive use of water in Chinese military tactics, including in the same region.[20] It is also not clear that the staff officers who organized the breaking of the levees knew that the city of Zhengzhou would not be hit by the floodwaters. When the Nationalist regime saw strategic advantage in wreaking disaster on cities they were willing to do so—as the thousands, perhaps tens of thousands, of urbanites killed in the bungled burning of Changsha later in 1938 discovered to their cost.[21] Rather than a rural-urban axis, it is more appropriate to see the spatial politics of Huayuankou in regional terms. After the retreat from Xuzhou in May, the Nationalist state focused on gaining the time needed to shift industrial and state apparatus to the redoubts of western China. Breaking the dikes abrogated responsibility for a large swathe of Central China, reducing it to the rather placeless "Yellow River flood zone" (Huangfanqu).

The dilatory Nationalist efforts at flood relief support this reading of regional abandonment. Those on the ground were overwhelmed by the scale of destruction. Surviving archival reports from the marooned villages of Zhongmu County and northeast Zheng County bring home the difficulty of even locating survivors in the flood zone, much less doing anything substantive to help. Relief worker Zhang Daqi spent the month of July traveling by boat across the floodwaters, disbursing relief funds in cash and meeting with surviving district heads (*quzhang*) as well as ordinary villagers. He found that there was "absolutely no local relief being organized"—just his small investigation team bringing in what they could from Zhengzhou. Zhang complained of a severe lack of funds and in terse reports appealed to the subprovincial commissioner (*zhuanyuan*) and the Provincial Relief Commission to release more aid.[22] According to Zhang

20. In 1128 the Song dynasty general Du Chong opened the Yellow River dikes in Henan in a failed attempt to forestall Jurchen invasion, and in 1642 both Li Zicheng and Ming forces tried to break the dikes to their advantage. See Sawyer, *Fire and Water*, 241–315. On 1128 and the negative construction of the river that made Du Chong's decision possible (a negative view of the Yellow River that ran all the way down to the Nationalist strategy of 1938), see Lamouroux, "From the Yellow River to the Huai."

21. See Hudson, "River Sands/Urban Space," 299–311.

22. "Zheng Xian, Zhongmu, Weishi deng xian guanyu Huanghe jizhen gongzuo baogao," Henan Provincial Archive, M8-08-0194, esp. the letter of July 9, 1938 (p. 10) and the undated letter on p. 19.

Fang (1886–1966), head of the provincial relief agency, in the three months after the flood only 320,000 yuan had been spent on support for Henan's 1.2 million flood victims.[23]

This regional sacrifice of summer 1938 set the tone for the spatial politics of the Nationalist war effort. Henan was at the center of the war, as local historian Xie Xiaopeng puts it: "the hinterland of China, the gateway to the Northwest, the screen for Central China, and the crossroads between northern and southern fronts."[24] Micah Muscolino has shown how Henan's fragile environmental infrastructure was unable to cope with the pressures of the long war. As well as Muscolino's story of the energy demands of modern armies, this should also be read as a deeply political story of the Nationalist neglect of frontline regions. The achievements for which the Nationalist war effort has received praise—state building, the ability to keep fighting, avoiding hyperinflation, successful retreat to and reconstruction in western China—are the very things that brought human catastrophe to Henan and precipitated Nationalist collapse in the province in spring 1944. Henan bore a disproportionate burden: in terms of soldiers, providing nearly two million Nationalist troops, more than any province apart from the rear province of Sichuan; in terms of refugees, at more than 40 percent of the population, a higher proportion than anywhere else in China; in terms of millions of civilian dead, at a rate of population loss similar to the wartime demographic collapse within the borders of prewar Poland. But as this chapter shows, the political and economic resources of the Nationalist war effort were concentrated far from the frontline. For Zhengzhou, this led to a contradictory wartime spatial politics: a military frontline pivot but also an isolated outpost, deeply and deliberately cut off from the new core of Nationalist-held western China.

Zhengzhou on the Front Line: Isolation and Adaptation

Although the Huayuankou flood had kept Zhengzhou in Nationalist hands, the city was within a few kilometers of the watery front line to

23. Zhang Fang, "Guomin Zhengfu Henan sheng zhenwuhui guanyu Huanghe juekou Weishi Xian beizai qingxing cheng," September 18, 1938, reproduced in Zhongguo di'er lishi dang'anguan, *Zhonghua minguoshi dang'an ziliao huibian*, 5.2.14, no. 64 in overall series, 509–14.

24. Xie Xiaopeng, "Kangzhan shiqi Henan," 139. For a helpful discussion of Nationalist spatial strategy, see Van de Ven, *War and Nationalism*, 229–35.

its north and east (see map 3.1). The Zhengzhou region was therefore at the geographical heart of the whole continental struggle, as it had been for many previous conflicts in China. But the changing nature of war meant that such frontline areas were in some ways less important. For the Nationalist authorities, rear area industry, economic management, and resource mobilization were more important in the long term than frontline areas—particularly given that they were a state on the defensive. The Nationalist state's temporary capital was at Chongqing in Sichuan Province, which became the new core of the war economy. State spending per capita in Sichuan was more than three times higher than in frontline Henan; even remote Gansu Province in Northwest China saw per capita budgets averaging almost twice those of Henan.[25]

This focus on rear areas was exacerbated by the Nationalist sabotage of Zhengzhou and its transport links. The scorched earth policy began in the chaotic days of early June 1938, when it looked as if the city would fall and most of the civilian population fled westwards. According to Canadian missionary George Andrew (1883–?) demoralized troops "started to loot and did their work pretty thoroughly. Then, in order that the enemy might derive no gain from their occupancy of the city, they blew up most of the remaining buildings that the bombs had not taken." Nor did nearby rural areas escape: "villages within a radius of a mile or two around the city have been burned [by Nationalist troops] and much of the wheat crop either carried off or destroyed."[26] But sabotage continued even after it was clear that Zhengzhou would remain in Chinese hands. Nationalist troops ripped up the Long–Hai railroad from Zhengzhou

25. Provincial budgets for 1939–1942 inclusive show that state spending per capita was an average of 3.2 times higher in Sichuan than in unoccupied parts of Henan. Per capita spending in Gansu averaged 85 percent higher across the same period. Raw data are from Zhongguo di'er lishi dang'anguan, *Zhonghua minguoshi dang'an ziliao huibian*, 5.2.1, 594–95. For per capita calculations, I estimate Sichuan's population in the first half of the war at around 47 million (including Chongqing) and Gansu at 6.6 million. See Hou Yangfang, *Zhongguo renkou shi*, 6:134 (for Gansu) and 202 (Sichuan). I estimate that 60 percent (17.6 million) of Henan's population was under Nationalist control. A 1943 provincial government report claimed that 61 percent of the provincial population was in unoccupied Nationalist-held territory. See "Henan sheng minzhengting 1943 niandu minzheng tongji," Henan Provincial Archive, M-12-01-0005.

26. George Andrew, letter to Canon Gould, June 20, 1938, Andrew Correspondence, 1916–1940, MSCC Records, box 77, folder 1, General Synod Archives, Anglican Church of Canada.

almost as far as Luoyang, using the tracks to extend the line toward Gansu in the better-protected Northwest. This meant that the hundreds of thousands of troops in the frontline counties around Zhengzhou could only be supplied locally or by the rudimentary roads—which themselves had been sabotaged and only half-repaired.[27]

A report of 1940 sums up the city's isolation: "To the north and the east, Zhengzhou is cut off by the river, and to the south and the west the Jing–Han and Long–Hai railroads have been dismantled. Communication routes are inconvenient and transportation difficult."[28] Not only had the center of gravity of the Nationalist state and war effort shifted to China's western regions, but the same process occurred within Henan itself. The western city of Luoyang, with its intermittent rail connection to Shaanxi, was the commercial and political center of unoccupied Henan; once-peripheral southwestern areas of the province such as the Funiu Mountains south of Luoyang and the Nanyang Basin also rose to strategic prominence. Zhengzhou received little of the attention it had attracted before Huayuankou. Of the Henan Provincial Government's eleven road-building projects between 1939 and 1942, almost all connected Luoyang or Nanyang, with only one short road in the Zhengzhou region (Zhengzhou to Dengfeng).[29] "Not only is it difficult for important officials to come here," noted one visiting journalist in 1940, "but there is also very little trace of cultural figures or patriotic troupes. . . . In most people's minds, Zhengzhou is already like a deserted island (*huangdao*)."[30]

Apart from refugees, only a few thousand people were still living in Zhengzhou in the summer of 1938, and it was not clear what form of urban civilian life would survive.[31] The disruption was particularly stark at the fringes of the city. The Long–Hai Gardens were again repurposed, this time as headquarters of the Third Group Army.[32] In a reversal of

27. Liu Hui, *Tielu yu Zhengzhou chengshihua*, 92. Before Japan's Ichigo attack of 1944, there were up to four hundred thousand Nationalist troops stationed in the eleven frontline counties around Zhengzhou, mostly of the Thirty-Eighth Army. Admittedly, this figure seems high, since it assumes the units were at numerical strength. See Huang Zhenglin, Zhang Yan, and Su Zhigang, *Jindai Henan jingjishi*, 2:278.

28. "Zhengzhou de jingji gaikuang," 5–6.

29. Huang Zhenglin, Zhang Yan, and Su Zhigang, *Jindai Henan jingjishi*, 2:296.

30. Zhen Mou, "Huanghe xianshang de Zhengzhou," 10a.

31. Zhen Mou, "Huanghe xianshang de Zhengzhou," 10a.

32. Zheng Xiangqian, "Zhengzhou zuizao de gongyuan," 144–45.

the earlier urban-to-rural flight from bombing raids, rural refugees from the Huayuankou flood moved to the city in search of safety. Within a month of the flood, between 20,000 and 25,000 refugees were camped out around Zhengzhou.[33] On the western edge of the city, refugees assembled makeshift shelters on abandoned railroad land or sheltered in bomb craters in the open fields beyond.[34] A local relief committee tried to provide some assistance, but in August 1939 Zhengzhou was hit with flash flooding—not from the Yellow River flood but from the small Jinshui River on the northern edge of the city. Water poured into the downtown, hundreds of shacks were destroyed, and homelessness and infectious disease stalked the city afresh.[35]

Despite this isolation and human suffering, the urban life and spatial politics of wartime Zhengzhou were more complex than simply a "deserted island." Although there were occasional bombing raids and periodic rumors of Japanese incursions across the Yellow River flood, Zhengzhou was usually safe for civilian activity: "apart from the fact that enemy aircraft can swiftly be over the city (*xunsu fei lin shi kong*) in just four or five minutes, which creates danger, there is nothing else that creates any unhappiness."[36] Those still living in Zhengzhou adapted to the destruction of the city's railroad role and forged local networks of production and trade. With larger factories having fled town, Zhengzhou's small workshops found niches in cloth, oil, leather, and cigarettes, buoyed by demand from military units stationed nearby. In 1940—a difficult year for Nationalist China as a whole—the Henan Farmers' and Workers' Bank cheerfully noted that in Zhengzhou "the marketing of these local products (*tuchan*) is certainly flourishing more and more, and it is not difficult to compete with goods coming from outside."[37] There were more than three hundred handicraft operations in town as well as hundreds

---

33. "Zheng Xian, Zhongmu, Weishi deng xian guanyu Huanghe jizhen gongzuo baogao," Henan Provincial Archive, M8-08-0194, 1–2 in folder.

34. Zhengxie Zhengzhou shi Erqiqu weiyuanhui, *Yuanqu zhi jiyi*, 56.

35. "Henan sheng diyi qu dierci shuizai jiuji huiyi jilu" (September 1940), reproduced in Zhongguo di'er lishi dang'anguan, *Zhonghua minguoshi dang'an ziliao huibian*, 5.2.14, no. 64 in overall series, 528–30. See also Zhao Fuhai, *Lao Zhengzhou: Shangdu yimeng*, 85–88.

36. Zhen Mou, "Huanghe xianshang de Zhengzhou," 10a.

37. "Zhengzhou de jingji gaikuang," 5b.

of households producing hand-rolled cigarettes.[38] Amid the dearth of consumer goods in Nationalist-held China, wartime Zhengzhou provides a curious instance of a frontline zone supplying rear areas despite the city's isolation: "Although the large factories have closed," one journalist noted in 1940, "all kinds of small handicrafts have already sprung up to replace them: hand-rolled tobacco, woven cotton goods, cosmetics. . . . Not only does this supply the needs of the locality; a fair amount is also shipped out to Luoyang, Xi'an, and Lanzhou."[39] That June, the Chamber of Commerce even held a festival showcasing the best of Zhengzhou's products, with a program of celebratory events and an evening banquet.[40] By then the city's population had recovered to an estimated seventy thousand people—around half the prewar total and including thousands of refugees but a significant recovery from the devastation of 1938.[41]

The key to this minirevival was the city's rural-urban connections, with the major sectors of cloth, oil, leather, salt, and cigarettes all reliant on production in the hinterland. Rural-urban tensions remained—following the Jinshui flood of 1939, villagers north of Zhengzhou protested that the new channel protected the city while exposing them to flood risk—but the sabotage of long-distance rail connections made Zhengzhou's economy newly reliant on its rural hinterland.[42] Although parts of the urban edge were occupied by the Nationalist garrison, such as the Long–Hai Gardens and the Bishagang memorial park, this control was far from complete—indeed, with Feng Yuxiang's support the civilian district commissioner even won back control of the Bishagang site.[43] Nor did Zhengzhou experience the strict control on rural-urban exchange seen in some wartime Chinese cities, particularly those under

38. The number of people employed in such workshops had fallen by over 20 percent compared to before the war (from 2,164 in 1936 to 1,644 in 1941) but accounted for a much larger proportion of the city's reduced population. Figures from Zhengzhou shi gongshangye lianhehui, *Zhengzhou gongshangye xingshuai*, comparing 38–46 and 50–53.

39. Zhen Mou, "Huanghe xianshang de Zhengzhou," 10a.

40. Zhao Fuhai, *Lao Zhengzhou: Shangdu yimeng*, 28–29.

41. Zhen Mou, "Huanghe xianshang de Zhengzhou," 10a.

42. A joint army-civil government project during the 1939–1940 winter diverted the Jinshui River away from the city center to the north and the west as part of a work-for-relief program. See "Henan sheng diyi qu di'erci shuizai jiuji huiyi jilu" (September 1940), in Zhongguo di'er lishi dang'anguan, *Zhonghua minguoshi dang'an ziliao huibian*, 529; on rural complaints, see Zhao Fuhai, *Lao Zhengzhou: Shangdu yimeng*, 185–90.

43. Wu Huimin, "Shengde Zhongxue zai Bishagang de shimo," 20–21.

occupation. Zhengzhou's handicraft producers found both raw materials and markets in the counties close to the city—Sishui, Xingyang, Mi County—that had hitherto been left behind by Zhengzhou's railway boom. The combination of revived handicrafts, good grain harvests, and the opening of coal seams brought economic growth to these nearby counties in 1939 and 1940. Strikingly, with industrial production disrupted, rural cloth production more than doubled in Nationalist-held Henan compared with before the war; in Zheng County, small-scale wartime village improvement schemes included brickworks, fruit and fish farms, as well as weaving.[44]

If Zhengzhou's revival after 1938 was based in part on local handicraft production, the second strand of its recovery restored the city's role in interregional trade. Although the loss of rail connections limited the city's role in processing and wholesaling bulk goods, Zhengzhou became an important hub for smuggling routes across the front line.[45] The very proximity to the front, which had hit the city's prewar commercial links, proved to be a boon in the rather separate realm of the smuggling business. Illicit trade between occupied and unoccupied China was lucrative, binding together occupier, collaborator, and resister, and has duly attracted the attention—and sometimes the admonition—of historians.[46] What is less well understand is how smuggling routes affected towns in the contested zones of Central China.

44. "Henan sheng ge xian ni ban xiangzhen zaochan xiangmu tongjibiao," Henan Provincial Archive, M12-001-0005, 57–58 in folder. Most prewar rural projects in Zheng County fell into abeyance, but a fruit center and nursery did continue at Guanhutun, 5 kilometers north of the city. See "Henan sheng nongye gaijinsuo sannianlai gongzuo gaikuang," 1943, Henan Provincial Archive, M27-001-0015, 7 in folder. On cloth production, see Huang Zhenglin, Zhang Yan, and Su Zhigang, *Jindai Henan jingjishi*, 2:263. For the classic statement of rural advantage in the first phase of war (before widespread taxation in kind), see Eastman, *Seeds of Destruction*, 45–70.

45. I follow contemporaries in using the term "smuggling" (*zousi*), although cross-front trade was not always illegal from all perspectives. In July 1939, the Nationalist government made it legal to bring in most goods from occupied China on payment of tax duty, even though any collusion or contact with the enemy was still officially illegal. For a local list of banned items, see "Xiuzheng qudi jinzhi jinkou wupin shangxiao banfa," Henan Provincial Archive, M08-46-1268, 104–19. On the occupied side, the economic blockade of unoccupied China meant that export of goods to such areas was officially illegal throughout.

46. For a full-length study, see Qi Chunfeng, *Zhong-Ri jingjizhan zhong de zousi*. See also Schoppa, *In a Sea of Bitterness*, 261–84; Thai, *China's War on Smuggling*, 165–204.

The smuggling routes across the flooded Yellow River to Zhengzhou took off during 1939. Consumer shortages and high prices in Nationalist-held China offered big profits for all kinds of transportable goods: Nationalist official Zhang Zhonglu (1895–1968) remembered watches, pens, medicines, clothing, and even bicycles, along with a steady flow of opiates.[47] A bank report from Zhengzhou notes that it was easier and cheaper to get gasoline from occupied territory than from rear areas.[48] Unlike before the war, though, Zhengzhou was not quite the main center for long-distance trade in north-central China. That honor belonged to the smuggling boomtown of Jieshou, 230 kilometers southeast of Zhengzhou (see map 3.1), where one official-turned-smuggler reckoned in 1941 that more than a million yuan worth of goods were changing hands each day—more than the central government's daily budget for education, health, and welfare combined.[49]

Zhengzhou was the meeting point of three smuggling routes, replicating its prewar junction role, and became an important pivot for funneling goods toward Nationalist-held rear areas. The first of these routes was from Jieshou, via Luohe and northwards up the route of the sabotaged Jing–Han railroad. According to the collaborationist official Xing Hansan, much of this trade was directly or indirectly controlled by Tang Enbo, Nationalist general and hero of the victory at Tai'erzhuang.[50] The second route was directly westwards from occupied Kaifeng, where the old China hand Sakurai Tokutarō (1897–1980) controlled much of the smuggling trade in collusion with Sun Tongxuan (1895–1978), Nationalist commander of the Third Army Group at Zhengzhou.[51] It took two or three days to cross the floodwaters of the Yellow River, staying overnight in the marooned villages of no-man's

47. "Zhengzhou de jingji gaikuang," 6a; Zhang Zhonglu, "Guanyu 1942 nian Henan da jihuang," 68.

48. "Zhongyang yinhang Zhengzhou fenhang," report of November 16, 1942, Henan Provincial Archive, M54-001-0085, 45.

49. Peck, *Two Kinds of Time*, 237. Budget figures from Young, *China's Wartime Finance*, 333.

50. Xing Hansan, *Riwei tongzhi Henan*, 176.

51. In summer 1940, Sun's brother, Sun Tongfeng, was arrested by the Kempeitai (Japanese military police) on a trade visit to Kaifeng. Sakurai was able to spirit him out of prison and back to unoccupied territory. See Shi Sutan, "Kangzhan qijian Rikou zai Kaifeng," 402–6.

land in Zhongmu County. With official connivance on both sides, military patrols were happy to let traders through for a small fee. According to an official Ministry of Finance report, in summer 1939 the cost of smuggling 100 *jin* of goods between Kaifeng and Zhengzhou was 15 yuan, roughly equivalent to two weeks' wages for an unskilled male laborer. Ninety percent of these goods were Japanese-made, with huge profits reported in Zhengzhou.[52] The third route was south from occupied Xinxiang, crossing the Yellow River upstream from the breach at Huayuankou, and was controlled by Nationalist commander Wu Shaozhou (1902–1966). The American war photographer Harrison Forman described a "regular fair" in operation at the riverside, with goods being resold and taken into Zhengzhou on wheelbarrows. Orders placed for goods in Zhengzhou would arrive from Xinxiang within three days.[53] With these three routes converging in Zhengzhou, they were then carried overland westwards to rear areas: according to a 1940 report, "they then get transported to Xi'an, where they can be sold off for a large profit (*ke huo hou li*)."[54]

It is difficult to quantify the impact of the smuggling trade on Zhengzhou. Although ultimately controlled by regional military powerholders, smuggling helps explains why the city's civilian population numbers stayed so buoyant during the first half of the war. Most goods did not stay in Zhengzhou, but there was something of a boom for commercial agents (*xintuo shanghang*), firms helping long-distance traders with accommodation, marketing, goods storage, and encounters with bureaucracy. By 1941 there were twenty such outfits in the city—even more than before the war—supporting some 360 independent merchants as well as taking part themselves in trade across the front line.[55] When the American journalist Graham Peck (1914–1968) visited in late 1941, he found that "the remains of the petty middle class—artisans and small shopkeepers—were in it on a retail scale, trundling their wheelbarrows off to the front to see what they could buy." Peck was told that "the

52. "Caizhengbu guanyu chajin Huang-Huai lianghe zousi zhi Jingjibu dai dian" (August 1939). Reproduced in Zhongguo di'er lishi dang'anguan, ed., *Zhonghua minguoshi dang'an ziliao huibian*, 5.2.11, no. 61 in overall series, 720–21.
53. Forman, "Harrison Forman Diary," 58.
54. "Zhengzhou de jingji gaikuang," 6a.
55. Zhengzhou shi gongshangye lianhehui, *Zhengzhou gongshangye xingshuai*, comparing 44 and 52 with 92–94.

peasant refugees who camped on the outer fringes of Chengchow stayed because they could make some kind of living by hauling smuggled goods on into the interior."[56]

Zhengzhou's remarkable survival as a frontline city, a railroad town without a railroad, was thus built on twin spatial adaptations of local handicraft production and long-distance smuggling. Those around the front line, whether generals, rural weavers, or refugees-turned-haulers, made the most of new opportunities to make, move, and sell goods. With a porous front—crossed by laborers, missionaries, and spies as well as traders—Zhengzhou was part of an adaptive war economy in central China separate from the control of Chongqing. However, this "wartime normal" of 1938–1941 was built on delicate foundations. When the military struggle for space and resources in Henan became more intense, these adaptations broke down, with catastrophic consequences for those in Zhengzhou and its hinterland.

Before dawn on October 2, 1941, the Japanese 110th Division advanced across the Yellow River floodwaters. Zhengzhou was attacked in a pincer movement and fell two days later. This first occupation of Zhengzhou was short-lived—Nationalist forces recaptured the city at the end of the month—and is only a small footnote in the wider war. But accounts of the period show how this burst of military activity changed the spatial struggles and strategies for Zhengzhou's residents. Within the occupied city, even very local movement became dangerous. During the day, residents faced the hazards of Japanese checkpoints; after dark, with Nationalist forces having sabotaged the generator for street lighting, occupation troops retreated to walled compounds and left the streets in the hands of looters.[57] The occupiers militarized the urban edge, ringing it with barbed wire, throwing up blockhouses, and burning the straw huts of the 1938 flood refugees. A no-entry zone was imposed around Zhengzhou, and sentry posts confiscated goods from farmers trying to bring in produce for sale.[58] In the Anglican mission compound, things were desperate: "we got down to food for just three more days and there was no going out into the country parts or coming

56. Peck, *Two Kinds of Time*, 331–32.
57. Peck, *Two Kinds of Time*, 337–38.
58. *Henan minbao*, November 9, 1941; on the burning of shacks, Peck, *Two Kinds of Time*, 337–38.

in either to get more. Sentries and wire fences surrounding the whole place prevented that."[59]

Apart from joining in the looting, the main survival strategy of Zhengzhou's residents was flight to the nearby countryside. Under conditions of extreme military violence, this response brought its own risks. According to Graham Peck—who, admittedly, brought his own narrative of social and political collapse in Nationalist-held China—city residents told him that unlike in the air raids of 1938 they had found little refuge or solidarity in villages during the Japanese attack. Peck met a merchant-smuggler who had been robbed by a rural Red Spears (Hongqianghui) militia group, and another resident, the widow of a railway engineer, reported that she "had spent the whole month in a little farm village with many other refugees from the city. The refugees helped each other a little, loaning cooking utensils, but the farmers were very cruel . . . They would not even let us pick leaves from their trees." Only the nightsoil collector, who was well known by his customers in nearby villages, was treated well.[60] The very worst atrocities during October 1941 also seem to have taken place outside of town, away from the efforts of the urban Peace Preservation Committee (Zhi'an weichihui) to restore order through collaboration with the occupying force.[61] Civilian casualty figures in some Zheng County villages reportedly ran into three figures, most seriously in the brutal reprisals that followed attacks on Japanese troops at Shilipu and Wulibao.[62] Conditioned by the horrors of Nanjing, today the strongest images of Japanese atrocities in wartime China are urban, but most victims were rural people caught up in these "pacification" campaigns, launched from urban command centers like Zhengzhou under the "Three Alls Policy" of murdering civilians, destroying infrastructure, and looting resources.

When Graham Peck visited Zhengzhou a few days after the Japanese retreat, he found a city almost totally destroyed, different from the countryside primarily in the aesthetics of its ruins:

59. George Andrew, letter to Canon Gould, November 21, 1941, Andrew Correspondence, 1916–40, MSCC Records, box 77, folder 1, General Synod Archives, Anglican Church of Canada.

60. Peck, *Two Kinds of Time*, 329, 341–42.

61. On the Zhengzhou committee, see Luo Jiurong, "Lishi qingjing."

62. *Henan minbao*, December 9, 1941; Peck, *Two Kinds of Time*, 339; Xu Lianshan and Wang Zongmin, *Zhengzhou kangzhan*, 92.

I have never seen a city look so strange. After two days' travel in the brown fading countryside . . . this wilderness of tall, rectangular, ruined buildings for a moment made the very fact of a city, any city, seem fantastic. . . . [With] deserted and blasted factories, warehouses and blocks of flats, clumsily porticoed and corniced in the styles common to any European or American railway town . . . in the last cold glow of the dark sunset, their elaborate decaying walls were streaked with the light, ice-cream colors of a big modern city—pistachio, mint, lemon, strawberry.[63]

Peck's first impression from a distance sounds almost picturesque, but up close Zhengzhou at the end of 1941 presented an ugly scene. What had not been sabotaged by Nationalist forces was removed or destroyed by Japanese troops. Returning Chinese journalists found a city stripped of food stores, movable equipment, and even electricity wires.[64] A report from a local bank branch describes a newly militarized city, with trenches and checkpoints around a town that had "become a military outpost where it is impossible to feel at ease (*buneng anxin*)."[65] District Commissioner Wang Guanglin moved his headquarters out of Zhengzhou to nearby Xinzheng, noting that the "former energy of the area has been ravaged and almost completely exhausted (*zhuosang daijin*)."[66] After November 1941 the city's population only recovered to around half of its pre-October level and a quarter of the prewar total—perhaps much less.[67]

A shadow urban life continued—that is, some density of structures and activity—clustered around the shell of the bombed-out commercial districts, but the local handicraft production that had brought a pale prosperity to Zhengzhou had been shattered by the bombing, flight, and

63. Peck, *Two Kinds of Time*, 331–32.
64. Guan Weiming, "Cong Luohe dao Zhengzhou," *Henan minguo ribao*, November 13–14, 1941, reproduced in Chen Chuanhai and Xu Youli, *Rijun huo Yu ziliao*, 109–10.
65. "Zhongyang yinhang Zhengzhou fenhang," report of November 26, 1942, Henan Provincial Archive, M54-001-0085, 51.
66. Wang Guanglin, "Wunianlai gongzuo jiyao," July 1, 1947, Zhengzhou Municipal Archive, *jiu* 03-38-001.
67. Andrew estimated fifteen thousand people in the city in 1942. Another resident told Harrison Forman that the population was a little less than fifty thousand in summer 1942, but this may include refugees coming to Zhengzhou in the early stages of the 1942–43 famine. See, respectively, Christensen, *In War and Famine*, 96; Forman, "Harrison Forman Diary," 70.

looting of October 1941.[68] Both sides tightened the front line and reduced the pace of smuggling. With Zhengzhou "under a stricter material blockade," reported the press in occupied Shanghai, its "function as an artery (*shu xue guan*) to the rear areas is reduced."[69] Peck found nothing but the shattered fragments of Zhengzhou's material modernity: "in the pitted fields between the Chengchow ruins, swarms of tattered people seemed also to be mocking urban life, for they were building hovels out of massive carved tables, cupboards and other big-city furniture." For Peck, Zhengzhou in 1941 was "modern war at its lowest ebb"—or, perhaps, as he seems to hint, its logical endpoint.[70]

"All Well. Famine Raging": Spatial Perspectives on Famine

Yet Graham Peck was wrong: conditions in and around Zhengzhou were about to get worse. During 1942–1943 Henan suffered one of the worst wartime famines of modern history.[71] The Nationalist authorities in unoccupied Henan did not react to the poor spring 1942 wheat harvest, hoping that, as in previous years, the fall harvest of sorghum, millet, and tubers would be sufficient to see farmers through the winter. Instead, the long drought of 1942 brought the almost complete failure of these autumn crops. Across both 1942 harvests, nominal food availability in Nationalist-held Henan fell to just under half that of previous years.[72] More than one million people suffered starvation-related deaths and a further three million fled their homes.[73]

---

68. "Zheng xian shiqing gaikuang: san si yuefen," *Jingji huibao*, no. 4 (1942): 285.

69. *Shenbao*, April 20, 1943.

70. Peck, *Two Kinds of Time*, 331 and 340–41.

71. "All Well. Famine Raging" in the heading comes from a George Andrew telegram to Canon Dixon, October 26, 1942, Andrew Correspondence, MSCC Records, box 77, folder 1, General Synod Archives, Anglican Church of Canada.

72. Using yield estimates from the Farmers' Bank of China, I estimate 48.5 percent of the 1938–1941 average. For data, see Xu Daofu, *Zhongguo jindai nongye shengchan*, 19–22.

73. This death toll estimate is a more pessimistic interpretation of Anthony Garnaut's figure of a little less than one million (Garnaut's food estimates for food availability are a little more optimistic than my own). Garnaut, "Quantitative Description," 2032–36. Muscolino, *Ecology of War*, 87, gives a higher figure of 1.5 to 2 million excess deaths, but the report that forms part of this estimate may include outmigration.

SPATIAL POLITICS OF FAMINE

The struggles over food in Henan during 1942–1943 can be interpreted along several axes: the multiple armies in the province competing for food, the struggle of civilian society to resist food expropriation by state authorities, tension between producers and consumers of food, and local residents competing for food with famine refugees. Amid this complex picture, recent surveys of the war have tended to downplay the culpability of the Nationalist state.[74] This trend goes too far. Famine in Henan was partly caused by Nationalist military requisitioning, which amounted to around one-fifth or one-sixth of 1942 total food production in the unoccupied parts of the province and tipped nominal food availability below starvation levels.[75] Rather, the famine should be seen not just in terms of tension between Nationalist military and civilian society but as part of a wider story of the spatial politics of the Nationalist war effort. As at Huayuankou in 1938, famine was exacerbated by Nationalist neglect of the frontline regions of Central China—both unoccupied Henan in general and frontline Zhengzhou in particular. Zhengzhou and its hinterland was one of the worst-hit districts but received almost no aid until well into 1943. Crucially, when relief did—belatedly and temporarily—become a Nationalist priority in the spring of 1943, the state showed that it could marshal inputs for the frontline famine zone but that it had chosen not to do so until it was, for many, too late. I here examine this

74. Rana Mitter concludes that "individuals could have behaved differently, but overall the result was inescapable." See Mitter, *Forgotten Ally*, 273; see also Lary, *Chinese People at War*, 124–26. Although my reading of 1942 famine causality is similar to that of Micah Muscolino, I lay slightly more stress on central and provincial Nationalist culpability during the 1942–43 winter. Compare Muscolino, *Ecology of War*, 105–11.

75. I estimate that requisitioning in 1942 reduced nominal daily per capita food availability to around 800 to 920 calories (even if perfectly distributed). This estimate includes taxation in kind (*zhengshi*), compulsory purchase (*zhenggou*), and additional levies (*tanpai*). According to official statistics, following partial tax remission, 3.74 million *shidan* (市擔, not the volume measure 市石) of wheat was requisitioned by land tax and compulsory purchase. See Henan sheng zhengfu tongjichu, *Henan sheng tongji nianjian*, 142–44. This amounted to around one-sixth of the wheat harvest, possibly an underestimate, but the suggestion that the authorities took half the wheat crop seems too high; see Garnaut, "Quantitative Description," 2025. This wheat harvest figure omits ongoing levies and requisitioning of fall crops. Following Muscolino, these were as much as or more than wheat procurement (*Ecology of War*, 98–99), bringing requisitioning to my estimate of one-fifth to one-sixth of total production.

process at three spatial scales: first at the level of the province, then of the local area around Zhengzhou within unoccupied Henan, before turning to the rural-urban dynamics of the famine around Zhengzhou.

The Provincial Scale: Henan in Unoccupied China
During the depths of the desperate 1942 winter, Henan newspaper editor Li Jingzhi (1901–1989) bemoaned the lack of aid entering the province: what was required, Li argued, was "for the famine to be seen as a major question for the whole of China (*kancheng yige quanguoxing de da wenti*)."[76] Li was writing six months into famine conditions, but his appeal was still wishful thinking. It was not that the central government did not know about conditions in Henan. Provincial governor Li Peiji (1886–1969) had cabled Chongqing as early as June 1942 asking—without success—for the province to be excused from the burden of compulsory grain purchase.[77] In the fall, Chiang Kai-shek discussed shortages in Henan and pledged a reduction in tax demands as well as 200 million yuan in relief funds.[78] Yet military requisitioning continued well into 1943, and, even six months after the pledge, only 40 percent of promised funds had arrived, their value much reduced by inflation.[79] Even the official press admitted that by March 9 just 5.1 million *jin* of grain had entered Henan on the Long–Hai railroad—only enough to keep the estimated 3.8 million most desperate famine victims alive for a few days, even if it could reach them.[80] This drift between the fall of 1942 and spring 1943 cost hundreds of thousands of lives in Henan. At this crucial juncture, provincial official Zhang Zhonglu argued, "There was nobody from Henan to speak out at the GMD [Nationalist Party] center."[81] The contrast with food shortages in Sichuan is striking. Faced with hunger in this core area of unoccupied China following a poor rice harvest of 1940, Chongqing swiftly found

76. *Qianfengbao*, December 11, 1942.
77. *Henan minbao*, June 25, 1942.
78. Song Zhixin, *1942: Henan dajihuang*, 14.
79. For levies around Zhengzhou in 1943, including of famine foods such as animal feed, wheat husks, and millet straw, see "Henan shengzhengfu Minzhengting 1943 niandu minzheng tongji," Henan Provincial Archive, M12-001-0005, 131–39; on slow arrival of funds, White and Jacoby, *Thunder Out of China*, 164.
80. *Henan minbao*, March 19, 1943. On the figure of 3.8 million across fifty-eight unoccupied counties, see "Henan shengzhengfu Minzhengting 1943 niandu minzheng tongji," Henan Provincial Archive, M12-001-0005, 98–99.
81. Zhang Zhonglu, "Guanyu 1942 nian Henan da jihuang," 296–97.

alternative sources of supply for the military and for Sichuan's cities.[82] I do not mean to suggest that residents of Sichuan had an easy time during the war—Isabel Crook and Xiji Yu found deep state-society tension over tax, conscription, and attendant local corruption[83]—but dearth in Sichuan was an existential threat to the state in a way that the Henan famine, in a distant and expendable frontline area, was not.

It was clear to those on the ground what needed to be done. The newspaper editor Li Jingzhi offered solutions as early as September 1942: the end of requisitioning, transfer of surplus grain from other provinces, and the large-scale subsidized sale of grain (*pingtiao*).[84] This program was within the capacity of the Nationalist state, as was demonstrated when the relief effort finally swung into action. Partly prompted by reporting in the *Dagongbao* newspaper in Chongqing and *Time* magazine in New York, a large-scale aid effort began in late February and March 1943, closely chiming with Li's prescriptions of six months earlier. In the final six weeks before the 1943 harvest, government-organized relief made a real difference. Up to a million people were receiving free grain from soup kitchens (*zhouchang*) as well as benefiting from subsidized grain.[85] Although much of it may not have reached Henan before the harvest, the efforts of the civil and military apparatus yielded between 35 million and 52 million *jin*. If distributed perfectly, this was enough to keep the most desperate three million people in Henan alive for between three and five weeks—a crucial bridge to the wheat harvest in May and early June.[86] Yet

---

82. Zhang complained that Sichuan got "top place in the whole country" (*quanguo shouwei*). Zhang Zhonglu, "Guanyu 1942 nian Henan da jihuang," 297. On 1940 in Sichuan, see Tsung-han Shen, "Food Production and Distribution."

83. Brown Crook, Gilmartin, and Yu, *Prosperity's Predicament*, 225–49.

84. For Li's proposals, see editorial in *Qianfengbao*, September 3, 1942.

85. Su Xinliu, *Minguo shiqi Henan shui han zaihai*, 156–58. Su urges caution on these county-by-county relief figures, noting that by spring 1943 officials were incentivized to exaggerate famine relief efforts.

86. This is assuming that a further 7 million *jin* scheduled from Shaanxi arrived, making 14 million *jin* in civil relief. In addition, Muscolino calculates that Henan's military units donated or (mostly) loaned a further 21.3 million *jin*. Muscolino, *Ecology of War*, 111. Local newspapers suggest that this figure may be an underestimate: including some pledges from military units stationed outside the province, I conservatively estimate the total at 38 million *jin*—although it is not clear how much of or when these donations reached those in need. On total relief pledges, see *Henan minbao*, May 8, 1943. United China Relief coordinator Ernest Wampler concurred that the Nationalist response was effective when it occurred, but it was simply too late. Wampler, *China Suffers*, 230.

this eventual success of Nationalist relief work sheds a dark light on the failure to support this frontline region during the preceding nine months of famine. For local journalist Li Rui (1911–1998), the Nationalist state was neglecting the "minimal responsibility" (*qima de zeren*) of statecraft: keeping citizens alive. "Previously, the blood and sweat of these famine victims was poured out, drop by drop, for the War of Resistance and for the state, but now they are starving to death."[87]

The Local Scale: Zhengzhou in Henan Province
Provincial official Fang Ce (1886–1945) toured the famine zone in spring 1943 and declared that "the Henan disaster is worst in the Zhengzhou district; within the district, Zheng County, Xingyang, Guangwu, and Sishui are especially hard hit."[88] The statistics of death bear out Fang's assessment: the first Nationalist attempt to count famine mortality reckoned that more than a third of deaths were in this Zhengzhou region.[89] The American journalist Theodore White's description of Zhengzhou in March 1943 still has the power to shock: "Death ruled Chengchow, for the famine centered there. . . . It had the half-destroyed air of all battlefront cities. Rubble was stacked along the gutters, and the great buildings, roofless, were open to the sky. Over the rubble and ruins the snow spread a mantle that deadened every sound. We stood at the head of the main street, looked down the deserted way for all its length, and saw nothing."[90] The reporter Li Rui cycled to Zhengzhou a few weeks later and found a situation of endemic violence: suicides, occasional food riots, petty theft, and rumors of cannibalism. Echoing White, Li reported that "the famous streets of Datonglu, Dehuajie, and Fushoujie have all become desolate places (*huang chang*)" (figs. 3.1 and 3.2). He heard that more than a thousand people had died in the city in the previous two weeks.[91]

87. Quotes from *Qianfengbao*, respectively April 21, 1943; April 6, 1943.
88. Quoted in Song Zhixin, *1942: Henan dajihuang*, 70.
89. Zhang Guangsi, "Zhang Guangsi guanyu Henan sheng hanzai qingkuang ji jiuzai qingxing de diaocha baogao," September 27, 1943, reproduced in Zhongguo di'er lishi dang'anguan, *Zhonghua minguoshi dang'an ziliao huibian*, 5.2.14, no. 64 in overall series, 560–67.
90. White and Jacoby, *Thunder Out of China*, 161.
91. *Qianfengbao*, April 6, 1943, and April 21, 1943. George Andrew reported that around one hundred people were dying in the city each day. Letter to Canon Dixon,

FIGURE 3.1. Dehuajie, March 1943. Photograph by Harrison Forman. Reproduced with permission from the American Geographical Society Library, University of Wisconsin–Milwaukee Libraries.

FIGURE 3.2. Datonglu, March 1943. Photograph by Harrison Forman. Reproduced with permission from the American Geographical Society Library, University of Wisconsin–Milwaukee Libraries.

The appalling conditions in and around Zhengzhou between summer 1942 and summer 1943 were a product of wartime spatial politics, not just chance. Rainfall conditions were not markedly worse here than elsewhere in the province.[92] The problem was the place of the frontline zone in the Nationalist war effort. With Chongqing increasingly demanding self-sufficiency of individual armies, rural producers around Zhengzhou faced worsening pressure on their resources: corvée labor, tax-in-kind (rolled out in 1941–1942), compulsory purchase, ad hoc levies, and in some places Japanese grain raids. A 1942 appeal from twelve notable citizens of Zhengzhou, including the head of the chamber of commerce, gives some idea of how years on the front line had reduced disaster resilience, when compared with parts of the province further from the front: "since the war started in Zhengzhou, transport has been cut off, many troops have been stationed here, requisitions have been frequent, and supply does not meet the demand; in particular, grain for military supply has been the main aspect of suffering among the people (*minjian tongku daduan*)."[93] In the push for extraction and despite the desperately poor crop, Zheng County met almost three-quarters of its wheat requisitioning quota in 1942.[94]

With Zhengzhou cut off by Nationalist sabotage of the rail lines, the 120-kilometer journey to the city from the railhead at Luoyang took White and the photojournalist Harrison Forman three days in March 1943, even traveling part of the way by truck; a cart carrying grain would take longer.[95] That month, at the height of the famine, prices in Zhengzhou were two and a half times higher than in railroad-connected Luoyang.[96] Just as Henan's voice at Chongqing was marginal, so the provincial government, from May 1942 operating from its mountainous

February 28, 1943, Andrew Correspondence, MSCC Records, box 77, folder 1, General Synod Archives, Anglican Church of Canada.

92. On rainfall, see Su Xinliu, *Minguo shiqi Henan shui han zaihai*, 28–30.

93. Letter to the Central Relief Committee (Zhongyang jiuji weiyuanhui), reproduced in Xu Lianshan and Wang Zongmin, *Zhengzhou kangzhan*, 156–58.

94. "1942 nian Henan gexian maishou zaiqing tongjibiao," reproduced in Zhongguo di'er lishi dang'anguan, *Zhonghua minguoshi dang'an ziliao huibian*, 5.2.14, no. 64 in overall series, 265–74; Forman, "Harrison Forman Diary," 36–37.

95. White and Jacoby, *Thunder Out of China*, 160.

96. Forman, "Harrison Forman Diary," 18 (informed by relief worker Ernest Wampler).

redoubt in Lushan, was slow to respond to petitions from Zhengzhou. In August 1942 the former commissioner of Zhengzhou (along with his Xuchang counterpart) decided, in frustration, to bypass the provincial government and travel to Chongqing to appeal directly to the central authorities—albeit with limited success.[97] As the next part of this chapter shows, the relief effort by authorities beyond Zhengzhou did not bring substantial amounts of food to the city until seven months later, in late March 1943.

Rural and Urban in the Henan Famine
The rural-urban dimensions of famine are less clear than its provincial and local patterns. In the first attempt to reconstruct from patchy data, Anthony Garnaut cautiously suggests that the effects of famine may have been worse in Henan's urban areas than in the countryside. This is doubtful, partly because Garnaut misreads his own figures—rural areas are slightly worse hit—but also because of the difficulties in identifying a stable urban cohort of the 1940s in later census data.[98] If anything, the rural-urban dimensions of the famine around Zhengzhou may have favored the city, although the difference is much less stark than the clear antirural bias of the Great Leap Forward famine a generation later (1958–1961, see chapter 5). Most of Zhengzhou's remaining urban residents seem to have fled early in the famine. Already by June 1942, the business press was reporting the departure of Zhengzhou's traders in the face of drought and slack trade.[99] The city's poorer residents left along with merchant groups. Local journalist Li Rui found that most of Zhengzhou's sex workers had long since left, and the number of rickshaws in the city—five thousand before the war,

97. Yang Yifeng (1898–1974) of Zhengzhou and Liu Jiyan (1880–1961) of Xuchang. *Henan minbao*, August 5, 1942.

98. Garnaut, "Quantitative Description," 2036–39. This estimate uses 1982 census data to compare cohort loss in cities (*shi* units) with rural prefectures (*diqu*). In Garnaut's data, the 1942 cohort loss for rural prefectures (average 28.2 percent) is slightly worse than the eight prefectural-level cities (23.25 percent). Urban units of the 1982 census do not map well onto the cities of the 1940s. For Zhengzhou, post-1949 growth means that most of the "city" unit of 1982 covers not the wartime city but the rural county that was so hard hit in 1942–1943. This discrepancy, rather than high mortality among the small number of long-term urban residents, may explain why Zhengzhou had the worst 1942 cohort loss (32 percent) of the eight cities surveyed.

99. "Zheng xian shiqing gaikuang, liu yue," *Jingji huibao*, no. 6 (1942): 101.

and still over 3,500 in the early part of the war—had fallen to just a couple of dozen.[100]

With most long-term urban residents having fled the worst famine zone, those who died in or around Zhengzhou seem overwhelmingly to have been rural in origin, whether they died in their home villages, along roads, or in the city. Though conditions were bad in Zhengzhou, things were perhaps even worse in the surrounding countryside. Li Rui described a cannibalism case in East Chen Village, just outside the city. Three kilometers farther out, the missionary Greta Clark reported that forty people had died in a hamlet of only twenty-five households.[101] In early spring 1943, Zheng County officials told Li that more than 90 percent of the remaining households had absolutely no food of their own.[102] When Li traveled to his home district in neighboring Sishui County, he found that most inhabitants had either already died or fled. Others were huddled in their homes to preserve energy: "Going from one village to the next, for several *li* I didn't encounter anyone. . . . In the village there was no crow of chickens, no bark of dogs . . . home after home was locked up, some blocked up with mud bricks; others stood open, but most of them did not even have a door. With nothing left to steal inside, the inhabitants had torn off the doors to sell as firewood."[103]

The final argument for a slight urban bias in the 1942–1943 famine is the flight of victims from the rural hinterland to the city in the hope of finding food. By spring 1943, Theodore White reported that there were almost forty thousand people in Zhengzhou, the majority of whom were famine refugees from the surrounding countryside.[104] It should not be taken for granted that movement to the city was a clear-cut strategy for farmers around Zhengzhou. As well as the risks and calorific demands of the journey, an outbreak of epidemic disease could have turned Zhengzhou into a death trap.[105] Nor was the city a welcoming place for rural

---

100. *Qianfengbao*, April 21, 1943.

101. *Qianfengbao*, April 21, 1943. Greta Clark, letter to Canon Dixon, December 30, 1943, Clark Correspondence, MSCC Records, box 77, folder 4, General Synod Archives, Anglican Church of Canada.

102. *Qianfengbao*, April 21, 1943.

103. *Qianfengbao*, April 16, 1943.

104. On spring 1943 population, see White and Jacoby, *Thunder Out of China*, 161.

105. Zhengzhou saw only a mild outbreak of cholera in spring 1943. Wampler, *China Suffers*, 249.

refugees. Unlike in some cities, the 1928 removal of Zhengzhou's city wall meant they could not be physically excluded, but one missionary source reports the authorities trying to "shoo the starving off the street so they die outside the city"; it is no surprise, then, that Li Rui found corpses scattered around the urban edge.[106] Yet tens of thousands made the calculated decision that Zhengzhou contained a greater concentration of calories—and opportunities for obtaining calories—than the surrounding countryside.

There were three reasons for this concentration of resources in the city. First, food was still available in the city—albeit for sky-high prices. A portion of military and civil grain rations filtered through to urban markets. Famine foods like grasses and bark, by spring 1943 obtainable in the countryside only after long, energy-sapping forages, were also for sale in Zhengzhou.[107] Second, the city offered opportunities for the pilfering or begging of small quantities of grain. In the ruins of Zhengzhou, the very fabric of the city offered a chance of survival, with famine refugees tearing down abandoned buildings to sell wood, bricks, and corrugated iron for a pittance. George Andrew reports "the dismantling of houses of windows, doors and even roofs to be sold for food."[108] The city was also the best place to try to convert material possessions or labor into calories. Li Rui found rural refugees clustered amid the faded grandeur of Changchun Road trying to exchange their clothes, blankets, and farm tools for small quantities of grain.[109]

106. Elvera Carlson journal, April 27–28, 1943, quoted in Christensen, *In War and Famine*, 113; for corpses on the edge of Zhengzhou, see *Qianfengbao*, April 21, 1943. In Luoyang, the authorities banned famine refugees from entering the gates in the name of "tidying the appearance of the city," and many died outside the walls. Chen Chuanhai and Xu Youli, *Henan xiandai shi*, 272. Note, though, that the policy of keeping refugees outside cities was not new. For a discussion from the early nineteenth century, see Lillian Li, *Fighting Famine in North China*, 158.

107. The Catholic bishop in Luoyang estimated that between a quarter and half of requisitioned state grain eventually found its way to market. See Forman, "Harrison Forman Diary," 13–14.

108. George Andrew, "Annual Report for 1942," MSCC Records, box 77, folder 1, General Synod Archives, Anglican Church of Canada. For a wider discussion of using the urban environment for survival in the Second World War, see Laakkonen et al., "Epilogue" 292–94.

109. *Qianfengbao*, April 21, 1943. Changchun Road ran from the center of the commercial city to its northern edge.

Third, relief efforts were concentrated in the city. By September 1942 the missionary-run United China Relief was feeding four thousand people each day, with a further fifteen hundred living in their camps.[110] During the winter, Zhengzhou's local authorities teamed up with merchants to bring in grain from Luoyang and sell it at below-market prices in Zhengzhou.[111] With the belated arrival of government assistance from outside the province, Li Rui reported "six or seven" new grain-disbursing points opening in the city just before his arrival in April 1943. Li calculated that the burst of aid in Zhengzhou could keep eleven thousand people alive until the harvest—though this was still not enough for all the refugees in the city.[112] For those beyond the city, help was even slower to arrive. The official provincial newspaper admitted that even in April relief was desperately inadequate in nearby county seats, which by then usually had at least one relief institution in operation, let alone rural areas.[113]

As Kathryn Edgerton-Tarpley has pointed out, the wartime exploitation of Henan's resources was underpinned by a Nationalist discourse of sacrifice and national identity.[114] Though this language was present across unoccupied China, the wartime state treated some of its most economically and ecologically vulnerable populations in frontline regions as cheap lives, expendable for marginal strategic gain. This treatment was

110. Wampler, *China Suffers*, 243. Note that one of United China Relief's four soup kitchens was outside the city, on the road west toward Xingyang. On refugee camps, see Bill Simpson letter to Canon Dixon, December 14, 1942, MSCC, box 79, folder 3, General Synod Archives, Anglican Church of Canada.

111. By the end of February 1943 district (*zhuanyuan*) and county officials around Zhengzhou had organized five rounds of relief from Luoyang stocks. Some of this relief did reach rural areas. Commissioner Wang Guanglin claimed to have organized some assistance to half a million people in the twelve counties under his control; see Wang, "Wunianlai gongzuo jiyao," July 1, 1947, Zhengzhou Municipal Archive, *jiu* 03-38-001, 1–3. The Zheng County government was able to distribute a small amount of grain (15 *jin*) to its twenty thousand most desperate households. See *Henan minbao*, February 28, 1943. Crucially, amid wartime stress and displacement there are few signs of the local elite aid found by Pierre Fuller in the 1920–1921 North China famine. Fuller, *Famine Relief in Warlord China*. For an exception from Xigang Village, see Xigang cunzhi bianzuan weiyuanhui, *Xigang cunzhi*, 117 and 121. For more on the limits of elite aid in nearby Xuchang, see Ruchen Gao, "Tobacco, Western Education, and the Japanese Army," 175-88.

112. *Qianfengbao*, April 21, 1943; May 6, 1943.

113. *Henan minbao*, April 15, 1943.

114. Edgerton-Tarpley, "Saving the Nation, Starving the People?," 344–48.

facilitated—and here James Tyner's observations on space and genocide are a useful pointer—by the marginalization of vulnerable populations across both psychological and physical space.[115] The Nationalist state's wartime spatial politics were not exceptional. Conditions were similar in Japanese-occupied parts of Henan, except where the 1942 drought was less intense.[116] Britain, with much greater resources at its disposal, revealed an appallingly racialized politics of priority during the Bengal Famine of 1943–1944.[117] But with food surpluses available elsewhere in unoccupied China, it is reasonable to censure the Nationalist neglect of this frontline region without reviving the "Stilwell-White paradigm" of Nationalist incompetence.[118] It is instead a question of where the Nationalist authorities placed their limited but very real governing capacity. The wartime Nationalist state was in many ways highly competent: strong enough to keep fighting, to penetrate and extract from rural society, and to tighten economic control. But without corresponding inputs, it was precisely these successes in state strengthening that caused so much damage, particularly in neglected frontline regions. A more measured approach to mobilization, taking on regional military interests and reducing numbers unnecessarily under arms, could have saved hundreds of thousands of lives in Henan—and perhaps allayed the collapse of Nationalist rule in the province in spring 1944.

Occupied Zhengzhou, April 1944 to August 1945

The worst stage of famine in Henan came to an end with the spring wheat harvest of 1943. Though not as high as originally hoped, yields helped reduce the epidemic of starvation to the more "normal" state of endemic destitution. Food prices fell sharply, and many refugees were able to return home.[119] Around forty thousand people were still resident in Zhengzhou during 1943 and early 1944, with a third of those in the refugee camps scattered around the urban edge. Although there were

---

115. Tyner, *Genocide and the Geographical Imagination.*
116. Garnaut, "Quantitative Description," 239–41.
117. Mukherjee, *Hungry Bengal.*
118. For a critical summary of this approach, see Van de Ven, *War and Nationalism,* 3–4.
119. By June 1943, wheat prices in Zhengzhou had fallen to less than a quarter of their peak. "Zheng xian shiqing gaikuang: liu yuefen," *Jingji huibao,* no. 6 (1943): 83.

rumors of possible famine that winter, timely rain ensured there was no repeat of 1942–1943.[120]

Nationalist rule in much of Central China was swept away by the Japanese Ichigo offensive of spring and summer 1944. Zhengzhou was the first target of this last great Axis advance of the war. The advance began at Zao Village in Zhongmu County on April 18, 1944, and Zhengzhou fell to the Japanese Twelfth Army within a few days. Unlike in the 1941 advance, Japanese forces were able to drive westwards from Zhengzhou, taking Luoyang a few weeks later—hardly slowed down by the 1938 Nationalist sabotage of infrastructure that had left Zhengzhou isolated for so long.[121] But this was more than a military retreat. Resentment against the burdens of Nationalist rule spilled over into civilian violence against the military, with retreating units attacked and disarmed by groups of rural people. It is hard to know the scale or location of these incidents—Theodore White's report that fifty thousand troops had been disarmed in this way was based on hearsay—but there seems little doubt that such attacks occurred: Nationalist commander Jiang Dingwen (1895–1974) himself reported it, and Chiang Kai-shek openly discussed the phenomenon in a heartfelt speech.[122]

This last year of the long war is somewhat overlooked by historians, told as either an abbreviated endnote to the Sino-Japanese War or a prelude to the civil war to come. China's jostling for diplomatic position among the Allies tends to dominate at the expense of domestic problems. The story of territory newly occupied by Japanese forces is particularly obscure. Yet this murky last year of the war was an important period for Zhengzhou, with a desperate struggle for control of territory and

120. An official population survey of 1943 gives 41,420 in the city, with only 150 able-bodied men (*zhuangding*) left on the rolls for conscription and corvée labor. See "Henan shengzhengfu Minzhengting 1943 niandu minzheng tongji," Henan Provincial Archive, M12-001-0005, 40–45. For the estimate that a third of the population were refugees, see Elizabeth Chen He-Chih, "An Unforgettable Journey," undated manuscript, Yale Divinity School Special Collections, China Records Project Miscellaneous Personal Papers Collection, record group 8. On 1943, see Rewi Alley, "Honan Famine Situation: Autumn 1943," August 20, 1943, United China Relief Papers, box 2, folder 4, New York Public Library.

121. Most sources date the takeover of Zhengzhou to April 22, but the collaborationist press reported April 20. *Xin Henan ribao*, May 4, 1944.

122. White and Jacoby, *Thunder Out of China*, 169; Chiang Kai-shek quoted in Song Zhixin, *1942: Henan dajihuang*, 35; also noted in Mitter, *Forgotten Ally*, 320–24.

resources around the city. As the first city to fall in the Ichigo attack, it became a key springboard for the Japanese military presence in western Henan, which in some ways restored Zhengzhou's function as a logistical center. The city was operations headquarters of the Japanese Twelfth Army and de facto seat of the so-called special district of newly occupied Henan territory.[123] Remarkably, the occupiers also managed to marshal sufficient corvée labor and materials to restore Zhengzhou's railway access. The Long–Hai line to Kaifeng was patched up, with a pontoon bridge crossing a narrow point of the Yellow River flood zone, and before the Japanese surrender there was also a resumption of service on part of the Zhengzhou–Luoyang section. Partial restoration of the Jing–Han line, to the north bank of the Yellow River and south to Xuchang, restored Zhengzhou's status as a railway junction.[124]

But it would be premature to suggest that rail access prompted a return to prewar commerce or even the more limited wartime prosperity of Zhengzhou prior to the first Japanese incursion of 1941. The occupation authorities strictly controlled the movement of goods, and makeshift railroad repairs were vulnerable to attacks from the air and by guerrillas on the ground. After years of Japanese bombing, Zhengzhou was hit several times by Allied bombs.[125] All the same, Zhengzhou's restored logistical functions brought opportunities for some in the occupation economy. As in its first boom of the 1910s, the opium and sex trades boomed, while missionaries heard from contacts in Zhengzhou that with restored connections to Tianjin and Shanghai, business in the city was brisk.[126] At least according to the collaborationist press, by June 1944 Zhengzhou's population was almost back to pre-Ichigo level.[127]

123. See Xu Lianshan and Wang Zongmin, *Zhengzhou kangzhan*, 174–75. Some twenty-one counties fell under partial Japanese control in this district. Down to the last months of the war, there were some limited attempts to introduce a collaborationist civil administration. See *Xin Henan ribao*, April 17, 1945.

124. See Henan sheng difang shizhi bianzuan weiyuanhui, *Henan sheng zhi*, 24–25; Zhengzhou tielu fenju shizhi bianzuan weiyuanhui, *Zhengzhou tielu fenju*, 111.

125. There has been very little study of US Air Force bombing of Chinese cities. On Zhengzhou, see, for instance, *New York Times*, July 30, 1944.

126. Augustana Synod Board of Missions, *Thirty-Fifth Conference*, quoted in Erleen Christensen, *In War and Famine*, 181.

127. *Shenbao*, June 11, 1944.

If the city itself was restored to some importance, a rural-urban perspective on occupation exposes both the limits and the violence of Japanese rule after Ichigo. The period of Japanese occupation, which it is easy to dismiss as sui generis, marked an extreme case of patterns of coercion that recurred across the twentieth century: tight control of the urban edge, suspicion of rural-urban mobility, and use of the city as a springboard for rural extraction—patterns that reached an apogee during the Great Leap Forward (see chapter 5). Like other iterations of the local state, Zhengzhou's occupiers tried to project power from the city into the rural hinterland of Zheng County, using collaborationist military units to take over village-level militia and collecting in-kind land tax to feed the occupation force.[128] Japanese firms in North China, including Mitsui and Mitsubishi, used this territorial control to buy up cotton and tobacco in newly occupied or semioccupied zones and ship out the products through Zhengzhou. Relying on this rural link, a hundred or so people in the city were able to keep producing hand-rolled cigarettes down to the very end of the war.[129]

As far as most residents were concerned, though, occupation cut off Zhengzhou from its hinterland. Permanent Japanese control only existed in Zhengzhou, its most immediate environs, and other occupied county seats. Even in Zheng County, the rival Nationalist government was able to remain within the county boundary.[130] Zhengzhou therefore could not serve as a "normal" central place for the region, instead functioning as a launchpad for violent antiguerrilla and grain-seizing expeditions into the rural hinterland. Like in 1941, the Japanese military declared the immediate outskirts of the city a no-go "depopulated zone" (*wurenqu*), and sentry posts (*gangshao*) sprang up to guard the urban boundary. According to Nationalist District Commissioner Wang Guanglin, movement into and out of the city under the occupation required not just a "good citizen card," as in other occupied cities, but

128. *Xin Henan ribao*, May 27, 1945; Xu Lianshan and Wang Zongmin, *Zhengzhou kangzhan*, 176.

129. On Japanese firms, see *Xin Henan ribao*, May 27, 1945; on tobacco rolling in Zhengzhou, see Huang Zhenlin, Zhang Yan, and Su Zhigang, *Jindai Henan jingjishi*, 2:273.

130. The shadow Nationalist county government was at Meishan in the far south of the county. Wang Guanglin, "Wunianlai gongzuo jiyao," July 1, 1947, Zhengzhou Municipal Archive, *jiu* 03-38-001, 28.

a specific transit permit (*tongxingzheng*) signed by the Japanese military authorities.[131]

Zhengzhou's nearby villages were badly affected. Numerous buildings were knocked down to construct a ring of blockhouses, and the occupation force commandeered local villages to build a new airstrip in the city's eastern suburbs.[132] Across the city in the western outskirts, the village of Caiwang was taken over as a Japanese depot and vehicle repair point. Barbed wire surrounded Caiwang as well as nearby Mifengzhang and the Muslim village of Duizhou. Those villagers who had not already fled were banished outside the ring of barbed wire. They were allowed back in daylight to farm, but the whole area was an exclusion zone at night, and they were left to survive as best they could in the city.[133] A little to the south, the occupation forces seized some 600 *mu* of land in the villages of Caozhai and Genghe, setting up an agricultural company to provide vegetables and animals exclusively for the use of the Japanese Twelfth Army garrison.[134]

This hypermilitarization of Zhengzhou's urban edge and nearby villages was designed to protect the strategic node of the city but resulted in isolation from its hinterland. In the early years of the war, Zhengzhou's long-distance railroad links had been lost, but traders and handicraft producers in the city adapted with greater reliance on its nearby rural areas; under Japanese occupation, this pattern was reversed, with long-distance connections tenuously restored but the city cut off from its more local role. This separation had political as well as economic and social effects. Nearby Sishui, Xingyang, Mi County, and parts of Zheng County itself had become confusing battlegrounds of a multisided struggle between occupation-collaborationist forces, Nationalist guerrillas, and Communist armies. In places it was Communist groups gaining the upper hand: parts of Zhengzhou's hinterland did not return to effective Nationalist control after the Japanese surrender of August 15, 1945. The city of Zhengzhou, though, returned to Nationalist hands within

131. Wang Guanglin, "Kangzhan shengli zai Zhengzhou shouxiang," 79–81.
132. Zhonggong Henan shengwei dangshi yanjiushi, *Henan sheng kangzhan sunshi diaocha*, 2:7. This airfield evolved into Zhengzhou's main airport until 1997 (see chapter 7).
133. Zhengxie Zhengzhou shi Erqiqu weiyuanhui, *Yuanqu zhi jiyi*, 69–74.
134. Ji Fu, "Rijun Zhengzhou shucai zhushihuishe," 82.

a few days. The next month, at Zhengzhou's Anglican mission church, Provincial Governor Liu Mao'en (1898–1981), and General Hu Zongnan (1896–1962) accepted the formal surrender of Lieutenant General Takashi Takamori's (1888–1968) 43,000-strong force.[135]

Zhengzhou had been a fulcrum of military conflict for over seven years. The maintenance of any kind of urban life here is remarkable and underlines the capacity for human adaptation and the importance of mobility in survival strategies. But Zhengzhou and its region had paid a heavy cost. Through mortality and flight, the city and its surrounding county had both lost around two-thirds of their prewar population. District Commissioner Wang Guanglin reported that "all the streets and buildings were in a state of terrible collapse and completely broken (*lingluan daota, canpo bukan*)"; a statistical survey calculated that 70 percent of Zhengzhou's buildings were severely damaged. This was the worst proportion of any major town in this devastated frontline province.[136] The spatial politics of the Nationalist war effort had placed an enormous burden on this frontline region, sacrificing people, resources, and places for the sake of state survival. Yet this was not a one-off occurrence. Within a generation, both the Chinese Civil War and Mao's Great Leap Forward would reprise in very different ways some of the sacrifices and spatial inequalities of the War of Resistance.

135. Wang Guanglin, "Kangzhan shengli zai Zhengzhou shouxiang," 79–81.
136. Wang Guanglin, "Wunianlai gongzuo jiyao," July 1, 1947, Zhengzhou Municipal Archive, *jiu* 03-38-001; Zhonggong Henan shengwei dangshi yanjiushi, *Henan sheng kangzhan sunshi diaocha,* 2:625–26.

CHAPTER FOUR

Reconstructions and Revolutions, 1945–1958

The decade after Japanese surrender was a period of alternating reconstruction and revolution in Zhengzhou. The reconstruction of the Nationalist postwar was quickly overtaken by civil war. Political revolution followed on October 22, 1948, when Zhengzhou fell to Communist forces. Yet even compared with other cities, early CCP (Chinese Communist Party) rule in Zhengzhou was more reconstructive than revolutionary, particularly from a spatial perspective. Priorities included restoration of the city's markets, built environment, and economic networks. A new spatial strategy for Zhengzhou came only after 1952, when the city's favored place in the planned economy revolutionized its economic and political role. Along with similar inland cities of Middle China, Zhengzhou was a site for intense investment under China's First Five-Year Plan (1953–1957). The State Planning Commission designated Zhengzhou a "base of new industrial construction," opening six large textile mills by 1956. In 1954 the city's political role was also transformed when it replaced Kaifeng as capital of Henan Province. Zhengzhou's population nearly tripled in the five years after 1952, reaching almost half a million. The broken city of 1945, with its war-damaged, low-rise buildings and transient refugee population, was transformed into a center of large factories, multistory apartments, and a permanent urban working class. Zhengzhou was now the hegemonic city of north-central China.

This chapter begins with a focus on the short-term continuities of Zhengzhou's double postwar, revealing similarities between Nationalist restoration (1945–1948) and early Communist rule (1948–1951). The CCP takeover of cities has been carefully studied for many years, but the immediately preceding Nationalist rule is less well understood.[1] This

1. See, for instance, Lieberthal, *Revolution and Tradition*; James Zheng Gao, *Communist Takeover*; Wakeman, "'Cleanup.'"

chapter argues that the restored Nationalist administration (in 1945) and Communist rule (in 1948) followed a similar pattern of spatial politics, beginning with promises of rural-urban reconnection but shifting toward rural-urban disconnection and a more urban-centered politics. In the Nationalist case, these conditions resulted from the demands of civil war; under Communist rule, they were part of the transition to the planned economy. The chapter goes on to explore the consequences of this latter shift. Studies of this period have usually explored Communist rule in China's largest cities, but fast-growing Zhengzhou, one of the medium-sized inland "winners" from the Five-Year Plan, is a particularly good example of how the planned economy brought highly unequal results across space.

These alternating moments of reconstruction and revolution brought rapid-fire changes to Zhengzhou in the decade after 1945. But behind these abrupt transformations there can be discerned underlying forces of spatial politics that ran across much of the twentieth century. Similar competing impulses remained from before 1949—to connect or disconnect across space, to distribute or concentrate resources—and just as before, a state with limited resources chose to focus its development efforts at certain urban centers. The key difference from the 1930s was that Zhengzhou rather than Kaifeng was the center of political and economic investment in the region (see chapter 2). As this chapter and the next illustrate, the resulting inequalities took new shape in the priorities and spatial contradictions of the planned economy. First, booming Zhengzhou was designed to pull along Henan as a new core region of inland China, but the concentration of investment here left other cities far behind—especially the former capital of Kaifeng. Second, Zhengzhou's rapid growth made the fringes of the city a newly stark front line of rural-urban inequality. Third, Communist revolution promised an end to rural-urban inequality, but the planned economy was built on extraction for the city at the expense of the rural hinterland—even in the relatively privileged villages within the Zhengzhou municipal boundaries.

Spatial Politics in Postwar and Civil War

Zhengzhou's future as a socialist industrial center was a world away from the shattered city of summer 1945. But the city's resilience and ability to bounce back—noted from the 1920s onwards—were in evidence again after the Japanese surrender. The revival of transport links restored Zhengzhou's interregional role, connecting the former unoccupied zone of western China to eastern regions previously under Japanese occupation. Zhengzhou once again became a center for wholesale trade, primary product processing, and a large drifting population. During wartime, the key long-distance entrepôt of Central China had been the smuggling center at Jieshou, but with railroads restored, many Jieshou merchants moved to Zhengzhou. Most businesses that had fled in 1938 did not return, including the flagship Yufeng spinning mill, and into their place stepped a variety of workshops and trading houses, including flour mills and a boom in machine-rolled cigarettes.[2] By the time journalist Wang Shoumei (1913–1994) visited in fall 1946, he found a lively commercial city recovering from its wartime trauma: "after having had the chance to stay here two days and take a good look at the city, I felt very happy: it is 'chaotic' and 'dirty,' but everywhere is being improved and is full of vigor (*chongman zhe shengqi*)."[3] Between early 1946 and fall 1947, Zhengzhou's population more than doubled to an estimated 112,000, not far from its prewar height.[4] Zhengzhou's postwar importance was political as well as commercial. Like the recent Japanese occupiers, the Nationalist authorities tried to use Zhengzhou as a springboard for rural control across the region. Although the provincial capital remained at Kaifeng, from early 1946 Zhengzhou hosted the important regional Pacification Headquarters (Suijing gongshu) under former Henan governor Liu Zhi (1892–1971). From Datonglu in downtown Zhengzhou, Liu plotted the defeat of Communist forces across four provinces of inland China.[5]

Zhengzhou's postwar prominence makes it all the more surprising that there was still no municipal government in the city. Although the Nationalist authorities were setting up municipal governments across China (reaching sixty-nine by the end of 1947, compared with just thirteen in 1932), Zhengzhou was still administered as part of Zheng County,

2. See Wang Guanglin, "Wunianlai gongzuo jiyao," July 1, 1947, Zhengzhou Municipal Archive, *jiu* 03-38-001, esp. 102–3; Zhengzhou shi dang'anguan, *Zhengzhou jiefang*, 30.

3. *Shenbao*, October 15, 1946.

4. *Zhongyang ribao*, October 21, 1947, citied in Liu Yongli, "Minguo shiqi Zhengzhou chengshi renkou," 38. Liu attributes this earlier demographic growth to economic renaissance as opposed to the later refugee influx.

5. Wang Yongchuan, "1945 nian zhi 1948 nian Zhengzhou jianwen," 100–104.

as it had been since the abolition of Feng Yuxiang's short-lived municipality in 1931.[6] The city was divided into three subcounty "towns" (*zhen*),
each of which also included a handful of nearby villages. This made
city-level coordination difficult, but moves within the city for the rees-
tablishment of municipal government were fiercely opposed by Zheng
County's rural-dominated Consultative Assembly (Canyihui).[7] Postwar
urban governance seems to have been the purview of District Commissioner Wang Guanglin, who, like Feng Yuxiang two decades earlier, tried
to tackle the sex work, entertainment, and *jianghu* district of Laofengang
on Zhengzhou's northwest edge. Like Feng, Wang was fiercely critical
of Laofengang, describing it as full of "degenerate soldiers and people"
(*buxiao junmin*), a place that could really "cause trouble" (*zhaoshi*).
Working with the city police, he rebranded the area the "Zhengzhou
City Citizens' Market" (Zheng shi guomin shichang) and introduced
new regulations to control the area. Trying to kill two birds with one
stone by "improving" the rest of the city as well as Laofengang, Wang's
office opened an expanded zone of five hundred new stalls and ordered
the itinerant traders and tea sellers from other parts of Zhengzhou to set
up permanent pitches in the newly controlled zone of Laofengang.[8]

While this Laofengang project tried to build on and control existing
urban space, a similar impulse was at work on a much bigger scale in
the Nationalist government's design for a future Zhengzhou. In 1947 the
Zhengzhou City Revival Plan Guidance Committee (Fuxing guihua
zhidao weiyuanhui) drew up a new blueprint for the city, the first urban
plan in Zhengzhou for almost twenty years.[9] This design is a good insight
into postwar Nationalist thinking and shared similarities with urban planning under both Feng Yuxiang and the People's Republic (see chapter 2
and later sections of this chapter). At its heart was a critique of the existing
city, particularly the "chaotic" (*luan*) area around the rail station, where
dense, narrow streets had sprung up in the first years of the railroad. This

6. Zhonggong Henan shengwei dangshi yanjiushi, *Henan sheng "yiwu" jihua*, 15.
Among the core eighteen provinces of China, only Henan did not have a single munic-
ipal authority down to the end of Nationalist rule on the mainland. For a full list, see
Xu Xuelin, *Zhongguo lidai xingzheng quhua*, 302–7.

7. Fan Shiqin, "Mantan Zhengzhou," 15.

8. Wang Guanglin, "Wunianlai gongzuo jiyao," July 1, 1947, Zhengzhou Municipal
Archive, *jiu* 03-38-001; Zhao Fuhai, *Lao Zhengzhou: minsu shengdi Laofengang*, 14–15.

9. Published in *Zhengzhou ribao* over the course of a week, June 23 to June 29, 1947.

anxiety was shared by Feng Yuxiang's 1928 plan and ran through urban planning all the way to the reform period forty years later.[10] As in many plans for the city, the solution lay not in reconstruction of Zhengzhou's urban heart, but in expansion at the city's edge, to which the dense downtown population could be "dispersed" (*shusan*). As in the late 1920s, the committee behind the 1947 scheme proposed resettling the urban poor on the fringes of the city, in this case in a "victory village" (*shengli xincun*).[11]

As in the plan of 1928, the west side of the Jing–Han railroad was earmarked for a dramatic expansion. But where Feng Yuxiang's urban planners had advocated building a whole city from scratch across the railroad, this 1947 scheme proposed using this area only as an industrial zone.[12] In that sense, the 1947 plan looks like a transition between prewar Republican urban planning and that of the People's Republic. Its proposal for an industrial zone is strikingly similar to the development of Zhengzhou west of the Jing–Han railroad during the First Five-Year Plan, although I have seen no evidence that any 1947 planners worked with the Soviet-led urban design teams of the 1950s (see below). There was, however, one key difference between these plans of the late Republic and the early People's Republic: Zhengzhou's industrial suburb of the 1950s included work unit housing within or adjacent to factory compounds; in the 1947 plan, Zhengzhou residents were promised a comprehensive system of municipal public housing separate from the industrial zone.[13] As part of the welfarist turn in Nationalist thinking, the stress was on housing and the habitability of the city, with industrial and residential zones "completely split up (*juedui fenli*). . . . Between the two zones there should be a permanent zone of green."[14] This green space included surviving agricultural plots that had been incorporated into the city, making the plan of 1947 the only twentieth-century design for Zhengzhou to include food production within the built-up area—although it would later be pursued as an ad hoc strategy to combat famine in the wake of the Great Leap Forward.

10. *Zhengzhou ribao*, June 23, 1947.
11. *Zhengzhou ribao*, June 29, 1947.
12. *Zhengzhou ribao*, June 24, 1947.
13. *Zhengzhou ribao*, June 27, 1947.
14. "Shoufuqu chengzhen yingjian guihua," no date (summer 1946?), Henan Provincial Archive, M08-25-0723, 43–44 in folder.

As with the 1928 plan, the scheme of 1947 was overtaken by civil war and never built. But as in the 1920s, its ambitions underline how Zhengzhou's strategic position as a transport pivot generated excitement for the city's future. One commentator argued, in a strategy similar to that of twenty-first-century policy makers, that Zhengzhou could drag the entire Central Plains region back to the prosperity of its Tang dynasty heyday.[15] As in the 1930s, Zheng County authorities tried to spread urban financial resources to the nearby countryside, promoting cooperative loans for cotton growing, cloth, and oil production.[16] This optimism reached a peak in spring 1947, with the closing of the 1938 Yellow River breach at Huayuankou. For the first time in almost a decade, floodwaters no longer cut off Zhengzhou from the provincial capital at Kaifeng. On May 4, thousands of officials and students from Zhengzhou traveled north to the riverbank to watch Chiang Kai-shek preside over a lavish ceremony.[17]

This confidence was overtaken by events on the battlefield. The month after Chiang Kai-shek visited Zhengzhou, PLA (People's Liberation Army) forces under Liu Bocheng and Deng Xiaoping crossed the restored Yellow River and joined up with Chen Yi's East China Field Army. Communist summer offensives followed across Henan.[18] By late 1947, PLA units were able to maneuver across much of the province, ending Zhengzhou's strategic importance in preventing movement between North and Central China. In December, the fighting came close to Zhengzhou for the first time. One eyewitness described a chaotic scene "of clamor and fear in people's hearts. The roads were filled with people pouring into the city from the surrounding countryside (*sixiang*) and urban residents trying to get of the city."[19]

The cautious Communist forces pulled back, and the next phase of civil war in and around Zhengzhou was less a military conflict and

15. Fan Shiqin, "Mantan Zhengzhou," 15.

16. "Zheng Xian xianzhengfu hezuo zhidaoshi sanshiliu nian wu yuefen gongzuo baogao," Zhengzhou Municipal Archive, *jiu*, 03-046-008. After a devastating decade, the cultivated area for cotton in Zheng County was less than half that of the immediate prewar years. See "Henan sheng gexian sanshiliu niandu zhi mian mianji yuding biao," no date [1947], Henan Provincial Archive, M08-28-0781, 85–94.

17. *Zhengzhou ribao*, May 5, 1947.

18. On the significance of summer 1947 in Henan, see Edgerton-Tarpley, "River Runs through It," 164–69.

19. Lu Yunsheng, "Cheli Zhengzhou," 6.

more a struggle for resources between local residents and the Nationalist authorities. This tension was also a deeply spatial one, centered on state control of movement, space, and populations as the Nationalist authorities sought the full-scale mobilization of the diminishing areas under their control.[20] This phase of Nationalist mobilization and coercion was short-lived, but it was part of a wider pattern across the middle decades of the twentieth century: barriers to rural-urban exchange, extraction from a weak rural sector, and efforts to control the movement of people. The mobilization of Zhengzhou for civil war repeated not only the inequalities of Nationalist rule in the Second World War but also patterns of Japanese occupation in 1944–1945 and even, in some ways, the tight control over space and movement in the Great Leap Forward era (see chapter 5). In the intense civil war period of 1947–1948, this strategy of the Nationalist state manifested itself in three ways. In each case, the effects on individuals and households were marked by a spatial arbitrariness—that is to say, inequality of outcome depended in part on location, with those at the urban edge and nearby villages particularly badly affected.

First, the Nationalist authorities in Zhengzhou depended on rural extraction close to the city to feed armies and state employees. After a brief reprieve in 1945, in-kind land tax collection resumed and was then supplemented by the revival of the compulsory purchase system implicated in the 1942–1943 famine (now rebranded as "unified purchase," *tonggou*). As well as grain, requisitioning of firewood and fodder for horses also resumed, with neighborhood leaders in the *baojia* mutual responsibility system facing punishment for the nonfulfillment of quotas. Purchase prices were rendered derisory by runaway inflation.[21] After almost a decade of conflict against Japan, a devastated rural economy around Zhengzhou was once again bearing the burdens of total war. In addition to flood damage in the northeast, Zheng County was still depopulated and riddled with trenches and other scars of the earlier conflict. In summer 1947, hailstorms and drought damaged harvests,

---

20. For a longer discussion, see Baker, "Civil War."

21. Wang Guanglin, "Wunianlai gongzuo jiyao," July 1, 1947, Zhengzhou Municipal Archive, *jiu* 03-38-001, 37–38 and 62–63; on monetary and fiscal collapse, see Huang Zhenglin, Zhang Yan, and Su Zhigang, *Jindai Henan jingjishi*, 434–42.

and the authorities reported distress all over the county.[22] The following year, with Communist advances across the province, the rural burden was getting worse for those still under Nationalist rule. By the time of the military requisitioning of the 1948 spring wheat harvest, only three and a half of Zheng County's six townships were under secure Nationalist control, increasing pressure on the city's closest villages.[23]

Second, the local Nationalist state used old and new systems to tighten control of Zhengzhou's population. As well as updating the household registers, in 1946 Zhengzhou was an experimental site for China's new individual ID cards (*shenfenzheng*), complete with photographs and fingerprints. Residents were subject to police spot checks, which raised difficulties for rural people visiting the city: at first even nearby villages under the jurisdiction of the Zhengzhou police were excluded from the ID card scheme.[24] The other group worrying the city police was refugees, who were placed on a "floating population register" (*liudong renkou dengji*). Some refugees still dated from the 1937–1945 conflict, but by the end of July 1947 about one hundred thousand new arrivals had registered in Zhengzhou, mostly in flight from Communist advances north of the Yellow River.[25] Control of movement tightened during the crunch summer of 1948. Everyone passing between city and countryside was checked, and those without identification papers were taken into custody: in mid-September, the authorities arrested several thousand people in Zhengzhou who had simply attracted suspicion or did not have the right paperwork.[26]

Third, the pressures of civil war brought a struggle for control of

22. "Zhengzhou nongmin weiji yanzhong," 2.

23. "Lengyan wang Bian Zheng," *Shibao* (Xi'an), July 27, 1948.

24. *Guominbao*, June 8, 1946. On efforts to roll out ID cards in rural areas, see "Henan sheng qingcha hukou zhengbian baojia shishi banfa," no date [May 1947], Henan Provincial Archive, M08-14-0434, 3.

25. On the floating population register, see *Zhengzhou ribao*, July 29, 1947. On numbers, see *Zhengzhou ribao*, July 26, 1947. This does not necessarily mean there were one hundred thousand refugees in the city at any one time. A surviving list of 169 refugees on the north side of Zhengzhou reveals that more than half (90) were from Hebei or Shandong, and most of the rest were from Henan north of the Yellow River. "Zhengzhou Datongzhen juzhu nanmin hukou xingming ce," September 28, 1947, Zhengzhou Municipal Archive, *jiu* 03-057.

26. Zhengzhou shi dang'anguan, *Zhengzhou jiefang*, 36; for a sample case, see Zhengzhou Municipal Archive, September 8, *jiu* 17-002-032.

space at Zhengzhou's urban edge. The tension arose because the fringes of the city had been occupied by refugees but were commandeered by the Nationalist military for defensive fortifications. Even as refugees were settling on the urban edge, Zhengzhou's City Defense Committee began an intensive militarization of the same space. In late 1947 the committee received 400 million yuan from the central authorities to shore up defenses, but most of the budget was raised locally through ad hoc levies.[27] The Nationalist garrison ringed Zhengzhou with similar installations to those of the Japanese occupation period. According to a CCP report spirited out of the city by underground agents, by summer 1948 Zhengzhou was guarded by more than four hundred cement pillboxes, gun batteries, and concealed strongpoints. A map of their distribution shows two loose rings of defenses.[28] The inner ring encircled the key sites of the urban edge: cotton baling factories, granaries, railroad yards, temples, and, in the south of the city, the long-ruined Long–Hai Gardens. The outer ring connected Zhengzhou's closest villages, which one newspaper declared "have become strong fortresses," complete with earth walls, perimeter trenches, tree barricades (*luzhai*), blockhouses, earth tunnels, and anti-aircraft emplacements.[29] Just as under Japanese occupation, the suburban village of Caiwang was used as a military depot; neighboring Duizhou housed a Nationalist field hospital. In these villages, ringed with barbed wire, the inhabitants were either forcibly removed or unable to leave and enter the village without proving their identity at military checkpoints.[30]

This militarization of the urban edge was a ruthless process. One eyewitness reported that soldiers simply tore down houses that impeded defense works.[31] The military authorities enforced emergency levies, cut down any remaining trees around the city, and imposed corvée labor

27. "Tan dian Zhengzhou chengfang gongshi daikuan si yi yuan zhunbei an," November 21, 1947, Zhengzhou Municipal Archive, *jiu* 10-032-019; on the raising of nine billion locally, see *Shenbao*, November 2, 1947.

28. "Zhongyuan junqu silingbu guanyu Zhengzhou shoudi bingli ji bufang qingkuang diaocha," Henan Provincial Archive, reproduced in Zhengzhou shi dang'anguan, *Zhengzhou jiefang*, 88–91.

29. "Lengyan wang Bian Zheng," *Shibao* (Xi'an), July 27, 1948.

30. "Lengyan wang Bian Zheng," *Shibao* (Xi'an), July 27, 1948; on Duizhou and Caiwang, see Zhengxie Zhengzhou shi Erqiqu weiyuanhui, *Yuanqu zhi jiyi*, 70–74.

31. Compensation was in the form of food relief and a cash payment. See Mark Lu, "From Kaifeng to Chengchow," *China Weekly Review*, August 21, 1948.

duties on all residents. In summer 1948, several neighborhood *bao* leaders wrote to the civil authorities to protest against conditions and ask for exemptions. In *bao* number 6, more than two-thirds of the population were impoverished refugees camping on the edge of the city, having been thrown off adjacent railway land: "when it comes to raising levies from the people living there," the *bao* head warned, "there are a host of difficulties."[32] Kong Fanmao, head of a poor neighborhood along the Jinshui River, estimated that 20 percent of residents had lost their homes in the construction of city defenses.[33] Strict control on rural-urban movement also impeded ordinary civilian life in the city. When the Zhengzhou police tried to move nightsoil storage sites out into the nearby countryside for sanitary reasons, it proved impossible: "because of all the sentry posts (*shaokou*), it is not convenient to get in and out of the city."[34] The City Defense Committee also imposed an additional 10 percent levy on goods coming in and out of Zhengzhou, further raising prices and exacerbating the city's isolation.[35] Despite the rising population, swollen to almost two hundred thousand by summer 1948, half of Zhengzhou's flour and oil merchants had had to close, blamed in part by observers on the severing of rural-urban connections.[36]

With the PLA advances of early 1948, Zhengzhou lost its roles as both long-distance transport center and hub for a regional hinterland. A series of towns on the Jing–Han line south of Zhengzhou fell to Communist forces, and Luoyang to the west was taken at the beginning of April. Nationalist troops around the city found themselves sabotaging roads that had only recently been repaired after the conflict with Japan.[37] By the long, hot summer of 1948, Zhengzhou was under a near-blockade, if not quite the terrible siege conditions faced by residents of Changchun

32. "Zhengxian Changchunzhen di liu bao cheng," August 8, 1948, Zhengzhou Municipal Archive, *jiu* 17-001-082.
33. "Zhengxian Changchunzhen di shiliu bao chengwen," August 9, 1948, Zhengzhou Municipal Archive, *jiu* 17-001-084.
34. "Zhengzhou jingchaju di er fenju cheng," May 2, 1948, Zhengzhou Municipal Archive, *jiu* 07-028-004.
35. "Zhengzhou chengfang gongshi weiyuanhui zhengmuzu kaipi chengfang kuan yuan banfa," no date [1948], Zhengzhou Municipal Archive, *jiu* 06-006-001.
36. "Zhongyuan fenghuo hua Zhengzhou," *Shibao* (Xi'an), June 7, 1948.
37. On roads, see Huang Zhenglin, Zhang Yan, and Su Zhigang, *Jindai Henan jingjishi*, 446.

or Taiyuan. The tension of summer 1948 came to an end in September, when Liu Bocheng ordered the "total conquest of the Central Plains."[38] Although most residents had apparently expected Zhengzhou to be "defended to the death" (*sishou*),[39] in the event Nationalist commander Liu Zhi lacked the appetite for the sabotage and sacrifice of 1938, preferring instead to pull out most Nationalist forces intact. Zhengzhou was defended by a motley remnant of the Fortieth Army, war-weary troops who had fought variously under the banners of Feng Yuxiang, Chiang Kai-shek, and in some cases the collaborationist government of Wang Jingwei.[40] The tight control of the city finally relaxed: one observer noted in mid-October that "the official organs did not have the strict atmosphere (*senyan qixiang*) of previous days, and even the sentries had abandoned their posts."[41] The fortifications that had imposed such a burden on the residents were not put to the test. On October 21, Chen Yi's Communist troops took control of Zhengzhou's closest villages and, under cover of darkness, sneaked into the northeast corner of the city. By dawn the following day the rump Nationalist garrison had fled, only to be wiped out in afternoon skirmishes on the banks of the Yellow River.[42]

Rural and Urban in Early Communist Rule

Zhengzhou's residents emerged on the morning of October 22, 1948, to find Communist troops on the city streets. As in other Chinese cities, PLA units were given a cautious welcome, but as even the Nationalist official Yang Zhenxing admitted, the overwhelming emotion was one of relief: "The people were worried . . . expecting at the least a fierce struggle for the city (*menglie gongfang zhan*). . . . From the viewpoint of the state, to abandon Zhengzhou without extracting any kind of price for it really is regrettable (*wanfen kexi*); but, from the viewpoint of citizens, in that there was no damage to life or property, it can be counted fortunate."[43]

38. Zhengzhou shi dang'anguan, *Zhengzhou jiefang*, 64.
39. "Zhongyuan fenghuo hua Zhengzhou," *Shibao* (Xi'an), June 7, 1948.
40. Zhao Guangyu, "Zhengzhou 'jiefang' hou de zhenxiang," *Zhongguo xinwen* (Nanjing), December 16, 1948.
41. Yong Mu, "Gege cong Zhengzhou lai," 10.
42. Zhengzhou shi dang'anguan, *Zhengzhou jiefang*, 64–65.
43. Yang Zhenxing, "Zhengzhou tuoxian ji," nos. 111 and 112, December 5 and 8, 1948.

Historians have long been interested in early Communist state building in urban China, albeit usually focused on cities much larger than
Zhengzhou. On the question of rural-urban relations, Jeremy Brown
has explored dynamics between early Communist Tianjin and its wider
hinterland.[44] Rather than repeat Brown's work, then, I focus more specifically on Zhengzhou's urban edge and the villages within the municipal
boundary. Evidence from Zhengzhou in this period reveals the spatial
contradictions already running through urban Communist governance in
its early months and years. On the one hand, unlike the Nationalist practice of using Zhengzhou as a springboard to control its rural hinterland,
Communist forces had built a revolution from rural areas, "surrounding
the city from the countryside" and promising rural-urban unity. Zhengzhou's new rulers vowed to reverse Nationalist mistakes, which had "not
met the needs of the mass of peasants but broken the material exchange
of rural-urban relations (*pohuai le chengxiang wuzi jiaoliu guanxi*)."[45] On
the other hand, the Communist takeover of Zhengzhou occurred just as
the new regime was shifting emphasis from rural areas to China's cities.
Even in these first years of Communist Zhengzhou, the contours of an
urban-centered program of modernization can be seen in the rise of city
cadres, ambitious urban planning, and the neglect of even the villages
closest to the city and within its municipal boundary.

This is not to say that the CCP promise of improved rural-urban relations was simply a trick. The city's new rulers were quick to roll back
the tight spatial control of the last months of Nationalist rule. Zhengzhou's governing military committee ordered the de-militarization of
the urban edge within forty-eight hours of takeover. Nationalist official
Yang Zhenxing, still hiding in the city, described how the new authorities
"mobilized various local ruffians and hooligans (*dipi liumang*) and some
ignorant traders to tear down the defensive walls and all the blockhouses
and fortifications."[46] The PLA garrison declared the city open within a
week of takeover: "For the ease of industry and commerce, and for the
flourishing of markets, from October 28 you can move freely in and out
of the city."[47] That same day, military control passed to new civil author-

44. Brown, *City Versus Countryside*, esp. 15–28.
45. *Zhengzhou ribao*, October 31, 1949.
46. Yang Zhenxing, "Zhengzhou tuoxian ji," no. 113, December 11, 1948.
47. "Zhengzhou Jingbei silingbu guanyu shi nei wai tongxing yu wuzi yunchu guid-

ities. Regional chief Deng Zihui (1896–1972) also emphasized rural-urban exchange, noting that Henan's industry was much more closely connected to agriculture than the heavy industry of Manchuria that had been the basis of much previous CCP urban experience. Mutually beneficial exchange, Deng argued, could only be rooted in the revival of cash crops and their processing and marketing in cities.[48] A year after the CCP takeover, *Zhengzhou Daily* reported strong informal trade in the center of the city, reminiscent of descriptions of the early days of the railroad in the early 1900s: "every day, Xiguan Dajie [the main street in Zhengzhou's commercial district] is filled with carts carrying cotton and salt, packed with peasant women carrying wicker baskets and peasants leading animals carrying sacks of grain to sell, and people pulling carts full of coal for sale."[49]

Behind this positive picture, though, rural-urban movement was by no means smooth. Despite the language of open connection, those moving between city and countryside were still subject to inspections at the urban edge, at the "entry and exit points" (*churu chu*) on Zhengzhou's main roads, and at the railroad station.[50] Nor was rural-urban movement a panacea for the economy. After the initial recovery of trade at the end of 1948, commerce in Zhengzhou ran into difficulties during the first half of 1949. City mayor Song Zhihe (1915–2013, in office 1948–1956) felt that that one of the hurdles was the slow speed of "opening up relations between city and countryside."[51] The local press also noted the problem of poverty around the city, suggesting that weakness in hinterland markets was a

---

ing," October 27, 1948, reproduced in Zhengzhou shi dang'anguan, *Zhengzhou jiefang,* 187–88. See also Zhao Guangyu, "Zhengzhou 'jiefang' hou de zhenxiang."

48. Deng Zihui, "Kaifeng shi gejie daibiaohui," 1–4. Deng was chairman of the Central Plains Provisional Government based at Kaifeng, among other posts. Note that Deng later admitted to Mao Zedong that CCP policy in Zhengzhou in the early months had been marked by "Right deviations," even in the context of the cautious standards of 1948. See "Deng Zihui tongzhi guanyu jieguan Zhengzhou, Kaifeng de jingyan yu Zhongyuan xinqu de nongcun gongzuo gei Mao Zhuxi de zonghe baogao," January 16, 1949, reproduced in Wang Liqi, *Zhongyuan jiefangqu,* 84–89.

49. *Zhengzhou ribao,* October 31, 1949.

50. "Zhengzhou Jingbei silingbu guanyu shi nei wai tongxing yu wuzi yunchu guiding," reproduced in Zhengzhou shi dang'anguan, *Zhengzhou jiefang,* 187–88.

51. Song Zhihe, "Zhengzhou shi renmin zhengfu guanyu yinianlai gongzuo baogao," November 20, 1949, reproduced in Zhengzhou shi dang'anguan, *Zhengzhou jiefang,* 248–49.

factor in the closure of so many businesses in Zhengzhou—almost two hundred in April 1949 alone.[52]

In addition to economic difficulties, political relations between city and countryside also cast doubt on rural-urban unity. The takeover of Zhengzhou was part of a wider shift in Communist prioritization of cities, as Mayor Song told cadres of the new municipality in an echo of Mao's formulation: "the age of the countryside encircling the cities is over; from now on it will be the city leading the countryside (*chengshi lingdao xiangcun*)."[53] Where the CCP had previously built institutions from rural areas to the cities, they now repeated patterns of Zheng-zhou's earlier rulers in using this railroad junction city as a launchpad for regional control: "now we are first capturing the cities and major transport routes," noted Deng Zihui in January 1949 in a report to Mao Zedong, "and then spreading into the countryside (*tuiguang nongcun*)."[54] This strategy risked reducing the role of rural areas. Deng nodded to the formula of urban work "serving rural construction" (*wei nongcun jianshe fuwu*), but his thinking was rooted in the extraction of rural resources, in language that both points back to the military demands of the 1942–1943 famine and forward to requisitioning under the planned industrial econ-omy: "the countryside . . . is our main source of soldiers and food, and in addition we need rural production to develop as a precondition for national industrialization (*guojia gongyehua de qianti tiaojian*)."[55] Grain requisitioning around Zhengzhou restarted a few days after this report.[56]

This tilt toward an urban focus was accompanied by tensions between city cadres and their rural counterparts around Zhengzhou. Deng Zihui reported that although it had once been difficult to persuade cadres to take on urban work, by early 1949 cadres in Zhengzhou and Kaifeng had

52. On problems in spring 1949, see the economic review of the year in *Zhengzhou ribao*, October 31, 1949.

53. "Gu Jingsheng tongzhi baogao jianshe xin Zhengzhou jihua," December 5, 1948, reproduced in Zhengzhou shi dang'anguan, *Zhengzhou jiefang*, 219.

54. "Deng Zihui tongzhi guanyu jieguan Zhengzhou, Kaifeng de jingyan," January 16, 1949, reproduced in Wang Liqi, *Zhongyuan jiefangqu*, 88.

55. "Deng Zihui tongzhi guanyu jieguan Zhengzhou, Kaifeng de jingyan," repro-duced in Wang Liqi, *Zhongyuan jiefangqu*, 88. Note, though, that during the Great Leap Forward Deng was a staunch defender of rural interests. See Xiao-Planes, "Un contestataire de la politique agricole."

56. Zhengzhou shi difang shizhi bianzuan weiyuanhui, *Zhengzhou shizhi*, 1:91.

developed "the erroneous tendency to lay stress on the cities and regard the countryside as unimportant."[57] A few months later these tensions came to a head over the issue of rural cadres arriving in Zhengzhou to arrest "bandits and bullies" (*feiba*) who had sought refuge in the city. Officials in Zhengzhou complained that this practice upset urban social order—not least because a target for arrest in the countryside might be playing a positive role in the city's economic recovery. For their part, rural cadres seem to have felt ill-treated by urban officials, many of whom were themselves of rural origin: "as for the municipal organs, when it comes to the quite correct requests peasants make of them, they lack enthusiastic assistance or the attitude of promptly solving the problem; worst of all, there are some who treat the peasants who have come into the city coldly and contemptuously (*lengdan qingshi*)."[58] In May 1949, provincial party head Zhang Xi (1912–1959) arranged a meeting of all the cadres involved. Zhang emphasized the importance of rural-urban unity, while admitting that differences in policy might generate "rural-urban contradictions" (*chengxiang maodun*). Rural cadres should consult with urban colleagues in advance, Zhang insisted, and he warned against anticity feeling in the countryside; for their part, officials in Zhengzhou should receive rural cadres "like honored guests and make the peasants feel as if they have arrived in their own government."[59] There is some evidence that better communication was achieved—soon after, a joint body was set up to handle the cases of "bandits" and "local bullies"—but the bigger picture of friction between rural and urban interests emerging during 1949 was more difficult to reverse.[60]

These emerging tensions were mirrored by new administrative distinctions between city and countryside. Apart from the brief interlude of municipal government in 1928–1931, Zhengzhou had always been governed as part of the surrounding county. But with the new

57. "Deng Zihui tongzhi guanyu jieguan Zhengzhou, Kaifeng de jingyan," reproduced in Wang Liqi, *Zhongyuan jiefangqu*, 87–88.

58. *Zhongyuan ribao*, May 27, 1949.

59. *Zhongyuan ribao*, May 27, 1949.

60. "Zhengzhou shi chengxiang jiehe qing fei zhihuibu zuozhan mingling," July 25, 1949, reproduced in Zhengzhou shi dang'anguan, *Zhengzhou jiefang*, 331–32. On 1949 efforts to reduce this new urban orientation of cadres and maintain strong rural links, see James Zheng Gao, *Communist Takeover of Hangzhou*, 99–108; for the more antirural pattern in 1949 Tianjin, see Brown, *City Versus Countryside*, 17–22.

emphasis on urban work, Zhengzhou's incoming rulers established a municipal government less than a week after their arrival. Municipal government did not mean, however, that urban administration could be wholly divorced from the countryside. The nascent municipality still needed revenue transfers from rural areas, and there were still agricultural areas within the boundaries of the city. Even the tightly drawn municipal boundary of October 1948—which simply adopted the three subcounty "town" units of Nationalist rule—included eighteen nearby villages with 1,009 rural households (*nonghu*). At the end of 1949, Zhengzhou's boundary expanded from Bishagang in the west to the airfield in the east, encompassing over a hundred villages—effectively the city's "diurnal hinterland," nearby countryside within an easy daily journey of the city.[61]

Control of nearby villages raised questions on the nature of urban rule: Should this municipal countryside be governed in the same way as the city or as other rural areas? How could this zone best serve the city? How should the municipality tackle rural-urban inequality within its boundary? These have been important questions for Zhengzhou's rulers throughout the People's Republic, but they were slow to be answered during the first period of Communist rule. Reviewing the first year of municipal work, Mayor Song Zhihe admitted that "our work in the municipal countryside has been the weakest link of all (*zui boruo de yihuan*). . . . Not only have we not yet done the work of reducing rent and reducing interest, but also the clearing out bandits and local despots (*qing fei fan ba*) has not even started."[62] This delay was partly caused by the complexity of Zhengzhou's mixed suburban districts, where warehouses and railway land were interspersed with agricultural fields, and many residents participated in both rural and urban labor. But it was also because villages close to the city were not vital for Communist power. Unlike previous regimes, which followed Charles Tilly's "center-out" pattern, using the city as a springboard for hinterland control,

61. Song Zhihe, "Zhengzhou shi renmin zhengfu guanyu yinianlai gongzuo baogao," November 20, 1949, 254; on municipal expansion, see "Zhengzhou shi renmin zhengfu guanyu kuoda benshi xiaqu de bugao," December 15, 1949, reproduced in Zhengzhou shi dang'anguan, *Zhengzhou jiefang*, 296–97.

62. Song Zhihe, "Zhengzhou shi renmin zhengfu guanyu yinianlai gongzuo baogao," November 20, 1949, 254.

Communist power was already entrenched across the Henan countryside (in Tilly's terms, "periphery-in"). Although CCP rule was shifting in 1949 to a "center-out" model, the building of revolution from the ground up meant that Zhengzhou's nearby villages, so prominent as rural laboratories under Feng Yuxiang, were not needed as experiments in state building.[63]

Both the low priority and the complexity of Zhengzhou's nearby villages become clear in the issue of suburban land reform, something usually missing from both urban and rural histories of this period.[64] Although Zheng County had been in the first wave of land reform in Henan during the 1949–1950 winter, redistribution stopped at the municipal boundary.[65] The regional party headquarters raised the issue of suburban land reform around the same time but noted that medium-sized cities like Zhengzhou and Kaifeng brought "complications very different from Beijing and Tianjin."[66] "Much of this land is held by those in the city, including foreign missions, medium and small capitalists, free professionals (*ziyou zhiyezhe*), independent laborers, and poor people (*pinmin*)." Many of those renting land did not fit into neat categories. "In addition to poor peasants, there are more than 30 percent whose main income is from handicrafts, transportation, or peddling but who also farm a little land." "Strictly speaking," the report concluded, "they should not be classified as peasants (*buying huawei nongmin*)."[67] The authorities were particularly concerned that workers might be mislabeled as rich peasants or landlords because they owned land in nearby villages. In the municipality's draft regulations, only those directly involved in agriculture for at least four months each year were to be given a rural classification and exposed to the risk of negative class labels. Farmland owned by urban merchants, businesses, or religious organizations was

63. Tilly, "Town and Country," 289–90.
64. The exception is suburban land reform in Beijing, which has received some attention. See Liu Yigao, "Chengshi jiaoqu tudi gaige," and Shaofan An, "Suburban Revolution."
65. Sun Jianguo, *Xiandai Henan jingjishi*, 30.
66. "Huazhongju guanyu chengshi jinjiao tudi wenti chuli banfa de qingshi," December 24, 1949, Zhongguo dangdai zhengzhi yundongshi shujuku (hereafter ZDZYS).
67. "Huazhongju guanyu chengshi jinjiao tudi wenti chuli banfa de qingshi," December 24, 1949, ZDZYS.

redistributed, but small-scale landownership by workers or profession-als was allowed to continue.[68] Rent negotiation was encouraged, but, wary of formally overseeing conflict between workers and peasants, the regulations did not force landowning urban workers to lower their rents. In their own words, the authorities admitted that they were harming the interests of farmers (*yingxiang liyi*) to safeguard urban interests and vegetable supplies.[69]

Once the principles of suburban land reform were established, noth-ing happened for several months. In Zhengzhou, land reform began only in August 1950, in twenty-two experimental villages west of the city, and was rolled across the municipality by November.[70] At the same time, the city government broke the power of Zhengzhou's "shitlords" (*fenba*)—the labor bosses who dominated the notoriously exploitative business in removing nightsoil for sale as fertilizer and whose influence had crossed the rural-urban boundary.[71]

What did that urban edge look like in the late 1940s and early 1950s? Already in the prewar period, Zhengzhou's rural-urban fringe interspersed railroad land, warehousing, industrial workshops, market gardening, temples and Christian missions, as well as the *jianghu* district of drifters, petty criminals, street entertainers, beggars, and sex work-ers at Laofengang; since 1938, refugee camps had also sprung up at the urban edge, contracting or expanding according to patterns of the Sino-Japanese War, famine, and civil war. Perceptions and meanings of the rural-urban edge must have differed according to individual experience,

68. "Zhengzhou shi renmin zhengfu guanyu jiaoqu tudi gaige shishi banfa (cao'an)," no date, 1950, reproduced in Zhengzhou shi dang'anguan, *Zhengzhou jiefang*, 414–18.

69. "Huazhongju guanyu chengshi jinjiao tudi wenti chuli banfa de qingshi," December 24, 1949, ZDZYS; see also the central government's response: "Zhonggong Zhongyang guanyu chengshi jinjiao tudi wenti chuli banfa gei Zhongnanju de pifu," January 6, 1950, ZDZYS. Note that, as across China, confiscated suburban land passed to state control and was leased out to cultivators. In November 1950 it was decreed that all land under urban district governments was state land.

70. "Zhengzhou shi renmin zhengfu guanyu zai Zhengzhou jiaoqu Duizhou xiang, Xinglongpu xiang, Zhutun xiang shixing tugai de tonggao," August 21, 1950, repro-duced in Zhengzhou shi dang'anguan, *Zhengzhou jiefang*, 409.

71. A municipal commission was established in late 1950 to organize the removal of waste. See Zhang Qixian and Wu Xiaoya, *Dangdai Zhengzhou chengshi jianshe*, 138–39. For more on nightsoil reform in Beijing, see Joshua Goldstein, *Remains of the Everyday*, 72–77.

but one resident of 1940s Zhengzhou later remembered his perception of the everyday rural-urban edge as both distinct place and boundary:

> The southern edge of Zhengzhou was what is now the south side of Yimalu and Longhailu. Previously, the north side of the railroad had a large poplar tree, and, in those days, south of the tree was into the countryside, the villages of Xiaozhaozhai and Mazhai. . . . In summer, there were always lots of people sitting at the bottom of the tree. Those leaving the city and those coming into the city all enjoyed resting (*xie xie jiao*) under the tree. There were usually some tea sellers and snack peddlers under the tree, and local children often played around it.[72]

Away from this everyday sense of the urban boundary, Zhengzhou's edges presented a challenge for the new authorities, and in the short term Song Zhihe's administration reprised the playbook of their predecessors. The always-troublesome Laofengang *jianghu* neighborhood underwent its third rebranding in 1950 as the "Aid the People Market" (Yimin shichang). As under Feng Yuxiang, its prostitutes were housed and retrained, more than five hundred from the licensed brothels alone.[73] The Communist municipality also followed the "new village" phenomenon of both the Feng and the Nationalist periods, building three model settlements for the urban poor on the city's edge.[74] But the settlements made only a small dent in the city's housing crisis, and the new authorities were also as keen as their Nationalist predecessors had been to remove Zhengzhou's refugees and drifters, many housed in long-standing shack settlements at the urban edge. Zhengzhou's population had ticked up from 160,000 at Communist takeover to 181,000 a year later, sparking what would be the first of many efforts under the People's Republic to control the migrant population. Between September 1949 and the end of the year, the municipality detained and deported (*shourong qiansong*) almost 27,000 beggars, refugees, migrant unemployed, and former soldiers.[75] Indicative of a desire for the "right" kind of working class, in 1950 the long-standing refugee camp west of the Jing–Han railroad

72. "Lao Zhengzhou san ti," *Zhengzhou jiyi*, June 21, 2010.

73. On early Communist social policy in Zhengzhou, see Zhang Nan, "1948–1953 nian Zhengzhou shi." On sex work and Laofengang, see 17–20.

74. Zhang Qixian and Wu Xiaoya, *Dangdai Zhengzhou chengshi jianshe*, 45. For the most famous example of this phenomenon, see Van Duyn, "Building Socialist Shanghai."

75. Fan Futang et al., *Zhengzhou liudong renkou yanjiu*, 137.

was knocked down to make way for Soviet-style apartments for railway workers.[76] By the end of 1952, some 113,000 people had been repatriated from Zhengzhou.[77]

That these experiments at Zhengzhou's edge followed an older pattern underlines the limits of urban transformation in the first years of the People's Republic, especially in smaller cities with limited urban infrastructure. For all the lauding of the city's potential since the arrival of the railroad half a century before, Zhengzhou in 1951 was still an unprepossessing town of small workshops and low-rise alleyway houses. The most ambitious scheme, for a piped water supply, had been shelved for lack of funds; just as before 1948, officials had to settle for digging more wells.[78] Zhengzhou was still hemmed in by its two railroads and had not expanded across either the Long–Hai or Jing–Han line. Even the first urban plan for Communist Zhengzhou closely resembled Republican-era planning. The 1950–1951 design of Beijing-based urban planners Chen Wo and Zhong Hanxiong owed much to ideals of the Euro-American garden city. Chen and Zhong proposed a low population density city of one million people, with most land designated for residential zones and green space and only a small industrial zone. Large-scale manufacturing was to be banished south of the city around the village of Fengzhuang.[79] This was a world away from the Soviet-style growth that would transform Zhengzhou just a few years later, where industry was at the heart of the new city, and residential areas were integrated into work unit compounds. This early People's Republic planning staked an important claim for Zhengzhou's potential, but it envisaged a mode of politics—where power would lie with the municipal government—that was about to be overtaken by the power of industrial work units in the emerging planned economy.

76. Zhengxie Zhengzhou shi Erqiqu weiyuanhui, *Yuanqu zhi jiyi*, 53.
77. Zhengzhou shi difang shizhi bianzuan weiyuanhui, *Zhengzhou shizhi*, 7:459. This figure includes people deported on multiple occasions.
78. Zhang Qixian and Wu Xiaoya, *Dangdai Zhengzhou chengshi jianshe*, 58–59.
79. On 1950–1952 planning, see Hao Pengzhan, "Lun jindai yilai Zhengzhou," 40–45; on the twists and turns of urban design in the 1950s, see Duanfang Lu, *Remaking Chinese Urban Form*, 19–46.

Making a Socialist Boomtown

Zhengzhou was transformed during China's First Five-Year Plan, with political power and economic resources concentrated in the city as never before. Zhengzhou was one of the eighteen "focus cities" of the plan, described by the State Planning Commission as a "base of new industrial construction" (*xinjian gongye jidi*), with a specialization as one of China's six centers for textile production. This designation brought urban industrialization at a breakneck pace. Zhengzhou became one of the fastest-growing cities in China, rising from a population of 161,000 to over 450,000 between 1952 and 1957, at a growth rate ten times faster than China's total urban population.[80] In 1954 Zhengzhou replaced Kaifeng as Henan's capital, overturning an administrative hierarchy dating back to the creation of provinces in the thirteenth century. By 1957 Zhengzhou's built-up area was eight times larger than on Communist takeover in 1948.

Historians have explored several key themes in the emergence of socialist cities in China's 1950s, including urban planning, industrialization, and the work unit (*danwei*) system.[81] The case of Zhengzhou adds to this work in two ways. First, it illustrates the scale and pace of change in the medium-sized, newly industrial cities most revolutionized by the planned economy. Below I explore the unequal consequences, particularly in Zhengzhou's new industrial district, the "western suburb" (*xijiao*). Second, Zhengzhou underlines how the political construction of spatial inequalities under socialism were about more than just rural-urban relations. Even as the planned economy was shifting industrial growth inland, it was underpinned by stark inequality of resource allocation between cities such as Zhengzhou and those left behind, especially the abandoned provincial capital at Kaifeng.[82]

---

80. *Zhengzhou shizhi*, 1:345–46. China's urban population rose only 28 percent over this period (at least officially). Kwok, "Trends of Urban Planning and Development," 154.

81. See, for instance, Bray, *Social Space and Governance*; Duanfang Lu, *Remaking Chinese Urban Form*; Samuel Y. Liang, *Remaking China's Great Cities*; Hirata, "Mao's Steeltown." For the new industrial cities of the Five-Year Plan, see Li Hao, *Ba da zhongdian chengshi guihua*.

82. On rural-urban relations, see especially Brown, *City Versus Countryside*, 15–52. On inequality between adjacent cities, see the highly gendered example recently explored by Robert Cliver in *Red Silk*.

ZHENGZHOU AND KAIFENG IN THE FIRST FIVE-YEAR PLAN

Why was Zhengzhou such a prominent beneficiary of the First Five-Year Plan? The answer lies in the drive to move away from the capitalist and colonial version of modernity represented by China's coastal cities, instead spreading industry to new sites inland where it would be easier both to mold the new political economy and to defend in the event of invasion. The center of China's economic gravity shifted north and west, with 79 percent of major construction projects designated for inland areas, along with fourteen of the eighteen "focus cities."[83] Henan Province—inland but accessible by rail—was one of the key sites for this shift. The largest heavy industrial projects in the province were mostly around Luoyang, 110 kilometers west of Zhengzhou and in the top echelon of China's eight "key cities" of socialist planning. But Zhengzhou was not far behind, with industrial investment rising three times over during 1953 alone and by a further 56 percent the following year.[84] Like the developmental efforts of the 1930s, the limited resources of the planned economy were concentrated in certain cities, but unlike under Nationalist rule, neighboring Kaifeng was almost wholly neglected. Zhu Junxian calculates that across the Five-Year Plan period, Zhengzhou accounted for 31 percent of Henan's entire capital construction investment. Kaifeng, at the beginning of the period still Henan's provincial capital and largest city, received just 1.5 percent.[85] Kaifeng was the only large city (population two hundred thousand or more) outside the Lower Yangzi region that was not even earmarked for "ordinary" levels of urban growth in the First Five-Year Plan. The only other provincial capital to suffer this fate was the former Nationalist capital of Nanjing.[86]

This low investment in Kaifeng was not without economic logic. Kaifeng's strength lay in light agricultural processing, which had only minor status in this first stage of the planned economy. As a railroad

83. He Yimin and Zhou Mingchang, "156 Projects." These fourteen cities include four in Jilin and Heilongjiang Provinces, then designated part of the Central Region.
84. *Henan minbao*, July 21, 1954. For more on the geography of the Five-Year Plan in Henan, see Sun Jianguo, *Xiandai Henan jingjishi*, 83–91.
85. Zhu Junxian, "Bianyuan yu zhongxin de huhuan," 105.
86. He Yimin and Zhou Mingchang, "156 Projects," 59–60. Other cities that in 1953 had lost or were about to lose status as provincial capitals (Guilin, Baoding, Zhangjiakou, Chengde, and Jilin City) were all designated for growth. The only exception was the small city of Ya'an (capital of Xikang Province, abolished in 1955).

junction relatively close to both coal fields and cotton-growing areas, Zhengzhou was well suited to the state-owned textile sector. But the startling level of Kaifeng's neglect suggests something more political was at work, particularly when coupled with the move of the provincial capital to Zhengzhou in October 1954. The shift was officially attributed to the convenience of Zhengzhou's central location and rail links within the province.[87] But the discourse around the relocation also points to a politicized elevation of Zhengzhou, emblematic of the new, productive socialist city, and a similarly political condemnation of its neighbor.[88]

This brings us to the heart of the relationship between the two cities. Zhengzhou had been an important logistical and commercial center throughout the first half of the twentieth century, but Kaifeng remained the dominant political, cultural, and education center of the province. It is true that the idea of moving the provincial capital away from Kaifeng had been raised before, particularly after it was hit by the Yellow River flood of 1841.[89] One geographer of the early Republican period noted that fast-growing, conveniently located Zhengzhou might be an alternative capital.[90] But apart from its wartime occupation, the provincial administration remained at Kaifeng, which on the eve of the First Five-Year Plan was almost two-thirds larger than its neighbor. Retired cadre Wen Jiuyu later insisted that in the early 1950s "Zhengzhou was definitely no rival for Kaifeng (*juedui ganbushang*)."[91]

Zhengzhou's status as a railroad junction was a major factor in its selection as Henan's new capital, but as Wu Pengfei shows, it was insufficient without the political critique of Kaifeng in the People's Republic. As well as being a "consuming city"—which was applied to almost all cities—Kaifeng was criticized for having a particular "feudal" (*fengjian*)

87. For a good example of the official explanation, note the account offered by Jiang Xin, mayor of Kaifeng, reproduced in *Henan minbao*, October 19, 1954.

88. Although there are several cases of new provincial seats in the Mao period, including Nanning (1950), Hohhot (1952), Changchun (1954), and Shijiazhuang (1968), historians have paid little attention to these shifts. On Henan, see Xie Xiaopeng, "1954 nian Henan shenghui." On the peripatetic Hebei administration, see Jin Lingxia, "Zai Jing Jin Ji zhijian."

89. See Dodgen, "Salvaging Kaifeng."

90. Lin Chuanjia, *Da Zhonghua Henan sheng*, 71.

91. Quoted in *Dahebao*, January 10, 2007. The 1952 population figures (161,000 in Zhengzhou and 264,000 for Kaifeng) are from, respectively, *Zhengzhou shizhi*, 1:345–46; Cheng Ziliang and Li Qingyin, *Kaifeng chengshi shi*, 323.

character; in other words, it had a long history of elite cultural traditions and luxury consumption dating back to its period as China's capital.[92] Its recent past was also anathema, as a hub of collaboration under Japanese occupation and as a center of Nationalist rule. Although Kaifeng had seen social and economic changes during the Republican period, these were glossed over in discussions around the move of the capital and by commentators for decades afterwards: pre-1949 Kaifeng was "an unbearably dilapidated city of consumption," wrote one historian in 1980.[93] The provincial party promoted Zhengzhou as a more appropriate environment: "the meaning of the shift in the capital to Zhengzhou is to criticize that kind of luxurious living and pleasure-seeking individualist thinking (*tantu xiangshou de gerenzhuyi sixiang*)."[94] Zhengzhou did not escape criticism, being described in the provincial press as "an exploitative marketplace (*panbo shichang*) for bureaucratic capital and speculating merchants."[95] But the new provincial capital avoided the designation of "feudal" and, as the center for the 1923 Jing–Han railroad strike, also supplied one of the few urban proletarian memories in early Communist Party history.

The move of the capital was confirmed in September 1953 by the Government Administration Council (Zhongyuan zhengwuyuan, the forerunner of the State Council). The core facilities of the new administrative district—the main office buildings, most cadre dormitories, the water system, and new roads—were ready by fall 1954.[96] Against the feverish backdrop of the First Taiwan Strait Crisis, the Transfer Committee (Qianyi weiyuanhui) selected ten days in the middle of October for the bulk of the move. The various organs of provincial government were divided into four batches to make the transfer across the ten-day period, moving the 60 kilometers between the two cities by a mixture of train and truck.[97] Somewhere between thirty and forty thousand officials and dependents were eventually transferred to Zhengzhou, and in 1955 the new capital outstripped Kaifeng in population. Zhengzhou was now the

92. Wu Pengfei, "Kaifeng chengshi shengming," 124–26.
93. Wu Sizuo, *Zhongyuan chengshi shilüe*, 94.
94. Directive from the Henan Provincial Party Committee (*shengwei*), September 23, 1954, quoted in *Dahebao*, January 10, 2007.
95. *Henan minbao*, October 14, 1954.
96. *Henan minbao*, October 14, 1954.
97. Xie Xiaopeng, "1954 nian Henan shenghui," 43.

largest city Henan had seen since the devastation of Kaifeng in the 1642 Yellow River flood.[98]

The loss of provincial capital status had serious effects on Kaifeng. During the 1954 move, Kaifeng's mayor, Jiang Xin, admitted that there would be "temporary problems" but insisted these were merely "the difficulties of a victorious advance" and urged residents to avoid such slanderous statements as "Kaifeng has no future prospects" (*Kaifeng meiyou qiantu*).[99] By 1957, though, with its industrial output barely a quarter of Zhengzhou's, cadres in Kaifeng were already complaining about the effects of the shift in provincial capital. Several leading officials in the city later wrote self-criticisms for airing these grievances, but history proved them right.[100] Under the planned economy, there was little mechanism for Zhengzhou's industrial expansion to spill over into Kaifeng. During the Second Five-Year Plan (1958–1962), Kaifeng became something of a production center for chemicals and small machinery, but the failures of the Great Leap Forward limited the gains from these sectors.[101] By the end of the Mao period, Kaifeng was one of the three medium-sized cities in China that had grown the least since 1949 (out of a total of seventy-one).[102] For historian Yang Min, even by the early twenty-first century, Kaifeng had still not recovered from 1954: "the vitality of Kaifeng was badly damaged, with its energy gone, as if its muscles had cramped up (*xiang bei choule jin yiyang*)."[103]

By contrast, Zhengzhou offered a new start for the provincial government, a chance to build a model, productive city of socialist modernity. But the reality was not so straightforward. Resources were limited, and the emphasis lay on rapid increases in production, not urban refinement. Zhengzhou was not a blank slate but an overcrowded and impoverished

---

98. Comparing Zhengzhou shi difang shizhi bianzuan weiyuanhui, *Zhengzhou shizhi*, 1:345–46 (Zhengzhou) and Cheng Ziliang and Li Qingyin, *Kaifeng chengshi shi*, 323 (Kaifeng).

99. *Henan minbao*, October 19, 1954.

100. "Henan shenghui cong Kaifeng dao Zhengzhou dabanqian," *Dahebao*, January 10, 2007.

101. Zhang Yiwen, "Kaifeng chengshi jianshe fazhan," 7–9; Cheng Ziliang and Li Qingyin, *Kaifeng chengshi shi*, 291–99.

102. Tōdaishi kenkyūkai, *Chūgoku toshi no rekishiteki kenkyū*, 27–28. The others were the Republican-era growth towns of Dandong (Liaoning) and Bengbu (Anhui).

103. Yang Min, "Kaifeng, Kaifeng!," 14.

city. So how did Zhengzhou's overstretched authorities try to build a city fit for its place in the planned economy?

The first step was to make a new urban plan for the city's future. In 1953 the Soviet architect and planner A. S. Mukhin (1900–1982) ripped up the garden city–inspired plan of 1950–1951 and drew up the first design for socialist-industrial Zhengzhou. Mukhin had to wrestle with the same questions as previous urban plans: what to do with the existing city, how to incorporate rural space, and whether to expand Zhengzhou across the Jing–Han and Long–Hai railroads. Mukhin was the most cautious of the three prominent Soviet urban planners working in China at the time. In Beijing, he had been a key ally of Liang Sicheng's (1901–1972) unsuccessful effort to preserve the city wall.[104] With this orientation toward incorporating local environments, it is perhaps not surprising that Mukhin planned an industrial Zhengzhou closely linked to the existing city. Unlike most previous urban plans for the city (such as those of 1928, 1947, and 1950–1951), Mukhin proposed keeping Zhengzhou's expansion entirely north of the Long–Hai and east of the Jing–Han railroads, promising ease of movement and avoiding the problems of a city divided by railroads.[105]

But Mukhin's design for Zhengzhou did not work out as planned. Preliminary investigations for the No. 1 State Cotton Factory showed that the water table east of the Jing–Han line was too high for large-scale industrial use. With the oversight of deputy mayor Wang Junzhi (1916–) and the input of another Soviet planner, D. D. Baragin, the 1953 plan was adapted by moving the industrial zone to the slightly higher and more stable ground west of the Jing–Han railroad.[106] In a few short years this patch of ground, 4.4 kilometers by 2.4 kilometers, became one of the flagship zones for state-owned industry in Mao's China. After flattening out the undulating ground, Zhengzhou's state construction companies laid out three east–west roads and pushed the city beyond Feng Yuxiang's memorial park at Bishagang. By the end of the First Five-Year Plan, this new western suburb boasted five state-owned textile mills on its north side. A cluster of schools and colleges were located to the south,

---

104. See Wang Jun, *Beijing Record*, 174–97; on A. S. Mukhin, see also 344. On the three major Soviet planners, see Li Hao, "'Yi wu' shiqi de chengshi guihua."

105. Zhengzhou shi jianshe weiyuanhui, *Zhengzhou shi jianshe zhi*, 15–16; Hao Pengzhan, "Lun jindai yilai Zhengzhou," 45–51.

106. Zhengzhou shi jianshe weiyuanhui, *Zhengzhou shi jianshe zhi*, 15–17.

with the East German–backed grinding wheel factory in the far west (see map 4.1). This was the first major expansion of Zhengzhou since the 1910s, and Baragin's plan for the city was the first to be realized.[107] Poet and historian Guo Moruo (1892–1978) praised Zhengzhou's ancient past and its industrial future:

> Zhengzhou is a ruined Shang city,
> Perhaps it was the capital of King Zhong Ding.
> Below the ground the ancient city lies deep and thick,
> the relics from its tombs are luxurious and special.
> . . . .
> But what I love most is the newly built west side of the city,
> where the factories stand like a forest and connect with the
> heavens.[108]

ZHENGZHOU'S WESTERN SUBURB: SPACE AND EDGES

What did this rapid urbanization and industrialization—history speeded up—mean for space in Zhengzhou? First, it produced new spatial divisions within the city. As map 4.1 shows, Zhengzhou was now divided into three distinct zones: the industrial western suburb, the new administrative zone to the north, and the pre-1952 built-up area. The latter was now referred to as the "old city" (*laocheng*), an appellation that had previously been applied to the prerailroad walled area.

Divisions within the city were not new. Commentators in the Republican period had been struck by the social divide between the old walled city and the flourishing commercial town, and in 1928 Feng Yuxiang ordered the removal of the city wall to connect the two parts of Zhengzhou (see chapters 1 and 2). The municipal authorities in the 1950s faced a more difficult task. The new industrial and administrative districts operated in very different political economies from the pre-1952 city, being dominated by work units answerable to provincial authorities or central government ministries rather than the municipal government. The city

107. Zhonggong Henan shengwei dangshi yanjiushi, *Henan sheng "yiwu" jihua*, 291–93. The sixth state-owned cotton factory (the No. 2 works) was east of the Jing–Han line, reconstituted on the site of the Yufeng mill. For an excellent recent study of gender and labor in the Zhengzhou mills, see Yige Dong, "From Mill Town to iPhone City."

108. This and other poems referencing Zhengzhou are available at Li Gangtai's online collection: http://blog.sina.com.cn/ligangtai.

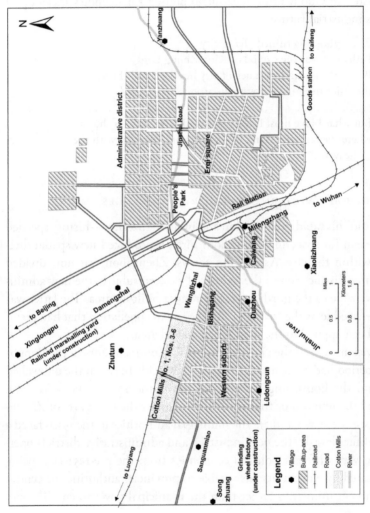

MAP 4.1. Urban Zhengzhou, mid-1950s. Adapted from "Zhengzhou shi jie tu" [Street map of Zhengzhou City] 郑州市街圖, no date, mid-1950s. Map by Jogu Gopinath.

authorities were more prominent in the old town, but its financial weaknesses prevented it from doing much to improve living conditions. This disparity gave the intracity inequality of the Mao period a sharply spatial dimension in Zhengzhou, as in other rising industrial centers such as nearby Luoyang. In the wide, straight streets of the new Zhengzhou, cadres and industrial workers enjoyed the higher pay and welfare benefits of state employment, including work unit housing. The concentration of government organs and state factories ensured that Zhengzhou enjoyed a much higher rate of privileged state employment (81 percent) than the national urban average (62 percent). But in the twisting lanes of the pre-1952 city, most residents were employed by lower-wage urban collectives, which were struggling to increase productivity in the 1950s.[109]

Divisions of political economy within the city were exacerbated by physical disconnection. Zhengzhou's wide railroad tracks posed more formidable barriers than the city wall had done in 1928. The main link between the industrial and administrative zones, the new Jinshui Road, was a crowded bottleneck, its railroad crossing frequently blocked by passing trains.[110] Zhengzhou's mass of railroads and railway yards created miniperipheries in several pockets of the city and at its urban edge. The lineside village of Mazhai was only half a mile from downtown Zhengzhou but was surrounded by railroad infrastructure and cut off from the urban core. Residents faced a long walk to either the north or the south crossing point of the Jing–Han line—though in practice many just climbed over the wall marking the edge of railroad land and scrambled across the tracks.[111] Transport between the west and east sides of the city was also rudimentary. Construction worker Luo Jiaquan remembered riding donkeys to get into downtown Zhengzhou when working on the No. 1 Cotton Factory in 1953.[112] The following year, Zhengzhou's first bus route linked the two sides of the city, carrying thirty-one passengers on a refitted US Army truck, but even in 1957 the local party admitted in an

109. For numbers in state employment in Zhengzhou, see Zhang Qixian and Wu Xiaoya, *Dangdai Zhengzhou chengshi jianshe*, 239–40; across China, see Bray, *Social Space and Urban Governance*, 94. Both figures are for 1957.
110. The problem was eased in 1960 with the opening of the Jinshui Road bridge over the Long–Hai line. See Zhengzhou shi difang shizhi bianzuan weiyuanhui, *Zhengzhou shizhi*, 1:125.
111. Zhengxie Zhengzhou shi Erqiqu weiyuanhui, *Yuanqu zhi jiyi*, 61.
112. "Zhengzhou Xijiao de bianqian," *Zhengzhou jiyi*, June 21, 2010.

internal document that the new districts were poorly linked to the rest of the city.[113] In these early years, the western suburb felt remote to many of its residents, particularly the tens of thousands of skilled workers who had arrived from larger cities. One Mrs. Wu, a textile worker from Shanghai, later remembered that "at that time the western suburb was all fields, and the No. 1 factory was an isolated island (*gudao*) with no roads around. In the evenings no one dared go out (*mei ren gan chuqu*)."[114]

Mrs. Wu's fear of her new surroundings raises a second important aspect of the spatial implications of Zhengzhou's industrial growth. In addition to connections to the existing city, how did the industrial suburb interact with village communities west of the Jing–Han railroad? Perhaps surprisingly, this flagship new industrial district was not so different from Zhengzhou's earlier, much less planned, urban expansions: like the original "western suburb" around the railroad station of the 1900s and 1910s, the new western suburb of the 1950s was a zone of mixed activity encompassing industry, housing, agriculture, and marketing—albeit on a different scale and in a very different kind of economy. Large industrial work units and prestigious new educational institutes were intermingled with agricultural plots in a new suburb which straddled the rural-urban division of the planned economy.

This mixed zone was not what had been imagined in the Soviet plan for Zhengzhou, which envisaged a neatly bounded district monopolized by industry, workers' housing, and new schools. But construction of the western suburb proved haphazard and inefficient. Zhengzhou's municipal government had little oversight over work unit activities. In Zhengzhou, as in other 1950s boomtowns, this lack of oversight produced what Duan-fang Lu calls a "jigsaw puzzle" of walled, self-contained factories rather than a cohesive urban district.[115] Reports of the construction process sound more like the chaotic expansion that marked Zhengzhou's first boom of the 1910s than a carefully planned district. The provincial finance ministry found massive failures at construction companies, with major delays and

113. Zhonggong Henan shengwei ji Zhengzhou shiwei, *Zhengzhou shi gaikuang (neibu wenjian)*, 2; on buses, "Zhengzhou shi de shoupi gongjiaoche," *Zhengzhou jiyi*, June 21, 2010.

114. "Zhengzhou Xijiao de bianqian," *Zhengzhou jiyi*, June 21, 2010.

115. Duanfang Lu, *Remaking Chinese Urban Form*, 13.

huge discrepancies between real and reported profits.[116] In one industrial school, poor building work led to a student strike in 1956. Ominous posters appeared in the college, declaring, "CCP rule for ten thousand years; that's ten thousand years without freedom (*you wansui bu ziyou*)."[117] "The urban area has been blindly expanded (*mangmu kuoda*)," reported the provincial government in May 1954, "and much land has been wasted." Large gaps appeared in the sprawling new zone of the city as work units grabbed as much land as they could. One work unit procured over 400 *mu* of farmland and enclosed it with a wall but left most of the compound as wasteland.[118] The juxtaposition of factories, schools, and farming plots became even more complex in 1959, when, amid tightening food supplies, the municipality tried to roll back the land grab, ordering unused areas to be returned to agricultural production.[119] The messy construction of the new zone inadvertently achieved what the Nationalist city plan of 1947 had been aiming for: the "intangible" inclusion of suburban cultivated land into the expanded city.

Many farmers did lose some or all of their access to land—an estimated 3,700 in the municipality by the end of the First Five-Year Plan.[120] But the eight villages in and around the new industrial zone did not simply disappear or lose their separate identities. Central government orders on Zhengzhou's urban planning dictated that village housing "should as far as possible not be knocked down" (*jin keneng bu chaiqian*).[121] Given the relentless march of the industrial economy during the First Five-Year Plan, this may seem surprising, but pressure on housing meant that neither work units nor the municipal authorities wanted to take responsibility for rehousing villagers. The village of Mifengzhang, which had been on the edge of Zhengzhou since the 1910s, retained its village identity even at the crossing point of two major new roads in the

116. *Henan minbao*, October 8, 1954.

117. "Zhengzhou fasheng bake shijian," *Xuanjiao dongtai*, October 30, 1956, ZDZYS.

118. *Henan minbao*, June 8, 1954. Fabio Lanza notes a similar pattern in Beijing. See Lanza, "City of Workers?," 46–47.

119. Zhengzhou shi jianshe weiyuanhui, *Zhengzhou shi chengshi jianshe guanli zanxing guize*, 3.

120. Zhengzhou shi difang shizhi bianzuan weiyuanhui, *Zhengzhou shizhi*, 1:114.

121. "Guojia jianwei dui Zhengzhou shi chubu guihui de pifu," February 22, 1956, reproduced in Zhengzhou shi jianshe weiyuanhui, "Zhengzhou shi chengxiang jianshe zhi," 320.

new industrial zone. At Caiwang, where part of the village was in fact knocked down and which lost most of its land, a vegetable work team survived into the mid-1980s.[122]

How does this mixed suburban zone fit into the wider picture of the deepening divisions between rural and urban China during this period? In one sense it complicates that story. The haphazard nature of the new industrial suburb made Zhengzhou's rural-urban boundary less stark than that proposed by Soviet planners. Some villagers benefited from low-end jobs—janitors, gatekeepers, cleaners—in the new state work units. In these first years of the western suburb, there was also some social mixing between rural and urban residents. In 1951, Chen Zemin moved from Nanjing to Zhengzhou's western suburb, where his cadre father was involved in setting up the Artillery College. With no work unit schools yet available, Chen attended the local primary school at Wanglizhai, where the schoolyard doubled as the village threshing ground.[123] Even when work unit facilities were established, it was this rural proximity that gave street life to Zhengzhou's western suburb beyond the walls of work unit compounds. New open-air markets sprung up, near Bishagang and at Lüdongcun on the edge of the new district, where nearby producers were able to sell items outside the state grain monopoly: vegetables, tofu, and other rural sidelines.[124]

This optimistic reading of connection does not disguise the fact that Zhengzhou's western suburb was on the front line of rural-urban division in the planned economy. As Jeremy Brown points out, rural-urban contact can itself reinforce a sense of difference.[125] Even when he was sharing a classroom with village children in the early 1950s, Chen Zemin was acutely conscious that his clothes were superior to those of his farming classmates; once the new district was better established, the world of urban industry and state employment lay behind the gates and walls of work unit compounds.[126] As Duanfang Lu points out, the proliferation of walls in this period was in part about keeping the countryside and its

122. Zhengxie Zhengzhou shi Erqiqu weiyuanhui, *Yuanqu zhi jiyi*, 54 and 70–71.
123. "Sanquan laozong shai xiaoxue biye zhao, 60 nian qian Zhengzhou daochu shi 'lü de,'" *Zhengzhou jiyi*, May 9, 2014.
124. "Zhengzhou Xijiao de bianqian"; "Lao Bishagang shichang: wo tongnian de tiantang," *Zhengzhou jiyi*, June 21, 2010.
125. Most explicitly in Brown, "Crossing the Rural-Urban Divide," 41.
126. "Sanquan laozong shai xiaoxue biye zhao, 60 nian qian Zhengzhou daochu shi 'lü de,'" *Zhengzhou jiyi*, May 9, 2014.

inhabitants at arm's length.[127] Although city growth brought marketing opportunities for nearby villagers that were not available to their
counterparts farther from Zhengzhou, these openings were usually at
the margins of the urban economy.

"All to Supply the Needs of the City": Municipal Countryside in the Planned Economy

Zhengzhou's western suburb saw in microcosm the rural and urban division that underpinned China's planned economy. Such divides were not
new, even for a small city such as Republican period Zhengzhou, where
urban commercialization had had only a limited impact on rural Zheng
County (see chapter 1). State spending in the 1950s was concentrated in
urban areas, even in overwhelmingly agricultural Henan, but this also
continued a pattern seen under Nationalist rule (see chapter 2).[128] What
was new in the First Five-Year Plan period was the systematic and state-
controlled subordination of the rural sector to urban and state interests
in a way that had not occurred under Nationalist rule, even in wartime.
During the first year of the plan, unified state grain purchase (*tonggou
tongxiao*) was introduced across China, reaching Zhengzhou in November 1953. This unified system was advertised as helping rural producers
escape the clutches of grain merchants but was primarily a response to
urban supply difficulties: in Zhengzhou and Kaifeng it was celebrated in
internal party documents for having "settled down the mood" of city residents (*qingxu wending*).[129] Like its Nationalist predecessor, this compulsory purchase secured procurement of grain from rural areas, while its
price scissors of low prices extracted value from the agricultural economy;
unlike the Nationalist system, it effectively controlled all grain surpluses

127. Duanfang Lu, *Remaking Chinese Urban Form*, 136.
128. In the First Five-Year Plan, only 10.7 percent of investment in Henan was
earmarked for agriculture (including irrigation), compared with 31.4 percent for industry and 24.3 percent in the rest of the urban economy. Zhonggong Henan shengwei
dangshi yanjiushi, *Henan sheng "yiwu" jihua*, 6. In practice, with a sense of rural crisis in
the mid-1950s, agriculture's share of investment across the period was higher than first
planned (16.9 percent). Sun Jianguo, *Xiandai Henan jingjishi*, 91–92.
129. "Quanguo gedi liangshi tonggou tongxiao gongzuo qingkuang," November 27,
1953, printed in *Neibu cankao*, December 3, 1953, ZDZYS. For a propaganda piece celebrating *tonggou tongxiao* and the end of merchant power, see *Henan minbao*, November
14, 1954.

and urban distribution. Soon afterwards, this division between rural and urban economies was underpinned by the tightening restrictions on movement between the two. Although not yet at its strictest, the *hukou* household registration system had been rolled across rural China by the end of 1955 and its definitions of rural and urban residency finalized.[130]

This story of rural-urban division is now well known, but what did these changes mean locally for connections between Zhengzhou and its nearby countryside? In early 1953, Zheng County was dissolved and its more than eight hundred villages brought under municipal control as a new administrative district called simply the Suburbs (Jiaoqu).[131] Relative to more distant rural areas, those in Zhengzhou's expanded "municipal countryside," particularly the vegetable belt around the city, seem to have benefited from proximity to the city. Zhengzhou's urban population growth drove a 2.5-fold increase in the cultivated area for vegetables during the first two years of the Five-Year Plan.[132] Given that vegetables were under less tight state control than grain, producers were able to benefit from rising urban demand—just as in the railroad boom of the first decades of the century. Several vegetable coops became highly profitable enterprises, celebrated nationally in *People's Daily*. Xiaolizhuang, just to the south of Zhengzhou, became the model for vegetable production, with experiments in high-yield varieties and cadres sent to Beijing for specialist training.[133] Available data suggest that unlike in the Republican period, farming households in Zhengzhou enjoyed higher incomes than the regional average.[134]

130. For an interpretive survey of the new food system, see Oi, *State and Peasant in Contemporary China*, 13–65; on the emerging *hukou* system, see Brown, *City Versus Countryside*, 40–52.

131. From this point, my use of "suburbs" in this book follows a shift in contemporary sources and refers to this rural area under municipal administration rather than to the urban fringe. Capitalized "Suburbs" and "Suburban District" refer to this administrative district, which included almost all the villages and farmland in the municipality. Note that the municipality of 1953 was slightly larger than Zheng County, expanding to the west.

132. Zhonggong Henan shengwei ji Zhengzhou shiwei, *Zhengzhou shi gaikuang (neibu wenjian)*, 16. On shifting of grain to outer suburbs, see Zhengzhou shi jiaoqu liangshiju, *Zhengzhou shi jiaoqu zhi: liangshi zhi*, 173–74.

133. *Renmin ribao*, August 7, 1957; Zhengxie Zhengzhou shi Erqiqu weiyuanhui, *Yuanqu zhi jiyi*, 84.

134. Rural net income per capita in Henan in 1957 was an estimated 64 yuan. Sun

However, as even this apparent success story shows, Zhengzhou's "municipal countryside" was placed in an explicitly subordinate role, serving the city and its new industrial economy. In the very first years of Communist rule in Zhengzhou, local propaganda pieces had emphasized the importance of mutual assistance between city and countryside. With the planned economy, the rhetorical emphasis shifted to rural production in the service of the urban economy: "the socialist cities will thus lead the countryside to enter socialist society," readers of *Henan Daily* were told.[135] Farmers around Zhengzhou were urged by deputy mayor Wang Junzhi to achieve "great growth in grains and develop production of vegetables . . . all to supply the needs of the city and support the state's socialist industrialization."[136] Relative to urban residents, who from November 1953 were guaranteed a grain ration, villagers around Zhengzhou were being left behind. Urban wages in Zhengzhou during the first years of the Five-Year Plan were rising almost twice as fast (16 percent per year average) as rural incomes (8.25 percent). In 1956, the disposable per capita incomes for Zhengzhou's urban residents were 2.83 times those of their rural counterparts in the Suburban District. One might expect tightly drawn municipal units such as Zhengzhou to have a smaller rural-urban income gap than China as a whole, but this figure was even worse than the national rural-urban income ratio (2.59 in 1957).[137] The municipal achievements of the period—road building, sewage disposal, expansion of electricity, and finally, in 1956, Zhengzhou's first piped water system—did not reach beyond the city, even though these systems often appropriated rural land and labor in their construction.[138] Similarly, even as Zhengzhou's urban

---

Jianguo, *Xiandai Henan jingjishi*, 146. I have not seen a 1957 estimate for rural per capita net income in Zhengzhou municipality, but the 1956 figure was 80.2. Zhengzhou shi difang shizhi bianzuan weiyuanhui, *Zhengzhou shizhi*, 7:588.

135. *Henan minbao*, November 2, 1954.

136. *Henan minbao*, November 1, 1954.

137. Urban wages in Zhengzhou rose 48 percent, 1952–1955; rural incomes rose 33.1 percent, 1952–1956. Not adjusted for inflation. Zhengzhou shi difang shizhi bianzuan weiyuanhui, *Zhengzhou shizhi*, 7:573. Urban-rural per capita income gap compares *Zhengzhou shizhi*, 7:586 and 588. It should be stressed that raw income figures do not give a full picture of welfare and standards of living in a socialist economy. See Dillon, *Radical Inequalities*.

138. Zhonggong Henan shengwei ji Zhengzhou shiwei, *Zhengzhou shi gaikuang (neibu wenjian)*, 2–3; Zhang Qixian and Wu Xiaoya, *Dangdai Zhengzhou chengshi jianshe*, 58–61. It is true that some intercounty roads gradually crossed Zhengzhou's rural

water supply problem began to be solved, the city's waste water was still being dumped into rivers, leaving downstream rural communities east of Zhengzhou to deal with the toxic consequences.[139]

In the drive for production to serve the city, other economic functions were lost. As Jacob Eyferth shows, the conflation of village life only with agricultural production was a dangerous trend, leading to the loss of handicraft skills and incomes needed to survive difficult times.[140] In Sanguanmiao, on Zhengzhou's new western edge, the end of village cloth manufacture was told in the provincial press as a gender liberation, something to be celebrated: "the once-common spinning wheels and weaving looms have fallen silent, and the women can now also take up a sickle or a hoe."[141] In nearby Songzhuang, villagers who bemoaned the end of cloth manufacture were taken on a tour of the No. 1 Cotton Mill, where "everyone had their ideas straightened out (*dajia kaiqiao le*). . . . Ten women put down their spinners and looms and instead took part in agricultural labor." Only very specific kinds of sidelines closely linked to agriculture and serving the city—in Songzhuang, making tofu to sell to textile workers—were deemed acceptable.[142] After less than a decade of Communist rule, agricultural sidelines as a proportion of rural production around Zhengzhou had slumped by almost a quarter.[143]

In addition to food supply, Zhengzhou's boom was also built on the exploitation of rural labor in the city. This fact is often obscured in local histories, which have tended to concentrate on higher skilled workers from industrial Hubei, Manchuria, and the Lower Yangzi region. There was indeed a significant migration, with at least ten thousand people transferred in the textile sector alone in the first years of the plan.[144] In the long-run pattern of regional inequality in China, such people lost out.

Suburban District, but even here the first all-weather surfaced road (to Mi County) opened only in 1956.

139. See Zhonggong Henan shengwei ji Zhengzhou shiwei, *Zhengzhou shi gaikuang (neibu wenjian)*, 2.

140. Eyferth, *Eating Rice from Bamboo Shoots*.

141. *Henan minbao*, September 30, 1954.

142. *Henan minbao*, September 30, 1954.

143. From 17.5 percent of production to 13.5 percent. Zhengzhou shi jiaoqu zhi bianzuan weiyuanhui, "Zhengzhou shi jiaoqu zhi, nongye zhi," 129–30. As Eyferth also explores, this did not in practice mean the end of rural cloth production. See Eyferth, "Liberation from the Loom?," 144–47.

144. "Zhengzhou Xijiao de bianqian," *Zhengzhou jiyi*, June 21, 2010.

Textile workers from Shanghai took a 20 percent pay cut in what was officially a voluntary move inland; startlingly, by the early twenty-first century, their pension income was only a third of that of former colleagues in Shanghai.[145] But most migration to Zhengzhou was lower paid, often insecure labor from its rural hinterland—just as in its other boom periods of the 1910s and the later reform era. Even in the textile-dominated western suburb, around two-thirds of new residents were from within Henan, largely from rural and small-town backgrounds and some on temporary contracts.[146] Construction firms posted appeals across Henan for temporary contract workers, and migrants could hope to pick up work at the casual labor market just north of the railroad station. Some "temporary" work lasted for years. The expansion of railway yards on the north side of Zhengzhou employed almost three thousand unskilled laborers over several years during the First Five-Year Plan. They were housed in temporary accommodation around the urban edge villages—Damengzhai, Xiaomengzhai, and Xinglongpu—that in the late 1920s had been Feng Yuxiang's model rural district (see map 4.1).[147]

Unlike long-distance migrants or periurban vegetable producers who were lionized in the media, these temporary contract workers are almost invisible in contemporary sources. But this phenomenon underlines the importance of rural-urban mobility in the 1950s, both for China's economy and for individual households, whose long-term fate could rest on spatial strategies during these short years of rapid urban growth. For some, well-timed movement to Zhengzhou could be an opportunity to find a foothold in the city and, for those able to find permanent employment, an urban household registration (*hukou*). Yet even as they were necessary for Zhengzhou's rapid growth, migrant workers discovered that their freedom to move into the city was being curtailed. After a lull in deportations during the frenetic growth of 1953–1954, the arrival of the provincial government put pressure on Zhengzhou to become a model for urban control and remove those coming "blindly" into the city.[148]

145. "Zhengzhou Xijiao de bianqian," *Zhengzhou jiyi*, June 21, 2010.

146. "Zhengzhou Xijiao de bianqian," *Zhengzhou jiyi*, June 21, 2010.

147. On casual labor markets, see Zhao Fuhai, *Lao Zhengzhou: Shangdu yimeng*, 104–5. Local historian Zhao Fuhai spent part of his childhood in these temporary worker camps. See pp. 76–78.

148. See, for instance, Deputy Mayor Wang Junzhi's speech warning against "blind migration" to the new provincial capital. Reproduced in *Henan minbao*, November 1, 1954.

In 1955, with growth and spending beginning to tighten, the municipal government organized a new drive to expel not only beggars but also casual laborers and rural migrants looking for work. But with urban incomes in Zhengzhou some three and a half times the Henan rural average, migrants continued to come into the city, whether for temporary work or, as in 1956, fleeing disaster conditions in rural Henan.[149]

The Anti-Rightist Campaign of 1957 also brought a new clampdown on the mundane business of rural-urban exchange, now mostly criminalized by state monopolies. In the space of six months, police in Zhengzhou uncovered almost three hundred cases of black-market goods being sold in the city by rural producers. Grain, cotton, medicines, and even peanuts were all monopoly goods being sold in the cracks of the planned economy. In one case, nineteen-year-old Chen Benyuan from rural Runan County was found to have been back and forth to Zhengzhou and Beijing seven times in the space of half a year, making so much money he just "lazed around" (*youshou*) smoking all day and refusing to take part in agricultural production. At one guesthouse in the southern fringes of the city, Zhengzhou police found almost one hundred rural visitors carrying out these illicit trades, often with the connivance of whole rural cooperatives.[150] The clampdown of 1957 on longer-distance rural-urban exchange might have benefited some villagers in Zhengzhou's most proximate, diurnal hinterland, who were still able to move to the city on a daily basis.[151] But for most rural residents in Henan, the screw was tightening on movement from countryside to city.

By 1957, Zhengzhou had undergone several rounds of revolution in the twelve years since Japanese surrender. In both 1945 and 1948, Zhengzhou's new regimes began processes of urban design and rural improvement.

---

149. Zhengzhou shi difang shizhi bianzuan weiyuanhui, *Zhengzhou shizhi*, 7:459–61.
150. "Sheng gongxiaoshe dang fenzu guanyu nongcun ziyou shichang hunluan de baogao," September 21, 1957, ZDZYS.
151. Tiejun Cheng and Mark Selden similarly suggest that growing restrictions on migration meant that villages close to the city enjoyed the bulk of the temporary labor opportunities. See Cheng and Selden, "Origins and Social Consequences," 654. It is hard to assess the extent of such travel around Zhengzhou, but it certainly occurred. For example, villagers in Xigangcun traveled into the city throughout the 1950s for casual work, in some cases even making enough money to buy bicycles for the commute. Xigang cunzhi bianzuan weiyuanhui, *Xigang cunzhi*, 186–87.

In both cases, the promise of renewed rural prosperity and beneficial rural-urban relations proved hollow: most damaging for the long term, an urban-centered political economy had emerged by the end of this period. The People's Republic was constructing socialist modernity on the basis of spatial inequality—and, as the case of Kaifeng shows, this inequality occurred between urban areas as well as between city and countryside. The coming of the Great Leap Forward in 1958, with its utopian promises of universal growth and rural-urban unity, threw some of the assumptions of the early planned economy into question and seemed to offer a new start. But, as the next chapter shows, with the rise of rural extraction and subsequent collapse of agricultural production, the Great Leap brought not rural-urban unity but new divisions, extracting a heavy cost in human lives and living standards in rural Henan.

CHAPTER FIVE

The Maoist Model

Utopia and Its Limits, 1958–1978

In 1974 the French spatial theorist Henri Lefebvre praised China's efforts to unify city and countryside. Lefebvre saw under Mao, unlike the staid Soviet Union of Brezhnev, the vision "to draw the people and space in its entirety into the process of building a different society. . . . The dichotomy between town and country with all its attendant conflicts will dissolve thanks to a transformation of both poles."[1] This sentiment is easy to dismiss as willful New Left naïveté, but Lefebvre reflects real strands of egalitarian spatial politics in the two decades after the break with Soviet economic models.

The idea of rural-urban unity had both radical and more cautious iterations. In the first, radical, version, the Great Leap Forward of 1958–1960, collectivization promised to close the rural-urban inequalities that had been preserved and even exacerbated by the planned economy of the 1950s. Zhengzhou was at the forefront of this vision, as capital of the Great Leap's model province and the first city in China to experiment with urban communes. After the retreat from the Leap, China turned to a more cautious route to spatial redistribution by tilting the economy away from urban industry toward the rural sector. From the late 1960s, the countryside around Zhengzhou enjoyed the strongest rise in productivity and incomes yet seen in the twentieth century, while the city faced strict limits on economic growth, population, and wages. At the same time, Zhengzhou's young people were "sent down" to rural areas to take part in agriculture and undergo revolutionary reeducation from China's peasants. Beginning in summer 1968, more than 130,000

1. Lefebvre, *Production of Space*, 421–22.

young people were sent out from Zhengzhou, ostensibly to help bridge the gap between urban and rural life.

Although such impulses to close the rural-urban gap were real, this chapter shows that it was not the dominant mode of spatial politics in these two decades. When other imperatives came to the fore, egalitarian policies to spread resources across space were sidelined. Behind the utopian language of equality, the Great Leap was a ruthless drive to extract from agriculture for the urban industrial sector. The effects on rural citizens were devastating: "villagers starved so that urban dwellers could live," writes Yang Jisheng.[2] In the ensuing famine, somewhere between two and three million people died in Henan, one of the worst-hit provinces in China. Although Zhengzhou's urban residents also faced difficulties, they were largely protected from the devastation of famine by state grain rations. Even the rural turn after 1961 was only a partial rebalancing. Restrictions in the rural sector meant that growth in output around Zhengzhou did not yet translate to economic takeoff, and the experiment of "sent-down" youth ended in frustration and a desperate rush back to urban life. Although no longer a key city in the planned economy, Zhengzhou's urban living standards continued to far outstrip those of even the relatively favored rural areas within its municipal boundary, let alone the rest of its Henan hinterland. Per capita urban incomes in Zhengzhou fluctuated between 2.5 and 3 times those of the municipality's rural residents, and, taking urban welfare systems into account, the gap was wider still.[3]

How do Zhengzhou's spatial politics of this period fit into the bigger picture of the twentieth century? In a narrow sense, they can be understood as contradictions within Chinese socialism, between a revolutionary movement built in rural China and an economic model wedded to the minority interest of state-owned industry. But as this book shows, this pattern is part of a wider story of spatial tension in China's successive modernization projects, between state impulses to connect and equalize across space and the countervailing production of disconnection and spatial inequality. The impulse to connect across space has important parallels in both the Republican and the post-Mao periods. Promoting rural industrialization, encouraging cultivation within the city, sending

2. Yang Jisheng, *Tombstone*, 340.
3. Zhengzhou shi difang shizhi bianzuan weiyuanhui, *Zhengzhou shizhi*, 7:579–93.

young people and technical expertise from city to countryside, fostering exchange between Zhengzhou and its nearby villages: none of these was exclusive to the "High Maoism" of this period. At the same time, the competing and usually dominant impulse of disconnection and spatial prioritization also echoes before and after this period: spatial politics in Zhengzhou were marked across much of the twentieth century by the concentration of economic growth in the city, rural extraction via the fiscal system and/or price scissors, the dominance of an urban political center over smaller towns, a focus on showcase rural projects over wider diffusion of resources, and restrictions on movement (though the last of these was a wartime-only phenomenon before 1949). Although the Great Leap famine carried the heaviest human cost in modern China, it was not an aberration but the most extreme manifestation of longer-running inequalities.

Communism in One City: Communes and Famine in the Great Leap Model

Recent research on the Great Leap Forward and subsequent famine has placed it at the center of PRC history, even the whole trajectory of China's twentieth century. It has also created some understanding of how the Leap years were experienced by urban residents, particularly in Tianjin.[4] But Zhengzhou was the model city of the Leap, driven by the radical provincial leadership of Wu Zhipu (1906–1967).[5] Not only were the first rural communes in Henan, but in August 1958 Zhengzhou was the first city in China to establish communes for urban residents. Between 1958 and 1960, Zhengzhou was visited by almost every important political figure, in a procession never seen before or since: Mao Zedong, Liu Shaoqi, Zhou Enlai, Peng Dehuai, Lin Biao, Peng Zhen, Deng Xiaoping, and Zhu De. Zhengzhou's rural suburbs even became a site for national policy making when Wu hosted the central leadership for two work conferences, constructing a lavish conference

---

4. See, for instance, Thaxton, *Catastrophe and Contention*; Yang Jisheng, *Tombstone*; Manning and Wemheuer, *Eating Bitterness*. On the urban experience in Tianjin, see Brown, "Great Leap City," 226–50; Paltemaa, *Managing Famine, Flood and Earthquake*, 18–91.

5. On Henan's political prestige during the Great Leap, see Heberer and Jakobi, "Henan—the Model," 16–20.

center for the purpose 12 kilometers north of the city. Underlining the Great Leap's separation from rural realities, attendees arrived by a specially constructed railroad, and villagers from nearby Qingzhai and Yangzhuang were kept out by high compound walls.[6]

Zhengzhou is therefore a key site for interrogating the spatial politics of the Leap, a model site for utopian closing of the rural-urban gap but one that as provincial capital of Henan also presided over some of China's worst rural suffering. It exemplifies the contradictions between what was both a state socialist movement of extraction for industry and a communist movement trying to break down divisions between rural and urban, industry and agriculture. The trajectory of the Great Leap, from serious thinking on rural-urban unity to ruthless extraction from the agricultural sector—ending in failure, famine, and retreat—was a key moment in China's spatial politics and, despite the rebalancing toward the rural sector from the end of 1960, enshrined inequalities for the rest of socialist period.

SUMMER OF FIFTY-EIGHT: CONNECTING RURAL AND URBAN IN THE GREAT LEAP

This Great Leap contradiction can be traced to its aims, seeking simultaneously to close the rural-urban gap and to ensure more efficient extraction from the rural economy. Both issues were apparent around Zhengzhou before rural collectivization in summer 1958. Criticism of the authorities highlighted rural poverty. At a cadre training school in late 1957, anonymous "reactionary" big-character posters expressed anxiety about rural conditions: "oppose hunger" (*fan ji'e*) ran one poster; another declared that "we are appealing for justice for the peasants."[7] At the same time, though, municipal officials were anxious about food supplies for an urban population that had almost tripled in the space of five years (from 161,000 in 1952 to 450,000 in 1957). A more moderate agricultural policy from late 1956 had caused problems in Zhengzhou, with authorities expressing concern about the "reverse flow" (*daoliu*) of vegetables from the city to the countryside, where the relaxation of restrictions on

6. Zhao Fuhai, *Lao Zhengzhou: Shangdu yimeng*, 266–72.
7. Chen Jian, "Zhengzhou weisheng di'er ganbu xuexiao zai zhuanru zhengfeng disan jieduan zhong chuxian le daliang de jiduan fandong de dazibao," November 23, 1957, printed in *Neibu cankao*, November 26, 1957, ZDZYS.

marketing had raised rural prices.[8] Henan's radicalism was in part an effort to escape these difficulties. In the second half of 1957, ultraleftist provincial governor Wu Zhipu used the Anti-Rightist Campaign to gain the upper hand over the more moderate provincial party secretary Pan Fusheng (1908–1980). Henan's pioneering wave of collectivization began in April 1958, with experiments in agricultural communes in Suiping County, 170 kilometers south of Zhengzhou.[9] Other parts of the province followed, and on August 6 to 8, Mao Zedong toured Henan and visited rural communes around Zhengzhou. He publicly endorsed rural collectivization a few days later.[10] Five rural communes were established in the Zhengzhou Suburban District (Jiaoqu), each bringing a couple of hundred villages into a single economic unit.

Breaking down barriers between rural and urban was part of the heady cocktail of summer 1958. Zhengzhou's five rural communes were dotted with the ubiquitous "backyard" blast furnaces and other small industrial workshops.[11] The city itself expanded into a wider hinterland, with the municipality absorbing five nearby counties and establishing a new satellite urban district just over 30 kilometers from the city proper. This was Shangjie, centered on a vast aluminum smelting plant (constructed in 1958–1966; for location see map 6.2). Shangjie was the first effort in Zhengzhou to take industry out of the urban area, just one of several such developments running all the way to the "iPhone City" export zone of the 2010s (see chapter 7). During the Great Leap, Shangjie resident He Zhongcha later remembered, there were close connections with villagers, with workers lodged in village households and their children, as in the early days of Zhengzhou's industrial western suburb, attending rural schools (see chapter 4).[12]

The other facet of rural-urban connection in the first phase of the Great Leap was the surge of migration to Zhengzhou. This movement was a rapid about-face from the previous policy of restricting urban population. Beginning in summer 1957, new restrictions on movement

8. *Henan ribao*, August 24, 1958.
9. Wemheuer, *Steinnudeln*, 87–93; Domenach, *Origins of the Great Leap Forward*, 123–27, 149–56.
10. *Henan ribao*, August 12, 1958. Mao's endorsement of rural communes appeared in *Henan ribao* the following day.
11. *Henan ribao*, November 2, 1958.
12. He Zhongcha, "Zhongyuan chuge."

were imposed across China. In Zhengzhou almost three thousand young people were sent to join agricultural production teams in the Suburban District.[13] But in summer 1958 Great Leap industrial investment brought a return of the rapid migration to Zhengzhou seen during the city's boom of the mid-1950s. Over one billion RMB was slated for industrial investment in Zhengzhou (almost twice that of the First Five-Year Plan) in the only moment of truly heavy industry in the city's history. As well as four abortive iron and steel works, Zhengzhou's forty-seven new enterprises included a cable factory and machine works for mining and engineering tools.[14] Zhengzhou's population duly boomed. In 1959, net migration to the city was 148,000 (including temporary work permit holders), with a population increase of 29 percent in a single year. Zhengzhou faced a severe housing shortage.[15]

Zhengzhou's municipal authorities therefore faced the ideological task of bringing together this massive urban industrial expansion with the Great Leap rhetoric of rural-urban unity. In January 1959 Zhengzhou Party Secretary Wang Lizhi (1921–2014) tried to square the circle with the most radical plan in the city's history. Wang proposed replacing much of pre-1949 Zhengzhou with a mixture of agriculture and parks, and dispersing the city's industry to effect the "urbanization of the countryside." Ultimately, the city of Zhengzhou would cease to exist in any recognizable form, with the population scattered into satellite towns, "like many small islands indistinct in a sea of green" (*xiang yigege de xiaodao, yinyue zai lü hai zhong*).[16] A more detailed design later that year built on Wang's ideas, with large wedge-shaped areas of orchards, vegetable plots, and experimental agricultural stations extending into the downtown to "create the conditions for eliminating differences between

13. "Zhengzhou shi zhishi qingnian," 1. On national policy, see Tiejun Cheng, "Dialectics of Control," 105–13.

14. Zhang Qixian and Wu Xiaoya, *Dangdai Zhengzhou chengshi jianshe*, 11–12.

15. Zhengzhou shi difang shizhi bianzuan weiyuanhui, *Zhengzhou shizhi*, 1:353. By way of comparison, Jeremy Brown found that net migration increased Tianjin's (admittedly much larger) population by only 9 percent in the same year. Brown, "Great Leap City," 228. On housing, see Zhang Qixian and Wu Xiaoya, *Dangdai Zhengzhou chengshi jianshe*, 42–45.

16. Wang Lizhi, "Zaitan chengshi renmin gongshe wenti," *Zhongzhou pinglun*, reproduced in *Henan ribao*, January 19, 1959.

city and countryside (*xiaomie chengxiang chabie*)."[17] Neither scheme was realized or sent for formal approval, but this does not mean there was no substantive thinking about how such visions could be realized—indeed, for Wang Lizhi, Zhengzhou already possessed the building blocks for his mixed rural-urban utopia: city communes.

Zhengzhou's Urban Communes

On August 17, 1958, some seventy thousand villagers from around Zhengzhou came into the city for a rally marking the establishment of agricultural communes. The very same evening, eighty thousand city residents paraded down Jiefanglu (Liberation Road) to celebrate the creation of their own urban communes (*chengshi renmin gongshe*)—the very first in China.[18] Historians have recently shown how China's short-lived city communes, overlooked for decades, were a tool for tackling urban contradictions, whether welfare inequalities (Nara Dillon) or the competing imperatives of raising production and improving the lives of poorer city residents (Fabio Lanza).[19] The Zhengzhou case reveals a further friction: the tension between city communes as a mode of urban governance and as a vehicle to close rural-urban divisions.

It is not quite clear why Zhengzhou became the pioneering site for urban collectivization. Janet Salaff attributed it to Zhengzhou's close rural-urban connections, as a city at the heart of an agricultural region that had seen rapid migration in the 1950s.[20] There may be something in this, but city communes would not have occurred without the radicalism of provincial and municipal authorities. Although accounts of the movement from just a few months later emphasize bottom-up spontaneity, the very earliest discussions in 1958 make it clear that the initiative came from the Municipal Party Committee.[21] The first commune was not in the industrial vanguard of Zhengzhou's new textile district but in the oldest and perhaps the poorest area of town: the tightly packed lanes of the northern part of the former walled city, close to Zhengzhou's oldest

17. Zhengzhou shi jianwei guihua guanlichu, "Zhengzhoushi de chengshi guihua," 16.
18. *Henan ribao*, August 18, 1958.
19. Dillon, *Radical Inequalities*, 237–51; Lanza, "Search for a Socialist Everyday."
20. Salaff, "Urban Communes," 90.
21. *Zhengzhoushi zenyang ban chengshi de renmin gongshe*, 1.

mosque and inhabited by many Hui Muslims (see map 1.2). Zheng-zhou's Hui community accounted for 10 percent of the city's population in 1948 but had since been marginalized both demographically by the growth of the city's Han majority and economically by official suspicion of their occupational niches as small traders, shopkeepers, and restaurant owners.[22]

That suspicion of small commercial traders perhaps accounts for the municipal government's push for neighborhood collectivization around Zhengzhou's main mosque. In July 1958, a handicraft cooperative merged with nearby residents' teams to form a "socialist community" (*shehuizhuyi dajiating*) that communalized childcare and cooking and operated small workshops. In mid-August, following Mao's endorsement of rural collec-tivization, the municipal authorities encouraged its rebranding as the Red Flag Commune, claiming three thousand members.[23] Early propaganda for Zhengzhou's communes emphasizes their role in boosting control and production in nonstate parts of the urban economy. Municipal offi-cials heralded the power communes brought over "small workshops, small traders, and individual craftspeople . . . completely eliminating the remaining elements of private production and blocking off (*dusi*) the capitalist road."[24] Given the spatial divisions within Zhengzhou, private economic activity was a particular concern in the pre-1949 parts of the old commercial town, where the new state-owned industry was less import-ant. One celebratory article described a tamed, productive version of the former walled city: "previously, in walking from Shifuqianjie to Dongda-jie or Nandajie, it was full of small vendors selling cigarettes and all kinds of odds and ends, but now it is workshop upon workshop."[25] Within a few days of the establishment of the Red Flag Commune, a second type of urban commune was established, based not on old neighborhoods but on the state-owned firms, government organs, and educational institu-tions of Zhengzhou's post-1949 districts. The stress here was bringing the dependents of state employees into productive activity. The pioneer was

22. Zhu Xiangwu, "Wo zai Zhengzhou shi." On the Muslim community in Zhengzhou, see Aaron Glasserman's recent study of Hui identity and mobilization in Henan, "Hui Nation," esp. 8–13, 73–77.

23. On the "socialist community," see *Henan ribao*, July 26, 1958; on the commune, *Henan ribao*, August 18, 1958.

24. Guo Ronghua, "Zhengzhou shi chengshi renmin gongshe," 20–21.

25. *Henan ribao*, September 26, 1959.

the Textile Machinery Factory (Fangzhi jixiechang), which established a commune with canteens, nurseries, and several small workshops.[26] By September 15, 98 percent of Zhengzhou's residents were urban commune members, at least on paper.[27]

These developments suggest that Zhengzhou's communes were a pragmatic response to problems of both urban governance and production. But urban communes also had a more idealistic aim. It is true that when *Henan Daily* listed the ten benefits of city communes in September 1958, five were concerned with raising production, and four of the rest were connected to political control. The tenth, though, suggested a more utopian goal: "eliminate the differences between city and countryside, industry and agriculture, and manual and intellectual labor."[28] In contrast to the usual mode of state building in the twentieth century, in which efforts to close the rural-urban gap were based on the extension of urban systems and resources to the countryside, Zhengzhou's communes display the unusual phenomenon of the city adopting a rural mode of organization.[29] At least in Zhengzhou, this rural-urban unity was more than just a communist cliché. The large "July First Commune," set up for the dependents of provincial officials, incorporated over 5,000 *mu* of nearby arable land within a few days of its establishment.[30] When Liu Shaoqi visited Zhengzhou in September 1958, he urged the city's communes to incorporate more nearby villages.[31] Liu's advice brought Zhengzhou's fringes to the forefront of experiments in rural-urban unity, perhaps benefiting from the mix of agriculture and industry that already existed at the urban edge (see chapter 4). By summer 1959, Zhengzhou's seventeen city communes encompassed twenty-seven agricultural work teams.[32] On a practical level, one propaganda piece declared, agricultural teams could supply vegetables for the members of the commune, who in

26. *Henan ribao*, August 18, 1958.

27. *Zhengzhoushi zenyang ban chengshi de renmin gongshe*, 1.

28. *Henan ribao*, September 3, 1958.

29. The historian of urban communes Li Duanxiang makes the similar point that, as in the revolution of 1949, agricultural collectivization of summer 1958 meant that cities were "surrounded" from the countryside by rural communes. Li, *Chengshi renmin gongshe yundong*, 257.

30. *Henan ribao*, October 8, 1958.

31. *Henan ribao*, September 21, 1958.

32. Guo Ronghua, "Zhengzhou shi chengshi renmin gongshe," 20.

turn could help when labor was needed in the fields. On a theoretical level, it "had great significance as a condition for the establishment of communism (*gongchanzhuyi chuangzao tiaojian*)."[33]

Zhengzhou's commune experiment was quickly replicated in other cities, especially in radical Henan but also in far-flung Guiyang, Tianjin, and Harbin. Yet, by the beginning of 1959, this first phase of city communes had run out of steam. News of Zhengzhou's urban communes virtually disappeared from local media, which admitted that they were "not yet very well consolidated" (*shangwei hen hao gonggu*).[34] These problems were partly due to internal failings in the urban commune system. Even in radical Zhengzhou, where urban communes had some political momentum, they achieved little real collectivization, and commune workshops were dogged by low investment, productivity, and output quality. In 1959 the total production by value of Zhengzhou's commune workshops was only 24 percent higher than cooperative workshops had achieved in 1957—despite much higher labor inputs.[35] As Party Secretary Wang Lizhi admitted, Zhengzhou's communes had struggled to establish an independent financial base or effective system of wages, or work out how they interacted with work unit services and municipal administration. As one internal report noted, local power remained in the hands of state-owned industries, which used their administrative dominance over urban communes in Zhengzhou to obtain cheap services and components from commune workshops without needing to take financial or welfare responsibility for commune workers (fig. 5.1).[36]

These early problems in urban communes might have been tackled but for a political shift away from city communes and the immediate ambition of rural-urban unity. When Tan Zhenlin (1902–1983), patron of Henan's radicalism at the party center, asked Mao Zedong his view on urban communes, the chairman was noncommittal.[37] The Wuchang

33. *Zhengzhou shi zenyang ban chengshi de renmin gongshe*, 15 and 27.

34. *Henan ribao*, June 2, 1959.

35. *Henan ribao*, April 26, 1960.

36. Wang Lizhi, "Zaitan chengshi renmin gongshe wenti," *Zhongzhou pinglun*, reproduced in *Henan ribao*, January 19, 1959. For the national picture, see "Quanguo chengshi renmin gongshe qingkuang diaocha," *Neibu cankao*, March 25, 1960, ZDZYS. For more on low wages and the benefits of low-wage commune workshops for state-owned enterprises, see Li Duanxiang, *Chengshi renmin gongshe yundong*, 212–19.

37. Li Duanxiang, *Chengshi renmin gongshe yundong*, 223.

Figure 5.1. Red Flag Commune workshop using waste products from cotton mills to produce MSG, 1960. *Henan xinwen,* available at https://www.ktmxneb.cn/55754.html, accessed March 31, 2023.

Conferences in November–December 1958 gave only a cautious endorsement of the experiment, passing a resolution noting that "there are differences between city and countryside." Amid the greater complexity of urban areas, the resolution stated, some residents had reservations about city communes—not that such misgivings had prevented the headlong rush to rural collectivization.[38] By the beginning of 1959, the impulse to close rural-urban division had been laid aside amid the need to maintain rural-urban difference for the purposes of agricultural extraction. This shift in spatial politics had devastating consequences. I do not intend to rehabilitate utopian thinking in the Great Leap, which was so culpable in its failure, nor to suggest that a blending of rural and urban economies could have been achieved through collectivization. It was clear by 1959 that China simply did not have the resources for simultaneous rural and urban growth, for radical equalization *and* industrial takeoff. But the response to that realization—abandoning the former to maintain the latter—was catastrophic. Had a stronger ethos of unity between city and

38. Wuchang resolution reproduced in *Henan ribao*, December 19, 1958.

countryside survived into 1959, the wavering Mao Zedong might have rowed back from the drive for grain procurement. Instead, as reaffirmed at the Lushan Conference that summer, the energies of the Leap were now more narrowly concentrated on agricultural extraction to fuel urban industry, with catastrophic consequences for Henan's rural citizens.

FAMINE GEOGRAPHY: PROVINCIAL SPACES

The Great Leap famine in Henan was deeper, longer lasting, and more widespread than the wartime famine of 1942–1943. The province was one of the worst hit in China. Henan suffered the third worst collapse in food production (1958–1961) and the fourth worst fall in rural grain availability per capita (1958–1962).[39] Official population figures, as extrapolated by Yang Jisheng, point to 1.70 million famine deaths, but Yang himself thinks this figure is too low. Felix Wemheuer estimates more than 2 million, whereas Cao Shuji calculates a figure of 2.94 million. In Cao's figures, Henan ranks as the third worst province for famine deaths (sixth worst as a proportion of population).[40]

What does the distribution of famine *within* Henan reveal about the spatial politics of the Great Leap? The most striking pattern is that of rural-urban inequality, even compared with elsewhere in China. After state procurement and transfers, average per capita grain availability in Henan's nonagricultural (i.e., mostly urban) sector was 80.5 percent higher than in rural communes. These are raw figures for state-controlled grain and do not mean that calorific intake was as much as 80 percent higher in Henan's cities, but they do suggest some of the worst inequalities in

39. On grain production, see Walker, *Agricultural Development*, 119; on rural grain availability per capita in Henan, see Ash, "Squeezing the Peasants," 997. This amounted to 582 grams per rural person per day before procurement and 496 grams per day after procurement (average across five years, 1958–1962). These figures are higher than my estimate of 1942–1943 per capita food availability in Nationalist-held Henan (312 grams per person per day before requisitioning, 267 grams per day after requisitioning) but were sustained over a much longer period. They are far below the 750 grams Robert Ash calculates was required for "basic human food consumption needs." See Ash, "Squeezing the Peasants," 972. By 1961, the figure in Henan was down to 380 grams per person per day. See Yang Jisheng, *Tombstone*, 399–400. These data also conceal important distributional differences. See Meng, Qian, and Yared, "Institutional Causes of China's Great Famine."

40. Yang Jisheng, *Tombstone*, 83–84 and 394–96; Wemheuer, *Steinnudeln*, 1.

China, where the nationwide grain gap was much lower (29.5 percent).[41] This pattern is mirrored in mortality. In the devastating year of 1960, Henan's rural death rate was more than double its urban counterpart, a worse disparity than for any province apart from neighboring Anhui.[42] That year, the rate of absolute population loss across Henan was 25.6 per thousand. In the urban districts of Zhengzhou, by contrast, the natural population change (i.e., excluding migration) saw a similar-sized increase (26.1 per thousand).[43] The famine hardly registers in the city's demographic data, apart from a marked (27 percent) fall in births during 1961 compared with the pre-Leap average, itself much less than the 51 percent drop in nearby rural counties.[44]

Through work unit and neighborhood rationing systems, Zhengzhou's urban residents received a sufficient—if far from lavish—food supply. By the end of the famine period, more than twelve thousand people in the city were surviving on direct welfare support from the municipality.[45] By contrast, the state abrogated responsibility for residents of rural communes. As in 1942, when the Nationalist authorities prioritized feeding soldiers and left farmers to their own fate, the state sacrificed rural citizens to fuel a hungry campaign, in the Great Leap case, a campaign not of war but of industrialization. The crucial difference is that the Nationalist authorities switched from extraction to relief in the spring of 1943; by contrast, the Communist state was more ruthless than its predecessor in extracting (nonexistent) surpluses over several harvests. By the second year of crisis, the Nationalist authorities had changed tack, but in summer 1959 there was little sign of a similar shift; instead, the policies resulting in famine were lucidly explained in the Henan press: "Nowadays there are people who say, 'Could the state procure a bit less grain and leave a bit more with the peasants?' That sounds good and on the surface would be good for both the state and the peasants, but in fact it is unworkable (*xingbutong*). Everyone knows, following the major advances in state industry, the popu-

---

41. Calculated from Walker, *Agricultural Development*, 139–43. Only Hebei shows a higher rural-urban grain gap.

42. Walker, *Agricultural Development*, 116.

43. On Henan, see Wemheuer, *Steinnudeln*, 102; on Zhengzhou, see Zhang Qixian and Wu Xiaoya, *Dangdai Zhengzhou chengshi jianshe*, 236.

44. Calculated from Zhengzhou shi difang shizhi bianzuan weiyuanhui, *Zhengzhou shizhi*, 1:350–51.

45. Zhengzhou shi difang shizhi bianzuan weiyuanhui, *Zhengzhou shizhi*, 7:453.

lation in cities and in mining areas has risen rapidly . . . all making large demands of the state for grain."[46] The next month, Mao renewed Great Leap radicalism at the Lushan Conference and plunged much of rural China into the devastating famine winter of 1959–1960.

Beyond rural-urban disparities, the regional distribution of famine in Henan also points to deeply unequal spatial politics. The famine in Henan was at its worst on the edges of the province. As Anthony Garnaut points out for China as a whole, semiperipheral but well-connected agricultural districts—that before the famine usually had a surplus and from which grain could easily be removed—were worst hit.[47] In Henan, it was rural areas around Nanyang in the southwest, Shangqiu in the east, and especially Xinyang in the south, all of which had escaped relatively lightly in 1942–1943, that were worst hit during the Great Leap disaster. It is perhaps not a coincidence that these were the same semiperipheral areas that had been zones of Communist Party strength between the 1920s and 1940s.[48] In Xinyang, under the control of radical cadres, more than a million people died during the desperate winter of 1959–1960 alone. By contrast, the provincial core around Zhengzhou, Luoyang, and Kaifeng was less hard hit.[49] Comparing average death rates of preceding years with the Great Leap famine, I calculate that the six rural counties around Zhengzhou saw just over ten thousand excess deaths.[50]

Henan's rural-urban and regional inequalities during the Great Leap famine were exacerbated by restrictions on movement of people and grain. More than bureaucratic overreach, these restrictions were at the heart of a rigid politics where access to food was tied to a particular place. In Henan's 1942–1943 disaster, mobility had been a key survival strategy, even if famine refugees were not always permitted to enter walled cities. By contrast, in 1959–1961, migration and access to grain were strictly controlled by the *hukou* system, and the charitable relief and market

46. *Henan ribao*, June 17, 1959. Felix Wemheuer calculates that the number of people receiving state grain in Henan had more than doubled in 1958 alone, from 1.1 to 2.4 million. Wemheuer, *Steinnudeln*, 97.

47. Garnaut, "Geography of the Great Leap Famine," 323.

48. Wou, *Mobilizing the Masses*, 383–84.

49. Garnaut, "Geography of the Great Leap Famine," 323–24. For a chilling account of Xinyang, see Yang Jisheng, *Tombstone*, 23–86.

50. Calculated from Zhengzhou shi difang shizhi bianzuan weiyuanhui, *Zhengzhou shizhi*, 1:350–51.

opportunities that had helped some famine migrants in 1942–1943 were largely absent.[51] In March 1959 the Central Committee ordered anyone entering a city without permission to be detained and repatriated— though this did not prevent people trying. In 1960 alone, an average of more than five hundred people were arriving in Zhengzhou every day and being deported to their places of origin.[52]

FAMINE GEOGRAPHY: SUBURBAN SPACES

The Great Leap famine in Henan was therefore driven by regional inequality, rural-urban division, and restricted movement, all in the name of industrial takeoff. But what were the spatial politics of famine at a more local level, in the villages around Zhengzhou (map 5.1)? Although there are now urban histories of the Great Leap famine, there has been little focus on or effort to quantify shortages in the immediate proximity of cities.[53] Did the experience of those in the Suburban District of Zhengzhou mirror the city or the wider Henan countryside? Did proximity to the city help or hinder Zhengzhou's nearby farmers?

Zhengzhou's Suburbs were badly hit by the dramatic falls in grain production during the Great Leap. Zhengzhou Municipality was something of a laggard in the overreporting frenzy of 1958, and was therefore supposed to achieve a fivefold increase in grain production in 1959.[54] Instead, data from the Suburban District Grain Bureau suggest that output in the Suburban District fell by 30 percent (compared with 22.9

51. On the foreclosure of famine survival strategies during the Great Leap, see Thaxton, *Catastrophe and Contention*, 157–97. Kathryn Edgerton-Tarpley shows that some relief strategies that had been successful in CCP-controlled areas during 1942–1943 were "disastrous" when deployed during the Great Leap: urging people not to flee, mobilizing disaster victims for productive projects, and promoting a "fervent faith in the power of the masses to save themselves." See Edgerton-Tarpley, "Saving the Nation?," 348–59, quote on p. 359.

52. On central government policy, see Yang Jisheng, *Tombstone*, 50; on Zhengzhou, see Zhengzhou shi difang shizhi bianzuan weiyuanhui, *Zhengzhou shizhi*, 7:460. Jeremy Brown reports similar numbers per day at Tianjin Railway Station. *City Versus Countryside*, 59.

53. The Great Leap studies of Tianjin mostly discuss its twelve subordinate counties rather than its suburban countryside. See Brown, *City Versus Countryside*, 53–76. There is some information on Tianjin's rural suburbs in Paltemaa, *Managing Famine, Flood and Earthquake*, 18–91.

54. *Henan ribao*, September 23, 1958.

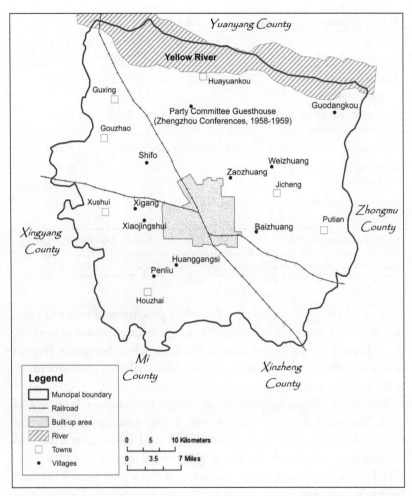

MAP 5.1. Zhengzhou Municipality in the Mao period. Adapted from Zhengzhou shi lianhe yunshu bangongshi, "Zhengzhou jiaotong tu" [Transport map of Zhengzhou] 郑州交通图, 1970. Map by Jogu Gopinath.

Table 5.1: Grain output during the Great Leap Forward (in tons)

	China-wide	Henan Province	Zhengzhou Suburbs
Average annual grain output, 1953–1957	181.6 million	11.75 million	74,850
Average annual grain output, 1958–1962	160.4 million	9.43 million	53,160
Grain output, 1961	136.5 million	6.85 million	33,260
1958–1962 as a percentage of 1953–1957	88.3	80.3	71.0
1961 as a percentage of 1953–1957	75.2	58.26	44.4

Source: China-wide and Henan Province figures from Ash, "Squeezing the Peasants," 994–95 (1953–1957 and 1958–1962 averages); Walker, *Agricultural Development*, 119–21 (1961). Suburban data from Zhengzhou shi jiaoqu liangshiju, *Zhengzhou shi jiaoqu zhi: liangshi zhi*, 77.

percent for the province as a whole), while procurement rose from 26.3 percent to 31.5 percent of the crop.[55] Taking the Leap period as a whole, the collapse in grain production in the Zhengzhou Suburban District compares unfavorably with provincial and national averages, particularly at the nadir of grain production in 1961 (table 5.1).

This bleak picture of production was partly attributable to loss of land. Zhengzhou's closest villages were hit by land requisitioning for the rapidly expanding city. Between 1958 and 1960, more land was requisitioned than in the whole of the urban boom of the First Five-Year Plan. Compensation was slashed, and for a brief period between November 1958 and January 1959, rural communes received no payment at all for lost land.[56] The collapse of grain output around Zhengzhou may also have been exacerbated both by a rise in vegetable production at the expense of grains and by the failure of an ambitious irrigation project to convert part of the northern suburbs to rice paddy (which failed because of the heavy silt content of water drawn from the Yellow River).[57] But reduction of grain area only accounts for around a third

55. Zhengzhou shi jiaoqu liangshiju, *Zhengzhou shi jiaoqu zhi: liangshi zhi*, 77; provincial figure from Walker, *Agricultural Development*, 121.
56. Zhengzhou shi difang shizhi bianzuan weiyuanhui, *Zhengzhou shizhi*, 3:171–73.
57. Zhengzhou shi difang shizhi bianzuan weiyuanhui, *Zhengzhou shizhi*, 1:117. The scheme was totally abandoned in 1964.

of the fall in production. Total grain output in the 1961 nadir fell to 44 percent of the 1953–1957 average, but yields per *mu* also collapsed, to 64 percent of pre-Leap levels.[58] By 1960, three-quarters of rural brigades in the Zhengzhou suburbs were officially categorized as short of food. Twenty brigades south of the city were the hardest hit, but edema was widespread across the whole Suburban District.[59] The next year, preprocurement grain availability in Zhengzhou's rural suburbs was down to 108.5 kilograms per person per year, or around a thousand calories per day. This level compares unfavorably with both the provincial averages for that year (138.8 kilograms) and the desperate drought year of 1942 (113.9 kilograms).[60]

This precipitous decline in food availability raises the question of why so few residents of Zhengzhou's rural suburbs seem to have died of famine-related causes. Local data suggest that the city and its rural Suburban District together—they are not separated in mortality figures—suffered "only" a few hundred excess deaths during the famine period. Even in 1960, when Henan's population suffered an absolute fall of 1.6 million, the rural population in Zhengzhou's Suburban District continued to grow slightly.[61] There are several tentative answers to this conundrum. Zhengzhou's very closest villages benefited from having one foot in the urban sector, coming under the administration of urban districts and forming agricultural production teams under urban communes. Local administrative records suggest that thirty-seven natural villages, around 5 percent of Zhengzhou's total, fell into that category during 1959–1960.[62] For villages farther out, in the ordinary rural communes of the Zhengzhou Suburban District, three other explanations point to the advantages of proximity to the city.

First, Zhengzhou's suburban communes were usually net recipients

58. Zhengzhou shi jiaoqu liangshiju, *Zhengzhou shi jiaoqu zhi: liangshi zhi*, 77.

59. Zhengzhou shi jiaoqu minzheng zhi bianxie zu, "Zhengzhou shi jiaoqu minzheng zhi," 6:34–35.

60. Calculated from Zhengzhou shi jiaoqu liangshiju, *Zhengzhou shi jiaoqu zhi: liangshi zhi*, 77. On 1942, see chapter 3, note 75, in this book.

61. Mortality figures in Zhengzhou shi difang shizhi bianzuan weiyuanhui, *Zhengzhou shizhi*, 1:351. Suburban rural population is from Zhengzhou shi jiaoqu zhi bianzuan weiyuanhui, "Zhengzhou shi jiaoqu zhi, nongye zhi," 92. Provincial comparison is from Walker, *Agricultural Development*, 117.

62. Zhengzhou shi jiaoqu minzheng zhi bianxie zu, "Zhengzhou shi jiaoqu minzheng zhi," 2:14.

from grain transfers. In four out of five years during the Leap (1958–1962), Zhengzhou's Suburban District received more grain in resales to communes (*tongxiao*) than had been procured, which brought per capita food availability from below the Henan rural average to a little (4 percent) above. In the crucial year of 1961, this influx of state grain raised nominal daily per capita food availability from a starvation level of less than 1,000 calories to around 1,250 calories, and must have played a vital role in limiting famine deaths.[63] But the marketing of state grain to Zhengzhou's rural suburbs is not enough on its own to explain the absence of widespread starvation-related deaths. Even after this redistribution, per capita grain availability in Zhengzhou's rural suburbs in 1961 was still nearly a quarter below the national average (76.4 percent).[64] In addition, these grain resales were not evenly distributed, with most earmarked for vegetable production teams, which were mostly close to the city and whose members at least in theory enjoyed higher grain entitlements than their grain-producing counterparts.[65]

Second, then, Zhengzhou's Suburban District received separate support from the municipal government in addition to *tongxiao* grain transfers. As early as May 1959, when it became clear that the wheat harvest was well below expectations, a 500,000 RMB municipal fund was set up to support grain-deficient brigades, with just over 20,000 RMB sent immediately to help the poorest rural residents. A further 368,000 yuan followed across 1960 and 1961.[66] These are not large sums relative to rural deprivation, but this support suggests that there were political imperatives to avoid mass starvation in the outskirts of the provincial capital—especially of a model province, a suburban site for dozens of foreign delegations.[67]

63. Calculated from Zhengzhou shi jiaoqu liangshiju, *Zhengzhou shi jiaoqu zhi: liangshi zhi*, 77.

64. Comparing Ash, "Squeezing the Peasants," 975, with Zhengzhou shi jiaoqu liangshiju, *Zhengzhou shi jiaoqu zhi: liangshi zhi*, 77.

65. Zhengzhou shi jiaoqu liangshiju, *Zhengzhou shi jiaoqu zhi: liangshi zhi*, 78. In Xigang, a vegetable-producing area close to the city, villagers received up to 250 grams per day in *tongxiao* grain during the worst period of famine. Xigang cunzhi bianzuan weiyuanhui, *Xigang cunzhi*, 213.

66. Zhengzhou shi jiaoqu zhi bianzuan weiyuanhui, "Zhengzhou shi jiaoqu zhi, nongye zhi," 23 (1959) and 119 (1960). On 1961, see Zhengzhou shi jiaoqu minzheng zhi bianxie zu, "Zhengzhou shi jiaoqu minzheng zhi," 6:57.

67. Zhengzhou's Suburban District received fifty-eight foreign delegations in

Third, proximity to the city also brought opportunities not readily available to most rural people in Henan. In the slight retreat from ultraradicalism in the first half of 1959, Zhengzhou municipality restored tiny private plots across the Suburban District—a policy only patchily employed elsewhere. Villagers in Xigang remembered that "from that time food wasn't too much of a problem, and life gradually got a bit better (*jianjian hao yixie*)."[68] Similarly, proximity to the city gave at least some opportunity for rural-urban movement and exchange. From 1958, the former *jianghu* neighborhood of Laofengang turned into a black-market site for the sale of fruit, vegetables, sweet potatoes, and grain between the city and nearby villages. Local historian Zhao Fuhai suggests that the municipal authorities turned a blind eye to such activity.[69] In Xigang, thirteen-year-old Cao Donghuan (b. 1947) made straw baskets to sell outside Zhengzhou railway station to help feed her family.[70] Even in the contracting economy of 1960, some short-term labor opportunities were available in the city. In the agricultural off-season, while other villagers were scavenging for grasses along the Yellow River, some 70 percent of carts from Zhengzhou's suburban rural communes were brought to the city to be used in haulage work.[71]

These opportunities may have softened the stark rural-urban divide around Zhengzhou, but they did not remove it altogether. As this discussion has shown, Zhengzhou's Suburban District operated in a very different political economy from the city and was still left in dire straits by state mismanagement and urban bias. The edge of Zhengzhou was on the front line of this rural-urban division, as underlined in a description from the unlikely source of Richard Crossman, staunch anticommunist of the British Labour Party, who visited in the early phase of the

---

1958 alone, though the number probably fell in the following years. Zhengzhou shi jiaoqu zhi bianzuan weiyuanhui, "Zhengzhou shi jiaoqu zhi, nongye zhi," 22. But it was still something of a showcase. Sympathetic foreigners were still being shown rural communes in the Zhengzhou Suburbs in 1960. See Greene, *Awakened China*, 154–79.

68. Xigang cunzhi bianzuan weiyuanhui, *Xigang cunzhi*, 28. On the policy across the whole Suburban District, see Zhengzhou shi jiaoqu zhi bianzuan weiyuanhui, "Zhengzhou shi jiaoqu zhi, nongye zhi," 117.

69. Zhao Fuhai, *Lao Zhengzhou: Shangdu yimeng*, 195 and 203.

70. Xigang cunzhi bianzuan weiyuanhui, *Xigang cunzhi*, 252.

71. Zhengzhou shi jiaoqu minzheng zhi bianxie zu, "Zhengzhou shi jiaoqu minzheng zhi," 6:35.

Leap: while being driven northwest to Guxing Commune, Crossman found himself in "another world, bouncing over perilous wooden bridges and pounding across endless low fields of cotton and maize. . . . It may only be twenty kilometers from Chengchow, but it has taken us fifty-five minutes of hard motoring and we might as well be in the middle of Central Africa."[72] Although for Crossman Guxing seemed impossibly remote, for those in Zhengzhou's rural suburbs, proximity to the city brought Great Leap conditions a little better than most in Henan, with a more secure food position than their counterparts on the hard-hit peripheries of the province.

Retreat and Rebalancing

The retreat from the Great Leap was a multistage process, from cuts in urban investment and food consumption in 1960 to the scaling back of rural collectivization in 1961 and the criticisms of Mao at the "Seven Thousand Cadres" conference in January–February 1962. These steps tilted the planned economy toward the rural sector, bringing lower gain procurement and a revival in agricultural production. In terms of Zhengzhou's spatial politics, these years were much more than just an interregnum between radical campaigns, a prelude to the Cultural Revolution. For Zhengzhou as a model radical city during the Leap, the retreat of 1960–1962 was particularly sharp, and the city fell from its short-lived fame: having been mentioned in *People's Daily* almost every day during 1958–1960, Zhengzhou featured only a few times per month in the post-Leap period.[73] This national prominence only returned when the State Council designated Zhengzhou a "National Central City" in 2016. In terms of rural-urban relations, the retreat from the Leap established a pattern that endured through the late 1970s. This post-Leap spatial distribution was less unequal than in the previous decade, with urban investment, incomes, and consumption all held down in the planned economy. However, the underlying dualism and inequalities between the city and its hinterland remained in place. The agenda of rural-urban

72. Crossman, "China Notebook," 19–20.

73. Zhengzhou was mentioned in *Renmin ribao* an average 329 times per year in 1958–1960, compared with 68 times per year in 1963–1965. Although this decrease is partly due to the smaller size of the post-Leap paper, by way of comparison, the number of mentions of Shanghai fell by less than half.

integration so prominent in the early Leap was largely off the table until its return, in a very different idiom, in the early twenty-first century.

Despite appalling famine conditions in the 1959–1960 winter, 1960 began with renewed efforts to maintain the Great Leap agenda. One of these policies was the curious revival of the urban commune experiment, which kept Zhengzhou in the national spotlight. After a near silence during most of 1959, in March 1960 city communes were endorsed by the Central Committee and the National People's Congress.[74] As communes spread across China's cities, in many cases for the first time, Zhengzhou's pioneering communes were subject to the attention that had been stifled by Mao's caution on urban communes in November 1958. The original Red Flag Commune was the subject of a lavish spread in *China Pictorial*, claiming 150,000 members and over a thousand workshops.[75] But for all the propaganda, the revival of city communes looks like a desperate strategy to cope with the consequences of catastrophic economic failure without abandoning the politics of the Leap altogether. Rather than a vision of rural-urban integration, the National People's Congress view of city communes entailed a doubling of output in neighborhood workshops to take the pressure off larger-scale state industry, with its higher demand for inputs.[76] Indicatively, the most high-profile visitors to Zhengzhou's urban communes in 1960 were Deng Xiaoping and Peng Zhen, soon to emerge as leaders of the post-Leap economic strategy.[77]

Insofar as Zhengzhou's city communes did foster rural-urban integration in the latter stages of the Great Leap, it was only via a sign of desperation: the mobilization of urban residents for food production. Mobilization had begun in late 1959, when provincial official and former Zhengzhou mayor Song Zhihe urged the city's residents to grow vegetables and even grain, promoting the slogan "self-reliance first; strive to

74. *Henan ribao*, March 31, 1960; Li Duanxiang, *Chengshi renmin gongshe yundong*, 88–103.

75. "Red Flag Commune Sets the Pace." The Red Flag Commune had—at least on paper—subsumed virtually all nonstate production in Zhengzhou.

76. National People's Congress 1960 economic plan, reproduced in *Henan ribao*, March 31, 1960.

77. *Henan ribao*, February 19, 1960. When Mao Zedong visited a few months later, he did not visit Zhengzhou's urban communes, inspecting only the wheat harvest at the nearby village of Yanzhuang. *Henan ribao*, May 12, 1960.

make outside assistance secondary (*waiyuan wei fu*)."[78] By the following spring, Zhengzhou's Red Flag Commune had almost a fifth of its urban workforce in agricultural production.[79] When the sympathetic American journalist Edgar Snow visited Zhengzhou later in the year, he was struck by the amount of space devoted to this task: "most of the new streets are broad and . . . principal highways are divided by parklike esplanades all of which are now being used as vegetable gardens."[80] The breaking down of rural-urban barriers, a communist hope of 1958, now meant little more than city residents trying to supplement their own dwindling rations. In 1961, Zhengzhou's work units, schools, and even military units were grabbing spare space in the city to grow vegetables and grain. Some 13,000 *mu* was found for food production on these parcels of land.[81] By then China's urban communes, which had kickstarted this food production drive, were themselves a dead letter. As part of the retreat from the Great Leap, from summer 1961 it was official policy that smaller cooperatives were preferable to communes in nonstate urban production.[82] Early in 1962, Zhengzhou's Guancheng District, which had been a single commune, restored subdistricts and eliminated the commune as the local administrative unit. That May, a party directive announced that any remaining communes "should in essence be disbanded."[83]

The winding down of urban communes was just part of the retreat from Great Leap collectivization. The solution that *Henan Daily* had declared "unworkable" in June 1959 proved the only way out: reduce the number of people receiving state grain, cut industrial investment, and improve terms of trade for the agricultural sector. Urban grain rations fell in Zhengzhou for the first time in September 1960, although they remained above food availability in the rural suburbs.[84] As across rural China, Zhengzhou's suburban communes were reduced in size (from five

78. *Henan ribao*, November 6, 1959. Urban food production is discussed in more detail in Paltemaa, "Serve the City!"

79. *Henan ribao*, April 7, 1960.

80. Snow, *Red China Today*, 494.

81. Zhengzhou shi difang shizhi bianzuan weiyuanhui, *Zhengzhou shizhi*, 1:126.

82. Wang Junwei, "Dui chengshi renmin gongshe lishi," 33–34.

83. Li Duanxiang, *Chengshi renmin gongshe yundong*, 266.

84. The cut was around 10 percent, depending on age, gender, and occupational status. See Zhengzhou shi jiaoqu liangshiju, *Zhengzhou shi jiaoqu zhi: liangshi zhi*, 82–84.

to thirty-eight communes), purchase prices for grain were raised by over a fifth (in May 1961), and household plots were enlarged (in November 1961).[85] These shifts brought major changes to the spatial distribution of resources in the planned economy. In the Zhengzhou Suburban District, grain procurement remained under 10 percent of the crop from 1961 all the way to the end of the Mao era, even as production recovered.[86] In Henan, the rural-urban grain availability gap dropped from a nominal 80 percent during the Great Leap to just 21.5 percent by 1962—and these figures do not include additional rural consumption from private plots.[87] Diagnosing a lack of rural-urban material exchange (just as they had during the civil war in 1948), the provincial government also expanded the very limited markets permitted in 1959 and allowed rural people into cities to sell meat, eggs, tofu, and fruit. Strikingly, there were still restrictions on movement for trade across county-level boundaries, but such limits helped those in Zhengzhou's rural suburbs, who being within the municipal boundary could enter the city without such restrictions.[88]

The corollary of revival in the agricultural economy was a downsizing of the urban sector. Economic planner Chen Yun aimed for the relocation of more than twenty million people to rural areas.[89] As a Great Leap boomtown, Zhengzhou was hit earlier and harder than most cities. According to Mayor Wang Junzhi, 145,000 people were forced to return to their place of origin in 1961 alone, mostly rural migrants who had moved to the city in the early phase of the Leap.[90] By 1962 Zhengzhou's population had fallen by 20.1 percent since 1960, twice the rate of decline in the national urban population as a whole. At half a million residents, Zhengzhou was almost the same size as before the Leap.[91] Behind the statistics lie human stories of missed opportunity. Liu Junfu was a third-

85. Sun Jianguo, *Xiandai Henan jingjishi*, 139–41.
86. Zhengzhou shi jiaoqu liangshiju, *Zhengzhou shi jiaoqu zhi: liangshi zhi*, 77.
87. Walker, *Agricultural Development*, 139–42.
88. Sun Jianguo, *Xiandai Henan jingjishi*, 151–52.
89. Brown, *City Versus Countryside*, 84.
90. Xiao Feng and Wang Junzhi, "Wushi niandai qianqi Zhengzhou shi," 92.
91. Zhengzhou shi difang shizhi bianzuan weiyuanhui, *Zhengzhou shizhi*, 1:357. Yin-Wang Kwok estimates a 10% fall in the urban population between 1960 and 1962 (13.2 million net reduction of an urban population of 130 million). Kwok, "Trends of Urban Planning and Development," 154. This figure tallies with Jeremy Brown's estimates, which are a little higher but are migration figures only (i.e., they do not include the 1962 boom in urban births). Brown, *City Versus Countryside*, 105–6.

year student at Zhengzhou Construction Engineering College when in autumn 1961 the whole school was closed as part of urban downsizing and its students returned to their places of origin. More than half of the class, including Liu, were rural *hukou* holders, and, when classes resumed in 1962, only students with urban household registration were permitted to return. Liu's home at Houzhai was only 9 kilometers from town, today just outside Zhengzhou's fourth ring road, but for the rest of his working life he was unable to jettison his rural registration.[92]

Zhengzhou's urban retreat was about more than just population cuts. Capital construction investment in Henan fell by three quarters in 1961, and Zhengzhou's shift toward heavy industry was stopped in its tracks.[93] Work on existing projects was put on hold, such as at the Shangjie aluminum plant, where construction stopped completely for more than a year, and production began only in 1966. The grinding wheel factory on Zhengzhou's western edge was also hit by long delays, although its East German technical staff did stay behind—the only foreign team remaining in the whole of China following the Soviet withdrawal in summer 1960—and the plant finally opened in late 1964.[94] In spatial terms, too, the tilt to the rural reduced the reach of the city. Work units had requisitioned over four thousand acres of land for construction projects during the Leap, many of which were never completed or even begun. In summer 1962 the municipal authorities began a drive formally to restore them to agriculture, and by the end of the year, 95 percent of unused land earmarked for urban expansion was back with rural production teams.[95] Suburban villages that had been brought under urban administration in 1958 were also returned to rural communes: twelve villages on the west side of the city in October 1961 and a further thirty-nine to the north and east in 1963.[96] Finally, the 1958 experiment of municipal control over nearby counties was quietly dropped in December 1961 and only revived under much the same principle—Zhengzhou pulling along

92. *Dahebao*, December 24, 2007.

93. Sun Jianguo, *Xiandai Henan jingjishi*, 140.

94. See Tao Chen, "Weathering the Storms."

95. Much of this land had already been used by urban work units for vegetable production. See Zhengzhou shi jiaoqu zhi bianzuan weiyuanhui, "Zhengzhou shi jiaoqu zhi, nongye zhi," 26–27.

96. Zhengzhou shi jiaoqu minzheng zhi bianxie zu, "Zhengzhou shi jiaoqu minzheng zhi," 2:13; Zhengzhou shi difang shizhi bianzuan weiyuanhui, *Zhengzhou shizhi*, 1:406.

its rural hinterland—more than twenty years later under the reform era regime.[97]

This multifaceted urban retreat lowered pressure on the rural economy but in some ways left divisions as deep as ever. Although urban wages were stagnant from 1957 onwards and China's overall rural-urban gap was falling slightly in the early 1960s, local data from 1965 suggest that the per capita income gap between Zhengzhou and its rural suburbs— admittedly, raw income figures are only a partial picture of living standards, particularly in a planned economy—was about the same as it had been a decade earlier (a ratio of 2.83).[98] The most appalling inequalities of the Great Leap famine had been reduced, but ideas of rural-urban integration were shelved, in part because of the association of the egalitarian radicalism of 1958 with subsequent disaster. Insofar as there was a post-Leap blueprint for rural-urban integration, it was not Zhengzhou but the new oil town of Daqing, promoted as an urban model from 1964. Daqing brought industry and agriculture together in a new, low-density landscape—in some ways this was comparable to Wang Lizhi's radical Zhengzhou plan of 1959—but was hard to replicate beyond the wide space of the Heilongjiang oilfield.[99] Holding back China's cities was predicated on strict enforcement of the *hukou* system and continued division of the rural and urban economies. Zhengzhou's population did tick up after 1962 but mostly (70 percent) as a result of natural increase. Net migration to the city between the end of the Great Leap and Mao's death averaged just six thousand people per year.[100] Vagrants and "blind" (*mangliu*) migrants arriving repeatedly in Zhengzhou were forcibly removed to a suburban farm, on poor land northeast of the city at Guodangkou, which could house two thousand *hukou* refuseniks.[101]

Meanwhile, village industries promoted in the early phases of the Great Leap as a facet of rural-urban unity were abandoned. In the post-famine drive for grain production, rural sidelines collapsed. In Xiaojing-shui, for example, workshops producing alcohol, tofu, and soy sauce all

97. The exception was Xingyang County, which returned to municipal administration in 1971.

98. Zhengzhou shi difang shizhi bianzuan weiyuanhui, *Zhengzhou shizhi*, 7:586–88.

99. See Li Hou, *Building for Oil*, 80–134.

100. Zhengzhou shi difang shizhi bianzuan weiyuanhui, *Zhengzhou shizhi*, 1:353 (no data for 1966–70).

101. Zhengzhou shi difang shizhi bianzuan weiyuanhui, *Zhengzhou shizhi*, 7:460.

Figure 5.2. Zhongzhou Hotel and Jinshuilu, 1960s. *Fenghuangwang* (Phoenix Network), available at https://news.ifeng.com/a/20160602/48902898_0.shtml, accessed August 4, 2023.

closed in 1960, with no nonagricultural activity until 1967.[102] The following year all commune workshops in the Zhengzhou Suburban District were ordered to close, apart from those directly connected with agriculture. Between 1959 and 1963, the value of rural sidelines in the district more than halved, to below 1949 figures, and only recovered to pre-Leap levels in the 1970s.[103] The seven rural towns in the Zhengzhou Suburban District—already limited in their growth throughout the first sixty years of the twentieth century—were now little more than grain collection points, tiny grassroots markets, and commune headquarters.

What did these post-Leap spatial politics mean for Zhengzhou on the

102. Xigang cunzhi bianzuan weiyuanhui, *Xigang cunzhi*, 123.

103. On closure of workshops, see Zhengzhou shi jiaoqu minzheng zhi bianxie zu, "Zhengzhou shi jiaoqu minzheng zhi," 1:29; for the value of nonagricultural output, see Zhengzhou shi jiaoqu zhi bianzuan weiyuanhui, "Zhengzhou shi jiaoqu zhi, nongye zhi," 129–30.

eve of the Cultural Revolution? In some ways Zhengzhou's economy did recover from the immediate urban austerity of 1961–1962. The shift away from heavier industry helped its textile sector, which enjoyed several years of strong growth after 1962.[104] Zhengzhou did retain more than a regional importance by virtue of its place as a transportation pivot, boasting China's fourth busiest railway station and the largest marshaling yard in all of Asia, running for several kilometers north from the downtown. By the middle of the 1960s, the hastily built new industrial and administrative districts of the mid-1950s had now been consolidated into the well-ordered, tree-lined avenues of a new socialist city (fig. 5.2).

With the removal of Henan's radical leadership, Zhengzhou was largely reduced to an ordinary medium-sized provincial capital, far from the model city of the early Great Leap. With the stark economic crisis in Henan, Zhengzhou's urban incomes had fallen back from well above the national average to a little below.[105] For all the success of its state-owned sector, the pre-1949 parts of Zhengzhou still endured poor urban services and few new facilities. Apart from the new districts to the west and the northeast, the city had hardly grown at all, with the same villages on the urban edge—Zhutun, Damengzhai, and Yanzhuang—as in the Republican and early PRC periods (see map 4.1).

Cultural Revolution: Campus, Suburb, and Beyond

Unlike in 1958, Zhengzhou and Henan Province did not play the vanguard role in the revolutionary summer of 1966. But, with its higher education institutions, factionalized provincial government, and radical recent past, events in Zhengzhou swiftly followed the pattern set by protests against party bureaucracy in Beijing. Following complaints over the role of official work teams that had been sent by Liu Shaoqi and Deng Xiaoping to schools to secure party control, Zhengzhou University became one of the most prominent campuses for early radical activity in

---

104. Sun Jianguo, *Dangdai Henan jingjishi*, 145.

105. In 1956, Zhengzhou urban residents enjoyed incomes 12 percent above the national urban average, probably owing to a high proportion of state employment. By 1965, they were 3 percent below. Comparing Zhengzhou shi difang shizhi bianzuan weiyuanhui, *Zhengzhou shizhi*, 7:586, and estimates in Nolan and White, "Urban Bias?," 57.

the provinces (along with Xi'an Jiaotong and Nanjing Universities).[106] On August 16, Henan Party Secretary Liu Jianxun (1913–1983) became the first provincial leader in China to back minority radical groups (those opposing official party bureaucracy). The next day Zhengzhou Party Secretary Wang Lizhi—he of the utopian urban plan of 1959— also swung behind the rebel faction, pulling work teams out of the city's schools.[107]

The stage was set for a turbulent decade of politics in Zhengzhou. Yet for all its radical language and attacks on systemic inequality, the Cultural Revolution and its aftermath did not cause a revolution in Zhengzhou's spatial politics. With a focus on Third Front development in western China, Zhengzhou saw little change in its scale or regional role. Unlike in 1958, there was little promise of bringing together rural and urban economies or lowering the barriers on rural migration to the city. The most prominent expression of rural-urban connection during this period was the transfer to the countryside of Zhengzhou's "educated young people" (*zhiqing*, hereafter untranslated)—almost 134,000 over the period—ostensibly to undergo revolutionary reeducation from Henan's peasants.[108] What is most striking about Zhengzhou's *zhiqing* program even compared with other cities in China is how rapidly it shed the goal of rural-urban integration. Zhengzhou's *zhiqing* projects quickly became little more than urban satellites in the rural Suburban District of the municipality. Contrary to Lefebvre's suggestion that late Maoism would lead to rural-urban unity by the "transformation of both poles," it is tempting to see this decade as the *stagnation* of both poles, held at arm's length apart by the strictures of the planned economy and the *hukou* system.[109] Yet this view is also a little too simplistic. Amid the noise of Cultural Revolution rhetoric, by the 1970s some of Zhengzhou's suburban villages were building closer economic links with the city, laying the foundations for a deeper transformation in the early reform period to come.

The first year of the Cultural Revolution in Zhengzhou pitted "rebel" Red Guards against "conservative" factions closer to official party commit-

106. Wu Caixia, "Shixi Henan sheng wenge de jige tedian."

107. "Liu Jianxun Wen Minsheng zai Zhengzhou shi dazhong xuexiao shisheng yuangong dahui shang de jianghua," August 17, 1966, accessed via ZDZYS.

108. Calculated from "Zhengzhou shi zhishi qingnian," 10.

109. Lefebvre, *Production of Space*, 421–22.

tees. This configuration was repeated across China, but as former rebel Red Guard Wu Caixia notes, what is striking in the Zhengzhou case is the prominence of Henan's recent history in the rebel agenda. On September 5, 1966, a mass meeting in Zhengzhou's City Stadium openly discussed the appalling Xinyang Incident of 1959–1960 and other Great Leap disasters in the province. Zhengzhou University rebel leader Dang Yanchuan sent a team to try to seize former party secretary Wu Zhipu to answer for his role in the Great Leap famine. The pronouncements of Dang's faction condemned both Leap and post-Leap politics, in an unconscious rhetorical echo of the appeals of the 1942–1943 famine: "the people of Henan . . . have been so squeezed they can no longer breathe (*chuan bu guo qi lai*). . . . Especially since 1958 there have been a series of extremely serious problems and appalling counterrevolutionary incidents (*hairen tingwen de fangeming shijian*)."[110] During fall 1966—coinciding with what Felix Wemheuer calls the "People's Cultural Revolution" of critique from below—factional struggle in Zhengzhou became something of a tussle over the legacy of the Great Leap. The official Cultural Revolution Committee at Zhengzhou University launched an alternative "Bombard the Headquarters" movement to defend the Great Leap and the record of the provincial bureaucracy.[111] It is easy to see events in this first year of the Cultural Revolution as a phenomenon concerned only with relatively privileged urban groups: students, workers, and cadres. In Zhengzhou, though, this radical demand for a reckoning with the rural famine deserves attention and serves as a reminder that, whatever its privileges, Henan's capital was not divorced from events elsewhere in the province.

These critiques from Zhengzhou's rebel factions did not survive their cooptation by rebel-supporting officials in 1967. That spring and summer saw bitter fighting in Zhengzhou's streets, factories, and schools between the rebel Red Guard February Seventh group, supported by a growing number of provincial officials, and a "moderate-rebel" grouping

---

110. Wu Caixia, "Shixi Henan sheng wenge de jige tedian." For a similar pattern in a village setting of using the Cultural Revolution to tackle Great Leap atrocities, see Thaxton, *Catastrophe and Contention*, 253–62.

111. Wu Caixia, "Shixi Henan sheng wenge de jige tedian." On the "People's Cultural Revolution," Wemheuer, *Social History of Maoist China*, 200–203. Note that Wemheuer adapts the phrase from Liu Guokai. See, for instance, Liu, *Renmin wenge lun*.

backed by the People's Liberation Army. After failed negotiations, Mao himself came to Zhengzhou in late September to impose a truce.[112] The deal favored the radical faction, and when the Provincial Revolutionary Committee was established in January 1968, it seemed to concentrate power in the hands of Zhengzhou's rebels. Seventeen of forty committee members were rebel Red Guards, including fourteen from Zhengzhou itself. But their power was illusory, with real authority in the hands of the People's Liberation Army and the coterie of provincial officials who had backed the rebel groupings. In August, the Revolutionary Committee ordered the dissolution of all Red Guard factions. The Cultural Revolution was over—or, at least, had moved to a very different phase, one with profound spatial as well as political consequences. On August 22, 1968, Zhengzhou's first consignment of young people was sent to join rural production teams in the far south of Henan Province. By the end of the year, almost no student Red Guards were left in the city.[113]

SPATIAL TRAJECTORIES OF "EDUCATED YOUTH"

Enforced transfers out of Zhengzhou were not new. Along with the removal of temporary work permit holders to their place of origin, permanent urban residents could be liable for transfer, particularly during the "Four Clean-Ups" movement of 1963–1966. In October 1965, a group of six hundred young people, most of whom had completed junior middle school but were unable to find jobs or advance to further study, were sent to Zhengzhou's northern rural suburbs. Others were school dropouts or "bad elements." The experiment was not a great success, with young people accused of doing little work and sneaking back to Zhengzhou without permission.[114] "I wanted to go home," remembered Zhang Guoxin decades later, "and I would wrap myself in my quilt and cry (*guozhe beizi ku*). But my *hukou* had already been transferred, and the

112. "Qi Benyu yu Henan 'Erqi Gongshe' daibiao de tanhua," June 28, 1967, ZDZYS; on Mao's visit, see "Liu Jianxun chuanda Mao Zhuxi shicha Henan shi de zuixin zhishi," September 26, 1967, ZDZYS. Joel Andreas suggests that Zhengzhou only avoided violence on the scale of the Wuhan Incident (July 1967) because of the weakness of the People's Liberation Army–backed faction. Andreas, *Disenfranchised*, 138–39.

113. Wu Caixia, "Shixi Henan sheng wenge de jige tedian"; Xia Yuan et al., *Zhugan hepan zhiqing*, 2–8.

114. "Zhengzhou shi zhishi," 10; Luo Huiwu, "Wo de zhiqing shenghuo."

work team cadres wouldn't let me leave." With a bad family background, Zhang was only able to return permanently to Zhengzhou sixteen years later, at the age of thirty-two.[115]

The Cultural Revolution movement of Zhengzhou's young people initially looks different from these earlier transfers, because of both its scale and the deeper radical discourse of a mutually beneficial relationship with the countryside, of boosted rural production in exchange for the revolutionary reeducation of Henan's peasants. On the face of it, this was the most significant effort at planned social integration between city and countryside throughout the twentieth century. But in terms of political economy, the pattern looks closer to the Great Leap Forward, with the state imposing a heavy human cost to keep a struggling urban system going. In this case, the cost was not rural famine to drive industrialization but the forced movement of young people to reimpose urban order and shift the burden of unemployment to the rural sector. As with the Great Leap, any initial goal of rural-urban reconnection did not last. By 1970 Zhengzhou's *zhiqing* program was not much more than an attempt to dump an undesirable demographic in the rural suburbs on the cheap —just as during the Four Clean-Ups a few years before. This points to a wider way to interpret the experience of China's sent-down generation. Despite its unique place in Chinese history and memory, in some ways the *zhiqing* program was not so different from other patterns of spatial exploitation—using spatial inequality to extract value—before and after this period.

The experience of Zhengzhou's *zhiqing* varied profoundly across space. Two self-published memoir collections give a good sense of this range of experience: first, the recollections of young people transferred in August 1968 to distant Luoshan County in Xinyang Prefecture, in the far south of Henan Province; second, the memoirs of those sent to Zhengzhou's rural suburbs in January 1971.[116] As one might expect (and should note with caution), the memoirs have much in common, including mixed emotions, profound nostalgia, and a strong sense of cohort identity.[117] But the spatial experience—particularly the encounter with

115. *Dahebao*, December 25, 2007.
116. On Luoshan County, see Xia Yuan et al., *Zhugan hepan zhiqing*; on the Zhengzhou suburbs, see *Zhiqing yinxiang*.
117. For a deeper discussion of memories and "memory entrepreneurs" of the sent-down generation, see Bin Xu, *Chairman Mao's Children*.

rural life and ongoing connections with the city—differed markedly between young people in the distant south of the province and those sent to Zhengzhou's rural suburbs.

The young people sent to Luoshan County were part of a batch of twenty-eight thousand students from the middle school graduating classes of 1966–1968. These cohorts were dispatched to agricultural production teams across much of the southern half of Henan in the last week of August 1968, in advance of a national policy that was confirmed only in December. The Jing–Han railroad, which in the summer of 1966 had funneled hundreds of thousands of Red Guards northwards through Zhengzhou to the mass rallies of Cultural Revolution Beijing, was now sending young people southwards to some of the poorest parts of the province. They had already surrendered their urban *hukou*, and—at least in their retelling of the story—expected to remain peasants for the rest of their lives.[118] The *zhiqing* assignment office placed the Luoshan group in a tight relationship with villagers, dispersing them in small groups averaging three to four across the commune's sixty-eight production teams.[119]

Although they were supposed to experience a revolutionary reeducation from villagers, what shines through in the Luoshan memoirs is their close encounter with the horrors of the Xinyang Incident, when more than a million people had died of starvation and state violence during the 1959–1960 winter. For the young people from the relative privilege of the provincial capital, this experience came as a shock. Xu Yiguang joined a new production team at the shell of Maowa Village, which had been almost completely wiped out by famine during 1959–1960, while female *zhiqing* Liu Aifang and Li Keye were horrified to find themselves living in an empty house where a family of four had starved to death less than a decade previously.[120] Meanwhile, another classmate enjoyed close ties with the villagers and was made accountant of his production team, but in a community where "the tragedy of every family losing people to hunger was etched in their memory" (*kegu mingxin*), he was soon doctoring the books to hide their surplus.[121]

118. Xia Yuan et al., *Zhugan hepan zhiqing*, 173.
119. Xia Yuan et al., *Zhugan hepan zhiqing*, 4–6.
120. Xia Yuan et al., *Zhugan hepan zhiqing*, 90, 239.
121. Xia Yuan et al., *Zhugan hepan zhiqing*, 157.

Young people sent down to Luoshan were cut off from life in Zheng-zhou 300 kilometers away. After an initial strict period without permis-sion for home visits, Xu Yiguang reckoned that he was able to visit Zhengzhou only two or three times a year—still more frequently than young people from China's very largest cities, who in this phase of the *zhiqing* program tended to be sent to provinces far from home. But it was not an easy trip, hitching a ride to the Xinyang railroad yard and then hiding in a northbound goods train. In 1971, Xu arrived in Zhengzhou in the dead of night and was picked up by the city police as a vagrant. Although he had been stripped of his urban *hukou*, his parents' work unit was able to vouch for him and release him from police detention.[122]

By the time of Xu Yiguang's run-in with the police, his long-distance rural experience was already unusual among Zhengzhou's *zhiqing*. After 1970 the majority of Zhengzhou's sent-down youth went no farther than the city's rural Suburban District or its satellite district 30 kilo-meters away at Shangjie. At the end of 1970, Zhengzhou's Revolution-ary Committee—then dominated by military figures—established ten suburban farms for the city's young people. More than twenty thousand were sent immediately as the founding cohort. Apart from a brief return to long-distance transfers during the radical renaissance of 1973–1974, they remained the key institutions for Zhengzhou's sent-down youth.[123] Zhengzhou's shift in *zhiqing* policy was pioneering, with its architect General Wang Hui (1923 or 1924–2010) later claiming to be the first in China to designate the rural suburbs as the default destination for a city's *zhiqing*, well before the flagship "Zhuzhou model" of 1972 promoted the same policy in Zhuzhou, Hunan Province. Wang later remembered: "at the provincial level there was much opposition, with people saying, 'Why are you setting up farms right outside their homes (*zai jia menkou ban nongchang*)?'" But Wang defended the policy on the grounds of cost, closer family connections, and the ease with which young people could be recruited by urban work units when openings arose.[124] It also brought

122. Xia Yuan et al., *Zhugan hepan zhiqing*, 98–100.

123. "Zhengzhou shi zhishi qingnian," 10.

124. Wang Yufeng and Cai Jiansheng, "Wang Hui jiangjun de Zhengzhou qingjie," 11–17. Wang Hui chaired the municipal revolutionary committee. On Zhuzhou as the model for keeping *zhiqing* in a city's suburban districts, see Honig and Zhao, *Across the Great Divide*, 131–33.

a large surplus labor force to Zhengzhou's rural suburbs, where, in the long-running—if not always successful—pattern of sending out urban resources for nearby agricultural improvements, they worked on labor-intensive projects of land reclamation, irrigation, and desalinization.

The largest *zhiqing* farm was 11 kilometers north of the city at Huayuankou. In the first few days of January 1971, more than 3,600 teenagers walked out of Zhengzhou to begin the task of cultivating wasteland along the Yellow River.[125] Proximity to the city did not mean life was easy. Like *zhiqing* in Luoshan, they faced local historical demons, in this case the task of removing the sandy deposits of the 1938 Yellow River flood. They spent the next few months leveling the undulating landscape, as the female *zhiqing* Wang Weidong remembered: "The winter was freezing, the north wind was howling, the earth was hard, and, when the pickaxes and shovels hit the ground, they just made a white speck [in the icy ground] (*tiexian he gaotou zadao dishang zhi shi yige baidian*)."[126] Zhengzhou's rural suburbs felt remote to the newcomers—a reminder of the limited reach of Zhengzhou's urban resources and infrastructure into nearby rural areas. Tian Xiaofang's No. 2 Brigade was quartered next to Liudicun, a hamlet "absolutely without brick and tile buildings, all just grass and mud huts."[127] Peng Tianzeng spent five years on marginal land north of Guxing town, still administratively in the Zhengzhou Suburban District but with only cave dwellings for accommodation and facing an hour's walk to the nearest communal *zhiqing* kitchen.[128]

In other ways, though, *zhiqing* on these suburban farms had a different rural experience from those in far-off Luoshan. Although some male urbanites were at first housed with local households, they did not usually work alongside them, and with recruitment back to the urban sector having already begun by the time of their rustication, they could have some confidence that they were not facing a rural life sentence. Although Zhengzhou's rural suburbs might feel remote, connections with the city were much more frequent than for those in the far south of the province. General Wang had envisaged suburban *zhiqing* visiting their families once a month, but after the initial burst of clearing

125. *Zhiqing yinxiang*, 234.
126. *Zhiqing yinxiang*, 4.
127. Tian Xiaofang, "Suiyue diandi," 261.
128. *Dahebao*, December 27, 2007.

wasteland, many seem to have visited more frequently. Most *zhiqing* at Huayuankou could walk home in three hours or catch the number 10 municipal bus. By 1973, the cash-strapped *zhiqing* farm was sending young people back to the city in rotation to collect urban nightsoil for fertilizer. Wang Ping remembered this as a "plum job" (*meichai*), despite the bad smell and cutthroat competition with the city's nightsoil cooperative: "you could go home, have a bath, make your life a bit better (*gaishan shenghuo*) and with a bit of luck even see a movie at the auditorium of the Yellow River Commission or at the Henan Cinema."[129] Zhengzhou's suburban *zhiqing* farms also forged links with urban work units, which opened opportunities unavailable to those joining ordinary rural brigades. Huayuankou's *zhiqing* performed all kinds of temporary jobs in Zhengzhou, including at the Agricultural College, at the vegetable wholesale market, and in the haulage sector.[130] Others worked on urban construction projects, including the memorial tower to the 1923 railroad strike and the vital Zhongyuanlu road tunnel, which crossed the railroad tracks to link the east and west sides of the city. In later memoirs, these *zhiqing* half-jokingly described themselves as the "first generation of peasant-migrant workers (*nongmingong*) coming into the city as laborers."[131] There is something in the comparison. As in the case of later migrant workers of the reform era, the municipal authorities did not usually object to their presence in the city—and were happy to exploit their cheap labor—as long as they did not have to take permanent responsibility for their food supply and welfare.

As well as sending young people for temporary urban work, the suburban *zhiqing* farms also developed formal economic connections with urban factories. At the Huayuankou *zhiqing* farm, the first workshops were established in 1973 and 1974, supplying components to a food processing plant and a tractor parts factory; in using low-paid labor to provide cheap inputs to state-owned factories, this role looks similar to the urban commune workshops of the Great Leap Forward.[132] In the last

129. *Zhiqing yinxiang*, 96; for more on going home, 78–80.
130. *Zhiqing yinxiang*, 85–88, 101.
131. *Zhiqing yinxiang*, 246. There was already a long history of peasant-migrant workers in twentieth-century Zhengzhou, particularly in the city's rapid growth periods of the first quarter of the twentieth century and in the 1950s, but the specific term *nongmingong* did not become common currency until the first half of the 1980s.
132. *Zhiqing yinxiang*, 255–57.

phase of the scheme, after 1978, Zhengzhou's suburban farms were run directly by urban work units themselves, such as the Textile Machinery Factory's *zhiqing* farm 8 kilometers south of the city at Penliu Village.[133] By 1980, when just two thousand young people were sent down to the rural suburbs, they were no longer liable for grain procurement and seem to have done little farming but were mostly employed in the workshops of *zhiqing* farms, subcontracting for state-owned enterprises as a stepping stone to urban employment. The very last *zhiqing* unit, run by the Zhengzhou Railway Bureau, finally closed in 1986. The great Cultural Revolution project to reconnect urban young people with China's countryside had ended in an ironic twist: as suburban satellite industries with little rural connection.[134]

This drawn-out ending to the *zhiqing* project underlines the unequal nature of young people's reabsorption by the urban sector. The Luoshan group of 1968 had all been sent back to the state sector—work units, higher education, or the army—by October 1972, although not all to Zhengzhou itself. By contrast, some of the Huayuankou cohort of January 1971 waited almost eight years to be recruited at the end of 1978.[135] Those with bad class backgrounds and without family connections or any other "back door" to the city found themselves languishing in the rural suburbs for years. "We used to say," Luo Huiwu remembered, "that being a *zhiqing* was not as good as being in a labor camp (*laogai*). . . . At least labor camp sentences have an end date, have something to look forward to (*you ge pantou*)."[136] By then, the *zhiqing* program was unraveling from below. Morale was down and tensions were rising, with "fights and brawls" (*dajia dou'ou*) both between *zhiqing* and villagers and among *zhiqing* themselves.[137] Some *zhiqing* drifted between suburban farms and spells in the city. With rising access to food through other sources, denial of on-farm grain rations does not seem to have prevented these disappearances. Li Xiongyi unofficially returned home to Zhengzhou's textile

133. Yue Guoding, "Houzhai zhiqing shiqilian."

134. On the Railway Bureau unit, see *Dahebao*, December 24, 2007. As Emily Honig and Xiaojian Zhao show, this phenomenon was not restricted to suburban areas. Honig and Zhao, *Across the Great Divide*, 133–35.

135. Xia Yuan et al., *Zhugan hepan zhiqing*, 30; *Zhiqing yinxiang*, 263.

136. Luo Huiwu, "Wo de zhiqing shenghuo," 298.

137. Zhengzhou shi jiaoqu minzheng zhi bianxie zu, "Zhengzhou shi jiaoqu minzheng zhi," 1:40.

district and hustled a living for several years with temporary jobs and by trading vegetables between rural and urban markets, while still registered in the countryside.[138]

Like almost all of Zhengzhou's *zhiqing*, Li eventually returned to the formal urban sector; he became a college teacher.[139] By contrast, almost five million "educated youth" in Henan who had been brought up in rural areas (and had always had rural *hukou*) were simply returned to their collectives at the end of their education. Like Liu Junfu at the end of the Great Leap Forward (see above), most faced limited options for social or geographic mobility for years to come.[140] This underlines the rather unrevolutionary nature of the last decade of the Mao period, not only enshrining existing arbitrary spatial inequalities in China's economy and society but also foreclosing possibilities for more equal patterns in the reform era to come.

ZHENGZHOU'S RURAL SUBURBS IN THE MAOIST TWILIGHT

With restrictions on investment and wages, Zhengzhou's urban economy was sluggish throughout the last years of the Mao period. The Zhengzhou Auto Factory on the south side of the city opened in 1969 producing light trucks, but after this milestone industrial growth flatlined all the way to 1976. Industrial wages in Zhengzhou were falling slightly, in both absolute terms and relative to living costs.[141] Although General Wang Hui tried to diversify the economy away from its dependence on textiles, such plans were stymied by the tense political conflict of the 1970s. Like other senior military figures, Wang himself came under heavy criticism following the fall of Lin Biao in 1971.[142] The city saw little by way of improvement projects, with all urban planning banned by the central authorities and the municipal planning bureau

---

138. "Zhengzhou Xijiao de bianqian," *Zhengzhou jiyi*, June 21, 2010; for more on *zhiqing* grain access and penalties for absconding, see Zhengzhou shi jiaoqu liangshiju, *Zhengzhou shi jiaoqu zhi: liangshi zhi*, 98.

139. "Zhengzhou Xijiao de bianqian," *Zhengzhou jiyi*, June 21, 2010.

140. Bernstein, *Up to the Mountains*, 24.

141. Zhengzhou shi difang shizhi bianzuan weiyuanhui, *Zhengzhou shizhi*, 1:27. Between 1967 and 1976 state wages in Zhengzhou fell 2.25 percent; retail prices fell 0.7 percent. *Zhengzhou shizhi*, 5:555.

142. Wang Yufeng and Cai Jiansheng, "Wang Hui jiangjun," 13–14.

"wearing the cap of revisionism."[143] The annual growth of Zhengzhou's built-up area was around a tenth that of the 1952–1960 boom and only half that even of 1961–1965. Held down by a strict *hukou* system and the removal of its young people, Zhengzhou's population of 680,000 in 1976 was hardly larger than it had been at its Great Leap peak in 1960.[144]

However, the last decade of the Mao period was not simply a time of stasis. Behind the larger pattern of stagnation, the most striking changes around Zhengzhou in the 1970s were taking place not in the city but in its rural suburbs. Beginning in around 1969, Zhengzhou's rural suburbs saw growth in both per capita output and living standards. After having largely missed out on the boom in much of China's agricultural economy in the 1910s (see chapter 1), Zhengzhou's Suburban District (the rural parts of the former Zheng County) was now experiencing its strongest sustained period of economic growth in the twentieth century. As Mobo Gao, Chris Bramall, and Joshua Eisenman among others have argued, behind the turmoil of high politics, the last decade of the Mao era brought real benefits to rural China, offering both immediate improvements in living standards and laying the preconditions for reform era growth.[145] What is striking in the Zhengzhou case is the concentration of these benefits in the Suburban District relative to the wider rural sector. China's overall rural-urban income gap was growing slightly between the mid-1960s and the late 1970s, but around Zhengzhou the income ratio was dropping (from 2.83 in 1965 to 2.53 in 1978). Having been less than 10 percent (9.6 percent) above the Henan rural average in the wake of the Great Leap, rural per capita income in the Zhengzhou Suburban District rose to 16.3 percent above by 1978.[146]

Explanations for this success underline the importance of proximity to the city. Following the model of self-reliance set by Daqing,

---

143. Henan sheng jiansheting chengjianzhi bianjishi, *Henan sheng chengjian shizhi gao*, 2:4.

144. On population, see Zhengzhou shi difang shizhi bianzuan weiyuanhui, *Zhengzhou shizhi*, 1:347–48. On built-up area over time, see Zhengzhou shi jianshe weiyuanhui, "Zhengzhou shi chengxiang jianshe zhi," 418–19.

145. Mobo Gao, *Gao Village*; Bramall, *Industrialization of Rural China*; Eisenman, *Red China's Green Revolution*.

146. Zhengzhou shi difang shizhi bianzuan weiyuanhui, *Zhengzhou shizhi*, 7:586–88; provincial figures from Henan sheng difang shizhi bianzuan weiyuanhui, *Henan sheng zhi*, 49:5–6.

cities across China tried to maximize agricultural production within municipal boundaries. This process led to a rise in procurement in the "municipal countryside" but also new inputs and investment.[147] Where production teams had been pulled out of vegetable cultivation following the Great Leap famine, by the late collective era almost a quarter of people in Zhengzhou's Suburban District were in specialist teams producing relatively high-priced vegetables for the city.[148] The rural suburbs also benefited from new projects to boost grain production. Some were typical of the rural sector—new crop varieties, improved terms of trade, fertilizer inputs—but some schemes were peculiar to the Zhengzhou suburbs. For example, north of the city, the effects of Yellow River flooding had stymied efforts to boost production both in the 1930s and during the Great Leap Forward, but the massive Mangshan project of 1970 mobilized more than eighty thousand people—including *zhiqing* in the Zhengzhou Suburban District—to draw water from the Yellow River. The results benefited both city and countryside, though to the detriment of the river and its ecosystems. When the water began to flow in 1972, 60 percent was designated for industrial and domestic use in the city, with 40 percent set aside for irrigation.[149] With Mangshan and smaller schemes, two-thirds of arable land in Zhengzhou's suburbs was now irrigated (compared to just 17 percent in 1962). The dream of large-scale rice production in Zhengzhou's northern suburbs, which had been an economic and ecological disaster in the Great Leap, was now realized.[150] Although growth in output across rural China was still mostly being eaten up by population growth, by the last years of the Mao period, per capita grain production in the Zhengzhou Suburban District had risen by 65 percent over the previous decade.[151]

147. For a near-contemporary discussion, see David Buck, "Policies Favoring the Growth of Smaller Urban Places," 138–46.

148. Zhengzhou shi jiaoqu liangshiju, *Zhengzhou shi jiaoqu zhi: liangshi zhi*, 89. On the 1970s vegetable boom, see Skinner, "Vegetable Supply and Marketing."

149. Zhengzhou shi difang shizhi bianzuan weiyuanhui, *Zhengzhou shizhi*, 1:142. On ecological damage in this period, see Pietz, *Yellow River*, 194–257.

150. Irrigation figures from Zhengzhou shi jiaoqu zhi bianzuan weiyuanhui, "Zhengzhou shi jiaoqu zhi, nongye zhi," 95. On rice, see Sheng Fuyao and Chen Daiguang, "Yuejin zhong de Zhengzhou," 5–7.

151. Comparing 1963–66 (inclusive) with 1973–76. Zhengzhou shi jiaoqu liangshiju, *Zhengzhou shi jiaoqu zhi: liangshi zhi*, 77; national figures suggest a rural per capita grain increase of 12.2 percent. See Ash, "Squeezing the Peasants," 648.

Despite this growth in output, grain and vegetables alone would not bring a major leap in rural living standards in the Zhengzhou suburbs, particularly under the restrictions of the collective economy. Although production had risen per capita, the tightening availability of arable land—sown area per person fell from 2.4 *mu* in 1962 to 1.52 *mu* in 1976—points to the limits of agriculture as a long-term strategy for rural development around Zhengzhou.[152] At the same time, then, collectives around Zhengzhou revived the rural "sidelines" that had been abandoned in the retreat from the Great Leap. Rural brigades reinvested collective income from gains and vegetables in workshops processing foods and producing small-scale consumer goods. This pattern was repeated across rural China, but villages close to cities seem to have benefited from slightly higher collective incomes, a nearby urban market, and the gradual spread of infrastructure such as electricity, paved roads, and public transport. By 1977, off-farm sidelines made up 16.7 percent of rural output in Henan but in the rural suburbs of Zhengzhou already accounted for over 30 percent.[153]

The village of Baizhuang demonstrates how this "walking on two legs" (rural industry and agriculture) could work in practice. Baizhuang lay 2 kilometers beyond the southeastern edge of Zhengzhou (see map 5.1). As with much of the east side of Zhengzhou, soil quality was poor, and the village had lost more than a third of its farmland to urban edge infrastructure: the city pig farm, the city horticulture farm, and the widening of both the Long–Hai railroad and the Zhengzhou–Kaifeng highway.[154] The cycle of collective accumulation in Baizhuang began with an effort to make up the lost land. Beginning in 1970, after the overthrow of the radical Cultural Revolution faction, Baizhuang's leadership under Bai Xichuan mobilized villagers to dig out 110 *mu* of sand next to the village. Taking advantage of the city's proximity, villagers then pulled the sand on carts to sell to Zhengzhou's construction sector, netting 400,000 RMB over the next seven years. This money was reinvested in irriga-

152. Zhengzhou shi jiaoqu zhi bianzuan weiyuanhui, "Zhengzhou shi jiaoqu zhi, nongye zhi," 95.

153. Zhengzhou shi jiaoqu zhi bianzuan weiyuanhui, "Zhengzhou shi jiaoqu zhi, nongye zhi," 130. For provincial figures, see Sun Jianguo, *Xiandai Henan jingjishi*, 180.

154. Zhengzhou shi jiaoqu zhi bianzuan weiyuanhui, "Zhengzhou shi jiaoqu zhi (zhengqiu yijian gao), Baizhuang zhi," 80.

tion and sideline projects producing fruit and fresh milk for the urban market. The production of apples for sale in Zhengzhou was reckoned to yield six times the income of state-controlled grain production (per unit of sown area), both boosting village incomes and, as chapter 6 demonstrates, accumulating capital for more ambitious collective industry in the early reform era.[155]

The place of rural suburbs in the late Mao era economy remains an ambiguous one. Peter Nolan and Gordon White have argued that "a strong case can be made for extending the notion of 'urban bias' to include the surrounding peasantry who benefit from relatively close proximity to large cities."[156] Evidence from Zhengzhou suggests that this view goes too far, although admittedly, Zhengzhou was not a particularly large or wealthy city. Rural incomes in its Suburban District did nudge farther ahead of the wider Henan region, and some villages close to the city such as Baizhuang fared even better. But this income growth was insufficient to close yawning rural-urban inequalities. Zhengzhou's urban incomes were still more than two and a half times those of its Suburban District at the end of the Mao period.[157]

Urbancentrism in political economy was far from unique to the People's Republic in the 1960s and 1970s.[158] But rural-urban divisions in some parts of the world, including in parts of the socialist world and in parts of Asia, were beginning to be narrowed by a range of infrastructures and social phenomena: a tilt toward relative support for agriculture; labor migration to cities; a boom of rural market towns; mass secondary education for rural children; widespread rural electrification; and rural ownership of radios, motorbikes, and even televisions.[159] Despite

155. Zhengzhou shi jiaoqu zhi bianzuan weiyuanhui, "Zhengzhou shi jiaoqu zhi (zhengqiu yijian gao), Baizhuang zhi," 4–7.

156. Nolan and White, "Urban Bias?," 76.

157. Zhengzhou shi difang shizhi bianzuan weiyuanhui, *Zhengzhou shizhi*, 7:586–88.

158. For the classic contemporary statement, see Lipton, *Why Poor People Stay Poor*. Note that China is largely missing from Lipton's diagnostics; he is more inclined to view Maoist China as a rural success story. Lipton might have revised this view had he had access to data from the People's Republic. Even at the relatively equal point of 1965, China's rural-urban income ratio (2.37) was worse than all but one of the six Asian countries in Lipton's survey. See p. 430.

159. For a recent study of Taiwan and South Korea, see Looney, *Mobilizing for Development*. For a less top-down example, note the 1970s fieldwork of S. Ann Dunham (also the mother of Barack Obama) on rural-urban links in Java; Dunham, *Surviving*

the promising growth in the rural sector during the 1970s and the emergence of some of this infrastructure (such as growth in rural electrification), the dual structures of the planned economy and a strict household registration system meant that most of these phenomena did not arrive in rural China until the 1980s. The Mao era city, as the Republican city before it, had not acted as a driving force to transform either its immediate hinterland or the wider regional economy. Nor was it clear that these signs of rural prosperity in the late Maoist period would be sustained. The fast-growing population of Zhengzhou's rural hinterland threatened to strangle long-run per capita economic growth, especially coupled with strict limits on mobility.

Factional conflict sharpened across China in the mid-1970s, driven by the rapid oscillations in Beijing between radical and moderate policy positions. With its strong radical faction in the crucial Railroad Bureau, Zhengzhou was one of the cities most seriously affected. But with stagnation in the urban economy, pressure was growing for political change and an end to late-stage Cultural Revolution radicalism. In April 1976, Provincial Party Secretary Liu Jianxun declared a "counterrevolutionary incident" after protesters laid flowers commemorating Zhou Enlai's death in Zhengzhou's Erqi (February Seventh) Square, as at Tian'anmen Square in Beijing. More than four hundred people were arrested, and, in the radical reassertion of power that followed, Zhengzhou's transport links were repeatedly shut down for weeks at a time by rebel worker groups in the Railroad Bureau.[160] But the political tides were soon to shift decisively against the radical movement. Within six months, a mass meeting was held in Zhengzhou's city stadium—site of many rebel meetings across the Cultural Revolution decade—celebrating the fall of the Gang of Four. By 1977, a full-scale purge of radical leadership was under way, eventually removing fifty thousand officials across Henan.[161] Zhengzhou's radical Mao era was over.

---

against the Odds. On the closing of the rural-urban gap in the Brezhnev era Soviet Union, see Wegren, "Rise, Fall and Transformation."

160. Heilmann, "Suppression of the April Fifth Movement." On radical faction politics and railroad stoppages in Zhengzhou, see Köll, *Railroads and the Transformation of China*, 281; Andreas, *Disenfranchised*, 153–59.

161. Zhengzhou shi difang shizhi bianzuan weiyuanhui, *Zhengzhou shizhi*, 1:145.

CHAPTER SIX

Reform Regimes

Inequalities Old and New, 1978–2003

In his recent survey of the Mao period, Felix Wemheuer notes that "post-1976 China is seldom studied as history."[1] This is beginning to change, including in urban history. With China under Xi Jinping having definitively entered a new era, a sharper historical lens on the reform period can reveal what was distinct about the first decades of post-Mao China. Work has begun on historicizing China's urban transformation, particularly in Beijing and the most striking coastal boomtowns of the reform era.[2] Away from those coastal flagships, most Chinese cities in the reform era still looked more like Zhengzhou: a gritty, medium-sized interior city still dominated by the state sector of the economy. Nonetheless, Zhengzhou was part of China's urban takeoff in the 1980s and 1990s, albeit in a less dramatic way than cities of the Lower Yangzi region or the Pearl River Delta. In some ways the city in these decades resembled that of the early twentieth century. Zhengzhou once again became a key wholesaling center and logistical link between the very different economies of a globally linked coastal China and interior regions; just as in the first years of the railroad, rapid unplanned migration changed the scale of the city, with the population almost tripling by the end of the twentieth century.[3]

1. Wemheuer, *Social History of Maoist China*, 282.
2. See, for instance, O'Donnell, Wong, and Bach, *Learning from Shenzhen*; Juan Du, *Shenzhen Experiment*; Evans, *Beijing from Below*; Joshua Goldstein, *Remains of the Everyday*, 144–222. Studies of less celebrated cities in other fields do use historical methods to explain reform era changes. See, for instance, the sociologist Andrew Kipnis in *From Village to City*, esp. 31–65.
3. In 1977 Zhengzhou's population was 689,000. Zhengzhou shi difang shizhi bianzuan weiyuanhui, *Zhengzhou shizhi*, 1:348. City population estimates in the reform

The People's Republic broke with patterns of the past to achieve remarkable long-run per capita economic growth during the 1980s and 1990s. But this chapter uses the example of Zhengzhou to show how and why this growth did not reverse the spatial inequality of the first three-quarters of the twentieth century. The fates of individuals were still profoundly conditioned by their location, and under the ongoing strictures of the *hukou* system, this inequality was only partially alleviated by labor migration. China in the reform era was still deeply, in some ways increasingly, divided: between regions, between different cities, and between the rural and urban sectors.

Given the growing role of the market in China's economy, it is tempting simply to attribute this pattern to "natural" forces: as proposed in the Kuznets curve, the takeoff phase of economic growth is marked by rising inequality.[4] Since, as Isabella Weber and Julian Gewirtz show, the course of China's economic reform was a contingent set of political choices, explanations for the extent and nature of spatial inequality must also be political.[5] The spatial disparities of China's economic takeoff were the result of both the legacy of Mao era rural-urban divisions and deliberate decisions under Deng Xiaoping's formula of "let some people and some regions get rich first." As across the whole twentieth century, this spatial politics was driven by a Chinese state that was deeply ambitious for economic development but, with still-limited resources, did not make it a priority to spread the benefits of growth across space. The spatial politics of the reform era instead stressed headline GDP figures, urban stability, and the exploitation and reproduction of a low-wage rural migrant labor force.

This chapter suggests that things could have been different—that much could have been achieved in economic terms while lowering the costs in spatial inequality and rural exclusion. I begin in this vein by

---

era are notoriously difficult, given uncounted migrants and a lack of clarity over boundaries. I estimate the population of Zhengzhou city proper in 1999 as 1.9 million. This is the total urban *hukou*-holding population of the urban districts (1.402 million) plus a long-term "floating population" (*liudong renkou*) of around five hundred thousand migrants. See *Zhengzhou tongji nianjian*, 2000:5. There is no "floating population" estimate for 1999, but the municipal statistics bureau reported 519,000 in the year 2000.

4. For a skeptical perspective on the Kuznets curve in China, see Ravallion and Chen, "Is That Really a Kuznets Curve?"

5. Weber, *How China Escaped Shock Therapy*; Gewirtz, *Never Turn Back*.

explaining the economic takeoff in Zhengzhou's immediate hinterland during the first years of reform, showing how the post-Mao era began with unprecedented equalization across space. I then turn to the rising inequalities of authoritarian market reform from the mid-1980s onwards, exploring the spatial politics of reform at three separate scales. First, Zhengzhou's urban edge by the end of the century had become a site for high-stakes struggles between periurban villages and the organs of a profit-seeking municipal state. Second, inequality sharpened between Zhengzhou and its hinterland, with the initial burst in village incomes outstripped by urban growth from the mid-1980s. Finally, migration from rural and small-town Henan Province to Zhengzhou transposed many of the burdens of Zhengzhou's economic growth to the province's impoverished countryside as the provincial capital benefited from a cheap, expendable labor force.

By the turn of the century, the inequalities of reform era spatial politics had brought rural China to a social and political crisis. The travails of Henan—rural poverty, local fiscal collapse, corruption, an HIV blood donation epidemic, the closure of state-owned industry—became emblematic of the unfairness of China's rapid economic growth. As the relatively privileged capital of a crisis-hit province but with its own collapsed state-owned textile sector, Zhengzhou was on a sharp and contentious fault line between relative winners and losers of economic reform. Partly as a result, the city became famous from the late 1990s for its neo-Maoist movement of workers and intellectuals, seeking an egalitarian route through these crises. This movement failed on its own terms, partly because it was not able to bridge the gulf between the city's urban workers and rural migrant workers. However, in a different idiom of infrastructure-led development, a series of new policies between 2003 and 2006 in and around Zhengzhou did promise to spread the benefits of growth. This program was part of the wider paradigm shift of the new Hu Jintao/Wen Jiabao leadership, from a dominant impulse of spatial division to a new emphasis on equalization across space. Chapter 7 explores the mixed results of this policy shift.

Reform and Its Winners in the Zhengzhou Hinterland

The first years of economic reform were particularly beneficial in China's rural sector, with some observers arguing that the entire reform process was driven from below by farmers.[6] The example of Zhengzhou shows why the rural suburbs around the city were well placed to benefit. In some ways, the benefits were an acceleration of existing trends, emerging from the commercial activities of the rural collectives in the 1970s. As chapter 5 has shown, rural brigades around Zhengzhou had been able to use proximity to the city to their advantage during the 1970s, using surplus resources of grain, labor, vegetables, and building materials to accumulate capital. Initial economic reforms of 1978 gave this process renewed energy. Even before the famous 20 percent hike in nationwide rural procurement prices that December, the Henan Provincial Government had permitted the opening of markets for over-quota grain and allowed local state organs to buy it up at higher "negotiated prices" (*yigou*). With ongoing restrictions on the movement of grain across administrative boundaries (until 1982), this policy was particularly beneficial to producers within Zhengzhou's municipal limits.[7] Mao era institutions were also beginning to disappear. In 1979, suburban Yanzhuang became Zhengzhou's experimental site for the abolition of class labels; symbolically, Yanzhuang was the village visited by Mao Zedong during his tour of 1960.[8] Decollectivization soon followed. Although in 1981 only a third of Zhengzhou's rural suburbs, mostly east of the city, had shifted full responsibility to the household (*bao gan dao hu*), they were markedly the most successful. More than 99 percent of households in Zhengzhou's Suburban District had switched to this household contract system by the time its rural communes were formally abolished in 1983.[9]

The rhetoric of the municipal government remained focused on grain: "serve the city, enrich the peasants, don't relax grain production" (*juebu fangsong liangshi shengchan*) was the slogan for Zhengzhou's rural suburbs during the early 1980s.[10] Although new incentives did boost

6. See Kelliher, *Peasant Power*; Kate Xiao Zhou, *How the Farmers Changed China*, esp. 46–105.

7. Zhengzhou shi difang shizhi bianzuan weiyuanhui, *Zhengzhou shizhi*, 5:159; for more on grain prices, see Christiansen, "Food Security," esp. 551–55.

8. Zhengzhou shi jiaoqu minzheng zhi bianxie zu, "Zhengzhou shi jiaoqu minzheng zhi," 1:44.

9. Zhengzhou shi jiaoqu zhi bianzuan weiyuanhui, "Zhengzhou shi jiaoqu zhi, nongye zhi," 120–21.

10. Zhengzhou shi jiaoqu zhi bianzuan weiyuanhui, "Zhengzhou shi jiaoqu zhi, nongye zhi," 128.

grain production—rising, in line with national figures, by an average of 20 percent per capita in the Suburban District across 1979 to 1984 compared with 1973 to 1978—the growth in rural incomes near Zheng-zhou was driven more by nongrain foodstuffs and rural sidelines.[11] The major windfall for suburban producers came with rising prices for vege-tables, which leapt by an average of 138 percent in Zhengzhou between 1977 and 1985. With the general cost of living rising only 28 percent in the same period, this was a stark reversal of intersectoral price scissors in favor of producers in the rural suburbs.[12] Not all cities experienced this growth: even in 1984 a study by Zuo Jinggang found that produc-ers around Luoyang were still suffering from enforced low prices and disincentives to produce vegetables.[13] Zhengzhou also had stresses in the vegetable supply system, but mostly to the benefit of producers, with prices over a third higher than in Luoyang. Long-established vegetable growers under Zhengzhou's jurisdiction were able to benefit from rising urban demand, limits on the long-distance movement of vegetables, and the low yields of new entrants to the sector, which ensured that supply was slow to catch up with demand.[14]

Zhengzhou's suburbs also benefited from the boom in rural enterprises (later called township and village enterprises, TVEs). Although Zheng-zhou's suburbs did not see a takeoff comparable to rural areas in parts of coastal China, its off-farm enterprises did boost incomes.[15] After ten years of reform, per capita agricultural production in the rural parts of Zhengzhou Municipality was still close to the Henan provincial aver-age, but its total per capita production (including nonagricultural activity

11. Zhengzhou shi jiaoqu zhi bianzuan weiyuanhui, "Zhengzhou shi jiaoqu zhi, nongye zhi," 77; compare Ash, "Squeezing the Peasants," 991.

12. Zhengzhou shi difang shizhi bianzuan weiyuanhui, *Zhengzhou shizhi*, 5:567–68 (overall price index) and 575 (vegetable market prices). Grain purchase prices rose much less slowly (for wheat, 36 percent between 1979 and 1985).

13. Zuo Jinggang, "Dui chengshi jiaoqu shucai shengchan."

14. On problems in the Zhengzhou system, see Xie Yingjun, Geng Zhanjing, and Li Qiaosong, "Dui Zhengzhou shi shucai." G. William Skinner reported that land newly converted to vegetables took five to eight years to produce a full yield. Skinner, "Vegetable Supply," 741.

15. As Peter Nolan discussed early in this process, high growth in the rural hinter-land of cities was particularly striking in the Pearl River Delta. See Nolan, *Growth Processes and Distributional Change*, 85–89. See also Chan, Madsen, and Unger, *Chen Village*, 267–87.

and processed food products) was 83 percent higher.[16] Some rural enterprises had their roots in the Mao era, including former *zhiqing* operations such as the textiles workshop at Huayuankou. Others were wholly new, benefiting from tax incentives and credit schemes within the municipal boundary.[17] Zhengzhou's most spectacular success story for rural industry was a mixture of old and new. The villagers of Baizhuang had found success in the 1970s selling first sand, then fruit and milk, to the nearby city (see chapter 5). In the early reform period Baizhuang built on this rising demand with expanded collective enterprises producing dried tofu and alcohol. By 1981, its village incomes were more than ten times the average rural income for Zhengzhou's suburbs.[18] In 1983 Baizhuang was able to build new homes for all residents: "the village streets look like the city," one report noted in 1985, "and their homes surpass those of urban residents (*shengsi shimin*)."[19]

Baizhuang's success may have been exceptional, but it points to a wider pattern of closer relationships between the city and its hinterland. Whereas in the 1920s and 1930s poverty in Zheng County had limited the benefits of rural-urban exchange (see chapter 2), in this period rising demand in both city and countryside made for closer, mutually beneficial connections. Although Zhengzhou's authorities had spent much of the twentieth century trying to force itinerant traders off urban streets, in 1980 the municipal government permitted, even encouraged, sellers to open stalls to boost the city's limited retail space. Five new markets were opened that year specifically for the sale of rural products.[20] One report of 1987 celebrated the effects of this rural-urban trade: "in the past, because of limits on peasants coming into the city, it was hard for urban residents to get hold of rural byproducts, but now the gates

---

16. *Henan tongji nianjian*, 1989:203. Note that this statistic represents the expanded Zhengzhou municipality (including six subordinate counties it absorbed in 1983), not the Suburban District only.

17. For examples, see Zhao Shuling, "Zhengzhou chengshi kongjian kuozhan," 52.

18. Zhengzhou shi jiaoqu zhi bianzuan weiyuanhui, "Zhengzhou shi jiaoqu zhi, nongye zhi," 121. Municipal rural average from Zhengzhou shi difang shizhi bianzuan weiyuanhui, *Zhengzhou shizhi*, 7:575.

19. Zhengzhou shi jiaoqu zhi bianzuan weiyuanhui, "Zhengzhou shi jiaoqu zhi, Baizhuang zhi," 3.

20. Zhengzhou shi jianshe weiyuanhui, "Zhengzhou shi chengxiang jianshe zhi," 1:400; Zhengzhou shi difang shizhi bianzuan weiyuanhui, *Zhengzhou shizhi*, 1:151.

of the city have been opened wide (*changkai le chengmen*). Suburban peasants come in to sell them in large quantities, and city dwellers are delighted."[21] A 1989 survey found 44,000 visiting traders in Zhengzhou. Almost 80 percent were of rural background, and 60 percent had arrived that day, mostly to trade in the city's 121 open-air markets.[22] In this early phase of market reform, it was often village entrepreneurs rather than city dwellers who provided the links with China's changing coastal economy. Villagers from Huanggangsi, 3 kilometers beyond the urban edge, became known for traveling to booming Wenzhou and Guangzhou to buy consumer goods, returning to sell them at a profit in Zhengzhou.[23]

The success story of rising rural incomes around Zhengzhou is mirrored in inequality data. During the collective era per capita incomes in the city were more than two and a half times those of the rural hinterland (see chapter 5). Even in 1980, after a decade of improved rural performance, urban incomes in Zhengzhou were still 2.64 times higher than their rural counterparts—a figure worse than the national rural-urban gap (2.36), and perhaps a legacy of high levels of state employment in Zhengzhou. At least according to official household sample data, this disparity had tumbled dramatically to a historic low of 1.51 by 1983, falling much faster than the national figure (1.85). The gap in consumer spending also narrowed, from a ratio of 3.4:1 in 1980 to 2.5:1 in 1985 (fig. 6.1).[24]

This pattern was not sustained. As figure 6.1 shows, rural-urban inequality within Zhengzhou municipality began to tick up in the mid-1980s. The next phase of economic reform backed the "winners" of spatial differences, as the rest of this chapter explores, with most inland and rural areas falling behind in what came to look like the natural pattern of state-led reform. It is tempting to see this first, prorural phase of reform as simply low-hanging fruit, a quick stimulus of release in a sector held back for so long. But this view downplays the importance of this period in kickstarting China's transition to rapid economic growth. It is ironic that whereas the long search for economic transformation had

21. Liu Yanpu et al., "1987 nian Zhengzhou shi liudong renkou," reproduced in Fan Futang et al., *Zhengzhou liudong renkou*, 255.

22. Fan Futang et al., *Zhengzhou liudong renkou*, 40–41.

23. Zhengxie Zhengzhou shi Erqiqu weiyuanhui, *Yuanqu zhi jiyi*, 122.

24. Chinawide figures from Knight and Song, *Rural-Urban Divide*, 28–29. Zhengzhou figures from Zhengzhou shi difang shizhi bianzuan weiyuanhui, *Zhengzhou shizhi*, 7:574 (consumption) and 7:586–88 (income).

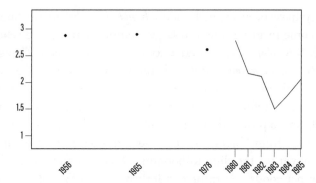

FIGURE 6.1. Urban-rural income ratios in Zhengzhou, 1956–1985. Data from Zhengzhou shi difang shizhi bianzuan weiyuanhui, *Zhengzhou shizhi*, 7:586–88.

centered on China's cities for almost the whole twentieth century, it was this anomaly of a more prorural policy that provided the springboard for a wider economic takeoff by increasing rural incomes. China's high-growth decades could hardly have avoided spatial disparities and social stresses altogether, but as the People's Republic continues to grapple with the legacies of both Mao era and reform era structural inequalities, the equalizing growth of these early years offers a glimpse of a reform road not taken.

Unequal Outcomes at the Urban Edge

The remainder of this chapter is organized thematically to explore three different aspects of spatial inequality between the mid-1980s and early 2000s: Zhengzhou's urban edge, its regional role, and the place of migrants in the city. This part of the chapter begins by examining how the urban fringe zone was reused and reimagined in the market economy. It then shows how the benefits of Zhengzhou's economic takeoff were unequally, even arbitrarily, distributed across space. By the 1990s, real estate speculation was driving the appropriation of rural land at Zhengzhou's urban edge, usually with low compensation for farmers relative to the value of their plots. The ability of former farmers to rent out rooms to migrant workers provided some financial reparation, but the farmers-turned-landlords of these "villages in the city" (*chengzhong-cun*) struggled to overcome cultural, institutional, and economic barriers to urban belonging.

Such high-value struggles were a distant prospect in the first phase of the reform era. Zhengzhou in the early 1980s was still at root the Soviet-designed city of the 1950s, with the three distinct zones of the pre-1948 city, the industrial western suburb, and the northern administrative district. Zhengzhou lacked adequate housing for almost a third of its population, and some of the appealing aspects of the socialist city—particularly the green space and tree-lined avenues—were being lost.[25] The provincial government was scathing in its report on Zhengzhou to the State Council: "The construction of the city has caused chaos in some areas, with the 'bones' [*gutou*, i.e., the grid of roads] and 'meat' [*rou*, i.e., the built-up area] unbalanced. Pollution is serious, the appearance of the city is untidy, and transport is chaotic." The blame was pinned on ultraleftism—"the chaos caused by Lin Biao and the Gang of Four"—but Zhengzhou's spatial problems were of a much older vintage.[26] As map 6.1 shows, the eastern and western halves of the city were still poorly connected, with only three bottleneck crossing points.

Even as the rural suburbs of Zhengzhou were enjoying unprecedented income growth, the city itself was slow to adjust to the new economy relative to other similar-sized cities. "Zhengzhou's economic place in the country slumped," notes local economist An Qian.[27] An rightly attributes this slump to the resurgence of coastal cities, but one might also add the longer neglect of Zhengzhou in the two decades after its heyday as a Great Leap model, even relative to other inland cities. By 1986 Zhengzhou's disposable income per capita ranked thirty-second of thirty-five provincial capitals and major cities.[28] Zhengzhou's social fabric was also threatening to tear apart, with the margins of the city a site of particular concern. At Erligang, on the southeast edge, unemployed young people (who could now avoid being sent down to the countryside) ran amok in

25. Zhang Qixian and Wu Xiaoya, *Dangdai Zhengzhou chengshi jianshe*, 15; on loss of green space, see Henan sheng jiansheting chengjianzhi bianjishi, *Henan sheng chengjian shizhi gao xuanbian*, 2:129.

26. "Henan sheng renmin zhengfu guanyu 'Zhengzhou shi chengshi zongti guihua' de qingshi," December 30, 1982, reproduced in Henan sheng jiansheting chengjianzhi bianjishi, *Henan sheng chengjian shizhi gao xuanbian*, 2:173.

27. An Qian, *Kuaisu chengshihua jincheng*, 170.

28. Ahead of only Jilin City, Taiyuan (two other industrial cities favored in the 1950s), and Nanchang. Zhengzhou shi difang shizhi bianzuan weiyuanhui, *Zhengzhou shizhi*, 7:581.

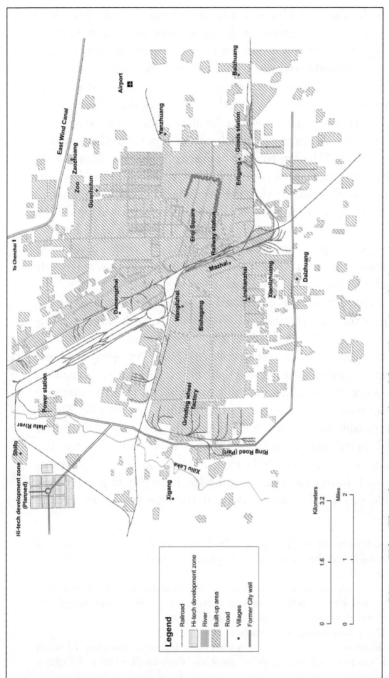

MAP 6.1. Urban Zhengzhou, 1988. Map adapted from *Zhengzhou shi chengshi guihua guanliju*, ed., *Zhengzhou shi chengshi fenqu guihua tuji*, 2–3. Map by Jogu Gopinath.

the warehouses and lanes around the railroad goods station. While waiting for jobs still occupied by their parents' generation, they joyrode on goods trains, took part in the black market, and engaged in petty theft. According to the official version of the story, order was only restored in the neighborhood by the arrival of a female cadre named Shao Yuhua, who organized them into a squad of construction workers.[29]

URBAN EDGE IN ZHENGZHOU'S TAKEOFF

From the relative low point of the mid-1980s, Zhengzhou's economy began to shift to a period of more rapid growth. One of the key drivers was Zhengzhou's reemergence as a site for wholesale exchange. With its place as a pivot in both rail and the increasingly important long-distance road networks, Zhengzhou linked the new coastal economy and interior markets. In a direct reprisal of its Republican era role, Zhengzhou was once again home to more than fifty wholesale cotton dealers, arranging the sale and transfer of cotton to the very same cities as in the 1910s and 1920s: Shanghai, Wuhan, Qingdao.[30] What was on a different scale from the Republican period was the strength of incoming trade for the wider Henan region. On the eastern edge of Zhengzhou, three large markets for consumer goods sprang up, where wholesalers from coastal China did business with traders from towns across Henan.[31] Zhengzhou's southern edge hosted the largest shoe market north of the Yangzi as well as one of China's five largest coal exchanges.[32] The wholesaling function was accompanied by a retail takeoff: according to official data from 1988, the size of the city's retail economy had risen by more than 60 percent in just three years.[33]

This growth of the mid-1980s rendered urban planning almost instantly out of date. Urban design work in Zhengzhou had been restored in 1979, but the full-scale plan for the reform era was approved

29. Chen Qiaoyan, "Zhengzhou yitiao jie."
30. Zhang Qixian and Wu Xiaoya, *Dangdai Zhengzhou chengshi jianshe*, 7.
31. Local historian Zhao Fuhai mentions in particular traders from Luohe, Zhumadian, and Shangqiu meeting those from Guangdong and Fujian. Zhao Fuhai, "Bainian Zhengzhou dayimin," *Zhengzhou wanbao*, November 21, 2007.
32. Zhengzhou shi difang shizhi bianzuan weiyuanhui, *Zhengzhou shizhi*, 1:35.
33. Henan sheng tongjiju, *Henan sheng, shidi, xian shehui jingji gaikuang*, 11. On the twists and turns of Zhengzhou's private sector in the reform era, see Yang Chunyu, "Zhengzhou shi fei gongyouzhi jingji."

by the State Council only in 1984. Its initial target population for the year 2000 was one million, but that landmark was passed just a year later, in the high-growth year of 1985.[34] With oversight from Mayor Hu Shujian (1934–2016), the city planning bureau hastily updated the plan, with a new focus on shaping development at Zhengzhou's urban edge to prevent "chaotic" expansion. The key to this 1986 scheme was Zhengzhou's first ring road, which was designed as a sharp urban boundary, with agricultural activity inside the ring road to be swiftly eliminated.[35] This strategy seems to have been at least partially successful. Although there is evidence of illegal construction and land speculation at the local level, Zhengzhou's urban edge did become a neater boundary as proposed in 1984–1986 planning. In a GIS study of Zhengzhou's morphology, Xia Baolin found that despite the city's rapid growth, Zhengzhou's urban edge was becoming more regular (with a "straighter" edge to the built-up area) between 1988 and the end of the century.[36]

This is perhaps surprising: given the rural-urban institutional divisions, local historians sometimes assume that the city had a tight spatial boundary during the Mao period and a reform era sprawl.[37] As seen in chapter 4, this was far from the case. Mao era expansion had been concentrated in Zhengzhou's northeast and southwest quadrants, and unplanned land grabs by work units had left patches of suburban agriculture around and even inside the built-up area (see map 6.1). On the southwestern edge of the city, the village of Luzhai (just east of Linshanzhai) had lost around two-thirds of its land during 1954–1980, but farming continued on the shrinking pockets of land into the 1990s. To the northwest, Wanglizhai was less than 3 kilometers from the heart of the downtown at Erqi Square and tucked up against factories and railroads,

34. Henan sheng jiansheting chengjianzhi bianjishi, *Henan sheng chengjian shizhi gao*, 2:171–72.

35. Zhengzhou shi jianshe weiyuanhui, "Zhengzhou shi chengxiang jianshe zhi," 1:311–12.

36. Xia follows Michael Batty and Paul Longley's use of the D-value in fractal geometry to calculate the spatial complexity of an urban fringe. See Batty and Longley, *Fractal Cities*, esp. 179–85. Xia's work is discussed in An Qian, *Kuaisu chengshihua jincheng*, 177–78. On land speculation beyond the designated zone, see an example from Weizhuang Village in Liu Weide, Feng Yunhuai, and Chen Jie, "Zhengzhou shi beijiao tudi liyong."

37. See, for instance, Zhao Shuling, "Zhengzhou chengshi kongjian kuozhan," 51.

but it was only accessible by a dirt track.[38] This whole northwest quadrant of the city was a local periphery cut off by multiple railroads and railway yards and had been hardly used during Zhengzhou's expansion of the 1950s: "This is one of the most backward (*luohou*) parts in the city," notes the neighborhood planning document of 1989. "It is on the rural-urban fringe, being in a rather remote position and overlooked for many years (*duonianlai zhongshi bugou*)."[39] Apart from some ribbon development along key arteries, Zhengzhou's late 1980s and early 1990s expansion is therefore best understood as a "filling-in" of the gaps left by Mao era growth. Luzhai's final patch of farmland was requisitioned by the telecommunications bureau in 1992.[40] Wanglizhai's transformation began with the opening of a fruit wholesale market in the mid-1980s, and its farmland had almost all disappeared by the end of the decade.[41]

This increasing spatial regularity of Zhengzhou's urban edge does not mean that the fringes of the city were homogeneous. At the end of the 1980s, the western edge of the city was still demarcated by the heavy industrial projects of the high Maoist era, whereas the fast-expanding northern edge was shaped by its numerous educational campuses and research institutions (more than twenty by 1988, plus the 1985 Zhengzhou Zoo). Expansion to the east was blocked by the airport until its 1997 relocation, and small factories and warehousing still predominated on the southeastern edges of the city, as they had during the Mao period. The northwest corner of Zhengzhou was becoming better connected but remained the least built-up quadrant of the city well into the twenty-first century. It was only the south side of Zhengzhou that had seen much sign of a phenomenon that was to dominate the urban edge in the decades to come: commercial housing projects.[42] The gradual re-marketization of urban housing had begun in 1985, and, with investment from Taiwan, Zhengzhou's first high-end real estate speculation soon followed on the southern edge of the city at Daizhuang. Numerous commercial housing zones on both the northern and southern edges of the city followed in

38. Zhengxie Zhengzhou shi Erqiqu weiyuanhui, *Yuanqu zhi jiyi*, 49.

39. Zhengzhou shi chengshi guihua guanliju, *Zhengzhou shi chengshi fenqu guihua tuji*, 40.

40. An Qian, *Kuaisu chengshihua jincheng*, 213.

41. Zhengxie Zhengzhou shi Erqiqu weiyuanhui, *Yuanqu zhi jiyi*, 49.

42. For detailed mapping of the urban edge, see Zhengzhou shi chengshi guihua guanliju, *Zhengzhou shi chengshi fenqu guihua tuji*.

the early 1990s, although Zhengzhou's spectacular real estate boom was still two decades away.[43]

HIGH GROWTH AND HIERARCHIES IN THE NINETIES

Local accounts of Zhengzhou's recent past tend to tell a story of smooth progress from the mid-1980s onwards.[44] But the transition to the fast-growing economy of the 1990s was more complex. Following the failed price reform of summer 1988, national economic policy shifted to retrenchment, a deliberate slowdown to deal with problems of overheating in the fast-growing Chinese economy. This retrenchment policy was designed for booming coastal areas but was ill-timed for Zhengzhou, where the commercial and construction sectors were forced to slow down almost as soon as they had begun to take off. As the municipal authorities discussed in their local neighborhood plans of 1987–1988, Zhengzhou's facilities and living space had failed to keep pace with rapid population growth. Wages were also falling slightly relative to the rising cost of living. It was an overcrowded, fractious city that saw the emergence and suppression of student and worker protest in the spring of 1989.[45]

Deng Xiaoping's "southern tour" (*nanxun*) in early 1992 is usually told as the relaunch of economic reform and rapid growth, but Zhengzhou's economy had been kickstarted a little earlier. China's very first experimental futures market was opened on the southwest side of the city in October 1990; illustrating Zhengzhou's role as a pivot between the rural, inland economy and the increasingly commercialized and financialized urban/coastal economy, this futures market specialized in trading on the agricultural products of Central China (especially cotton, wheat, and peanuts).[46] By 1991, Zhengzhou was receiving more investment per capita than the other provincial capitals of Middle China—Jinan, Hefei, Nanchang, Changsha, and even Wuhan—and in 1992 it was designated

43. On Daizhuang, see Zhengzhou shi jianshe weiyuanhui, "Zhengzhou shi chengxiang jianshe zhi," 1:60–61; on expansion to the north and south in the 1990s, see Wang Jianguo, *Zhengzhou dadu shiqu jianshe*, 111.

44. See, for instance, An Qian, *Kuaisu chengshihua jincheng*, 170–71.

45. Zhengzhou shi chengshi guihua guanliju, *Zhengzhou shi chengshi fenqu guihua tuji*, 8.

46. Zhengzhou shi jianshe weiyuanhui, "Zhengzhou shi chengxiang jianshe zhi," 1:604.

an "inland open city" (*neilu kaifang chengshi*), enjoying similar trading benefits to most coastal centers.[47] Zhengzhou's GDP growth hit a record high of 14.9 percent in 1995, with particularly strong performance in the service sector. In 1996, Laofengang, the urban edge entertainment and sex work district of the Republican period and black market of the Mao years, was relaunched as a vast retail center—one of the largest in China.[48]

This rapid growth pushed Zhengzhou's built-up area beyond the boundary of the late 1980s ring road. Aided by new regulations easing the reallocation of land away from agriculture, the second half of the 1990s witnessed the most rapid expansion of the city since the 1950s.[49] In addition to the new phenomenon of commercial housing, some of this expansion was of a familiar pattern, such as the boom in wholesale markets. Such markets were often still collective enterprises, such as the village-run Guanhutun (1991) and Chenzhai (1992) vegetable markets on the expanding northern edge of the city (see map 6.1).[50] But as in other major Chinese cities, the 1990s also saw urban edge schemes on a much larger scale. In Zhengzhou, a "High-Tech Industrial Development Zone" in the northwest (Gaoxin jishu chanye kaifaqu, approved 1991) was followed in 1993 by the "Economic and Technological Development Zone" (Jingji jishu kaifaqu) to the southeast. The latter was more successful, especially in vehicle assembly, food processing, and consumer goods.[51] Such zones were not wholly without precursors. Zhengzhou's first satellite district was the 1958 aluminum plant at Shangjie, and, in their commercial function, rights for foreign investment, and separate administrative powers, these development districts echoed the *shangbu* (trading port) zone of 1908.

These new districts were not the only echoes of Zhengzhou's first railroad boom. The rapid expansion, real estate speculation, and often murky land transactions of the 1990s and early 2000s also recall unequal patterns of Zhengzhou's railroad boom of the 1900s and 1910s (see chapter 1).

47. *Zhongguo tongji nianjian*, 1993:691–92.

48. On GDP, see Zhengzhou shi difang shizhi bianzuan weiyuanhui, *Zhengzhou shizhi*, 1:30; on Laofengang, see Zhao Fuhai, *Lao Zhengzhou: Shangdu yimeng*, 204.

49. Zhengzhou's built-up area increased by 23 percent between 1995 and 2000. *Zhengzhou tongji nianjian*, 2016:7.

50. Ishihara, "Kanan-shō Teishūshi ni okeru sosai," 33–38.

51. An Qian, *Kuaisu chengshihua jincheng*, 218–20.

222 Chapter Six

Urban growth was built on deep spatial inequalities, particularly regarding compensation for lost farmland. An arbitrary time/space hierarchy emerged, with the fate of former farmers deeply dependent on when their land was requisitioned and how close it was to the city. In 1985 Zhengzhou Municipality had adopted the most generous compensation scheme permitted by the central government, with payments per *mu* of grain land equivalent to almost three times the annual average urban salary plus well-subsidized job support schemes for former farmers. Relative to urban wages, this was a fourfold improvement on the compensation available in the mid-1970s (amounting to 80 percent of an average urban salary per *mu*), whereas some who had lost access to land during the Great Leap Forward had not been compensated at all—even at the level of the collective.[52]

The more generous 1985 scheme unraveled during the 1990s. Compensation fell markedly relative to the rising value of the land, and outcomes for suburban farmers varied depending on the negotiating position and political behavior of village committees and township officials. In the late 1990s and early 2000s, a series of cases exposed the inequalities of local corruption under the cover of a language of urban development and progress. In the High-Tech Development Zone on the northwestern edge of the city, journalist Jiang Xueqin found illegal land seizures and derisory, delayed compensation relative to both the value of the land and the length of farmers' leases.[53] As Zhengzhou's expansion intensified, responsibility for overseeing payments and reemployment passed from the municipal government to the patchier provision of development companies (until reclaimed by the municipality in 2011). In the same northwestern expansion zone, Zhang Wensheng found that although some training and subsidies were available for the former farmers of Gouzhao Village, they were inadequate to the challenge of integration into the urban economy. From the early 2000s, most in Gouzhao found themselves in a series of odd jobs, including at the new Zhengzhou University campus; like at the original university site in the new western suburb of the 1950s, those able to find jobs on campus were usually in the

52. On Great Leap Forward and 1980s arrangements, see Zhengzhou shi jianshe weiyuanhui, "Zhengzhou shi chengxiang jianshe zhi," 1:460–64; on 1970s compensation, see Zhengzhou shi difang shizhi bianzuan weiyuanhui, *Zhengzhou shizhi*, 3:171–72.
53. Jiang Xueqin, "Stealing the Land."

lowest-paid roles.[54] Inequalities over land requisitioning were also exacerbated by corruption in village committees. At Xigang, village leaders seized 510 *mu* of farmland without consultation, leasing it out in 2004 to a wholesale market in which they had private financial interests. Under self-trained lawyer and resident Gu Guo'an, villagers won the case in court and received national press attention—but did not get their land back. Instead, village leaders leased it out to another company in another unlawful contract, and residents suffered major financial losses when the firm stopped paying rent.[55]

Zhengzhou's former suburban farmers may have been losing out relative to land developers, the municipal government, and local leaders, but in other ways they benefited from the spatial inequalities of the reform regime. Villagers were able to capitalize on Zhengzhou's fast-growing "floating population" by letting out rooms to migrant workers. As with many other reform era phenomena, this pattern was not wholly new: as early as the 1910s villagers close to the city had been letting out rooms to railroad workers. Indeed, in some cases the "villages-in-the-city" (*chengzhongcun*, hereafter untranslated) of the 1990s were the very same villages as those at the urban edge in the Republican period. Liuloucun had lost farmland for the railroad station as early as 1904 but almost a century later still retained a separate identity as a lively *chengzhongcun*, full of food stalls and traders from Wenzhou. Because villages had rarely been demolished wholesale in either the Mao period or the reform era, settlements close to the downtown, such as Xichen, Mifengzhang, and Linshanzhai, became some of the most desirable *chengzhongcun* during the 1990s. Homeowners were able to charge higher rents than in *chengzhongcun* farther from the downtown, providing some recompense for the lower payments they had received for the loss of farmland in the Mao period, whereas villages such as Linshanzhai that had retained parcels of village-owned land within the city benefited collectively from rising rents.[56] At the urban edge, villagers began to build new housing blocks or

54. Zhang Wensheng, "Chengzhenhua jincheng zhong de jiaoqu nongmin," 17–18 (on employment in the early 2000s) and 24–29 (difficulties in transition).
55. Huang Jinping, "Zhengzhou Xigangcun."
56. See, for instance, Zhengxie Zhengzhou shi Erqiqu weiyuanhui, *Yuanqu zhi jiyi*, 40–41 (Xichen), 56 (Mifengzhang), and 58–59 (Liuloucun). On Linshanzhai, see *Dahebao*, May 8, 2014.

add stories to existing homes, sparking anxiety in the municipal government that "in the urban-suburban fringe zone (*chengjiao jiehebu*) there are many people renting rooms, but these areas are basically ungoverned (*jibenshang chuyu wu zhengfu zhuangtai*)."[57]

By not demolishing villages, even as farmland was requisitioned, the municipal authorities were able to solve—or, perhaps, able to ignore—problems of both migrant housing and the fate of Zhengzhou's former farmers. Former villagers experienced worse housing and facilities than other urban residents but enjoyed lucrative rental incomes. Li Jiashun's is a typical suburban story: born just north of Zhengzhou at Zaozhuang, he moved to the city as a twenty-year-old in 1981 to pick up casual work. After returning to the village to get married, he invested in several cows and sold fresh milk in the city each day. But by the end of the 1990s, Zaozhuang had lost all remaining land and become a *chengzhongcun*. From 2001 onwards Li was instead making a living as a landlord for migrant workers in his expanded, multistory home.[58] Li Jiashun's experience exemplifies the bigger inequalities of the high-stakes struggle at the urban edge, with villagers first gaining from proximity to the city in the early reform period, then losing the value of their land relative to urban institutions and development companies as the city expanded, but afterwards profiting from migrant workers at the very bottom of the reform regime's spatial hierarchy. The remainder of this chapter turns to those rural-urban inequalities and the place of migrants in the reform era city.

Rural-Urban and Regional Inequalities

Rural-urban inequality around Zhengzhou reached a historic low in 1983, with per capita incomes for urban residents just 51 percent higher than their rural counterparts.[59] In the same year, the Zhengzhou municipality expanded to include six nearby counties, resulting in the first-ever regional development plan (map 6.2). Apart from an abortive experiment of expanded municipalities during the Great Leap Forward, this

---

57. Kong Luyu, "Zanzhu renkou hukou guanli xianzhuang," in Fan Futang et al., *Zhengzhou liudong renkou*, 145.

58. "Zhengzhou chengzhongcun gaizao," *Zhengzhou jiyi*, November 5, 2015; for closer analysis of similar processes on Chongqing's periphery, see Smith, *End of the Village*, 71–102.

59. Zhengzhou shi difang shizhi bianzuan weiyuanhui, *Zhengzhou shizhi*, 7:575.

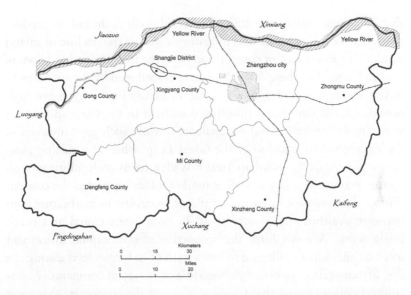

MAP 6.2. Zhengzhou Municipality, 1997. Adapted from Zhengzhou shi difang shizhi bianzuan weiyuanhui, ed., *Zhengzhou shizhi*, vol. 1, unpaginated front matter. Map by Jogu Gopinath.

expansion marked the first time since 1913 that the city of Zhengzhou had administrative responsibility for a large rural hinterland. The policy aimed further to close Mao era divisions between the rural and urban sectors. As one slogan of the time put it: "the two wings of the city and the countryside will rise together" (*chengxiang liang yi qi qifei*).[60]

The promise was not fulfilled. Even as great strides were made in the reduction of absolute poverty, municipal control of the countryside did not prevent rising inequality between Zhengzhou and its rural hinterland. As with China's overall rural-urban gap, income inequality in the expanded Zhengzhou grew steeply for the next decade. On a larger scale, the gulf also widened between the fast-growing provincial capital and the rest of Henan Province, reaching its most dramatic expression in the steep relative decline of neighboring Kaifeng.

There were several reasons for this growing inequality, all present at the national scale but particularly stark in inland agricultural provinces

60. Zhengzhou shi jianshe weiyuanhui, "Zhengzhou shi chengxiang jianshe zhi," 1:19.

such as Henan. Some were difficult to avoid, such as the gulf in productivity between agriculture and industry as well as the decline of inland
rural TVEs in the face of competition from the manufacturing boom of
coastal China. But these difficulties were exacerbated by the spatial politics of a state that underpinned rising inequality in the service of high
growth. In the reform era thinking dominant in the 1990s, disparities
were simply inevitable, and state efforts to close such gaps smacked of
the discredited utopianism of the Great Leap, while also risking post-
1989 regime stability in urban areas.[61] With a focus on headline growth
figures, economic policy as well as market forces supported the concentration of investment in particular places, widening infrastructure gaps
between wealthier and poorer areas, in both interregional and rural-
urban terms. Across China, the proportion of state capital investment
spent on agriculture collapsed to just a sixth of its former level during the
first fifteen years of reform.[62] A World Bank survey of comparative agricultural policies found that China was one of the economies that most
heavily penalized the farming sector (ranked fifty-fourth of fifty-seven
economies across all continents).[63] This imbalance was worsened by fiscal
decisions, where in the late 1980s and 1990s first fiscal decentralization
and then a partial recentralization of revenues (without reducing local
government spending responsibilities) led to a crisis of the local state,
particularly in inland rural areas, widening spatial gulfs in facilities,
welfare, and support for business. Given the rising role of educational
attainment in driving inequality during the 1990s, the gap was particularly serious in educational funding, where even at the level of compulsory primary schooling, per pupil spending in cities was almost double
that of rural areas.[64]

61. On urban bias following the protest movement of 1989, see Wallace, *Cities and
Stability*, 101–3.
62. Anagnost, "Strange Circulations," 514 (comparing 1979 and 1994).
63. China registered a nominal rate of assistance (NRA) for agriculture of -35.5
for 1985–1989. Only Zambia and Tanzania (also still emerging from Mao-style crash
programs of state industrialization) and the Dominican Republic show lower NRA
figures. See Anderson, *Distortions to Agricultural Incentives*.
64. For the effects on rural areas and regional inequality, see Xiaobo Zhang,
"Fiscal Decentralization and Political Centralization." In 1999, per pupil funding was
1,062 RMB in urban areas and 576 RMB in rural areas. Tsang and Ding, "Resource
Utilization," 10.

INEQUALITY IN THE EXPANDED MUNICIPALITY

Around Zhengzhou, these patterns concentrated economic investment and activity in the city, with relatively little trickle out into the six counties of the municipal hinterland. In the mid-1990s, the city proper received 72 percent of capital construction (*jiben jianshe*) spending and 61 percent of total state spending within the Zhengzhou municipality, despite only accounting for 34 percent of the population. The proportion of people with higher education was twenty-five times higher in the city than its subordinate counties.[65] By then, the relative rural-urban equality of the early reform period had been lost, with Zhengzhou's income gap rising sharply from the mid-1980s and reaching a peak in 1993–1995. A narrowing in the second half of the 1990s—the result of what Knight and Song call the "tardy and tortuous dismantling of the price-scissors policy"—was not sustained, and the gulf rose again in the first years of the new century, albeit less sharply than for China as a whole (where the urban-rural income ratio was over 3:1 by 2003; fig. 6.2).[66]

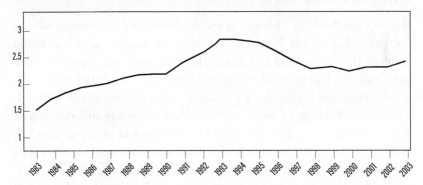

FIGURE 6.2. Urban-rural income ratios in Zhengzhou, 1983–2003. Pre-1990 data from Zhengzhou shi difang shizhi bianzuan weiyuanhui, *Zhengzhou shizhi*, 7:586–88; 1990s data from Zhengzhou shi difang shizhi bianzuan weiyuanhui, *Zhengzhou shizhi, 1991–2000*, 1:19; post-2000 data from *Zhengzhou tongji nianjian*, 2004:8.

65. *Zhengzhou tongji nianjian,* 1997:362–63. Numbers of university graduates from Zhengzhou shi difang shizhi bianzuan weiyuanhui, *Zhengzhou shizhi*, 1:367.
66. See Knight and Song, *Rural-Urban Divide*, 323.

These ratios also disguise sharp differences within the newly expanded municipality (see map 6.2). Aided by the presence of coal, Gong County (upgraded to Gongyi County-Level City in 1991) was one of Henan's flagship counties for rural growth, boasting GDP per capita more than double the provincial average in 1999. But to the east of Zhengzhou, Zhongmu County was much more reliant on agriculture and was left badly behind despite its closer proximity to the city. In 1976, Zhongmu's collectives had boasted incomes 30 percent above the average for counties around Zhengzhou, but, by the end of the century, the county's GDP per capita was almost 40 percent below.[67] This uneven distribution of economic growth translated into rural protest and social and political unrest during the 1990s and early 2000s. In 1993 rural residents were reported to be throwing up roadblocks on the Luoyang–Zhengzhou road to rob passing travelers. In 2004, more than a hundred people died in bitter communal clashes between Han and Hui residents in the isolated north of Zhongmu County.[68]

Zhengzhou's Suburbs

If living standards in Zhengzhou's wider hinterland fell sharply behind the city, what of the intermediate zone, the nearby rural hinterland between the urban edge and Zhengzhou's subordinate counties? These rural suburbs had enjoyed strong economic growth in the early years of reform, especially in the TVE sector. Soon afterwards, in 1987, the Zhengzhou Suburbs (Jiaoqu) was abolished as an administrative unit, with Zhengzhou's nearby hinterland broken up and absorbed into five ordinary urban districts. As with the takeover of adjacent counties, this administrative abolition of the Suburban District was heralded by local geographer Zhao Shuling as a breaking down of rural-urban divisions.[69]

---

67. *Henan tongji nianjian*, 2000:558. Zhongmu's 1976 figures calculated from Zhengzhou shi difang shizhi bianzuan weiyuanhui, *Zhengzhou shizhi*, 1:487–556.

68. Reported respectively in *Far Eastern Economic Review* 156, no. 32 (August 1993): 9; *New York Times*, November 1, 2004.

69. Zhao Shuling, "Zhengzhou chengshi kongjian kuozhan," 52. This was broadly the pre-1953 rural Zheng County that, with minor boundary changes, had been administered as the Suburban District (1953–1987) of the municipality. After 1987 it was divided between five urban districts, each of which contained part of the city and part of the nearby countryside (although Mangshan District in the far north was overwhelmingly rural). I continue to use the term "suburbs" to refer to the parts of these urban districts that were predominantly rural.

But did this proximity to and administrative unity with the city mean that Zhengzhou's closest countryside avoided the inequalities and sluggish growth of the nearby rural counties?

The short answer is no: data suggest that Zhengzhou's nearby rural suburbs did not join the city proper in surging ahead of the wider rural region (the other six county-level units under the municipal government). In 1990, rural incomes closest to the city were 14.6 percent ahead of the municipal rural average, but by 1997 they had seen a slight fall in relative terms (only 11.8 percent ahead). Over the same period (1990–1997), rural residents of Zhengzhou's nearby hinterland also saw their incomes slip back relative to their counterparts in the city proper (from a ratio of 1.89 in 1990 to 2.14 in 1997).[70] They were no more likely to own washing machines or color televisions than rural residents farther away from the city and were only half as likely to own these coveted items as their urban counterparts.[71] Much of the explanation lies in the fact that sectors that had boosted suburban incomes in the first half of the 1980s were no longer driving reductions in rural-urban inequality. Areas specializing in fruit and vegetables had lost their relative advantage owing to falling prices and the emergence of long-distance competition in wholesale markets.[72] Meanwhile, TVEs faced a period of much slower growth—in some sectors even a decline in the face of growing competition. By the second half of the 1990s, income from rural industry in the Zhengzhou suburbs was markedly *less* (14 percent) than the rural average for the wider municipality.[73]

As with Zhengzhou's subordinate counties, the spatial pattern in Zhengzhou's rural suburbs was deeply uneven, with economic outcomes in villages depending on factors such as skills, the trajectory of village specializations, and infrastructural links to the city. The most striking spatial difference was between the well-connected rural suburbs in the cardinal directions and poorer, more isolated "diagonals," particularly to the northwest and the northeast. Respectively due east and west

70. For 1990, see Zhengzhou shi difang shizhi bianzuan weiyuanhui, *Zhengzhou shizhi*, 7:575 and 593; for 1997, *Zhengzhou tongji nianjian*, 1997:608–9.
71. Ownership data per hundred households in *Zhengzhou tongji nianjian*, 1997:572–73 and 620–21.
72. On the diminishing place of local vegetable producers, see Ishihara, "Kanan-shō Teishūshi ni okeru sosai," comparing 32 and 38–40.
73. Calculated from *Zhengzhou tongji nianjian*, 1997:168.

of Zhengzhou, the expanding towns of Putian and Xushui emerged as key links between the city and rural economies (for their location, see map 5.1). This was not without drawbacks—the growth of Putian was partly driven by an effort to get polluting chemical industries out of the city proper during the late 1980s and 1990s—but given the underdevelopment of Zhengzhou's rural market towns throughout the twentieth century, this expansion marked an important shift.[74] Some villagers were able to take advantage of urban connections. Due west of the city, Cao Donghuan, the thirteen-year-old girl who sold straw baskets during the Great Leap Forward (see chapter 5), worked for a TVE in Xigang producing sofas and traveled frequently to the city to find customers. After a power struggle in the collective enterprise, Cao made the most of these city contacts to set up a private furniture factory.[75] These western suburbs also benefited from their proximity to Zhengzhou's industrial zone. Villagers around Xushui were able to obtain skills and technology from the nearby grinding wheel factory to set up lower-grade abrasive enterprises. At the peak of this expansion, some 280 small workshops in villages west of Zhengzhou were connected with the abrasives sector.[76]

However, most villages were in the "diagonals," away from major transport routes and fast-growing suburban towns. As in the Republican period, the cross shape of Zhengzhou's transport links had left these areas relatively isolated despite their proximity to the city, though changes in technology and living standards meant that nowhere around Zhengzhou was as cut off as in the Republican period. Ownership of bicycles and later motorbikes was becoming ubiquitous even in the poorer villages around Zhengzhou, expanding the "diurnal hinterland" of easy daily movement between city and countryside. But parts of the rural suburbs were still more remote from the city than mere distance would suggest. Surprisingly, public transport to the rural suburbs was becoming worse after 1985, when the municipal transport bureau decided to "stop suburban and county buses in order to strengthen urban transport capacity"

74. On Putian, see Zhengzhou shi jianshe weiyuanhui, "Zhengzhou shi chengxiang jianshe zhi," 1:306–7. For more on the environmental burden of periurban towns in the reform era, see Joshua Goldstein, *Remains of the Everyday*, 154–58.

75. Xigang cunzhi bianzuan weiyuanhui, *Xigang cunzhi*, 252–57.

76. Xigang cunzhi bianzuan weiyuanhui, *Xigang cunzhi*, 86–87.

(*jiao xian che tingyun, yi jiaqiang shiqu yunli*). Even in 1975 Zhengzhou's nearby rural hinterland had been linked to the city by nine bus routes, but by 1990 only six such links remained.[77] Whereas in the 1930s it was the southwest quadrant of Zheng County that was particularly remote (see chapter 2), in the reform period, it was the suburban areas to the northwest and northeast, toward the Yellow River that were left behind (see map 5.1). These districts had benefited from irrigation in the 1970s but struggled to build on this foundation. At Weizhuang in the northeast, Liu Weide found that villagers lacked the skills or technology to move beyond initial successes in fruit, vegetables, and fish farming.[78] To the northwest, the local authorities identified the cotton- and grain-growing area around Shifo and Guxing as a zone of relative deprivation from the mid-1980s.[79] In Gouzhao (between Shifo and Guxing), more than 80 percent of residents still earned most of their income from agriculture in 1990, compared with less than 30 percent in better-connected Xigang (note, though, that the Xigang sample is a few years later, from 1994).[80]

It was only in the early 2000s that incomes in Zhengzhou's rural suburbs surged ahead of their counterparts farther from the city. The small gap of 1997 (11.8 percent) jumped by 2003 to a remarkable 49 percent income advantage for rural residents of Zhengzhou's suburbs over villagers in nearby counties.[81] Yet on closer inspection, incomes from agriculture and off-farm employment were still similar in both Zhengzhou's suburban hinterland and more distant counties. Instead, three-quarters of the difference was made up of income from property and investments, including compensation payments for loss of land (which accounted for almost a third of the difference) as well as income

77. Zhengzhou shi difang shizhi bianzuan weiyuanhui, *Zhengzhou shizhi*, 3:440–44. Admittedly, informal private vehicles must have picked up the slack.

78. Liu Weide, Feng Yunhuai, and Chen Jie, "Zhengzhou shi beijiao tudi liyong," 17–18.

79. Zhengzhou shi jiaoqu zhi bianzuan weiyuanhui, "Zhengzhou shi jiaoqu zhi, nongye zhi," 121.

80. Zhang Wensheng, "Chengzhenhua jincheng zhong de jiaoqu nongmin," 17; compare Xigang cunzhi bianzuan weiyuanhui, *Xigang cunzhi*, 2.

81. *Zhengzhou tongji nianjian*, 1997:608–9; comparing *Zhengzhou tongji nianjian*, 2004:208–9.

from renting out rooms.[82] In other words, the higher incomes of rural residents in the Zhengzhou suburbs was an effect of urbanization rather than a narrowing of the rural-urban divide. Most residents of this zone still held rural *hukou*, but with Zhengzhou's rapid expansion of the early 2000s, the city's nearby hinterland was beginning a process of urbanization in situ (see chapter 7).

ZHENGZHOU IN HENAN PROVINCE

If rural parts of Zhengzhou's expanded municipality were being left behind by the city's rapid growth, the surge of the provincial capital relative to other parts of Henan was even more marked. Away from the industrial core of the province around Zhengzhou, Luoyang, and the northern coalfields, Henan was being held back by the worsening relative position of agriculture.[83] After more than a decade of reform, Henan was still China's fourth-poorest province and the second-poorest outside the western region (1991 figures).[84] Henan was receiving just 3.4 percent of state capital construction investment for its 7.6 percent of China's population, a victim of fiscal decentralization and the wider spatial policy of backing winners and concentrating resources.[85] Although Henan's position relative to other inland provinces improved slightly during the 1990s, it was on the wrong end of regional inequality between coastal and inland China, which widened all the way to 2005.[86]

Although it had become Henan's provincial capital and largest city in the mid-1950s, Zhengzhou in the late Maoist period was not yet *the* economic powerhouse of Henan. Even after a decade of reform, Zhengzhou's wages were only 10 percent above the urban provincial average.[87] But both William Hurst and Jeremy Wallace argue that the 1990s brought renewed bias to support provincial capitals—just as John Fitzgerald shows for the 1930s. For Wallace, there is a direct link to fears of unrest

---

82. *Zhengzhou tongji nianjian*, 2004:208–9.
83. Even in 2001, more than three-quarters of Henan's population were rural *hukou* holders (compared to a national figure of 64 percent). See Sun Jianguo, *Xiandai Henan jingjishi*, 367.
84. Guojia tongjiju, *Zhongguo tongji nianjian: 1993*, 40.
85. Guojia tongjiju, *Zhongguo tongji nianjian: 1993*, 149. The Henan population percentage includes *hukou* holders working outside the province.
86. Felix Haifeng Liao and Dennis Wei, "Regional Inequality."
87. *Henan tongji nianjian*, 1989:178.

in political centers following the 1989 student and worker movement.[88] The surge of Zhengzhou relative to the rest of the province supports their findings. In the space of a decade, Zhengzhou's urban wages rose from 10 percent to 33 percent above the Henan urban average, becoming by far the highest in the province.[89] Unlike in the 1930s, though, this bias for the provincial capital also aided nearby rural residents. Although rural incomes around Zhengzhou had been at the Henan average at the beginning of the reform period (1980), by the end of the century rural residents of Zhengzhou Municipality (including its subordinate counties) enjoyed average incomes 47 percent higher than their counterparts in the rest of Henan.[90]

Zhengzhou's new-found regional dominance is thrown into sharp relief by the relative economic collapse of nearby Kaifeng. The city that had been capital of Henan for more than six hundred years was still struggling following its political downgrading in 1954. Kaifeng was one of the few cities in China to have fared badly during both the planned economy and the reform era. The medium-sized state industries that had been allocated to Kaifeng as a sop to its loss of administrative status—chemicals, food processing, light machinery—struggled even before restructuring of state-owned enterprises in the mid-1990s. By 1992, Kaifeng's growth rate was rock bottom among Henan's seventeen city units.[91] The following year, the definitive local history of Cheng Ziliang and Li Qingyin offered a less-than-glowing endorsement of the city's place in the People's Republic: "compared to other cities, Kaifeng has offered up more and received less. It has developed others, while deferring its own development (*fazhan le bieren, yanhuan le ziji*)."[92] But even as Cheng and Li were writing, Kaifeng was slipping into another decade of crisis, with the closure of state-owned enterprises and fiscal difficulties. In the mid-1990s commentators across China began to speak of the "Kaifeng phenomenon" (*Kaifeng xianxiang*) as a warning for medium-sized cities that were being left behind in the

88. Hurst, *Chinese Worker*, 35–36; Wallace, *Cities and Stability*, 124.
89. *Henan tongji nianjian*, 2000:126.
90. 1980 figures from Henan sheng tongjiju, *Henan sheng, shidi, xian shehui jingji gaikuang*, comparing 4 and 10; year 2000 figures from *Henan tongji nianjian*, 2010:351.
91. Wu Pengfei, "Kaifeng chengshi shengming," 123.
92. Cheng Ziliang and Li Qingyin, *Kaifeng chengshi shi*, 285.

new economy.[93] Between 1978 and 2004 Kaifeng had slumped from the fifth-wealthiest city in the province to one of the poorest (fourteenth out of seventeen).

Although Zhengzhou and Kaifeng were just 60 kilometers apart, by the end of the century urban residents in the provincial capital enjoyed consumption levels almost twice those of Kaifeng (97 percent higher).[94] This divergence was most marked in the interurban inequality between the two cities, but it also affected their adjacent hinterlands. The process unfolded in two stages. First, when Zhengzhou Municipality expanded in 1983 to include nearby counties, it absorbed counties that had been transferred to Kaifeng Prefecture as partial compensation for its loss of provincial capital status in 1954. Some of these counties—Gong County, Mi County, Xinzheng—were already making strides in the TVE sector, leaving Kaifeng with overwhelmingly agricultural counties. For Kaifeng historian Wu Pengfei, their absorption by Zhengzhou was a matter of political muscle: "Relying on its systemic dominance as provincial capital (*yikao shenghui tizhi youshi*), Zhengzhou took away five strong economic counties that had belonged to Kaifeng."[95] Second, these counties surged further ahead following their absorption into Zhengzhou. In 1990, rural incomes in the Zhengzhou municipal unit were already 15 percent higher than in rural Kaifeng; a decade later, the gap was 34 percent.[96] The divergence was exacerbated by the very different levels of state support: by the end of the century, state capital construction investment was almost five times higher per capita in the infrastructure-rich Zhengzhou municipal unit than in crisis-hit Kaifeng next door.[97] For regional economist Liang Liuke, this pattern of rural poverty in Kaifeng's hinterland was in turn damaging economic growth in the city, in a vicious cycle of relative

93. Liang Liuke, *Kaifeng shi kechixu fazhan*, 41–45; on the "Kaifeng phenomenon," see Yang Min, "Kaifeng, Kaifeng!" 15.

94. *Henan tongji nianjian*, 2000:204.

95. Wu Pengfei, "Kaifeng chengshi shengming," 123. China's subprovincial prefectures were called *zhuanqu* before 1970 and *diqu* thereafter. They were replaced by expanded municipalities during the 1980s.

96. Figures for 1990 from Henan sheng tongjiju, *Henan sheng, shidi, xian shehui jingji gaikuang*, 10 (Zhengzhou) and 46 (Kaifeng); year 2000 figures from *Henan tongji nianjian*, 2000:219.

97. 1,116 RMB per head in Zhengzhou; 236.6 RMB per head in Kaifeng (1999 figures). *Henan tongji nianjian*, 2000:145.

decline.[98] In that sense, reform era Kaifeng looks something like Zheng-zhou in the 1920s and 1930s: a medium-sized city that was being held back by an impoverished hinterland and in turn failing to kickstart rural growth (see chapters 1 and 2).

SPACE AND CLASS

This is not to say that everything was straightforward in Zhengzhou at the turn of the twenty-first century. Although Zhengzhou had risen to regional dominance, it was wealthy only by the standards of strug-gling Henan Province. Per capita urban incomes were still less than 800 dollars per year. As with Kaifeng, the dismantling of the state manufac-turing sector hit Zhengzhou hard, particularly in its western industrial district. Zhengzhou's textile workers had received no increase in wages after 1994, despite the rising cost of living. After years of redundancies and closures, the remaining state mills filed for bankruptcy in 2003.[99] Zhengzhou became a center of grassroots leftist activism, with work-ers protesting against corruption and inequalities in the privatization process. In July 2001, workers at the Electrical Machinery Works occu-pied the factory to prevent the fire sale of state-owned assets. With the support of tens of thousands of workers from other factories, a tense standoff escalated into an hourslong pitched battle, the bitterest fighting in the streets and factories of Zhengzhou since the Cultural Revolution; indeed, some workers had been involved as teenagers in the movements of 1966–1967 (the unlucky "sent-down and laid-off," *xiaxiang xiagang*, cohort).[100]

Although some households and neighborhoods in Zhengzhou suffered badly during the running down of state industry, as with other provincial capitals, Zhengzhou was better placed than smaller cities to absorb the shock.[101] The workers' movement in Zhengzhou struggled to maintain its momentum in the 2000s, partly owing to state repres-sion but also because of the availability of an alternative, low-wage rural migrant labor force. Indicatively, the July 2001 struggle at the Electrical Machinery Works was not primarily between workers and police but

98. Liang Liuke, *Kaifeng shi kechixu fazhan*, 49–50.
99. See Guoxin Xing, "Living with the Revolutionary Legacy," 161–65.
100. For a summary, see Weil, "Conditions of the Working Classes," 28–29.
101. Hurst, *Chinese Worker*, 35–36.

between workers and rural migrants. "Peasants were hired as thugs," reported Robert Weil, and used by management to beat up workers and seize the factory's equipment.[102] This wider tension between China's rural and urban working classes demonstrates how spatial difference trumped class. In Maoist terms this was a "contradiction among the people"; for the authoritarian reform regime, it was a useful social and spatial division that Zhengzhou's labor movement was unable to bridge. The reform era state could have tackled this contradiction by taking stronger measures to address the rural-urban gap and/or implementing the *hukou* reform that might have enabled rural migrants to become part of the permanent urban working class. Instead, successive generations of leaders of the People's Republic chose to leave *hukou* half-reformed, preserving and exploiting the spatial inequality bequeathed by the Mao era to the intertwined benefit of capital and the state. As Alexander Day shows, just as in Mao era industrialization, the takeoff of China's urban economies was built on extraction and value suppression from the rural sector, which bore the costs of reproduction (since most dependents remained in the countryside) but received a small share of the rewards.[103] The state leveraged the *hukou* system to hold back a rise in wages, limit permanent rural-urban migration, and postpone equalization across space. This rural-urban inequality in turn pulled hundreds of millions of people into low-wage, insecure work on the margins of urban society. It was a vast story, involving hundreds of millions of Chinese citizens. This chapter closes on a more local level by examining how the spatial politics of this market authoritarianism affected patterns of movement and inequality in Zhengzhou itself.

Zhengzhou's Migrants and Their Place in the City

Studies of migration in the 1990s and early 2000s usually focused on long-distance movement to China's booming coastal regions.[104] Inland provinces such as Henan were discussed primarily as sites of migrant origin—with good reason. By the turn of the century, 6.8 million

102. Weil, "Conditions of the Working Classes," 28.
103. Day, *Peasant in Postsocialist China*.
104. See, inter alia, Solinger, *Contesting Citizenship*; Li Zhang, *Strangers in the City*; Jacka, *Rural Women*. Note that two of Solinger's six research sites were inland (Wuhan and Harbin).

Henanese people were working outside the province, often—in another facet of spatial inequality—at the bottom of migrant hierarchies and unfairly maligned in their destinations.[105] However, most migration was within provinces throughout the reform era, and inland cities such as Zhengzhou were important short- and medium-distance destinations. During the 1980s and 1990s migrant workers built a new Zhengzhou— one constructed on the spatial inequality of low wages and the insecurity of outsiders in the city.

Rural-to-urban migration was not new in Zhengzhou. Two earlier waves of migration, in the first quarter of the twentieth century and in the 1950s, had already built two iterations of the modern city. But such movement had been so restricted following the Great Leap Forward— just a few thousand temporary contract laborers per year—that reform era sources discuss it as if it were a new phenomenon. As in other cities, migrants began to drift into Zhengzhou for casual work in the late 1970s as strict restrictions began to unravel. In 1978 net migration to Zhengzhou was at its highest level since the Great Leap, and by 1979 more than 22,000 rural *hukou* holders were living in the city.[106] Over the next few years, municipal policies oscillated between clamping down on migrants and turning a blind eye, but net migration ran at an average of more than 25,000 per year during 1980–1987—more if undocumented movements are included.[107] In a period still overwhelmingly dominated by intraprovincial migration (80 percent in 1987), Zhengzhou was a magnet for migrants from across Henan.[108] According to a municipal report of 1987, Zhengzhou's long-term "floating population" was more than 200,000, with 119,000 rural people employed in construction alone—the muscle behind Zhengzhou's first reform era building boom. More than 16 percent of those living in Zhengzhou were not local *hukou*

---

105. The 6.8 million figure is from Li Hao, *Henan ren de shengcun*, 26; on the migrant hierarchy and the place of Henanese workers in Beijing, see Li Zhang, *Strangers in the City*, 31–36.

106. Fan Futang et al., *Zhengzhou liudong renkou*, 34.

107. Zhengzhou shi difang shizhi bianzuan weiyuanhui, *Zhengzhou shizhi*, 1:353–54. One study of a *chengzhongcun* in 1989 found that less than half of migrants (47 percent) had registered with the authorities. Fan Futang et al., *Zhengzhou liudong renkou*, 341.

108. Rural migrants from the rest of Henan outnumbered those from outside the province by about five to one. See Fan Futang et al., *Zhengzhou liudong renkou*, 3. The 80 percent figure is from Sidney Goldstein, "Urbanization in China," 684.

holders, a proportion similar to Shanghai and higher than most Chinese cities at the time.[109]

The 1987 municipal report on Zhengzhou's migrants took pains to note their contribution to the city. It pushed back against antimigrant feeling—"it is not true that they have 'stolen the rice bowls' (*qiang le fanwan*) of urban residents"—and even heralded a new era for rural-urban relations: "the increase in the migrant population . . . has broken through the separation of city and countryside."[110] But this rhetoric did not mean that divisions had been overcome in practice. Many migrants faced a tough life in the city during the 1980s. They did not qualify for the most basic welfare such as subsidies on food—another divisive legacy of the Mao period—and had to buy more expensive market grain. Even in winter, officials found more than two thousand people sleeping rough while trying to pick up casual work.[111]

Even Zhengzhou's flagship state textile industry was involved in the exploitation of migrant workers. Starting in 1985, Zhengzhou's textile mills used rural contract labor for the lowest-grade roles, at half the cost of urban workers. The No. 6 Mill, for example, used a labor contractor to hire five hundred young women from a cluster of villages in neighboring Xingyang County. These workers enjoyed few of the benefits of permanent urban workers and were subject to a "contract fee" of almost half a year's salary. Some 6,500 people were working in such conditions in Zhengzhou's textile mills by the end of the decade. An investigation by Wang Fuquan and Zheng Yinfang revealed that after living expenses and numerous administrative fees, contract workers arriving in the retrenchment years of 1988 or 1989 earned less than 6 yuan per month. Understandably, many fled before the end of the contract, but there were always more rural migrants to replace them—one factory received two hundred applications for forty contract labor positions.[112]

109. Fan Futang et al., *Zhengzhou liudong renkou*, 253–54. "Long-term" refers to those who had been in the city for more than six months. Note that the specific 119,000 figure in construction may include daily commuters coming from the rural suburbs for construction work. According to 1986 data, an average of 9.6 percent of those in China's cities were temporary residents (seventy-four cities surveyed). See Banister and Taylor, "China: Surplus Labor and Migration," 13. For direct comparison between Zhengzhou and other cities, see Fan et al., *Zhengzhou liudong renkou*, 238–43.

110. Fan Futang et al., *Zhengzhou liudong renkou*, 257–60.

111. Fan Futang et al., *Zhengzhou liudong renkou*, 4.

112. Fan Futang et al., *Zhengzhou liudong renkou*, 55–64.

As well as experiencing poor working conditions, migrants in Zhengzhou faced employment insecurity—just as in the Mao period. Although the 1987 municipal report had praised their economic contribution, Zhengzhou's migrants were up against a *hukou* system that had been relaxed enough for them to move to the city to sell their labor but still provided a formidable barrier to permanent urban belonging. The rural-urban division here was a stark one. Despite a stated preference for short-distance migrants, the 1985 regulations made it clear that even rural people from the suburbs had no more right to full urban citizenship than those from more distant areas (although they paid lower fees to the local government when they moved to the city).[113] From 1982 onwards, Zhengzhou's planners were anxious about controlling the growing "floating population" and urging tighter controls on movement.[114] Given the growing demand for cheap labor in the city, this policy was not quite followed in practice, but the Mao era institutions of the "Detention and Repatriation" (Shourong qiansong) system remained in operation: indeed, the detention facility in the city was in the same compound as it had been when the system was set up in 1949.[115] By the late 1980s, the deportation system in Zhengzhou was handling eight thousand people per year. Many of those awaiting removal or with nowhere to go were subject to coerced labor at a brickworks operated by the deportation office outside the city at Houzhai.[116]

It is true that those subject to deportation were usually Zhengzhou's most socially marginal, unregistered migrants. But even those not subject to clean-up campaigns could be levered out of the city, particularly during the economic retrenchment of 1988–89, when the number of migrant workers in industry and construction fell by more than half

---

113. "Zhengzhou shi zanzhu renkou guanli zanxing banfa," May 10, 1985, reproduced in Fan Futang et al., *Zhengzhou liudong renkou*, 264–70; "administrative fees" in the early 1990s were on a spatially unequal sliding scale: 1 percent of salary for rural migrants within the municipal unit; 2 percent for arrivals from within the province; 3 percent for interprovincial migrants. See Fan Futang et al., *Zhengzhou liudong renkou*, 290.

114. Zhang Qixian and Wu Xiaoya, *Dangdai Zhengzhou chengshi jianshe*, 243–44.

115. Fan Futang et al., *Zhengzhou liudong renkou*, 141.

116. Fan Futang et al., *Zhengzhou liudong renkou*, 141–42. Zhengzhou was a regional center for deportations, so the figure of eight thousand also includes those being deported from other cities and handled through the provincial capital.

of 1987 figures. The turbulent year of 1989 saw the smallest number of people moving to Zhengzhou since 1976.[117] At the same time, the official rhetoric that had been positive in 1987 turned against Zhengzhou's migrant population: "the good and the bad migrants are intermingled" (*liang you bu qi*), noted the report on the 1989 migrant survey, which emphasized problems of crime, public order, and the burdens of migrants on urban infrastructure.[118]

Soon afterwards, though, the renewed push for rapid economic growth overtook the antimigrant policies of 1988–1990. As in the short boom of the mid-1980s, Zhengzhou's rapid growth in the 1990s was built on the labor of rural migrants—and on a much larger scale. By 1993 there were four hundred thousand non-*hukou* holders in Zhengzhou (26 percent of the population).[119] This increase was accompanied by cautious steps in *hukou* reform. From 1995 Zhengzhou's temporary residence permit (*zanzhuzheng*) offered a more secure place in the city, and in 1998 a series of further relaxations made it possible to buy an urban *hukou*—albeit at prohibitive cost. But these beginnings of *hukou* reform seem to have done little to help "Zhengzhou floaters" (*Zhengpiao*) feel a sense of belonging in the city. In a study of the early 2000s, Jia Zhiqiang found that migrants in Zhengzhou felt little sense of identity either with their neighborhood or with the city, separated as they were from both local community participation and a share in the welfare and services of the city as a whole.[120] In a study of 145 workers, Cheng Xiuhong found higher levels of anxiety and much lower levels of self-confidence and job satisfaction among migrants than among locals. This discrepancy was also evident between rural *hukou* holders and migrants from other cities. Cheng reported that many felt like they were "begging" (*yaofan*), that, "no matter in dress, speech, consciousness, knowledge, awareness, or self-confidence, they could not be as good as urban people and could only take the lowest jobs." The official and unofficial workings of rural-urban division left many of Cheng's informants demoralized—

---

117. On employment by sector, see Fan Futang et al., *Zhengzhou liudong renkou*, 5. On net migration, see Zhengzhou shi difang shizhi bianzuan weiyuanhui, *Zhengzhou shizhi*, 1:354.

118. Fan Futang et al., *Zhengzhou liudong renkou*, 13.

119. Hao Pengzhan, "Lun jindai yilai Zhengzhou de chengshi guihua," 64.

120. Jia Zhiqiang, "Zhengzhou shi dushi cunzhuang."

particularly job advertisements stipulating "must have urban *hukou*" or "must have an urban *hukou* holder as guarantor (*danbao*)."[121]

Most rural migrants lived in Zhengzhou's fast-growing *chengzhong-cun*, those sites of marginality within the expanding city. The former vegetable-growing model village of Xiaolizhuang was already housing 3,000 migrant workers in 1989 but by early 2007 was home to 4,800 resident villagers, 5,500 urban *hukou* holders, and a "floating population" of more than 50,000.[122] That year, Zhengzhou had more than 140 such *chengzhongcun*, both long-absorbed settlements now close to the city center and villages recently drawn into the urban fringes.[123] As discussed above, these sites brought about an unequal exchange between two sets of former peasants, with locals receiving rent from new arrivals from villages that, apart from lacking proximity to a large city, had until recently not been so different from their own. With most incoming workers from Henan Province, there was not quite the same sociocultural gulf between migrants and locals seen in some parts of China— witness Joshua Goldstein's recent description of reform era Beijing as "two cities" divided between locals and migrants—but in Zhengzhou this sociocultural proximity underlines the spatial arbitrariness of their economic inequality. [124]

The unequal spatial politics of reform era Zhengzhou came to a head in the summer of 2002 over the humdrum issue of melons. Melon producers had long been in the habit of bringing fruit into the city for direct sale to consumers, particularly from impoverished Zhongmu County. But in 2002 the municipal government threw up new barriers to this practice, introducing a strict permit system for melon sellers on the grounds of "protecting markets and preserving the appearance of the city." Demand for permits far exceeded the number issued, and melon producers found they needed personal connections with their village committees to obtain one. Although they were residents of a county under the municipal government, Zhongmu melon sellers arriving in Zhengzhou with-

121. Cheng Xiuhong, "Zhengzhou shi weilai renkou," 27.
122. For 1989, see Fan Futang et al., *Zhengzhou liudong renkou*, 93; for 2007 figures, see Zhengxie Zhengzhou shi Erqiqu weiyuanhui, *Yuanqu zhi jiyi*, 87.
123. Li Huishan, "Zhengzhou shi jiaoqu jianshe guocheng zhong nandian wenti," 11.
124. Joshua Goldstein, *Remains of the Everyday*, 159–86.

out permits were turned back by police.[125] The dispute rumbled on for several summers. In 2004 seventy to eighty melon sellers from Zhongmu were blocked from entering Zhengzhou and staged a protest on the main Beijing–Shenzhen highway. A tense standoff ensued.[126] In 2005 the Zhengzhou municipal government imposed new restrictions, effectively banning all "farm vehicles" (*nongyongche*) from entering the city and forcing transactions to take place at wholesale markets on the urban edge.[127]

The ability of rural producers to enter Zhengzhou to sell their produce had long been a flashpoint, with controls on movement set up back in the 1920s by Feng Yuxiang, by Japanese occupiers of the 1940s, and by the Nationalist authorities during the civil war, as well as the restrictions of the collective period. Now, more than two decades after economic reform had seemed to open rural-urban relations, similar issues were being reprised; even Xinhua News Agency called the policy "unjustified" (*shuobuguoqu*) for "directly affecting the personal interests of the peasant masses."[128] The legal scholar Du Gangjian condemned the policy on both economic and human rights grounds. As Du pointed out, the dispute touched on several contentious issues: local corruption, the right of access to the city, and rural poverty.[129]

The Zhongmu melon controversy should be seen, therefore, not as an isolated incident but as part of the growth of critical commentary and social protest against the spatial politics of the reform period. As in the 1910s, commercialization and closer economic connections between city and countryside had not prevented rural-urban divisions. As in the 1920s and 1930s, agricultural crisis led to the "peasant question" becoming a focus of intellectual discussion and a political fault line. As in the 1950s

125. Du Gangjian, "Cong Zhengzhou guanong jincheng nan kan guizhi zhengce."
126. Zhang Jiangao, "Zhengzhou bu rang nongmin guache jincheng," *Xinhua meiri dianxun*, May 13, 2004.
127. Zhang Xingjun, "Zhengzhou: jinzhi nongyongche Jincheng," *Xinhua meiri dianxun*, May 26, 2005.
128. Zhang Jiangao, "Zhengzhou bu rang nongmin guache jincheng," *Xinhua meiri dianxun*, May 13, 2004. However, one must also be wary of simply panegyrizing the openness of the early reform period, when old-style animal carts had been banned from Zhengzhou's downtown. Zhengzhou shi difang shizhi bianzuan weiyuanhui, *Zhengzhou shizhi*, 3:394–95.
129. Du Gangjian, "Cong Zhengzhou guanong jincheng nan kan guizhi zhengce."

and 1960s, an industrializing economy had done little for the rural sector relative to its urban achievements, while the *hukou* system held back rural people from a place in China's cities.

By the turn of the century, the sense of rural crisis was growing, with a worsening rural-urban gulf in income, infrastructure, and public services, as well as the twin challenges of rural fiscal crisis and accession to the World Trade Organization. Henan became an emblem of this nationwide phenomenon. Cao Jinqing's 2000 exposé of poverty and corruption in rural Henan was one of the opening shots of the crisis discourse.[130] In 2003 the government was forced to admit that more than eighty thousand people—probably an underestimate—had been infected with HIV by contaminated blood plasma donation south and east of Zhengzhou. The scandal was read by Ann Anagnost as a metaphor for and a symptom of the subordination (and bloodsucking) of the rural in the reform era, with China's countryside reduced to what Julia Chuang calls a "holding pen for low-cost labor."[131] In short, Henan's spatial inequalities revealed how the growth-first policies of the reform period had generated perhaps the most serious challenge to Communist power and legitimacy in rural China since the collapse of the Great Leap. Chapter 7 shows how the state's response tried to overturn the twentieth-century patterns of spatial division and inequality—and how it has reshaped twenty-first-century Zhengzhou.

130. Cao, *China Along the Yellow River*. Cao's work was followed a decade later by another bestseller on the Henan rural crisis. See Liang Hong, *China in One Village*.
131. Anagnost, "Strange Circulations"; Chuang, *Beneath the China Boom*, 6. On numbers infected, see Wilson, *Tigers without Teeth*, 70.

CHAPTER SEVEN

Zhengzhou Unbound

World, City, and Region in the
New Spatial Politics, 2003–2020s

At the Nineteenth Communist Party Congress of 2017, President Xi Jinping heralded a "New Era" (*Xin shidai*) for the People's Republic. Scholars of contemporary China agreed that Xi's rule marks a break with the preceding decades, with a more ambitious foreign policy and tighter control in the economic, social, and political spheres.[1] But the major shift in China's spatial politics came not with the Xi Jinping era but a decade earlier under Hu Jintao and Wen Jiabao. Foucault's maxim of the 1960s—"the anxiety of our era has to do fundamentally with space"— rang especially true in the China of the early twenty-first century.[2] The reform era's pro-urban, growth-first orientation had bequeathed a crisis of inequality to the incoming Hu-Wen leadership: stark interregional and rural-urban gaps exemplified by the travails of the countryside in Henan Province (chapter 6). However, the rapid growth of previous years— China's economy grew four times over between 1990 and 2003—and the revenue recentralization beginning in 1994 also gave the new central leadership unprecedented resources to tackle these spatial inequalities.

In historical terms, the subsequent spatial shift under Hu and Wen combined the inland orientation of the First Five-Year Plan with the rebalancing to the rural sector following the collapse of the Great Leap Forward. In 2004, Premier Wen Jiabao launched a plan for the "Rise of Central China" (*Zhongbu jueqi*), promising renewed focus on provinces such as Henan that had been left behind by coastal regions and did not benefit from the earlier Great Western Development Strategy. The same

---

1. Economy, *Third Revolution*; Ding and Panda, *Chinese Politics and Foreign Policy*.
2. Foucault, "Of Other Spaces," 23.

year, the State Council approved plans for the nationwide high-speed rail network, aiming to reduce regional inequalities by compressing distance. In 2005, China abolished agricultural taxation and instituted greater subsidies for the farming sector. These and other prorural policies brought China's relative rate of assistance for agriculture (RRA) into positive territory for the first time, having seen decades of negative RRA (penalizing agriculture) since data began to be recorded in the Mao period.[3] The following year, the launch of the "New Socialist Countryside" offered unprecedented spending on rural infrastructure and greater rural-urban integration (*chengxiang yitihua*).

The effort to spread China's new wealth looks straightforward at the level of national policy but becomes more complex with a focus on its local effects in and around Zhengzhou. On the one hand, new measures promised to bring prosperity to those left behind by reform era growth in the provincial capital. In 2003, radical reform to Zhengzhou's *hukou* system seemed to open the city to rural migrants. Between 2004 and 2006, the provincial government launched plans for the Central Plains City Cluster, which aimed to spur on economic growth across north-central Henan. And in 2005, the launch of "Zhengzhou-Kaifeng Integration" promised to spread Zhengzhou's success to its struggling neighbor.

On the other hand, Zhengzhou's recent history also points to renewed concentration in the provincial capital. This tension had been formulated at the very beginning of the century, when local economists had stressed the need "to develop both Zhengzhou's cohering power and its radiating power (*ningjuli he fusheli*)."[4] Just as in the Republican period, they identified Zhengzhou as too small and too weak to transform its hinterland. Then, the city was only expected to pull along the immediate rural hinterland of Zheng County; in the twenty-first century, national planners gave Zhengzhou a much more significant role. Zhengzhou was the largest and most centrally positioned city in a huge, economically underperforming diamond-shaped swathe of inland China between Wuhan, Xi'an, Beijing-Tianjin, and the lower Yangzi. Zhengzhou was to be the economic driving force for the entire central part of this zone, including almost all of Henan and parts of neighboring provinces. State planning at the national and provincial level therefore backed Zhengzhou

---

3. Anderson, *Distortions to Agricultural Incentives*, 373.
4. Zhengzhou shi shehui kexuejie lianhehui, *Zhengzhou jingji shehui fazhan*, 14.

as a "winner" of the new inland spatial shift. By any growth measure—built-up area, population, GDP, investment, real estate—Zhengzhou has been one of the powerhouses of China's inland regional urbanization and now has the largest economy of any inland city north of the Yangzi valley. Yet during Zhengzhou's twenty-first-century takeoff, this concentration in the provincial capital worked against the competing imperative to spread growth across Henan. The City Cluster has so far had only limited impact in narrowing the gap between Zhengzhou and its neighbors, let alone more peripheral parts of the wider region. The real estate boom brought further capital concentration and accumulation in the provincial capital. There has been a partial dispersal of real estate growth into smaller regional cities, but demographic challenges and competition for labor, which Zhengzhou as regional powerhouse looks better placed to cope with, make for an uncertain future for cities farther down the still-rigid urban hierarchy.

This chapter examines these tensions in spatial politics in historical perspective. It argues that Zhengzhou's emergence as a megacity took advantage of existing spatial inequalities at the urban edge, before showing inequalities of migration in the twenty-first century and exploring ongoing spatial inequality between Zhengzhou and the rest of the Central Plains region. As in the twentieth century, Zhengzhou's recent spatial politics have been operating on dual impulses of concentration and dispersal. If the eye-watering real estate prices of contemporary Zhengzhou are anything to go by, the financial stakes may be higher; but in leaving behind the spatial politics of famine, war, and absolute poverty, the stakes in human lives have become thankfully lower. Unlike in most of the twentieth century, China's economic growth has allowed the dispersal of wealth and infrastructure in absolute terms, but the picture of relative equalization is much less clear. The life trajectories of individuals and families still depend on where as well as who they are—in other words, space remains an important independent variable besides being a reflection of other social inequalities. Although there was marked narrowing of inequality in the years between 2005 and 2015, progress has significantly slowed, and dimensions of spatial difference remain stubbornly high. The neat downward slope of the Kuznets curve, promising falling inequality as China shifts to an urbanized high-income economy, may be a bumpier road than it seemed at the beginning of the 2010s.

Zhengzhou Goes Global: The Urban
Edge in the Emerging Megacity

Even by the standards of China's rapid urbanization, Zhengzhou's expansion in the twenty-first century was spectacular. The built-up area of the city grew almost four times over between 2002 and 2019, and its population rose from 2.5 million to over 7 million (and more than 10 million in the metropolitan region).[5] Zhengzhou's economy rose from the twelfth largest of China's provincial capitals at the turn of the century to sixth in 2019 on the eve of the COVID-19 pandemic.[6] Zhengzhou's scale and spatial connections have both gone global. The value of its foreign trade rose a remarkable 55-fold between 2002 and 2015, much faster than that of China as a whole (which rose 8.5 times over during the same period).[7] Zhengzhou is now one of the fifty largest cities in the world. China's 2016 strategy of creating vast metropolitan regions has Zhengzhou at its heart, as the core city of the most populous megalopolis of them all: the 158 million people of the Central Plains City Cluster.

Zhengzhou's explosive growth was rooted in both the city's strategic location and in political support. During his tenure as Henan governor (1998–2004), future premier Li Keqiang identified a need to concentrate growth in Zhengzhou. Although it had surged ahead of other cities in Henan, Li felt that it was still inadequate, too small for its role as regional engine: "Zhengzhou should play the leading role (*fahui longtou zuoyong*) in the process of urbanizing the whole province, and its primacy within the province should be raised, particularly its share of provincial GDP."[8] It seems counterintuitive that a shift to a more equalizing spatial politics should drive a greater concentration in what was already the largest and wealthiest city in the region. But a team of researchers under economist Sun Xinlei agreed that Zhengzhou was too small to aid in the closing of China's coastal-inland and rural-urban

---

5. From 156 to 581 square kilometers. Comparing *Zhengzhou tongji nianjian*, 2003:223, and *Zhengzhou tongji nianjian*, 2020:219.

6. Zhengzhou shi shehui kexuejie lianhehui, *Zhengzhou jingji shehui fazhan*, 28 (1998 figures); 2019 figures available online at https://www.sohu.com/a/385307128_120607879.

7. Not adjusted for inflation. See *Zhengzhou tongji nianjian*, 2004:373 (2002 figures); *Zhengzhou tongji nianjian*, 2016:415 (2015 figures).

8. Zhengzhou shi shehui kexuejie lianhehui, *Zhengzhou jingji shehui fazhan*, 13.

divisions and that an underperforming province of almost one hundred million people needed a full-scale primate city to lead its economy.[9]

At the beginning of the twenty-first century, Zhengzhou's planners were still struggling to locate a central economic function to replace the now-defunct state textile sector. But the shift of economic weight inland ensured that, as in the early twentieth century, the crossing of north–south and east–west routes made Zhengzhou a key center for wholesaling, logistics, and processing functions—particularly when combined with its relatively low wages and large pool of nearby migrant workers. Zhengzhou became an important part of China's national spatial strategy for the first time since the 1950s, as one of the four inland node cities of the "two horizontal and three vertical" (*liang heng san zong*) core belts along major transport routes.[10] This logistical role became more than a domestic phenomenon. Zhengzhou had been repeatedly heralded throughout the twentieth century for the potential of its trans-Eurasian connections. But these links only came to fruition in 2013 with Zhengzhou's status as a key city in the Belt and Road Initiative (Yidai yilu). Cargo trains across Eurasia began that summer, and by 2020 an average of three trains were departing Zhengzhou for Europe each day.[11]

Zhengzhou's new economic importance brought more rapid urban growth than originally planned. At the beginning of the century, local planners had proposed a population of five million by 2020, but it was already clear that this figure would be outstripped well in advance.[12] By 2010, Zhengzhou was home to 4.3 million people (including long-term migrants) and was in the midst of a construction boom. In a study of thirteen large cities, Zhengzhou had the highest proportion of total fixed investment in real estate (56 percent, ahead of Beijing's 54 percent). In Huiji District, on the northern edge of the city, almost *half* of all employment (48 percent) was in construction.[13] When China's economic growth

9. Zhengzhou shi shehui kexuejie lianhehui, *Zhengzhou jingji shehui fazhan*, 13–15.

10. The other inland nodal cities were Chongqing, Xi'an, and Wuhan. Guo Xinxin, "Zhengzhou jianshe guojia zhongxin chengshi."

11. Figures released by Xinhua News Agency, January 6, 2021, available at http://www.ha.xinhuanet.com/news/2021-01/06/c_1126949908.htm.

12. Zhengzhou shi shehui kexuejie lianhehui, *Zhengzhou jingji shehui fazhan*, 42.

13. An Qian, *Kuaisu chengshihua jincheng*, 176 (population), 238 (investment figures), and 197 (employment by district).

slowed down in the 2010s, Zhengzhou was one of several inland cities continuing to surge ahead. Across the mid-2010s (2013–2018), Zhengzhou was ranked third of thirty-four major cities for per capita GDP growth, behind only Lanzhou and Chongqing, powerhouses of the fast-growing western region.[14] In 2016, Zhengzhou and Wuhan were designated the seventh and eighth National Central Cities, both describing their existing importance and prescribing their future role in sparking regional economic growth.[15]

High Stakes on the Urban Fringe

Behind the impressive growth statistics, though, Zhengzhou's early twenty-first-century boom was a fraught process, with murky politics and uneven results. The highest stakes came at the fringes of the city, where Zhengzhou's expansion accelerated the state takeover of collectively held rural land. As You-Tien Hsing and Xuefei Ren among others have shown, the expansion of Chinese cities was driven as much by local government profit as by local need.[16] By the second half of the 2010s, Zhengzhou's municipal government was making more money on selling use rights on state land than its entire fiscal revenue, with the net income from this source rising almost thirtyfold in a decade.[17] The ensuing tension over takeover, compensation, and relocation—what Hsing calls the deterritorialization of suburban land—gave rise to negotiation, protest, and resistance at Zhengzhou's urban edge. As this book has shown, Zhengzhou's fringes had often been a deeply contested space in the twentieth century, between urban authorities and farmers, traders, migrants, and refugees. But never before had there been such a rapid liquidation of village communities and with such huge profits to be made.

This transformation had profound environmental and spatial consequences on the ground. In 2010, an exposé by the prominent *Nanfang*

14. "Best-Performing Cities China," 2020.

15. For a skeptical reading of Zhengzhou's designation, see Guo Xinxin, "Zhengzhou jianshe guojia zhongxin chengshi."

16. Hsing, *Great Urban Transformation*; Ren, *Governing the Urban*, 35–55. For recent studies of these processes in the 2010s, see Smith, *End of the Village*; Chuang, *Beneath the China Boom*.

17. Xuefeng Wang and Tomaney, "Zhengzhou—Political Economy of an Emerging Chinese Megacity," 109.

zhoumo newspaper revealed that Xiliu Lake at the western edge of Zhengzhou was at risk of being damaged beyond repair. The lake was filling up with building rubble, and a 200-meter-wide protected zone around its perimeter was packed with illegal construction work.[18] In spatial terms, where the reform era had seen a "neater" morphology at the urban edge (see chapter 6), recent growth, economist Wang Jianguo argued in 2017, had been spatially chaotic and inefficient.[19] Although Zhengzhou's overall growth followed a 2006–2020 urban plan, at the local level the rush for profit made for a complex zone of transition at the urban fringe. High-rise estates, sometimes built well in advance of facilities and infrastructure, jostled with soon-to-be-demolished villages and semiformal migrant worker housing as well as patches of wasteland and surviving farmland. In this murky, fast-changing, investment-driven pattern, Zhengzhou's urban edge now resembled on a vast scale the speculation boom of its railroad suburb a century before.

In the complex process of urbanization, the fate of villages and households was still determined by a multiplicity of local factors, including village leadership, the value of land, the approach of district- and town-level government, the nature of building projects, and the actions of development corporations. This complexity led to arbitrary differences in outcomes across space. The case of Xigang Village provides an example of these inequalities and raised stakes. As discussed in chapter 6, the suburban village of Xigang had been subject to a corrupt deal over the leasing of collective land in the early 2000s. But this struggle over use rights was minor compared to the conversion of collective land to urban state land. By 2007 Xigang's land was worth 300,000 RMB per *mu* on the real estate market, driven by its proximity to the third ring road and the proposed route for Zhengzhou's first subway line (which opened in 2013). The village committee secretly sold collective land to a development company to be converted to urban housing but told villagers that the plot had only been leased. When the details of the sale emerged, it also transpired that the village collective had received only 60 percent of the market value of the land. Villagers launched multiple appeals and won a

18. Huang Jinping, "Zhengzhou Xigangcun."
19. Wang Jianguo, *Zhengzhou dadu shiqu jianshe*, 17; for a similar argument, see Zhao Jianhua, "Nongye duoyuan jiazhi," 53–55.

temporary success at the beginning of 2008, when the city government ordered a halt to construction. Yet this was a Pyrrhic victory and was followed by a campaign of intimidation, harassment, bribery, and even physical violence. Work on the site resumed, with the support of town-level officials and no sign of intervention from the municipal authorities.[20]

In 2009 investigations by villager Song Tiezhuang showed holes and evasions in the paperwork for the project, and it was eventually revealed that the land had been sold for an affordable housing project but was being used for twelve luxury villas and two high-end apartment blocks. The development company stood to make 100 million RMB in revenue, double that of the affordable housing scheme. Township officials and district government had all approved the deal, with a suspicion of personal kickbacks and links to organized crime. When a journalist contacted the municipal government, Deputy Urban Planning Director Lu Jun (1958–) refused to answer questions, asking, "Are you intending to speak for the party or for ordinary people?"—the implication being that journalists should speak for the party.[21] The phrase "speak for the party or speak for ordinary people?" (*ti dang shuohua, haishi ti laobaixing shuohua*) became a satirical internet catchphrase of 2009 and Xigang a notorious case of the power inequalities of urban expansion. Lu Jun was suspended, and Xigang villagers won some redress, but their collective rights were not restored. In December 2013, the village of Xigang was demolished and residents relocated.[22]

The major exception to this pattern of messy, locally determined expansion was the closer municipal planning of Zhengzhou's two flagship new districts. Zhengzhou already had two development zones from the reform era, but the East Zhengzhou New Area (Zhengdong xinqu, hereafter untranslated) and the Airport Economy Experimental Zone (Hangkonggang jingji zonghe shiyanqu) were altogether more ambitious, each around ten times the scale of their reform era precursors. Both have proved to be huge economic fillips for the city, but in different ways their success was built on ongoing spatial inequalities and the concentration of growth in the emerging Zhengzhou megacity. In the

---

20. For more details, see Lei Yushe, "Zhengzhou jingshifang tudi."
21. Lei Yushe, "Zhengzhou jingshifang tudi."
22. Xigang cunzhi bianzuan weiyuanhui, *Xigang cunzhi*, 10.

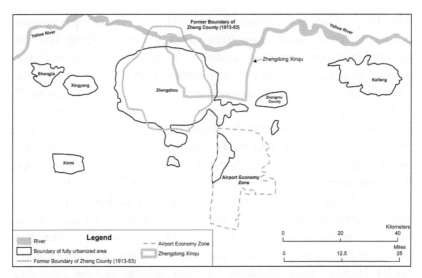

MAP 7.1. Zhengzhou as megacity, 2023. Adapted from OpenStreetMap and Google Maps. Map by Jogu Gopinath.

case of Zhengdong xinqu, the municipal authorities took advantage of the subaltern position of suburban villagers to obtain land at low cost relative to its market value; in the Airport Zone, they also took advantage of the relative poverty of Zhengzhou's rural hinterland to entice investors with the promise of a low-cost workforce (map 7.1).

A NEW CITY: ZHENGDONG XINQU

Zhengdong xinqu was part of China's "new cities" wave of the 2000s, a shift away from the development zone expansion of the 1990s in favor of building new city centers. Zhengdong xinqu made Zhengzhou a multicentric city for the first time. The long-mooted project to expand onto and beyond the former Zhengzhou airport (closed in 1997) was driven forward in 2000 under Governor Li Keqiang.[23] Kisho Kurokawa's (1934–2007) design for the first phase was confirmed in 2002, with a centerpiece financial CBD (Central Business District) flanked by zones for residential, commercial, logistical, and university use. In the single

23. Wang Jianguo, *Zhengzhou dadu shiqu jianshe*, 112.

year of 2003, Zhengzhou's built-up area increased by more than a third,[24] with the east of the city—neglected throughout the Republican, Socialist, and reform eras—now the center of investment and prestige, just as the last state-owned textile factories of the Mao era west of the city were filing for bankruptcy. The reversal in fortunes was poignant, not least because Zhengdong xinqu bears some comparison with that western industrial suburb of the 1950s, another urban edge district symbolizing and driving a new economic era.

In the spirit of its design, though, Zhengdong xinqu shared more with the "New Zhengzhou" scheme proposed under Feng Yuxiang in 1928 (see chapter 2). Unlike the industrial suburb of the 1950s, mostly controlled as it was by individual work units, the 1928 design had called for a new city driven by the municipal government, offering "chaotic" Zhengzhou a fresh start. The designs of the 1920s and the 2000s both proposed neat functional zones and an ordered, easily controlled urban environment. The founding discourse of Zhengdong xinqu even echoed some of the "ruralizing new city" rhetoric employed in 1928, with updated green slogans on the promise of urbanism: "ecological, symbiotic, metabolic," bringing together "traditions and contemporary life, urbanity and nature."[25] But as Charlie Q. L. Xue, Ying Wang, and Luther Tsai demonstrate, behind the harmonious language there was a Corbusierian utopianism running through Kurokawa's design, built on the tabula rasa of an obliterated rural space—just as in the "New Zhengzhou" plan of 1928.[26]

In the first phase of Zhengdong xinqu (2002–2008), forty-eight villages on the east side of Zhengzhou were demolished and more than 41,000 people relocated to apartments in four resettlement zones (*anzhiqu*).[27] The process was very different from that of the Xigang corruption case on the other side of the city. Villagers received the maximum compensation that was possible under national regulations, with higher payments than in other inland cities, such as those studied by Lynette Ong in Hefei. Li Huishan's study of resettled villagers in Zhengdong xinqu also found higher levels of satisfaction than in the

24. *Zhengzhou tongji nianjian*, 2004:219.
25. Xue, Wang, and Tsai, "Building New Towns in China," 225.
26. Xue, Wang, and Tsai, "Building New Towns in China," 226.
27. Li Huishan, "Zhengzhou shi jiaoqu jianshe," 12.

2011 Landesa survey of resettlement across seventeen provinces. Municipal officials hailed Zhengdong xinqu as a model for relocations, with a smoother rural-to-urban transfer of *hukou* status than in other sites on the city's fringe.²⁸

However, what is striking about Zhengdong xinqu is that, even in this case of model relocation for a flagship new district, the process was shot through with spatial inequalities. First, their rural status and the absence of full land ownership rights meant that residents received only a fraction of the value of their private and collective property. As across China, rural land was compensated on the basis of its agricultural output rather than its market value. Residential property was also undervalued. In the first phase of Zhengdong xinqu, rural homes were compensated on a fixed scale of 280 to 320 RMB per square meter, just a fifth of average property prices in Zhengzhou at the time. It was this level of compensation, more than the low payments for land relative to their value, that generated the strongest sense of dissatisfaction among displaced villagers.²⁹ It is true that the municipal government threw in additional sweeteners, including per head cash payments and contributions to pension and healthcare insurance schemes, but even so very little of the vast Zhengdong xinqu financing trickled down to those displaced. On the basis of these figures and assuming no malfeasance, a typical five-person household, including one grandparent and two children, with a 100-square-meter home and access to five *mu* of collective land, received compensation of 53,000 RMB per head. Though a large sum of money in the mid-2000s, as a proportion of investment per *mu*, this compensation represents just 4 percent of the capital being poured into Zhengzhou's new city.³⁰

Second, although displaced villagers were adequately rehoused, their status and income in the city remained marginal. Li Huishan points out

28. Li Huishan, "Zhengzhou shi jiaoqu jianshe," 30–35; Ong, "State-Led Urbanization in China," 167–68.

29. "Guanyu Zhengdong xinqu qibuqu Guancheng quyu jianshe zhengdi buchang shishi fang'an," December 12, 2002, reproduced by Guangdong waiyu waimao daxue tudi fazhi yanjiuyuan, available at https://illss.gdufs.edu.cn/info/1122/6395.htm.

30. By 2012, 160 billion RMB had been invested in building projects across 120,000 *mu*. See Li Huishan, "Zhengzhou shi jiaoqu jianshe," 12–13.

that the resettlement blocks were rather remote, often worse connected than the suburban villages they had replaced.[31] Although there was some job training, employment subsidies, and preferential access to commercial space, labor market outcomes were disappointing. In 2012, 62 percent of resettled families had a household income of less than 3,000 RMB per month, against a Zhengzhou urban average of 6,715 RMB.[32] Incentives for employers to hire former villagers were minimal (1,000 RMB per person), and Yuting Zhang discovered that the training schemes were small-scale and perfunctory.[33] Most former villagers found only low-end service sector jobs—the kind of work that many of them had been doing as suburban villagers before resettlement but without their previous additional farm and rental income streams. "Unstable income and irregular working time," Zhang writes, "have pushed landless peasants further away from a normal urban life and have widened the gap between regular citizens and landless peasants."[34]

The difficulties of displaced villagers had little bearing on the upward trajectory of Zhengdong xinqu. Although parts of the district were slow to take off, critical Western commentary was wrong to write off the scheme as a "ghost city."[35] During the 2010s, its high-rise towers filled with residents and businesses—the latter sometimes given a push by the municipal authorities—and from 2013 the new subway integrated the district into the rest of the city.[36] But as with other financial districts around the world, Zhengdong xinqu has not escaped the sense of separation from the lives of most people in the city and the wider region, let alone villagers who lost land to the project and migrant workers who built it. At one luxury hostess bar in the CBD, an average patron was reckoned to be spending 5,000 RMB in a single night in the early 2010s.[37] Already by 2011, property prices in the district were 20,000 RMB per square

31. Li Huishan, "Zhengzhou shi jiaoqu jianshe," 35.
32. Li Huishan, "Zhengzhou shi jiaoqu jianshe," 31. Zhengzhou-wide figure calculated from *Zhengzhou tongji nianjian*, 2013:5 and 151.
33. Yuting Zhang, "Employment Policy," 43–45.
34. Yuting Zhang, "Employment Policy," 46.
35. As pointed out in Wade Shepard, *Ghost Cities*, 52–55.
36. On the state role, see Xuefeng Wang and Tomaney, "Zhengzhou—Political Economy of an Emerging Chinese Megacity," 107–8.
37. The bar was busted in the early Xi era clampdown on prostitution. For a report on the investigation, see "'Huangjia yihao'an quanbu xuanpan wanbi."

meter—almost equal to per capita annual income in the city (22,477) and more than sixty times the compensation farmers had received for their homes less than a decade before.[38] Zhengdong xinqu succeeded in attracting investment, facilities, and prestige to the provincial capital, but two decades into the project the spatial and social distribution of these resources still seemed some way off.

iPhone City

If Zhengdong xinqu is of regional importance, Zhengzhou's second new district is one of the most extraordinary sites of the twenty-first-century world economy. The Airport Economy Zone, almost 30 kilometers from the old city center, is less impressive to look at, with its wide avenues, medium-rise dormitory blocks, and unprepossessing factory compounds. But since it opened in 2010, the Foxconn plant here has produced half of the world's iPhones, at the rate of half a million a day at peak production. At such busy times, its 350,000 workers make it the second largest production facility in the world by number of employees—behind only Foxconn's own Shenzhen plant.

The Foxconn Zhengzhou plant illustrates an important spatial tension in contemporary globalization. On the one hand, Foxconn assembly looks disembodied from its geographical context: components comprising raw materials from across the world are flown in tax-free to the special "bonded zone" of the Foxconn works. They are assembled behind the high compound walls of this Taiwanese firm before being sent across the world from the neighboring airport. Unlike in Republican era Zhengzhou, when much of the city's economic activity depended on hurdles and difficulties in transport, supply, and processing, the Foxconn plant is built on smooth connections and just-in-time systems. On the other hand, Foxconn Zhengzhou relies on and is deeply embedded in local social and political systems. Foxconn was wooed to Zhengzhou following a sustained campaign by the municipal and provincial governments. In the late 2000s, the Airport Economy Zone had not yet received State Council approval. Needing a flagship enterprise to get the project off the ground, local government invested US $1.5 billion in the site and offered

---

38. Xue, Wang, and Tsai, "Building New Towns in China," 230; per capita annual income from *Zhengzhou tongji nianjian*, 2012:151.

Foxconn a raft of subsidies, perks, and a decade of tax breaks.[39] The investment gamble has paid off. The Foxconn plant is now the centerpiece of a zone of transport, logistics, and assembly, running from the airport north through the former market town of Putian to Zhengdong xinqu and east into Zhongmu County.[40]

In addition to financial incentives, the provincial government tempted Foxconn with Henan's large pool of rural and small-town workers willing to work long hours for low pay—and offered state support for their recruitment and housing. Initial wage costs in Zhengzhou were 25 percent cheaper than at the Shenzhen plant, and labor supply was boosted by the more than three million Henanese migrants who had returned to the province after the 2008–2009 economic downturn hit coastal manufacturing.[41] Just as in Shenzhen, Foxconn was reliant on cheap labor from rural inland China, now employed even more cheaply in the interior itself. Foxconn Zhengzhou was also taking advantage of the discrepancy in wages between Zhengzhou city proper and its hinterland. Despite signs that China was coming to the end of rural surplus labor (the Lewis Turning Point) in the 2010s, leading to labor shortages and rising wages, Henan's still large rural workforce and the persistence of *hukou* barriers meant that Foxconn Zhengzhou was able to run a low-wage, high-pressure, high-turnover labor regime throughout the decade.[42] Even by 2018, Foxconn basic wages were only 2,100 RMB per month, rising with overtime to 4,000 RMB in the peak months of iPhone assembly, but with company rents, fees, and charges to be deducted.[43] Depending on the model, Foxconn Zhengzhou's assembly line workers were receiving just 0.46 to 0.66 percent of the purchase price of a new iPhone. By contrast, just a few kilometers away, average workers in Zhengzhou holding urban *hukou* were earning well over twice the Foxconn wages.[44]

39. A *New York Times* investigation concluded that the full amount of state support for Foxconn was effectively unknowable. *New York Times*, December 29, 2016; see also *South China Morning Post*, March 1, 2019.

40. Wang Jianguo, *Zhengzhou dadu shiqu jianshe*, 112–13.

41. *South China Morning Post*, March 1, 2019.

42. For a useful sense of the lives of Foxconn workers, see Jacobs, "Inside 'iPhone City.'" On rural surplus labor in the 2010s, see Zhang Xiaobo, Yang Jin, and Wang Shenglin, "China Has Reached the Lewis Turning Point."

43. China Labor Watch, "iPhone 11 Illegally Produced in China," 32.

44. Calculated from *South China Morning Post*, March 1, 2019, and China Labor

Inequalities of State and Market: Migration
and Housing in the Twenty-First Century

As the Foxconn case illustrates, one of Zhengzhou's main economic selling points was the large rural and small-town workforce of its Henan
hinterland. This was not new. The city's economy had benefited from
the low-wage labor of rural migrants throughout the twentieth century,
and under the People's Republic the restrictions of the *hukou* system
ensured that the municipal government did not bear responsibility for
their welfare, housing, or costs of social reproduction. As Julia Chuang
puts it, in such a political economy, "the stagnation of the hinterland
enables the dynamism of cities."[45] Zhengzhou's drive to megacity status
leveraged rather than overturned this deeply unequal spatial politics. In
addition to the ongoing barriers of the household registration system,
rising rents and the demolition of migrant housing created new challenges for arrivals in the city. The *hukou* and housing systems were deeply
contested political issues across the first two decades of the century, and
in both cases winners and losers were often determined by differences
across space.

Hukou and Fitful Reform

It is perhaps surprising that the *hukou* system remained a barrier to
rural-urban migration for so long, particularly in a fast-growing inland
city such as Zhengzhou. At the beginning of the twenty-first century, a
team of local economists were already urging its abolition: "If the people
cannot move freely . . . the city's society and economy will become like
a pool of stagnant water (*yitan sishui*)." "China's forty-year-old urban
household registration management and rural-urban divide system
should be completely scrapped," they continued, "removing all of the
former policy restrictions."[46] In August 2003, the municipal government
took their advice and launched what at the time was the most radical
reform of any provincial capital, abolishing the rural-urban distinction

---

Watch, "iPhone 11 Illegally Produced in China," 47. Foxconn assembly line wages fluc-
tuate across the year according to demand but seem to have averaged out at a little over
3,000 RMB per month in 2018, when average Zhengzhou wages were 6,929 RMB.

45. Chuang, *Beneath the China Boom*, 3.

46. Zhengzhou shi shehui kexuejie lianhehui, *Zhengzhou jingji shehui fazhan*, 31, 44.

within the municipal boundary (more than a decade ahead of national policy in 2014) and easing the conditions for long-term migrants to obtain urban *hukou*.[47] But in practice things were not so easy. After just twelve months, the reforms were reversed amid fears of urban services becoming overwhelmed and in the face of opposition from existing *hukou* holders and the local press. Among policy makers, Zhengzhou's abortive *hukou* relaxation became a byword for the dangers of a too-hasty approach.[48]

Following the 2004 reversal, Zhengzhou *hukou* were only available for those able to make large investments or property purchases. The importance of *hukou* in the mid-2000s came as something of a shock to those arriving in the provincial capital. Local researcher Cheng Xiuhong interviewed a Mr. Zhang from Tongbai County, in south Henan, who had arrived in 2004. "Before I came to Zhengzhou," Zhang recounted, "I'd heard that *hukou* didn't have so much use any more, that it didn't really matter (*wusuowei*)."[49] His experience proved the reverse. In his company wages varied by place of origin, with "regular" local workers earning double the pay of outsiders doing the same work. Although he was keen to settle in Zhengzhou, at just 1,500 RMB per month, Zhang's income was too low for anything but subsidized housing—for which he did not qualify. Even if he had been able to save up, new rules in 2005 meant that migrants had to have worked in Zhengzhou for at least three years to be able to buy property.[50] The tough post-2004 regime that Zhang encountered was gradually relaxed, with the 2007 residence permit system (*juzhuzheng*, replacing the old "temporary" permits) offering some access to local services. This relaxation provided a foothold in the city for many migrants but postponed the question of wider *hukou* reform.[51]

Hukou restrictions did not deter migrants from arriving in the booming Zhengzhou of the 2000s and 2010s. With further relaxations to the permit system, Zhengzhou was home to around 3.4 million non-*hukou*-holders by 2014, among provincial capitals second only to Guangzhou as

47. Yang Jianyun, "Zhengzhou huji jifen," 68.
48. Yang Jianyun, "Zhengzhou huji jifen," 68; see also Fei-ling Wang, "Renovating the Great Floodgate," 347–49.
49. Cheng Xiuhong, "Zhengzhou shi weilai renkou jiuye," 44.
50. Cheng Xiuhong, "Zhengzhou shi weilai renkou jiuye," 44.
51. For a review of *hukou* policy changes in the decade after 2004, see *Henan shangbao*, Novermber 13, 2014.

a proportion of the population.[52] Compared with a decade before, these *Zhengpiao* (Zhengzhou floaters) were a more diverse group, often with higher education and performing a wider range of jobs. But one 2018 memoir, titled "I Am What You Call a *Zhengpiao*," reveals that institutional barriers and anti-outsider feeling were still part of the migrant experience throughout the 2010s. The anonymous female author was from a rural area in Xun County, northern Henan. Her father had been away from home as a migrant worker for most of her own childhood in the 1990s and early 2000s. At first, her experience seemed very different from her father's, coming to Zhengzhou for university and graduating in 2012.[53] But as several studies demonstrated, relative equality in college ended with the graduate labor market.[54] Like many migrant graduates, she faced lower pay and more barriers to finding a job. Returning in the early hours of the morning to her shared room after a long overtime shift for low pay, the lived experience of her migrant twenties did not seem so different from her father's reform era life, white- or blue-collar work, college degree or no degree. It is true that the new migrant workers of the 2010s were often less socially or sartorially segregated from locals, and indeed the anonymous *Zhengpiao* looked to be heading toward marriage with her *hukou*-holding boyfriend, but at the crucial moment his parents declared that they disapproved and wanted him to marry a local woman. She toyed with the idea of returning to rural Xun County but decided to stay in the city, eventually scraping together enough for a down payment on a small apartment. Her future lay in Zhengzhou, despite the numerous pressures, long hours, and heavy interest payments: "If I had gone home at the beginning [after graduation], would I be more relaxed and happier? But in life there are no ifs (*rensheng meiyou ruguo*). . . . I decided to work in Zhengzhou, and here I will continue to strive (*jiu jixu fendou ba*)!"[55]

52. *Dahebao*, February 28, 2014. Note that this figure includes the whole municipal unit.

53. "Wo jiushi nimen kouzhong suoshuo de Zhengpiao," 111.

54. For example, Wen Wang and Peter Moffatt, "*Hukou* and Graduates' Job Search."

55. "Wo jiushi nimen kouzhong suoshuo de Zhengpiao," 112; on generational change, see also C. Cindy Fan and Chen Chen, "New-Generation Migrant Workers"; on the effects of rural-urban inequality on private life, see Wanning Sun, *Love Troubles*.

CHENGZHONGCUN DEMOLITION AND HOUSING CHALLENGES

The persistence of *hukou* barriers was exacerbated by the municipal government's wholesale demolition of *chengzhongcun*, the "villages in the city" that for decades had provided cheap accommodation for many of Zhengzhou's migrants. As in cities across China, this unplanned housing came to represent disorder and backwardness, something of a rural trojan horse in the ambitious twenty-first-century city: "these dirty and disordered places are not compatible with Zhengzhou's building of an international commercial metropolis (*yu Zhengzhou jianshe guoji shangdu buxiang fuhe*)," declared one unnamed official.[56] But for millions of Zhengzhou migrants, *chengzhongcun* made life in the city possible as well as providing sites for the entrepreneurship and creativity that in other spatial contexts the municipal government was eager to champion.

The municipal resolution to demolish *chengzhongcun* was passed in September 2003, after which there was little consideration of the more expensive alternative of upgrading these high-density neighborhoods. Village solidarity could improve compensation outcomes, but there was little sign in Zhengzhou of the successful resistance that stymied *chengzhongcun* demolition in some cities, especially in South China.[57] Of 143 *chengzhongcun* identified in 2007, demolition and development projects had been approved for 95 by early 2009.[58] This first phase of demolition included most of the villages discussed in this book, the urban edge villages of the Republican and Mao periods that had lost their last fields in the reform era but retained a collective identity and (usually) village committees as *chengzhongcun*: Mifengzhang, the old railside village where railroad workers had rented rooms in the early twentieth century; Feng Yuxiang's model villages of Damengzhai and Wulongkou; Caiwang, the Japanese and Nationalist military depot of the 1940s wars. The suburban village of Yanzhuang, where Mao inspected the 1960 spring wheat crop, had become an urban edge commercial zone in the late 1980s, then a high-density *chengzhongcun* as the city expanded beyond it. Yanzhuang

56. *Dahebao*, July 12, 2016.
57. Note, for instance, the much larger replacement homes reported from Xiaolizhuang than from nearby Caiwang. Zhengxie Zhengzhou shi Erqiqu weiyuanhui, *Yuanqu zhi jiyi*, 72, 87–88; compare village solidarity in Guangzhou in Ren, *Governing the Urban*, 56–90; Smith, *End of the Village*, 139–68.
58. Li Huishan, "Zhengzhou shi jiaoqu jianshe," 11.

FIGURE 7.1. Demolition of Chenzhai *chengzhongcun*, 2017. Reproduced with permission from Alamy.

was demolished in 2006 and replaced with the high-end Manhattan (Manhadun) housing development.[59]

The global economic downturn of 2008–2009 brought a hiatus in *chengzhongcun* demolitions. After 2010, the financial rewards of *chengzhongcun* sites spurred a renewed push for development. In 2012, eighty-five further *chengzhongcun*, mostly beyond the third ring road, were identified and slated for demolition. Zhengzhou's last major *chengzhongcun* was Chenzhai in the north of the city (see map 6.1). Chenzhai had first come to prominence in the 1990s as an urban edge vegetable wholesale market and home to many migrants from southern Henan.[60] In the mid-2010s, with other *chengzhongcun* disappearing fast, more than 150,000 people were crowded into the dense alleyways of this "little Hong Kong." But in summer 2016 this "starting point for the *Zhengpiao* pursuing their dreams" (*Zhengpiaomen zhui meng de qidian*) was also

59. For a full list of 2004–2012 redevelopments, see Li Huishan, "Zhengzhou shi jiaoqu jianshe," 11–12.

60. Ishihara, "Kanan-shō Teishū-shi ni okeru sosai," 35–38.

demolished (fig. 7.1).[61] By the end of the decade, the 228-village demolition program was almost complete.

As with the relocation of villagers for Zhengdong xinqu, the demolition and compensation system for Zhengzhou's *chengzhongcun* was hailed as a model but nonetheless was built on deeply unequal outcomes based on spatial difference. The municipal government's own slogan for this "Zhengzhou model" itself illustrates the problem: "the government gives up some of its profit, villagers gain, and businesses make a profit" (*zhengfu rangli, cunmin shouyi, qiye deli*).[62] There was no room in the slogan and little place in policy for migrant renters, who made up the vast majority of *chengzhongcun* residents. The fate of *chengzhongcun* villagers and migrants reflect deep hierarchies in the distribution of both cultural and economic capital—both spatially determined. In economic terms, the three hundred thousand original inhabitants of Zhengzhou's *chengzhongcun* received relatively high levels of compensation, albeit with the usual local variations. With property values taken into account, village members seem to have received a better deal than those in rural villages farther out. In Zaozhuang, just by the third ring road, Li Jiashun's family (see chapter 6) received more than 500,000 RMB as well as ownership of a replacement property when their home was demolished in 2014.[63] But as Megan Steffen shows, with a lack of cultural capital former villagers now faced stigmatization as *chai'erdai* ("second-generation demolishees"), with an uncertain discursive and social place in the city.[64]

By contrast, migrant renters were at the bottom of both cultural and economic hierarchies. The spatially determined inequalities between outside migrants and village members—already starkly reflected in landlord-tenant renting relationships—reached their climax at the point of demolition. As local journalists and scholars pointed out, the millions of migrant renters in *chengzhongcun* almost always received no compensation, instead facing rising rents and greater commuting distances as demolitions accelerated. The apartments that replaced *chengzhongcun*

61. *Henan ribao*, August 22, 2016.
62. Wang Yaowu and Zhang Yang, "Zhengzhou shi chengzhongcun yanjiu," 19–22.
63. "Zhenghou chengzhongcun gaizao," *Zhengzhou jiyi*, November 5, 2015. On better outcomes for displaced urbanites and villagers closer to the urban core (especially in South China), see also Hsing, *Great Urban Transformation*, 14–18.
64. Steffen, "Fruits of Demolition."

were beyond the reach of most migrants, with rents usually around three times the level of *chengzhongcun* living. *Henan Daily* reported the case of one migrant worker who had had to move four times between doomed *chengzhongcun*.[65] For local commentator Xiao Zhentao, the municipal government was simply using *chengzhongcun* development to drive out its most marginal migrants, despite their importance to the city's economy: "The current system is neglecting the interests of the lives of the floating population and is throwing all the contradictions of *chengzhongcun* onto migrants, simply taking the brutal method of driving them away (*hongzou de cubao fangshi*). This is nonsensical (*meiyou daoli*)."[66] Resentment was also sharpening over inequalities in the booming housing market—particularly after it was revealed that one senior official in a district housing office, Zhai Zhenfeng (b. 1963), had managed to acquire no fewer than thirty-one apartments for family members. To add insult to injury for Zhengzhou's *hukou*-less population, his twenty-year-old daughter not only had eleven properties to her name but had obtained them by illegally holding both Shanghai and Zhengzhou *hukou*.[67]

The Future of *Hukou* and Housing

The Zhai Zhenfeng scandal connected Zhengzhou's twin problems of *hukou* and housing policy. The first was a legacy of twentieth-century spatial politics; the second, a new problem generated by *chengzhongcun* demolition and the boom in property prices, which were rising three times faster than incomes.[68] In a period of emerging competition for labor, both local and external commentators were increasingly concerned that these twin barriers would hold back the final stages of Zhengzhou's drive to megacity status.[69] In practice, *hukou* issues have proved the easier to tackle; after several false starts, the municipality is still feeling its way toward a workable long-term housing policy.

Municipal housing strategy remained hesitant in the late 2010s, with few certainties apart from a firm line against the creation of new

---

65. *Henan ribao*, March 31, 2016.
66. Xiao Zhentao, "Zhengzhou shi chengzhongcun gaizao," 123.
67. *Dahebao*, December 19, 2014.
68. Xuefeng Wang and Tomaney, "Zhengzhou—Political Economy of an Emerging Chinese Megacity," 110.
69. *Henan ribao*, March 11, 2016; "China's Zhengzhou Banishes Ghosts."

chengzhongcun. Groups of villages were now demolished before being absorbed by the expanding urban area (*hecun bingcheng*). Zhengzhou's migrants, facing an uncertain future, could either pay higher rents at far-flung private apartments or, for those who were eligible, apply for the limited, sometimes unappetizing, subsidized public rental housing (*gonggong zulin fang*). This subsidized housing had seen a gradual expansion, but the 2016 cancellation of new public housing schemes—though only temporary—was a public relations disaster, adding fuel to Xiao Zhentao's view that the municipal government had still not given sufficient thought to the housing problem. Even the normally staid *Henan Daily* published a furious opinion piece calling the move an "extinguishing of hope" (*xiwang pomie*) for *Zhengpiao*.[70] It is true that the subsequent economic slowdown did take the heat off private rents, and the expanding subway network made lower-rent peripheries of Zhengzhou more accessible. But with limited growth in the supply of public rental housing (7,500 new units in 2019 for a fast-growing city of seven million people),[71] the risk remained of both freezing out low-paid outsiders and generating stark spatial divisions within the city based on class, with the further peripheralization of a migrant class permanently urbanized by *hukou* reform.[72] Most recently, the crisis in China's real estate sector in the 2020s—with Zhengzhou, epicenter of a 2022 mortgage boycott of buyers of unfinished units, at its heart—may bring some opportunities for migrant renters if the local state can convert additional properties for subsidized housing, but it also reveals the ongoing tensions and inequalities in the city's fraught housing sector.[73]

By contrast, Zhengzhou's *hukou* reforms since 2016 have finally whittled down many of the tenets of household registration that had been in place since the 1950s. This significant achievement should not be taken for granted: not only had previous rounds of *hukou* reform in China left most fundamental structures untouched, but with Zhengzhou's rapid growth, the city had fallen into ever-larger city categories, subject to a

70. *Henan ribao*, March 31, 2016; see also Xiao Zhentao, "Zhengzhou shi chengzhongcun gaizao," 122–23.

71. *Dahebao*, February 27, 2019. Note that public rental housing is separate from *baozhangfang*, social security housing for low-income groups.

72. On the risks of migrant peripheralization at an earlier period in Shanghai, see Ling, *Inconvenient Generation*.

73. "China Property Watch."

more cautious approach to *hukou* issues. But there was still some wiggle room, even in the more centralized policy making of the Xi era, and, although Zhengzhou was on the list of cities supposed to implement a points-based *hukou* system to select only the best migrant "talent" (*rencai*), it pointedly failed to do so. At the time of writing it was still the only designated city that had never introduced the points system.[74] Similarly, in December 2019, while national-level reform virtually abolished *hukou* barriers in smaller cities, Zhengzhou was designated one of the nine supercities with little scope for change.[75] Presumably not coincidentally, just a few weeks before the announcement, Zhengzhou's municipal government had implemented a dramatic opening up of *hukou* rights for migrant renters in the city. The qualification period for *hukou* transfer was reduced from five years to one year at a stroke.[76] Against a challenging economic backdrop, Zhengzhou announced further relaxations at the beginning of 2023, becoming the first major city to scrap a residency qualification period before a *hukou* application.[77] These relaxations did not mean that household registration had been altogether abandoned, and some of Zhengzhou's migrants—particularly poorer workers on temporary contracts—will continue to occupy a marginal place in the city. But unlike in many of China's largest cities, thus far Zhengzhou has been able to remove the most serious institutional inequalities of its *hukou* system.

These issues of migration, housing, and urban belonging were also deeply intertwined with Zhengzhou's relationship with its poorer hinterland. Could the city's twenty-first-century boom help the surrounding region? Did national-level promises of a more equal spatial politics translate to narrowing inequalities at the regional and local levels? And with Zhengzhou pulling along regional development, would the Central Plains be able to move beyond the politics of urban concentration and rural poverty that had overshadowed its twentieth century?

74. Yang Jianyun, "Zhengzhou huji jifen zhi," 67–71. For a critical view on the points system, see Yimin Dong and Goodburn, "Residence Permits and Points Systems."
75. Zhao Litao, "Chinese Society in 2019," 44.
76. "Te da chengshi fenfen fangkuan luohu."
77. *Dahebao*, January 4, 2023.

Zhengzhou Leading the Region: A Route to Social Harmony?

The answer to all these questions is a provisional "yes," particularly when set against Henan's rural crisis of the late 1990s and early 2000s. From the mid-2000s, the region saw a narrowing of spatial inequalities along several axes: a falling of rural-urban inequality around Zhengzhou, a slight narrowing of the gulf between Kaifeng and Zhengzhou, and some evidence of rapid growth in the provincial capital spilling over into the wider region. Beyond my scope here, the pervasive reform era inequality between China's coastal and inland regions also fell from around 2007.[78] The new spatial politics of equalization seemed to be bearing fruit, with a more sustained shift than the short years of rebalancing after the Great Leap Forward and in the early reform era. The discourse of this transition may have been banal, with the Henan provincial government calling for "rural-urban joint planning, social harmony, and the coordinated development of large, medium, small cities, small towns, and rural communities, all mutually promoting joint progress (*hu cu gong jin*)."[79] Behind the slogans lay a real pivot toward more equal government spending across space and efforts to foster equalizing market mechanisms.

These achievements are unlikely to be reversed, but in the second half of the 2010s, there were signs that the fall in inequality was slowing, even crawling to a halt in some dimensions. The rural-urban gap around Zhengzhou remained stubbornly high after 2015, even after infrastructure spending and the shift of most rural residents out of agriculture. Although the gap between Zhengzhou and Kaifeng cities had narrowed, Kaifeng's hinterland was left far behind, and in the late 2010s the wage gap between the two cities began to tick up again. Meanwhile, although the Central Plains City Cluster was designed to spread the benefits of Zhengzhou's growth across the region, there was little sign of reversing the concentration of investment and GDP growth in the provincial capital.

These issues in the later 2010s were not due to a major about-face under Xi Jinping: there has been more continuity in domestic spatial strategy than in other policy areas of Xi's "Third Revolution," although

78. Kanbur, Wang, and Zhang, "Great Chinese Inequality Turnaround," 471.

79. "Zhonggong Henan shengwei, Henan renmin zhengfu guanyu cujin zhongxin chengshi zutuan shi fazhan de zhidao yijian," *Yufa*, no. 11 (2011), quoted in Zhang Wensheng, "Chengzhenhua jincheng zhong de jiaoqu nongmin," 12.

the new paramount leader did lay more emphasis on tackling extreme poverty than overall spatial inequality.[80] More likely, it was simply that the low-hanging fruit of redistribution had been achieved, but the next phase was much more complex given the difficulties of unraveling territorial political interests, an unequal initial distribution of wealth, and behaviors clustering wealth and social capital. Based on Jeremy Wallace's view that moments of crisis precipitate a renewed focus on urban cores over rural peripheries (for reasons of political stability), the multilayered stresses of China's 2020s may lead to a further stalling of equalization across space.[81]

RURAL AND URBAN IN THE NEW SPATIAL POLITICS

Although rural areas under Zhengzhou's jurisdiction had avoided the worst crises of poverty, corruption, and HIV/AIDS prevalent in other parts of the Henan countryside (chapter 6), the beginnings of Zhengzhou's twenty-first-century economic takeoff had threatened to leave its rural hinterland behind. After a narrowing in the late 1990s, Zhengzhou's rural-urban income gap widened again, with urban residents 2.38 times better off than their rural counterparts by 2003. Rural off-farm employment meant that the gap between agricultural and nonagricultural incomes was even higher.[82] Besides noting income inequality, Sun Xinlei was concerned that rural and urban in Zhengzhou were still "two independent social and economic systems (*duli de shehui jingji xitong*)," identifying inequalities in services and infrastructure as well as a newly important digital divide.[83] Writing in a local Communist Party journal, Chang Heping diagnosed difficulties spreading capital from Zhengzhou to its rural hinterland—an issue first identified in the 1920s and 1930s: "There is very little credit available for small town infrastructure. . . . Because of distance or poor facilities, the development environment for smaller towns cannot compete with medium-sized or large cities (*wufa yu da zhong chengshi jingzheng*), and the scale of investment is very limited."[84]

80. For major policy shifts in other areas, see Economy, *Third Revolution.*
81. Wallace, *Cities and Stability*, 187–205.
82. *Zhengzhou tongji nianjian*, 2004:8.
83. Zhengzhou shi shehui kexuejie lianhehui, *Zhengzhou jingji shehui fazhan*, 32.
84. Chang Heping, "Zhengzhou shi chengxiang yitihua," 96.

It was these divisions that the municipal government tried to tackle from the mid-2000s. As development economists Liu Futan and Zhou Haichun put it, it was time for the industrial sector to "repay" (*fanbu*) agriculture for its support in the twentieth century, with a new shift to the "city supporting the countryside."[85] Such a shift was easiest to achieve within the municipal unit, where the strength of what Xuefei Ren calls the "territorial mode" of city governance could aid rural areas under its jurisdiction.[86] The policies of the New Socialist Countryside and Urban-Rural Integration brought new emphasis on agricultural subsidies, education, and infrastructure, with total state spending in Zhengzhou's rural areas rising 2.6 times over between 2003 and 2009 (even as the rural share of the municipal population fell from 43 percent to 36.6 percent).[87] The 104 model village projects in Zhengzhou Municipality included a range of schemes, including specialist cash cropping, rural industry, and the development of the service sector.[88] The rural-urban per capita income gap within Zhengzhou Municipality fell from a ratio of 2.38 in 2003 to just 1.90 a decade later, an earlier and faster fall than the rural-urban divide within Henan or China as a whole (fig. 7.2). Rising rural incomes also helped close Zhengzhou's digital divide— almost as soon as it had opened up. In 2003 urban residents had been twice as likely to own a cell phone, but by 2009 cell phones were ubiquitous across the whole municipality.[89]

These real achievements in the first decade of the new spatial politics did not mean that rural-urban differences were simply withering away. This was partly because of the top-down coercive aspects of New Socialist Countryside policies, which, much like their counterparts in the Nanjing Decade, tended to be dominated by the state's political and economic goals.[90] In places around Zhengzhou, such as in the experimental rural

85. Liu Futan and Zhou Haichun, *Zhongyuan chengshiqun zhanlüe*, 98.

86. Ren, *Governing the Urban*, esp. 9–10.

87. Comparing *Zhengzhou tongji nianjian*, 2004:89, and *Zhengzhou tongji nianjian*, 2010:67.

88. Feng Jingli, "Zhengzhou shi jianshe shehuizhuyi xin nongcun."

89. Comparing *Zhengzhou tongji nianjian*, 2004:161 (urban incomes) and 206–7 (rural), and 176 (urban cell phone ownership) and 215 (rural); *Zhengzhou tongji nianjian*, 2010:139 and 182–83 (incomes) and 151 and 191 (cell phone ownership).

90. Daniel Abramson suggests that the New Socialist Countryside was particularly top-down close to cities. See Abramson, "Periurbanization," 159. For more on

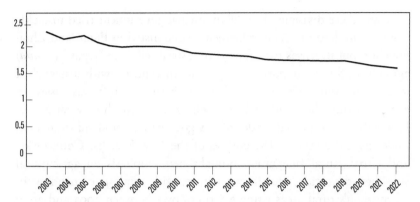

Figure 7.2. Urban-rural income ratios in Zhengzhou, 2003–2022. Data from Zhengzhou Municipal Statistic Bureau. Rural data: https://tjj.zhengzhou.gov.cn/ndsj/3093155.jhtml; urban data: https://tjj.zhengzhou.gov.cn/ndsj/3093156.jhtml. Accessed April 3, 2023.

area of Shangjie, the New Socialist Countryside entailed the wholesale demolition of villages and the consolidation of residents into new towns.[91] Studying the New Socialist Countryside in Zhengzhou, Gao Huifang warned in 2008 that enforced new rural towns risked "damaging the fundamental interests of peasants."[92] The New Socialist Countryside also tended to reproduce an antirural discourse. As one observer in Zhengzhou put it, the policy was about "encouraging the radiation of urban culture to the countryside (*chengshi wenming xiang nongcun fushe*)," something very different from the more prorural vision of the "substantivist" strand of thought explored by Alexander Day.[93]

In spite of the additional investment, Zhengzhou's rural areas still struggled to keep up with accelerating growth in the urban economy. Although direct state spending in rural areas rose sharply, massive private and state investment in Zhengzhou's booming urban economy meant that the rural share of investment was actually falling sharply after its early 2000s jump (from 25 percent in 2003 to less than 10 percent in

inequalities and disempowerment in this period, see Sorace, *Shaken Authority*; Looney, *Mobilizing for Development*; Chuang, *Beneath the China Boom*, 121–37.

91. "Jianzhi yange he dili gaimao," 3.

92. Gao Huifang, "'Chengxiang guanxi wenti,'" 72.

93. Wang Yan, "Guangyi chengxiang yitihua," 36; compare Day, *Peasant in Postsocialist China*, 154–85.

2009).[94] A 2011 study by Wang Yan revealed that although "rural-urban integration" around Zhengzhou was proceeding well in infrastructure, sharp gaps remained in social integration and economic performance.[95] By the mid-2010s, progress in income equality was slowing down, with almost no narrowing of Zhengzhou's rural-urban gap between 2016 and 2019 (down from a ratio of 1.80 to 1.79).[96]

This slower progress in tackling rural-urban inequality was repeated across much of China and gave rise to local and national debates about the rural future. Examining Zhengzhou's rural-urban fringe (*chengxiang bianyuanqu*), urban planner Zhao Jianhua argued in 2014 for the multiple economic, social, and ecological benefits of retaining rural life and agriculture close to the city.[97] In the mid-2010s, the policy pendulum was swinging away from Zhao's vision. Seeing urbanization partly as a panacea for inequality and partly as a driver for economic growth, the incoming Xi administration laid new emphasis on a breakneck program of rural urbanization. In 2013, new premier Li Keqiang announced that the People's Republic would create 350 million new urban residents by 2025.

To do so meant eliminating Zhengzhou's immediate rural hinterland and, farther out, in the county-level units, consolidating village populations into rural towns. In the mid- to late 2010s "Urban-Rural Integration" was abandoned as both policy and discourse around Zhengzhou in favor of wholesale "new-style urbanization" around the provincial capital. Building on New Socialist Countryside policy, municipal plans of 2017 revealed that Zhengzhou's rural residents (still numbering 2.7 million people, at least on paper) were to be concentrated in over 240 "new-style rural communities" (*xinxing nongcun shequ*) by 2030.[98]

94. Comparing *Zhengzhou tongji nianjian*, 2004:89, and *Zhengzhou tongji nianjian*, 2010:67.

95. Wang Yan, "Guangyi chengxiang yitihua," 37–38.

96. Zhengzhou shi tongjiju, "2019 nian Zhengzhou shi chengzhen jumin renjun kezhipei shouru shou po siwan yuan," April 7, 2020, available at http://www.zhengzhou.gov.cn/news4/121060.jhtml. China's Gini coefficient, which had been falling since 2008, also remained static over the same period. The rural-urban income gap did narrow further in the early 2020s, but this change was in part due to the heavy impact of COVID-19 restrictions on Zhengzhou's urban economy in 2020 and 2022.

97. Zhao Jianhua, "Nongye duoyuan jiazhi," 76–95.

98. Zhengzhou shi chengxiang guihuaju, *Zhengzhou chengxiang guihua 2017*, map after 117.

FIGURE 7.3. Demolition of Luosong Village, Zhongmu County, 2019. Photograph by Leonardo Ramondetti. Reproduced with permission.

Zhengzhou's first official experiments in this rural consolidation began in Dengfeng County in 2019.[99] The flagship zone for urbanization was Zhongmu County, where Leonardo Ramondetti found that the consolidated villages of the New Socialist Countryside period were already being superseded by the enforced new towns of the urbanization drive.[100] With the eastwards expansion of Zhengzhou and the westwards growth of Kaifeng, Zhongmu County in the late 2010s was in the throes of an urban revolution, with 102 villages being demolished to make way for a vast construction site of theme parks, logistics centers, housing estates, and transport infrastructure (fig. 7.3).[101]

This consolidation of hundreds of thousands of villages into towns was the most radical program for the transformation—some would say, the virtual elimination—of rural China since the Great Leap Forward.[102]

99. "Henan 'hecun bingju' you da dongzuo," December 8, 2020, reproduced at 163. com, https://www.163.com/dy/article/FTBD8CO305444ZOV.html.

100. Ramondetti, *Enriched Field*, 132–35.

101. *Renmin ribao*, December 26, 2017.

102. See Smith, *End of the Village*.

The Xi Jinping state in the mid-2010s gambled that urbanization would inevitably lead to rising incomes and lower inequality. There is much to commend this view, particularly if the People's Republic is firmly on the downward slope of the Kuznets curve. But breakneck urbanization is a crude instrument, and greater emphasis on "rural revitalization" in the 2020s (*xiangcun zhenxing*) suggests some rethinking away from one-size-fits-all urbanization and toward a stronger vision of a rural future.

The oscillation between "new-style urbanization" and "rural revitalization" matters less on the peripheries of Zhengzhou than in rural areas farther from the city. Close to the city, there has been relentless urban growth whatever the discursive and policy emphasis, with map 7.1 showing the almost total urbanization of Republican era Zheng County (which in 1953 became the Mao era Suburban District, or Jiaoqu). There is not quite a complete disappearance of the rural around the city: a "rurban" or "middle" landscape has been created with pockets of specialist, tourist-oriented agriculture interspersed with new housing along the Yellow River, in parts of Zhongmu County, and in the low hills southwest of the city.[103] Nor does this urbanization signify an end to spatial inequality around Zhengzhou—the last pages of this chapter point to the risk of new peripheries—but it marks the end of the rural-urban divide around the city as its major axis.

Good Neighbors? Pulling Along Kaifeng

In addition to the rural-urban gap Zhengzhou's neighboring city of Kaifeng has also been a challenge to spatial equalization. As discussed in chapters 5 and 6, the former provincial capital struggled badly under both the planned and reform era economies. By the beginning of the twenty-first century, Kaifeng had slipped to become one of the poorest cities in the province, with urban residents of Zhengzhou enjoying consumption levels almost twice those of their counterparts in Kaifeng (see chapter 6). This gap was often blamed by commentators on the cultural failings of Kaifeng's residents, accused by no less a figure than the head of Henan University's economics department of holding

103. Zhao Jianhua, "Nongye duoyuan jiazhi," 65–67, 109–10. For more on semirural landscapes around large cities, see Verdini, Wang, and Zhang, *Urban China's Rural Fringe*.

"backward concepts" (*gainian luohou*).[104] But local cultural essentialism was not necessary to explain Kaifeng's relative decline; rather, decades of political neglect and the collapse of its state-owned industry had left the city with few comparative advantages. In 2005, the travails of Kaifeng reached an international audience by virtue of its fame as the largest city in the medieval world. Writing in the *New York Times*, Nicholas Kristof used "dilapidated" Kaifeng as a warning to complacent New Yorkers of the rise and fall of the world's greatest cities, even if the "grimy and poor" city he described owed more to recent history than to its twelfth-century fall from grace.[105]

Even as Kristof was writing—and perhaps given a boost by his stinging critique of Kaifeng—the provincial government was formulating a new set of policies to aid the former capital.[106] In keeping with the new spatial politics of the mid-2000s, the aim was to spread the benefits of Zhengzhou's rapid growth with its neighbor under a policy of "Zhengzhou-Kaifeng integration" (*Zheng-Bian yitihua*). These measures improved infrastructural and business links between the two cities, encouraging an overspill of investment from Zhengzhou to cheaper Kaifeng. A new expressway between the two cities opened in 2006, and in 2014, the high-speed rail link cut journey times to less than half an hour. West of Kaifeng's walled area, expansion of the "Kaifeng New Area" pulled the city into the greater Zhengzhou metropolitan area by the end of the 2010s. Kaifeng's western expansion connected to the "Zhengzhou-Kaifeng New District" (Zheng-Bian xinqu), reaching from Zhengdong xinqu, straddling Zhongmu County, all the way to Kaifeng.[107] Kaifeng's economic revival was based on light industry and especially tourism, taking advantage of the earlier neglect that had enabled the survival of its fine city walls.[108] The policy of integration with Zhengzhou has helped kickstart Kaifeng's economy, and in the wake of Zhengzhou's mid-2010s boom, it was briefly one of the fastest-growing

104. Yang Min, "Kaifeng, Kaifeng!" 14.

105. *New York Times*, May 22, 2005.

106. "If it had not been for the American journalist's article in 2005," writes Kaifeng historian Wu Pengfei, "it is quite possible that Kaifeng would still be declining." Wu, "Kaifeng chengshi shengming," 128.

107. Wang Jianguo, *Zhengzhou dadu shiqu jianshe*, 112–13; Ramondetti, *Enriched Field*, 91–94.

108. Liang Liuke, *Kaifeng shi kechixu fazan*, esp. 212–20.

medium-sized city economies in China.[109] Kaifeng's population rose above one million for the first time since the Northern Song dynasty, and the urban income gap with Zhengzhou also narrowed slightly (from 39 percent to 34 percent, 2009–2018).[110]

This narrowing does not quite mean, however, an end to the inequalities between Zhengzhou and Kaifeng that have been a theme of this book. The fruits of over a decade of "Zhengzhou-Kaifeng integration" have in some ways been more disappointing than rural policy within the Zhengzhou municipal boundaries. Although some investment had spread to Kaifeng from Zhengzhou, after a decade of the integration policy real estate spending in Kaifeng per head was still well below the provincial average and less than a fifth of that of the booming provincial capital next door.[111] At the end of the 2010s, the wage gap between the two cities seemed to be rising again, and Kaifeng's economic performance tumbled back to the bottom quarter of China's medium-sized cities.[112] Even more serious than the divide between the two cities was the divergent fate of the county-level units under their jurisdiction. With the boost for investment and infrastructure around the provincial capital, GDP per capita in Zhengzhou's county-level units was more than double that of the still heavily agricultural counties under Kaifeng.[113] Even as the two adjacent cities were merging in space, the ongoing importance of municipal boundaries was contributing to a stark divergence in the fate of their hinterlands.

Zhengzhou and the Central Plains City Cluster

Zhengzhou-Kaifeng integration was part of a wider effort to encourage economic growth in medium-sized cities around the provincial capital. This Central Plains City Cluster was one of four such clusters

109. Kaifeng placed twelfth of 230 third-tier cities in the Milken Institute's 2018 rankings (on the basis of growth in jobs, wages, GDP, investment, and so on; data up to 2016). "Best-Performing Cities China," 2018:35.

110. Comparing *Henan tongji nianjian*, 2010:314; *Henan tongji nianjian*, 2019:251.

111. *Henan tongji nianjian*, 2016:476.

112. *Henan tongji nianjian*, 2019:124–25 (on wages). In 2020, the Milken Institute placed Kaifeng 178th of 228 third-tier cities (on the basis of 2018 data). "Best-Performing Cities China," 2020. Kaifeng was not included in the 2021 ranking owing to missing data.

113. *Henan tongji nianjian*, 2019:734–36 (county-level GDP data).

in inland China, aiming to use major cities as an engine for regional economies. Zhengzhou's growth was to "radiate out and drive (*daidong*) the economic development of the entire central region."[114] This growth would not only reduce the gulf between coastal and inland regions but also tackle inequality within Henan, one of China's most spatially unequal provinces.[115] The provincial government put forward a full plan for the city cluster in 2006, promising to develop high-speed road and rail to bring all eight cities within the cluster to less than an hour's journey from Zhengzhou. At the same time, the city cluster aimed to reduce barriers to mobility and investment across municipal boundaries, taking the pressure off the provincial capital by encouraging faster growth in other cities. In the original formulation of 2006, Zhengzhou was to see population growth of just 25 percent during the 2010s, with the other eight cities slated to grow on average two and a half times faster than the provincial capital.[116]

Yet this is not how the first phase of Central Plains City Cluster worked out in practice. As in much of the twentieth century, the impulse to spatial concentration rather than dispersal continued to dominate. As local geographer Feng Dexian argued in 2004, Zhengzhou was still too small to pull along the region: by one calculation, less than half the size needed for the primate city of a province with almost 100 million people.[117] Even as the cluster plan of 2006 spoke of spreading growth outwards from Zhengzhou, this aim was overtaken by concentrated development in the provincial capital. As shown in this chapter, Zhengzhou's economy boomed, subordinating the impulse to spread across the city cluster. In a single decade, Zhengzhou's urban population doubled in size relative to Luoyang, the second-largest city of the cluster, rising

114. Guo Xinxin, "Zhengzhou jianshe guojia zhongxin chengshi," 5.

115. In 2007, intraprovincial differences accounted for the majority (61 percent) of spatial inequality (at the county level). Depending on the measurement used, Henan was the second or third worst province for intraprovincial inequality. See Tsun Se Cheong and Yanrui Wu, "Intraprovincial Inequality," 193–95.

116. Henan sheng fazhan he gaige weiyuanhui, "Zhongquan chengshiqun zongti fazhan guihua," republished in Liu Futan and Zhou Haichun, *Zhongyuan chengshiqun zhanlüe*, 219–328, 241. The eight cities were Luoyang, Kaifeng, Xinxiang, Xuchang, Jiaozuo, Pingdingshan, Luohe, and Jiyuan.

117. Feng Dexian, "Cong zhongwai chengshiqun fazhan kan zhongyuan," 75–78; on Zhengzhou being half the required size, see Liu Futan and Zhou Haichun, *Zhongyuan chengshiqun zhanlüe*, 62.

from 1.51 times Luoyang's population in 2000 to 3.07 times a decade later. Zhengzhou's GDP growth was also 37 percent higher than that of the city cluster region as a whole (2000–2015).[118]

Whether or not a true primate city was strictly necessary, there was probably some truth in the diagnosis of the 2000s that Zhengzhou was too small to serve as an engine of growth for the wider region. By the 2010s, though, Zhengzhou had become the powerhouse of the region, and the overheating city economy should have encouraged the dispersal of economic activity. Unlike in China's very largest cities, there was still little sign of political pressure for an end to the concentration of growth in Zhengzhou. As the core of the city cluster, Zhengzhou may have sucked in resources more than it spread them. In the first half of the 2010s, the density of economic activity grew by 30 percent in the core around Zhengzhou but only 20 percent in the rest of the city cluster. Most striking is that economic activity in Henan's cities beyond the cluster, largely outside Zhengzhou's economic orbit, grew faster (24 percent) than the cities within the cluster.[119] During the 2010s, Zhengzhou's population doubled, rather than experiencing the 25 percent growth in the original 2006 plan, while the other cities in the cluster grew more slowly than slated.[120] Although the city cluster was supposed to spread prosperity, the urban per capita income gap between Zhengzhou and nearby cities grew slightly in the 2010s.[121]

These limited results of the city cluster policy are on the face of it surprising. Under the new spatial politics of the twenty-first century, as Jeremy Wallace points out, provincial governments have often aimed to avoid an overconcentration of growth in their capitals, with its attendant potential for generating instability.[122] As Anthony Gar-On Yeh

118. On the Luoyang and Zhengzhou disparity, see An Qian, *Kuaisu chengshihua jincheng*, 248. On GDP, see Feng Yunting and Zhang Yongfang, "Zhongyuan chengshiqun jingji zhongxin bianhua," 71.

119. Feng Yunting and Zhang Yongfang, "Zhongyuan chengshiqun jingji zhongxin bianhua," 71.

120. Henan sheng fazhan he gaige weiyuanhui, "Zhongquan chengshiqun zongti fazhan guihua," republished in Liu Futan and Zhou Haichun, *Zhongyuan chengshiqun zhanlüe*, 219–328, 241.

121. Urban incomes in Zhengzhou were 20.8 percent higher than those of the rest of the city cluster in 2009 and 21.9 percent higher in 2018. *Henan tongji nianjian*, 2010:314, and *Henan tongji nianjian*, 2019:251.

122. Wallace, *Cities and Stability*, 10–11.

and Zifeng Chen show, some city clusters in China have been effective in spreading growth beyond the core metropolis.[123] There are two key reasons for the ongoing concentration in Zhengzhou. First, state investment and support for Zhengzhou proved tricky to unravel, even when the city's economy was threatening to overheat. Political interests and municipal power made a real spread of resources difficult, particularly given that local government in Zhengzhou was fiscally reliant on the ongoing boom in the city. Provincial state expenditure was still weighted toward Zhengzhou, accounting for 21.5 percent of spending for only 10.6 percent of the provincial population.[124] Wang Jianguo argues that there was little real cooperation or effective division of labor between cities within the cluster.[125] The "territorial" strength of city government, which has helped alleviate rural poverty within Zhengzhou's municipal boundary, was proving a barrier to the spread of resources to neighboring jurisdictions.

Second, as commentators in the 2010s observed, Zhengzhou's rapid growth was of a type not easily spread across space. Endogenous growth remained weak, with much of the boom driven by real estate and direct or indirect support from the municipal government.[126] Property prices in Zhengzhou remained around twice as high as in other cities in the region, and despite a slowdown real estate still accounted for most (63 percent) investment in Zhengzhou at the end of the 2010s, more than twice the proportion of other cities in Henan. With slack demand elsewhere, market mechanisms had not yet taken the pressure off Zhengzhou.[127]

Zhengzhou's regional supremacy was not unusual by comparative standards. Indeed, in the first decade of the century it was less dominant than most provincial capitals, perhaps in part because of political pressure to bring growth to Henan's countryside, viewed as emblematic of China's rural crisis, as well as the sheer scale of Henan's population. Zhengzhou's growth numbers in the 2000s era did not match, for example, Kyle Jaros's study of Changsha as Hunan's booming hegemon.

123. Yeh and Chen, "From Cities to Super Mega City Regions," 647–48.
124. *Henan tongji nianjian*, 2019:222–23.
125. Wang Jianguo, *Zhengzhou dadu shiqu jianshe*, 5–6.
126. "China's Zhengzhou Banishes Ghosts."
127. Wang Jianguo, *Zhengzhou dadu shiqu jianshe*, 126. As proportion of investment, see *Henan tongji nianjian*, 2019:148–49.

But the pattern of concentration of growth and resources in Zhengzhou speaks to Jaros's wider concerns about uneven development and urban concentration in inland provinces, and in the years since Jaros's study ended in 2012, Zhengzhou's dominance has only increased, with its share of provincial GDP rising by almost 25 percent during the 2010s (from 17.4 percent in 2010 to 21.3 percent in 2019).[128]

A decade after the 2006 plan for the Central Plains City Cluster, China's State Council reformulated the strategy. In a vastly more ambitious scheme, the city cluster around Zhengzhou expanded in 2016 to include almost the entirety of inland north-central China: the whole of Henan Province plus portions of Shanxi, Shandong, Anhui, and Hebei. With 158 million residents, the revised city cluster was more than three times the original scale and, along with the Yangzi Delta, the most populous of China's nineteen city regions. Once again, this scheme was formulated in terms of spatial equalization, with Zhengzhou's breakneck growth now supposed to pull along Henan's provincial peripheries as well as poorer regions of neighboring provinces like northern Anhui and western Shandong. After over a century as the transport pivot of inland north-central China, Zhengzhou was now designated its economic engine.[129] In practice, it remains unclear how the expanded city cluster will operate across provincial as well as municipal boundaries. Zhengzhou remains the only large city in the cluster, and with a population four times that of the next largest monocentric cluster (centered on Xi'an), the revised cluster looks very different from any other city-region strategy in China. It is at best uncertain whether Zhengzhou will have much impact on the peripheries of the larger cluster, and at worst the regional development demands on Zhengzhou may lead to a further concentration and overheating of the city's economy as the People's Republic tries to kickstart economic growth in the mid-2020s.

These three scales of analysis—rural Zhengzhou, Kaifeng, and the Central Plains City Cluster—all reveal the difficulties of the new spatial politics of equalization in the twenty-first century. The picture here supports the suggestion of Ravi Kanbur, Yue Wang, and Xiaobo Zhang that it proved easier to narrow interprovincial inequalities and the gulf

128. Jaros, *China's Urban Champions*, 80–114 on Changsha.
129. Feng Yunting and Zhang Yongfang, "Zhongyuan chengshiqun jingji zhongxin bianhua," 67.

between coastal and inland areas than to tackle the politics of inequality in such inland regions.[130] Within Zhengzhou's municipal boundary, urbanization, consumption, and economic growth have formed a virtuous cycle, and some of the benefits have spread outwards from the urban core. But in relative terms these processes risk generating new inequalities, and the experience of recent years has shown the difficulties in unraveling the concentration of resources in a growing megacity.

Spatial Politics toward Midcentury

What does the future hold for Zhengzhou and China's spatial politics? This chapter has demonstrated that there are promising signs of a more equitable distribution of resources across space. Most measures of spatial inequality have fallen, and the easing of the path to Zhengzhou *hukou* has opened the provincial capital as never before. But differences across space still haunt China's economic and social policy. Levels of inequality remain high, with a stalling of progress since the mid-2010s, and as Andrew Walder shows, despite—or indeed because of—the state's power in the economy, it has proved difficult to tackle inequality by state redistribution mechanisms.[131] The challenges are both old and new. The party-state is simultaneously grappling both older issues of rural-urban inequality and more recent inequalities of higher income economies, including housing market/wealth inequity and what the anthropologist Li Zhang calls the "spatialization of class."[132] At the same time, with a slowing economy, aging population, and environmental challenges, China's households, cities, and the country as a whole could face a narrowing window of opportunity to achieve long-term prosperity. This drive for high-income status in the troubled 2020s risks generating an unequal distribution of wealth in the last phase of rapid economic growth that may be difficult to reverse.

For a city such as Zhengzhou, the goal of growing "fast and well" (*youhao, youkuai*)—for the most part successfully achieved in the 2010s—is not easy in the 2020s. The city's future as a regional megacity is already assured: its existing size, political weight, lack of nearby

130. Kanbur, Wang, and Zhang, "The Great Chinese Inequality Turnaround," 475–78.

131. Walder, "China's Extreme Inequality."

132. Li Zhang, *In Search of Paradise*, esp. 14–15.

FIGURE 7.4. Zhengzhou East high-speed rail station, looking east toward Zhongmu County, 2019. Photograph by Leonardo Ramondetti. Reproduced with permission.

rivals, and importance in logistics safeguard Zhengzhou's future as one of the major cities of China's midcentury. In the early 2020s, Zheng-zhou's contiguous built-up area stretched from Xingyang and Shangjie in the west to Zhongmu in the east, with a population not far from ten million—double what commentators had expected at the turn of the twenty-first century.[133] The new district of Zhengdong xinqu continues to expand and in the 2020s stretches east toward Zhongmu (fig. 7.4) and northwards as far as the Yellow River. This northeast expansion is urbanizing the last remaining corner of the old Zheng County, badly hit by flooding in 1938 and peripheral in both the socialist and reform eras (see map 7.1). At the beginning of the 2010s, residents were told that Zhengzhou will have expanded to a population of 15.5 million by 2050, including eight large satellite districts.[134] But Zhengzhou has exceeded every previous population prognostication, and with an economic logic of continuous expansion as well as intense intercity competition for migrants, the eventual figure may be higher.

133. For the expectation of a population of five million in 2020, see Zhengzhou shi shehui kexuejie lianhehui, *Zhengzhou jingji shehui fazhan*, 42.

134. *Dahebao*, November 5, 2011.

If Zhengzhou's regional role looks certain, the city's high-income future does not look quite so secure. If the city's advantages have been a strategic position and a rural hinterland labor force, it is uncertain if these strengths will translate beyond logistics, transport, and assembly to the high-end research, design, and information economy the municipal government aims to create. With hypercompetition between cities, the spatial politics of prestige continue to weigh against inland centers such as Zhengzhou. The city still compares poorly with its rivals in indices of innovation, high-end competitiveness, air quality, and the elusive "livability."[135] Having been one of China's best-performing cities in the mid-2010s, Zhengzhou fell back into the bottom half with a bump in the last years of the decade, with low GDP and wage growth. Commentators at the time warned against Zhengzhou's economic pattern, driven by debt-financed local infrastructure spending, real estate booms, and low-wage assembly that will not last forever.[136] Even Zhengzhou Foxconn was not immune to the slowdown of the late 2010s. The Apple downturn of 2018–2019 slashed production, with many temporary workers laid off and the workforce down to less than a third of its peak.[137] Although iPhone 12 brought a revival to the plant in 2020, the episode served as a reminder that footloose Foxconn may have its limits as a driver of growth.

Zhengzhou has had a troubled beginning to the 2020s, doing little to relieve the endemic anxieties, hierarchies, and unpredictability that Megan Steffen found in the city in the 2010s.[138] Against the simmering backdrop of the COVID-19 threat, the city suffered disastrous urban floods in 2021 and three significant protest movements in 2022: by account holders at rural banks, by mortgage holders of unfinished properties, and by Foxconn workers protesting over COVID restrictions and delayed pay. Taken together, these events risked making Zhengzhou perhaps unfairly emblematic of the multiple environment, social, and

135. In the latest air quality rankings, Zhengzhou was China's third worst provincial capital for pollution (after Xi'an and Wuhan). https://www.iqair.com/us/world-most-polluted-cities.

136. The Milken Institute index ranked Zhengzhou nineteenth of thirty-four major cities in 2020 (down from seventh in 2017). "Best-Performing Cities China," 2020. See also Xuefeng Wang and Tomaney, "Zhengzhou—Political Economy of an Emerging Chinese Megacity," 109–10.

137. *South China Morning Post*, March 1, 2019.

138. Steffen, "Unpredictability, Sociality, and Decision-Making."

political difficulties facing the People's Republic. City authorities and residents alike will be hoping for a strong recovery from the COVID-19 pandemic in the mid-2020s, but perceived inequalities and unfairness mean state-society relations may remain tense.

It is also unclear how governance of space and movement will operate in the Zhengzhou of the future. In an age of epidemics and techno-authoritarianism, there is a tension between different visions of China's cities, between individual-, leisure-, and market-oriented cities and a collective orientation toward production and control. Most relevant to this book, it is also unclear how Zhengzhou's residents and rulers will manage megacity issues of core-periphery division and housing inequality. The long-range plan for midcentury Zhengzhou assumes that those in its outer districts will enjoy the same services, education, and transport links as those in the city proper (*he shiqu yiyang*).[139] Although residents of the urban periphery can expect good facilities, it will be a trickier challenge to avoid spatially unequal outcomes for income, wealth, housing, and the labor market—let alone social capital—across the metropolitan area. Even if space loses something of its power as an independent variable, it will be hard to avoid other forms of inequality being reflected in spatial differences.[140]

The place of Zhengzhou in its wider region is also uncertain. Rural human capital growth means that Scott Rozelle and Natalie Hell go too far in their recent suggestion that rural-urban division "threatens China's rise"—though that was certainly the case in the first decade of the century—but inequality and tension between the Zhengzhou megacity and its Henan hinterland look likely to remain.[141] Daniel Abramson has outlined one version of China's rural-urban future, of "densely built, technologically complex urban hubs connected by high-speed rail lines that bypass vast stretches of rural land. These lands would in turn be largely depopulated . . . and reorganized for industrialized agriculture."[142] The booming high-speed rail hub of Zhengzhou looks

139. *Dahebao*, November 5, 2011.
140. Between 2009 and 2018, the income of Zhengzhou's richest 20 percent of households rose from less than four times the urban average to more than five, while the incomes of the bottom quintile fell relative to the city average. Compare *Zhengzhou tongji nianjian*, 2010:155; *Zhengzhou tongji nianjian*, 2019:162.
141. Rozelle and Hell, *Invisible China*.
142. Abramson, "Periurbanization," 158.

like a poster child for this vision. But the reality will be messier than this utopian (or dystopian) imagining, quite apart from the fact that there are still many alternative views on the rural future within the state as well as a lack of elite consensus on the dual impulses to concentrate or spread development across space.[143]

In the spaces between megacity and low-population agribusiness countryside, Zhengzhou's hinterland will remain a landscape of smaller cities, periurban neighborhoods, and peripheral rural towns. At best, as Hanchao Lu hopes, this layout may restore the more socially and economically fair continuum of late imperial China, a society united across different settlement sizes, perhaps as part of Hans Westlund's vision of a "post-urban world."[144] At worst, the result may be what Douglas Webster calls "stranded remnant landscapes" of an aging, recently urbanized underclass not so much solving China's rural-urban divisions as moving them to new small town and periurban spaces.[145] After decades of carefully preventing the creation of slum settlements for rural migrants, China's urban authorities must be mindful of the peripheries of less wealthy megacities as a site of social and political risk. In the wake of *hukou* reform, relatively isolated, perhaps stigmatized, townships for lower-paid urban workers at the megacity periphery are a governance challenge and site of potential political combustion. In a system of still strict urban hierarchies, Zhengzhou's influence, now stretching across north-central China as the region's only megacity, will not on its own be enough to avoid the creation of new peripheries. China's unequal spatial politics have changed in the twenty-first century and will continue to evolve, but they are by no means over.

143. Hayward, "Beyond the Ownership Question"; Jaros, *China's Urban Champions.*
144. Hanchao Lu, "Small-Town China," 49–51. Compare Westlund, "Urban-Rural Relations."
145. Webster, "An Overdue Agenda," 642; for similar concerns, see Yeh and Chen, "From Cities to Super Mega City Regions," 648–49.

Conclusion

I loved living in Zhengzhou while researching this book. Zhengzhou's residents were without exception welcoming, though I am keenly aware here that I write from a position of privilege. I loved both the quiet tree-lined streets and the sense of enormity of Zhengzhou's wide, straight avenues. I loved Zhengzhou's combination of pulsating energy and unpretentiousness. I especially loved exploring the city trying to discover traces of its history. This was sometimes a difficult task. Twentieth-century turmoil combined with the breakneck development of recent years means that Zhengzhou's past has often been not so much "displaced," like Joseph Allen's Taipei, as simply obliterated.[1]

But glimpses of the past still remain. In 2017 experts identified a cluster of surviving late Qing and Republican era buildings in the very center of Zhengzhou. The structures were hiding in plain sight around Toudao hutong, a long-forgotten corner of the old city, tucked up against the line of the city wall. Before their "discovery," these crumbling buildings were part of what local media called a shantytown (*penghuqu*) densely populated by rural migrants.[2] As part of an effort to promote a more distinctive historical narrative for Zhengzhou, municipal planners preserved these buildings and aimed to incorporate them in a new historic quarter along the southern line of the old city wall, including replicas of Shang era buildings and a rebuilt Kaiyuan Temple (destroyed during the Second World War).[3] The case of Toudao hutong is a reminder that

1. Allen, *Taipei*.
2. "Zhengzhou lao chengqu faxian jishi chu gu minju," *Zhengzhou jiyi*, June 26, 2017.
3. "Zhengzhou lao chengqu faxian jishi chu gu minju," *Zhengzhou jiyi*, June 26, 2017. For more on the proposals, see Zhengzhou shi chengxiang guihuaju, *Zhengzhou chengxiang guihua 2017*, 12–15. As of 2023, the new museum of Shang era Zhengzhou

Zhengzhou's twentieth-century past is not so far away as it can sometimes seem in the twenty-first-century city. It also illustrates that spatial
inequality operates on multiple scales, here connecting a two-block
microperiphery in the heart of the city with the much larger inequality between Zhengzhou and the rural hinterland origin of its migrant
inhabitants. With this past and these inequalities in mind, this book
has examined three spatial dimensions across the twentieth century and
beyond: Zhengzhou's urban edge, its immediate rural hinterland, and its
relationship with the wider region.

Zhengzhou's urban fringe has been a complex, contested zone since
the city burst beyond its walls in the first years of the twentieth century. It
has been on the front line of rural-urban difference, expressing in physical
form the division between city and countryside but in its mixed nature
softening that duality. At times the urban edge was a sharply defined
and militarized boundary, but more usually it was a messy, sometimes
sprawling transition zone. Pockets of agriculture have intersected with
migrant housing, railroad land, and Zhengzhou's many warehouses. It
has seen ambitious land speculation, experiments in social control, and
state-of-the-art production, from the vast Yufeng spinning mill to the
Foxconn works a century later. The urban edge has also been a site for
the marginal and maligned: the sex workers and *jianghu* of Laofengang,
the refugee-smugglers of the wartime years, the black marketeers of the
collective era, the "hooligan" young unemployed of the dying days of the
Mao period. This ambiguity has made Zhengzhou's urban fringe a site of
intense opportunity, exploitation, and unequal outcomes. At times, this
inequality has been exacerbated by struggles over land rights, the uses of
the urban edge, and the right to move across the rural-urban boundary.

Beyond the urban edge, Zhengzhou's immediate hinterland began
the twentieth century as an unremarkable rural county and ended it on
the cusp of full-scale absorption into an expanding megacity. Villagers
in the "diurnal hinterland" closest to the city usually gained from their
proximity, at least relative to their counterparts farther out: benefiting
from the high prices for rural sidelines in the first railroad boom, letting
out rooms to urbanites during Japanese bombing raids, enjoying the
relative protection of urban communes during the Great Leap famine,

---

has just opened, and the project of a reconstructed historical leisure and retail district
is ongoing.

using technology and expertise from nearby state-owned factories to set up successful TVEs during the reform era. Beyond a radius of a few kilometers, though, there is less sign of a positive impact from Zhengzhou. It is true that farmers in Zheng County (after 1953 the Zhengzhou Suburban District) were usually a little better off than most in this impoverished province, but the rural economy here was not transformed by the presence of urban Zhengzhou either before or after 1949. It was only in the very late twentieth and early twenty-first centuries that Zhengzhou's expansion brought major economic benefits to most of its nearby rural residents—at the moment of their urbanization—and even then, arbitrary differences across time and space made for an unequal windfall.

As for Zhengzhou's regional role, it was driven by three key factors. The first was the city's status as a railroad junction. In the first quarter of the twentieth century, Zhengzhou became a booming center for primary product processing and interregional trade. Multiple wars, political neglect, and the emergence of rivals partly threatened this commercial position by midcentury, but Zhengzhou's pivotal position in China's transport networks ensured that its logistical importance was secure. The second factor was a series of political decisions to support the city. On three occasions—under Feng Yuxiang in the 1920s, during the first decade of the People's Republic, and again in the twenty-first century—political authorities raised Zhengzhou's regional importance. But this was not a smooth upward trajectory, and in the 1930s and the 1960s authorities withdrew their patronage when political and economic circumstances changed. Thus, although Zhengzhou rose from being simply a commercial-logistical town to become a political center (and provincial capital in 1954), it remained a medium-sized, usually obscure provincial city until the first years of the twenty-first century.

This position points to the third factor affecting Zhengzhou's regional role: the gulf and disconnection between the city and its wider Henan hinterland, which was impoverished even relative to most of rural China. In the Republican period, Zhengzhou's role was geared toward funneling primary resources out to the coastal economy, with the city insufficiently large or wealthy to have much impact on the wider hinterland of Henan Province. Under the planned economy, Zhengzhou's urban economy became more important, but there was little mechanism to spread the city's resources to the wider region. In the Great Leap, Zhengzhou's residents escaped relatively unscathed while the provincial government in the city presided over a devastating rural famine. It was only in the reform period that market mechanisms opened for the more sustained spread of resources across space and for Zhengzhou to play a stronger economic role in pulling along the wider region. But in relative terms the results in Henan were disappointing, and much of Zhengzhou's regional hinterland faced a fiscal, social, and economic crisis at the end of the century.

These findings from Zhengzhou illustrate the importance of spatial politics in modern China. Both before and after 1949, differences across space have determined as well as reflected unequal outcomes. Such outcomes include the long-term neglect of Henan and "Middle China" as well as inequalities between Zhengzhou and both its rural hinterland and nearby cities such as Kaifeng. These inequalities are partly attributable to environmental differences and market forces but were also driven by the unequal spatial politics of the state. The city of Zhengzhou was sometimes a winner from this policy and sometimes a loser, but its rural hinterland almost always lost out, sometimes with devastating results. I do not mean to deny the reality of poverty or inequality within the city but simply to emphasize that the limited resources of economic wealth, social prestige, and political power were concentrated there.

The story of modern China has been about the gap between the ambitions of the state and its capabilities. Spatial inequality filled that gap. From the late Qing to the reform era, the Chinese state concentrated its resources in particular places with a view to accumulating the elusive "wealth and power" of modernity. It was able to do so by regimes of inequality that neglected and usually extracted from other, poorer places. Mobility as a strategy to even out this spatial inequality was rarely straightforward. These patterns reached their apogee in the Mao era but were not simply an aberration of the socialist economy: Mao period divisions were laid on top of existing inequalities of semicolonialism, wartime upheaval, and ideas of urban industrial modernization inherited from the Republican state. After Mao's death, the Dengist state retained Mao era institutions in the interests of capital accumulation and overlaid them with new inequalities of authoritarian market reform.

The additional resources of the twenty-first century enabled a break with this pattern. The new spatial politics promised infrastructure, support, and welfare for people and places left behind as well as greater opportunities for mobility, creating a society where the lives of individuals and households depend less on their location. The achievements in both absolute and relative spatial inequality have been impressive. Recent years have shown the scale of the challenge and perhaps thrown into question the political will to continue the drive to a fairer society. But from the point of view of both the Chinese state and its citizens, it is to be hoped that the new spatial politics succeed around Zhengzhou. As an old saying has it, "When the Central Plains are settled, the world is at peace" (*Zhongyuan ding, tianxia an*).[4]

4. Wang Jianguo, *Zhengzhou dadu shiqu jianshe*, 58.

BIBLIOGRAPHY

Archives, Journals, Newspapers, and Yearbooks

"Best-Performing Cities China." Milken Institute Asia Center, Singapore, 2015–2021. Available at https://www.best-cities-china.org/rankings.

The China Press. Shanghai, 1911–1949.

China Weekly Review. Shanghai, 1923–1950.

Dahebao 大河报. Zhengzhou, 1995–.

General Synod Archives. Anglican Church of Canada, Toronto.

Henan jianshe 河南建設. Kaifeng, 1934–?

Henan jiaoyu ribao 河南教育日報. Kaifeng, 1932–1934.

Henan minbao 河南民報. Kaifeng, 1927–1938; Luoyang, 1938–1942; Lushan, 1942–1944 (?); Kaifeng, 1945–1948.

Henan ribao 河南日報. Kaifeng, 1912–1914.

Henan ribao 河南日報. Kaifeng, 1949–1954; Zhengzhou, 1954–.

Henan sheng dang'anguan 河南省檔案館. Zhengzhou.

Henan tongji nianjian 河南统计年鉴. Beijing, 1984–.

Henan tongji yuebao 河南統計月報. Kaifeng, 1935–1937.

Kautz Family YMCA Archives. University of Minnesota. Available at https://www.lib.umn.edu/ymca.

Jingji huibao 經濟匯報. Chongqing, 1942–1945.

North China Herald. Shanghai, 1870–1941.

Qianfengbao 前鋒報. Nanyang, 1942–1947.

Shenbao 申報. Shanghai, 1872–1949.

United China Relief Papers. New York Public Library.

Xin Henan ribao 新河南日報. Kaifeng, 1938–1945.

Zhengzhou jiyi 郑州记忆. Zhengzhou, 2010–2021. Collected by Zhengzhou Municipal Library, available at https://www.zzlib.org.cn/culture/index?mid=67&nid=30.

Zhengzhou ribao 鄭州日報. Zhengzhou, 1931–1938; 1947–1948.

Zhengzhou ribao 鄭州日報. Zhengzhou, 1949–1963.

Zhengzhou shi dang'anguan 鄭州市檔案館. Zhengzhou.

Zhengzhou shizheng yuekan 鄭州市政月刊. Zhengzhou, 1928–1929.

Zhengzhou tongji nianjian 郑州统计年鉴. Beijing, 1992–.

Zhongguo dangdai zhengzhi yundongshi shujuku (ZDZYS) 中國當代政治運動史數據庫. Universities Service Centre for China Studies, Chinese University of Hong Kong.

Published Works

Abramson, Daniel. "Periurbanization and the Politics of Development-as-City-Building in China." *Cities*, no. 53 (2016): 156–62.

Alitto, Guy. *The Last Confucian: Liang Shu-ming and the Chinese Dilemma of Modernity*. Berkeley: University of California Press, 1979.

Allen, Joseph. *Taipei: City of Displacements*. Seattle: University of Washington Press, 2012.

An Qian. *Kuaisu chengshihua jincheng zhong chengshi "kongjian de shengchan" jizhi yu shizheng yanjiu – yi Henan sheng Zhengzhou shi wei li* 快速城市化进程中城市'空间的生产'机制与实证研究——以河南省郑州市为例 [A study of the mechanisms and evidence for the "production of space" in cities during the process of rapid urbanization: Taking Zhengzhou, Henan Province as a case study]. Chengdu: Xinan caijing daxue chubanshe, 2017.

An, Shaofan. "Suburban Revolution: Everyday Land Reform in Beijing Suburbs, 1949–1950." Ph.D. diss., University of Macau, 2020.

Anagnost, Ann. *National Past-Times: Narrative, Representation, and Power in Modern China*. Durham, NC: Duke University Press, 1997.

———. "Strange Circulations: The Blood Economy in Rural China." *Economy and Society* 35, no. 4 (2006): 509–29.

Anderson, Kym, ed. *Distortions to Agricultural Incentives: A Global Perspective, 1955–2007*. Washington, DC: Palgrave Macmillan and the World Bank, 2009.

Andreas, Joel. *Disenfranchised: The Rise and Fall of Industrial Citizenship in China*. New York: Oxford University Press, 2019.

Ash, Robert. "Squeezing the Peasants: Grain Extraction, Food Consumption and Rural Living Standards in Mao's China." *The China Quarterly*, no. 188 (2006): 959–98.

Baker, Mark. "Civil War on the Central Plains: Mobilization, Militarization and the End of Nationalist Rule in Zhengzhou, 1947–1948." *Twentieth-Century China* 45, no. 3 (2020): 266–84.

Ballantyne, Tony, and Antoinette Burton. "Empires and the Reach of the Global." In *A World Connecting: 1870–1945*, edited by Emily Rosenberg, 285–434. Cambridge, MA: Harvard University Press, 2012.

Banister, Judith, and Jeffrey Taylor. "China: Surplus Labor and Migration." *Asia-Pacific Population Journal* 4, no. 4 (1989): 3–20.

Barth, Gunther. *Instant Cities: Urbanization and the Rise of San Francisco and Denver*. New York: Oxford University Press, 1975.

Batty, Michael, and Paul Longley. *Fractal Cities: A Geometry of Form and Function*. London: Academic Press, 1994.

Beckert, Sven. *Empire of Cotton: A New History of Global Capitalism*. London: Penguin, 2014.

Bennō Saiichi. "Chūka minkoku zenki Chūgoku ni okeru nōsanbutsu seisan no kaiyō" 中華民国前期中国における農産物生産の概要 [An outline of crop production in China during the early Republican period]. *Kanazawa daigaku keizai ronshū* 金沢大学経済論集 33, no. 2 (2013): 75–101.

Bernstein, Thomas. *Up to the Mountains and Down to the Villages: The Transfer of Youth from Urban to Rural China.* New Haven, CT: Yale University Press, 1977.

Berry, Chris, Patricia Thornton, and Peidong Sun. "The Cultural Revolution: Memories and Legacies 50 Years On." *The China Quarterly*, no. 227 (2016): 604–12.

"Bian–Luo tielu chengbao benbu gezhan shangwu qingxing yilanbiao" 汴洛鐵路呈報本部各站商務情形一覽表 [A report submitted to the ministry: Schedule of the commercial situation at each station along the Kaifeng–Luoyang Railway]. *Jiaotong guanbao* 交通官報, nos. 22, 23, and 24 (1910): 32–39, 37–43, 34–40.

Bramall, Chris. *The Industrialization of Rural China.* Oxford: Oxford University Press, 2006.

Braudel, Fernand. *Civilization and Capitalism 15th–18th Century,* vol. 1: *The Structures of Everyday Life.* Translated by Sian Reynolds. London: Collins, 1981 [orig. 1979].

Bray, David. *Social Space and Governance in Urban China: The Danwei System from Origins to Reform.* Stanford, CA: Stanford University Press, 2005.

Brown Crook, Isabel, and Christina Gilmartin, with Xiji Yu; edited by Gail Hershatter and Emily Honig. *Prosperity's Predicament: Identity, Reform, and Resistance in Rural Wartime China.* Lanham, MD: Rowman and Littlefield, 2013.

Brown, Jeremy. *City Versus Countryside in Mao's China: Negotiating the Divide.* Cambridge: Cambridge University Press, 2012.

———. "Crossing the Rural-Urban Divide in Twentieth-Century China." Ph.D. diss., University of California, San Diego, 2008.

———. "Great Leap City: Surviving the Famine in Tianjin." In *Eating Bitterness: New Perspectives on China's Great Leap Forward and Famine,* edited by Kimberley Ens Manning and Felix Wemheuer, 226–50. Vancouver: University of British Columbia Press, 2011.

Buck, David. "Policies Favoring the Growth of Smaller Urban Places in the People's Republic of China, 1949–1979." In *Urban Development in Modern China,* edited by Laurence Ma and Edward Hanten, 114–46. Boulder, CO: Westview Press, 1981.

———. "Railway City and National Capital: Two Faces of the Modern in Changchun." In *Remaking the Chinese City: Modernity and National Identity,* edited by Joseph Esherick, 65–89. Honolulu: University of Hawai'i Press, 1999.

———. *Urban Change in China: Politics and Development in Tsinan, Shantung, 1890–1949.* Madison: University of Wisconsin Press, 1978.

Buck, John L. *Land Utilization in China*, vol. 2: *Atlas*. Nanjing: University of Nanjing, 1937.

———. *Land Utilization in China*, vol. 3: *Statistics*. Nanjing: University of Nanjing, 1937.

Cao Jinqing. *China along the Yellow River: Reflections on Rural Society*. Translated by Nicky Harman and Ruhua Huang. New York: RoutledgeCurzon, 2005 [orig. *Huanghe bian de Zhongguo—yige xuezhe dui xiangcun shehui de guancha yu sikao* 黄河边的中国——一个学者对乡村社会的观察与思考. Shanghai wenyi chubanshe, 2000].

Carroll, Peter. *Between Heaven and Modernity: Reconstructing Suzhou, 1895–1937*. Stanford, CA: Stanford University Press, 2006.

———. "Cities under Duress." *Journal of Urban History* 42, no. 2 (2016): 451–58.

Chan, Anita, Richard Madsen, and Jonathan Unger. *Chen Village: Revolution to Globalization*. Berkeley: University of California Press, 2009.

Chang Heping. "Zhengzhou shi chengxiang yitihua fazhan cunzai de wenti ji duice" 郑州市城乡一体化发展存在的问题及对策 [The development of rural-urban integration in Zhengzhou Municipality: Current problems and countermeasures]. *Zhonggong Zhengzhou shiwei dangxiao xuebao* 中共郑州市委党校学报, no. 114 (2011): 95–97.

Chen Chuanhai and Xu Youli, eds. *Henan xiandai shi* 河南现代史 [A history of contemporary Henan]. Kaifeng: Henan daxue chubanshe, 1992.

———. *Rijun huo Yu ziliao xuanbian* 日军祸豫资料选编 [Selected materials on the calamities brought to Henan by the Japanese Army]. Zhengzhou: Henan renmin chubanshe, 1986.

Chen Gengya. "Xibei shicha ji" 西北视察記 [Record of an investigation in the Northwest]. Reproduced in *Zhongguo xibei wenxian congshu* 中国西北文献丛书 [China Northwest documents series], vol. 4, part 132. Lanzhou: Lanzhou guji shudian, 1990 [orig. 1935].

Chen, Janet. *Guilty of Indigence: The Urban Poor in China, 1900–1953*. Princeton, NJ: Princeton University Press, 2012.

Chen Junren. "Zhengzhou mianhua shichang gaikuang" 鄭州棉花市場概況 [A survey of the Zhengzhou cotton market]. *Zhonghang yuekan* 中行月刊 2, no. 10 (1931): 13–17.

Chen Liusheng. "Dao Ningxia qu" 到寧夏去 [A journey to Ningxia]. *Haiwai yuekan* 海外月刊, no. 29 (1935): 30–44.

Chen Qiaoyan. "Zhengzhou yitiao jie" 郑州一条街 [A street in Zhengzhou]. *Liaowang* 瞭望, no. 4 (1982): 29–31.

Chen Shixing. "Kaifeng shi jianshe jihua" 開封市建設計畫 [A construction plan for Kaifeng city]. *Zhongguo jianshe* 中國建設 13, no. 5 (1936): 77–96.

Chen, Tao. "Weathering the Storms: East German Engineers in Zhengzhou, 1954–1964." *China Review* 19, no. 3 (2019): 39–64.

Cheng, Tiejun. "Dialectics of Control: The Household Registration (Hukou) System in Contemporary China." Ph.D. diss., SUNY Binghamton, 1991.

Cheng, Tiejun, and Mark Selden. "The Origins and Social Consequences of China's *Hukou* System." *The China Quarterly*, no. 139 (1994): 644–68.

Cheng Xiuhong. "Zhengzhou shi weilai renkou jiuye xinli zhuangkuang diaocha yu duice" 郑州市外来人口就业心理状况调查与对策 [The psychological state of Zhengzhou's outsider population regarding their work: Survey and countermeasures]. MA thesis, Zhengzhou daxue, 2007.

Cheng Ziliang and Li Qingyin, eds. *Kaifeng chengshi shi* 开封城市史 [A history of the city of Kaifeng]. Beijing: Shehui kexue wenxian chubanshe, 1993.

Cheong, Tsun Se, and Yanrui Wu. "Intraprovincial Inequality in China." In *Rebalancing and Sustaining Growth in China*, edited by Huw McKay and Ligang Song, 175–207. Canberra: ANU E Press, 2012.

China Labor Watch. "iPhone 11 Illegally Produced in China: Apple Allows Supplier Factory Foxconn to Violate Labor Laws." September 8, 2019, 1–51.

"China Property Watch—October 2022: Zhengzhou's Rescue Plan Helped to Revive Construction of Stalled Projects." Fitch Ratings report, October 31, 2022.

"China's Zhengzhou Banishes Ghosts but Struggles for Second Act." *Nikkei Asian Review*, September 26, 2017.

Christensen, Erleen. *In War and Famine: Missionaries in China's Honan Province in the 1940s*. Montreal: McGill-Queen's University Press, 2005.

Christiansen, Flemming. "Food Security, Urbanization and Social Stability in China." *Journal of Agrarian Change* 9, no. 4 (2009): 548–75.

Chuang, Julia. *Beneath the China Boom: Labor, Citizenship, and the Making of a Rural Land Market*. Oakland: University of California Press, 2020.

Cliver, Robert. *Red Silk: Class, Gender, and Revolution in China's Yangzi Delta Silk Industry*. Cambridge, MA: Harvard University Asia Center, 2020.

Cohen, Myron. "Cultural and Political Inventions in Modern China: The Case of the Chinese 'Peasant.'" *Daedalus* 122, no. 2 (Spring 1993): 151–70.

Cooper, Frederick. "Conflict and Connection: Rethinking Colonial African History." *American Historical Review* 99, no. 5 (1994): 1516–45.

Cronon, William. *Nature's Metropolis: Chicago and the Great West*. New York: W. W. Norton, 1991.

Crossman, Richard. "China Notebook." *Encounter*, no. 66 (1959): 11–22.

Cui Yanshou. "Liushi nian yuanlin suiyue" 六十年园林岁月 [Sixty years in gardens and parks]. *Zhengzhou wenshi ziliao* 郑州文史资料, no. 10 (1991): 27–135.

Dai Yifeng. "Chengshi shi yanjiu de liangzhong shiye: neixiangxing yu waixiangxing" 城市史研究的两种视野: 内向性与外向性 [Two perspectives on urban history research: inward-facing and outward-facing]. *Xueshu yuekan* 学术月刊, no. 10 (2009): 133–35.

Day, Alexander. *The Peasant in Postsocialist China: History, Politics, and Capitalism*. Cambridge: Cambridge University Press, 2013.

Deng Zihui. "Kaifeng shi gejie daibiaohui diwuci huiyi shang Zhongyuan renmin zhengfu Deng Zihui zhuxi de jianghua" 開封市各界代表會第五次會議上中原人民政府鄧子恢主席的講話 [Central Plains Government Chairman Deng Zihui's speech to the fifth meeting of the Kaifeng representative meeting for people from all aspects of society]. *Kaifeng jianshe* 開封建設 1, no. 3 (1949): 1–4.

Des Forges, Roger. *Cultural Centrality and Political Change in Chinese History: Northeast Henan in the Fall of the Ming*. Stanford, CA: Stanford University Press, 2003.

Di Fuyu. "Zhengzhou mianye zhi diaocha" 鄭州棉業之調查 [An investigation into Zhengzhou's cotton industry]. *Guoji maoyi daobao* 國際貿易導報 2, no. 12 (1932): 1–4.

Dillon, Nara. *Radical Inequalities: China's Revolutionary Welfare State in Comparative Perspective*. Cambridge, MA: Harvard University Asia Center, 2015.

Ding, Arthur, and Jagannath Panda, eds. *Chinese Politics and Foreign Policy under Xi Jinping: The Future Political Trajectory*. Abingdon, UK: Routledge, 2021.

Dodgen, Randall. *Controlling the Dragon: Confucian Engineers and the Yellow River in Late Imperial China*. Honolulu: University of Hawai'i Press, 2001.

———. "Salvaging Kaifeng: Natural Calamity and Urban Community in Late Imperial China." *Journal of Urban History* 21, no. 6 (1995): 716–40.

Domenach, Jean-Luc. *Origins of the Great Leap Forward: The Case of One Chinese Province*. Translated by A. M. Berrett. Boulder, CO: Westview Press, 1995 [orig. 1982].

Dong, Yige. "From Mill Town to iPhone City: Gender, Labor, and the Politics of Care in an Industrializing China (1949–2017)." Ph.D. diss., Johns Hopkins University, 2019.

Dong, Yiming, and Charlotte Goodburn. "Residence Permits and Points Systems: New Forms of Educational and Social Stratification in Urban China." *Journal of Contemporary China* 29, no. 125 (2020): 647–66.

Du Gangjian. "Cong Zhengzhou guanong jincheng nan kan guizhi zhengce de biduan" 从郑州瓜农进城难看规制政策的弊端 [Looking at the drawbacks in regulations and policy through the difficulties of Zhengzhou melon farmers entering the city]. *Juece shidian* 决策视点, no. 10 (2002): 39–40.

Du, Juan. *The Shenzhen Experiment: The Story of China's Instant City*. Cambridge, MA: Harvard University Press, 2020.

Dunham, S. Ann. *Surviving against the Odds: Village Industry in Indonesia*. Durham, NC: Duke University Press, 2009.

Eastman, Lloyd. *Seeds of Destruction: Nationalist China in War and Revolution, 1937–1949*. Stanford, CA: Stanford University Press, 1984.

Economy, Elizabeth. *The Third Revolution: Xi Jinping and the New Chinese State*. New York: Oxford University Press, 2018.

Edgerton-Tarpley, Kathryn. "Between War and Water: Farmer, City, and State in China's Yellow River Flood of 1938–1947." *Agricultural History* 90, no. 1 (2016): 94–116.

———. "A River Runs through It: The Yellow River and the Chinese Civil War, 1946–1947." *Social Science History* 41, no. 2 (2017): 141–73.

———. "Saving the Nation, Starving the People? The Henan Famine of 1942–43." In *1943: China at the Crossroads*, edited by Joseph Esherick and Matthew Combs, 323–65. Ithaca, NY: East Asia Program, Cornell University, 2015.

Eisenman, Joshua. *Red China's Green Revolution: Technological Innovation, Institutional Change, and Economic Development under the Commune*. New York: Columbia University Press, 2018.

Evans, Harriet. *Beijing from Below: Stories of Marginal Lives in the Capital's Center*. Durham, NC: Duke University Press, 2020.

Eyferth, Jacob. *Eating Rice from Bamboo Shoots: The Social History of a Community of Handicraft Papermakers in Rural Sichuan, 1920–2000*. Cambridge, MA: Harvard University Asia Center, 2009.

———. "Liberation from the Loom? Rural Women, Textile Work, and Revolution in North China." In *Maoism at the Grassroots: Everyday Life in China's Era of High Socialism*, edited by Jeremy Brown and Matthew Johnson, 131–53. Cambridge, MA: Harvard University Press, 2015.

Fan, C. Cindy, and Chen Chen. "The New-Generation Migrant Workers in China." In *Rural Migrants in Urban China: Enclaves and Transient Urbanism*, edited by Fulong Wu, Fangzhu Zhang, and Chris Webster, 17–35. Abingdon, UK: Routledge, 2014.

Fan Futang, Sun Jiansheng, Guo Tingbai, and Zhang Ying, eds. *Zhengzhou liudong renkou yanjiu* 郑州流动人口研究 [Research into Zhengzhou's floating population]. Beijing: Zhongguo tongji chubanshe, 1992.

Fan Shiqin. "Mantan Zhengzhou" 漫談鄭州 [Discussing Zhengzhou]. *Zhengyi* 正義 4, no. 4 (1948): 15.

Faure, David, and Tao Tao Liu, eds. *Town and Country in China: Identity and Perception*. New York: Palgrave, 2002.

Fei, Hsiao-t'ung. *China's Gentry: Essays in Rural-Urban Relations*. Chicago: University of Chicago Press, 1953 [revised and edited by Margaret Park Redfield].

Fei, Si-yen. "Ming Qing de chengshi kongjian yu chengshihua yanjiu" 明清的城市空間與城市化研究 [A study of urban space and urbanization in Ming-Qing cities]. In *Zhengguo shi xin lun: shenghuo yu wenhua fence* 中國史新論: 生活與文化分冊 [New perspectives on Chinese history: Life and culture], edited by Qiu Zhonglin, 317–41. Taipei: Zhongyang yanjiuyuan, 2013.

―――. *Negotiating Urban Space: Urbanization and Late Ming Nanjing.* Cambridge, MA: Harvard University Asia Center, 2009.

Feng Dexian. "Cong zhongwai chengshiqun fazhan kan zhongyuan jingji longqi—zhongyuan chengshiqun fazhan yanjiu" 从中外城市群发展看中原经济隆起—中原城市群发展研究 [The growth of the Central Plains economy from the view of city cluster development in China and beyond: A study of the Central Plains City Cluster]. *Renwen dili* 人文地理 19, no. 6 (2004): 75–78.

Feng Jingli. "Zhengzhou shi jianshe shehuizhuyi xin nongcun moshi yanjiu" 郑州市建设社会主义新农村模式研究 [A study into the pattern of building a new socialist countryside in Zhengzhou Municipality]. *Huanghe keji daxue xuebao* 黄河科技大学学报 9, no. 3 (2007): 39–42.

Feng Youlan. "Bian chengxiang" 辨城乡 [Distinguishing city and countryside]. Reproduced in *Xin shi lun* 新事論, 38–56. Shanghai: Shangwu yinshuguan, 1948, 3rd ed. [orig. 1939].

Feng Yunting and Zhang Yongfang. "Zhongyuan chengshiqun jingji zhongxin bianhua yu quyu jingji xietong fazhan" 中原城市群经济重心变化与区域经济协同发展 [Changes in the economic center of the Central Plains City Cluster and collaborative development in the regional economy]. *Dongbei caijing daxue xuebao* 东北财经大学学报, no. 119 (2018): 67–73.

"Feng Yuxiang liangci zhu Yu dashiji" 冯玉祥两次主豫大事记 [Record of major events during the two periods Feng Yuxiang controlled Henan]. *Kaifeng wenshi ziliao*, no. 14 (1994?): 94–101.

Feng Zhongli. "Cong fengshacheng dao lüman Zhengzhou de huigu" 从风沙城到绿满郑州的回顾 [Looking back: From a city of windblown sand to a Zhengzhou full of green]. *Zhengzhou wenshi ziliao* 郑州文史资料, no. 10 (1991): 1–26.

Finnane, Antonia. *Speaking of Yangzhou: A Chinese City, 1550–1850.* Cambridge, MA: Harvard University Asia Center, 2004.

Fitzgerald, John. "Provincializing the City: Canton and the Reshaping of Guangdong Provincial Administration, 1912–1937." In *New Narratives of Urban Space in Republican Chinese Cities: Emerging Social, Legal and Governance Orders*, edited by Billy K. L. So and Madeleine Zelin, 197–222. Leiden: Brill, 2013.

Forman, Harrison. "Harrison Forman Diary, China, December 1942–March 1943." Unpublished manuscript. Available at University of Wisconsin-Milwaukee Digital Collections. http://collections.lib.uwm.edu/cdm/ref/collection/forman/id/50.

Foucault, Michel. "Of Other Spaces: Utopias and Heterotopias." Translated by Jay Miskowiec. *Diacritics* 16, no. 1 (1986 [orig. 1967]): 22–27.

Fuller, Pierre. *Famine Relief in Warlord China.* Cambridge, MA: Harvard University Asia Center, 2019.

Funck, Marcus, and Roger Chickering. "Introduction: Endangered Cities." In *Endangered Cities: Military Power and Urban Societies in the Era of the World Wars*, edited by Marcus Funck and Roger Chickering, 1–11. Boston: Brill, 2004.

Gabbiani, Luca. "Connecting Urban Histories East and West." In *Urban Life in China, 15th–20th Centuries: Communities, Institutions, Representations*, edited by Luca Gabbiani, 11–25. Paris: École française d'Extrême-Orient, Études thématiques, 2016.

Gao Huifang. "'Chengxiang guanxi wenti' de sikao" '城乡关系问题' 的思考 [Reflections on the "urban-rural relations problem"]. *Shehui zongheng* 社科纵横 23, no. 3 (2008): 70–75.

Gao, James Zheng. *The Communist Takeover of Hangzhou: The Transformation of City and Cadre, 1949–1954*. Honolulu: University of Hawai'i Press, 2004.

———. *Meeting Technology's Advance: Social Change in China and Zimbabwe in the Railway Age*. Westport, CT: Greenwood Press, 1997.

Gao, Mobo, *Gao Village: A Portrait of Rural Life in Modern China*. Honolulu: University of Hawai'i Press, 1999.

Gao, Ruchen. "Tobacco, Western Education, and the Japanese Army: Globalization in a Northern County in China, 1900–1950." Ph.D. diss., University of Minnesota, 2022.

Garnaut, Anthony. "The Geography of the Great Leap Famine." *Modern China* 40, no. 3 (2014): 315–48.

———. "A Quantitative Description of the Henan Famine of 1942." *Modern Asian Studies* 47, no. 6 (2013): 2007–45.

Gerth, Karl. *Unending Capitalism: How Consumerism Negated China's Communist Revolution*. Cambridge: Cambridge University Press, 2020.

Gewirtz, Julian. *Never Turn Back: China and the Forbidden History of the 1980s*. Cambridge, MA: Harvard University Press, 2022.

Giersch, C. Patterson. *Corporate Conquests: Business, the State, and the Origins of Ethnic Inequality in Southwest China*. Stanford, CA: Stanford University Press, 2020.

Glasserman, Aaron. "Hui Nation: Islam and Muslim Politics in Modern China." Ph.D. diss., Columbia University, 2021.

Goldstein, Joshua. *Remains of the Everyday: A Century of Recycling in Beijing*. Oakland: University of California Press, 2020.

Goldstein, Sidney. "Urbanization in China, 1982–87: Effects of Migration and Reclassification." *Population and Development Review* 16, no. 4 (1990): 673–701.

Gong Yusong. "Zhongguo jindai chengxiang guanxi de jianlun" 中国近代城乡关系的简论" [A brief discussion of China's rural-urban relations in the modern period]. *Wenshizhe* 文史哲, no. 6 (1994): 31–36.

Greene, Felix. *Awakened China: The Country Americans Don't Know.* Garden City, NY: Doubleday, 1961.

Grove, Linda. *A Chinese Economic Revolution: Rural Entrepreneurship in the Twentieth Century.* Lanham, MD: Rowan and Littlefield. 2006.

Guan Wenbin [Man Bun Kwan]. "Qingmo minchu Tianjin yu Huabei de chengshihua: yige wangluo xitong de fenxi" 清末民初天津与华北的城市化: 一个网络系统的分析 [Late Qing, early republican Tianjin and the urbanization of North China: A network system perspective]. *Chengshi shi yanjiu* 城市史研究, no. 21 (2002): 49–66.

Guinness, G. Whitfield. "The Province of Honan." In *The Chinese Empire: A General and Missionary Survey*, edited by Marshall Broomhall, 149–63. London: Morgan and Scott, 1907.

Guo Ronghua. "Zhengzhou shi chengshi renmin gongshe tongji gongzuo jianli yu kaizhan qingkuang," 郑州市城市人民公社統計工作建立与开展情况 [The establishment and development of statistical work in the Zhengzhou city communes]. *Zhongguo tongji* 中国統計, no. 5 (1960): 20–21.

Guo Xinxin. "Zhengzhou jianshe guojia zhongxin chengshi de wenti he duice" 郑州建设国家中心城市的问题和对策 [Issues and countermeasures regarding construction of Zhengzhou as a National Central City]. *Jiangsu keji xinxi* 江苏科技信息, no. 17 (2017): 5–6.

Hao Pengzhan. "Jijin yu baoshou: minguo qijian Zhengzhou liangci chengshi guihua de bijiao" 激进与保守: 民国期间郑州两次城市规划的比较 [Radical and conservative: A comparison of two city plans for Zhengzhou during the Republican period]. *Zhongguo mingcheng* 中国名城, no. 11 (2012): 44–51.

———. "Lun jindai yilai Zhengzhou de chengshi guihua yu chengshi fazhan" 论近代以来郑州的城市规划与城市发展 [City planning and city development in modern Zhengzhou]. MA thesis, Shaanxi shifan daxue, 2006.

Harms, Erik. *Saigon's Edge: On the Margins of Ho Chi Minh City.* Minneapolis: University of Minnesota Press, 2011.

Harrison, Henrietta. *The Man Awakened from Dreams: One Man's Life in a North China Village, 1857–1942.* Stanford, CA: Stanford University Press, 2005.

Hayford, Charles W. *To the People: James Yen and Village China.* New York: Columbia University Press, 1990.

Hayward, Jane. "Beyond the Ownership Question: Who Will Till the Land? The New Debate on China's Agricultural Production." *Critical Asian Studies* 49, no. 4 (2017): 523–45.

He Hanwei. *Jing–Han tielu chuqi shilüe* 京漢鐵路初期史略 [Outline history of the early years of the Beijing–Hankou Railway]. Hong Kong: Zhongwen daxue chubanshe, 1979.

He Yimin. *Cong nongye shidai dao gongye shidai: Zhongguo chengshi fazhan yanjiu* 从农业时代到工业时代: 中国城市发展研究 [From the agricultural age to the industrial age: Studies in China's urban development]. Chengdu: Sichuan chuban jituan, 2009.

He Yimin and Zhou Mingchang. "The 156 Projects and New China's Industrial and Urban Development." In *Selected Essays on the History of Contemporary China*, edited by Zhang Xingxing, 54–70. Leiden: Brill, 2015.

He Yiping. "Zhongguo nongcun jingji de gaizao wenti" 中國農村經濟的改造問題 [Issues of reform in China's rural economy]. *Henan daxue nongxueyuan yuankan* 河南大學農學院院刊 (1936): 176–95.

He Zhongcha. "Zhongyuan chuge" 中原楚歌 [Songs of Hubei on the Central Plains]. *Shangjie wenshi ziliao* 上街文史資料, no. 2 (2011): 41–50.

Heberer, Thomas, and Sabine Jakobi. "Henan—The Model: From Hegemonism to Fragmentism: Portrait of the Political Culture of China's Most Populated Province." Duisberg Working Papers on East Asian Studies, no. 32, 2000.

Heilmann, Sebastian. "The Suppression of the April Fifth Movement and the Persecution of 'Counter-Revolutionaries' in 1976." *Issues and Studies* 30, no. 1 (1994): 37–64.

"Henan ge xian wuchan zhuangkuang diaocha: Zheng xian" 河南各縣物產狀況調查:鄭縣 [A survey of the state of produce in each county in Henan: Zheng County]. *Gong shang banyuekan* 工商半月刊 6, no. 4 (1934): 83–85.

Henan sheng difang shizhi bianzuan weiyuanhui, ed. *Henan sheng zhi* 河南省志 [Henan Province gazetteer]. 65 vols. Zhengzhou: Henan renmin chubanshe, 1991–1997.

Henan sheng jiansheting, ed. *Henan jianshe gaikuang* 河南建設概況 [Survey of construction in Henan]. Kaifeng: Henan sheng zhengfu jiansheting, 1934.

Henan sheng jiansheting chengjianzhi bianjishi, ed. *Henan sheng chengjian shizhi gao xuanbian* 河南省城建史志稿选编 [Draft selections for the historical gazetteer of city construction in Henan]. 2 vols. Zhengzhou: internal circulation (*neibu ziliao*), printed by Zhonghua yinshua chang, 1987.

Henan sheng mianchan gaijinsuo, ed. *Henan mianye* 河南棉業 [Henan's cotton industry]. Kaifeng: Henan sheng mianchan gaijinsuo, 1936.

———. *Henan sheng mianchan gaijinsuo gailan* 河南省緬產改進所概覽 [An overview of the Henan Province Cotton Improvement Bureau]. Kaifeng: Henan sheng mianchan gaijinsuo, 1937.

Henan sheng tongjiju, ed. *Henan sheng, shidi, xian shehui jingji gaikuang: 1980–1990* 河南省、市地、县社会经济概况, 1980–1990 [A survey of society and economy in the cities, prefectures and counties of Henan Province, 1980–1990]. Beijing: Zhongguo tongji chubanshe, 1991.

Henan sheng tongji xuehui, ed. *Minguo shiqi Henan sheng tongji ziliao* 民国时期河南省统计资料 [Statistical materials on Henan Province in the Republican period]. 2 vols. Zhengzhou: Henan sheng tongji xuehui, 1986.

Henan sheng zhengfu tongjichu, ed., *Henan sheng tongji nianjian: minguo sanshiwu nian* 河南省統計年鑑: 民國三十五年 [Henan Province statistical yearbook: 1946]. Kaifeng: Henan zhengfu tongjichu, 1947.

"Henan Zhengzhou zhi Yufeng shachang" 河南鄭州之豫豐紗廠 [Henan Zhengzhou's Yufeng cotton mill]. *Shiye zazhi* 實業雜誌, no. 33 (1920): 88–89.

Hirata, Koji. "Mao's Steeltown: Industrial City, Colonial Legacies, and Local Political Economy in Early Communist China." *Journal of Urban History* 49, no. 1 (2021): 85–110.

Ho, Virgil. *Understanding Canton: Rethinking Popular Culture in the Republican Period*. Oxford: Oxford University Press, 2005.

Holston, James. *The Modernist City: An Anthropological Critique of Brasilia*. Chicago: University of Chicago Press, 1989.

Honig, Emily, and Xiaojian Zhao. *Across the Great Divide: The Sent-Down Youth Movement in Mao's China, 1968–1980*. Cambridge: Cambridge University Press, 2019.

Hou, Li. *Building for Oil: Daqing and the Formation of the Chinese Socialist State*. Cambridge, MA: Harvard University Asia Center, 2018.

Hou Yangfang. *Zhongguo renkou shi, di 6 juan, 1910–1953 nian* 中国人口史, 第6卷, 1910–1953年 [Population history of China, vol. 6, 1910–1953]. Shanghai: Fudan daxue chubanshe, 2001.

Hsing, You-tien. *The Great Urban Transformation: Politics of Land and Property in China*. Oxford: Oxford University Press, 2010.

Hsü, Immanuel. "The Great Policy Debate in China, 1874: Maritime Defense vs. Frontier Defense." *Harvard Journal of Asiatic Studies*, no. 25 (1964–1965): 212–28.

Hu Puqing. "Kaifeng shi mofanqu jihua dayi" 開封市模範區計劃大意 [Outline plan for Kaifeng Model District]. *Henan zhengzhi* 河南政治 4, no. 12 (1934): 1–7.

"'Huangjia yihao' an quanbu xuanpan wanbi" '皇家一号'案全部宣判完毕 [Sentencing complete in the "Huangjia yihao" case]. *Jinghua shibao* 京华时报, May 30, 2015.

Huang Jinping. "Zhengzhou Xigangcun: bu zhong zhuangjia zhong fangzi" 郑州西岗村:不种庄稼种房子 [Zhengzhou Xigang Village: Not planting crops but planting houses]. *Nanfang zhoumo* 南方周末, April 16, 2010.

Huang Mingyuan. "Zhengzhou de dangpu 'gonghedian'" 郑州的当铺'恭和典' [The Zhengzhou pawnshop: "Gonghedian"]. Reproduced in *Zhengzhou wenshi ziliao* 郑州文史资料, no. 3 (1987 [orig. 1965]): 184–94.

Huang Zhenglin. "Zhidu chuangxin, jishu gaige yu nongye fazhan—yi 1927–1937 nian Henan wei zhongxin de yanjiu" 制度创新, 技术改革与农业发展——以 1927–1937 年河南为中心的研究 [Institutional innovation, technological reform and agricultural development: A study focused on Henan, 1927–1937]. *Shixue yuekan* 史学月刊, no. 5 (2010): 28–44.

Huang Zhenglin, Zhang Yan, and Su Zhigang. *Jindai Henan jingjishi (xia)* 近代河南经济史 (下) [The economic history of modern Henan (vol. 2)]. Zhengzhou: Henan daxue chubanshe, 2012.

Hudson, James J. "River Sands/Urban Spaces: Changsha in Modern Chinese History." Ph.D. diss., University of Texas at Austin, 2015.
Huenemann, Ralph. *The Dragon and the Iron Horse: The Economics of Railroads in China, 1876–1937.* Cambridge, MA: Council on East Asian Studies, 1984.
Hurst, William. *The Chinese Worker after Socialism.* Cambridge: Cambridge University Press, 2009.

Isherwood, Christopher, and W. H. Auden. *Journey to a War.* London: Faber and Faber, 1973 [revised edition, orig. 1939].
Ishihara Hiroshi. "Kanan-shō Teishū-shi ni okeru sosai oroshiuri shijō no hatten" 河南省鄭州市における蔬菜卸売市場の発展 [The development of vegetable wholesale markets in Zhengzhou City, Henan Province]. *Nara daigaku chiri* 奈良大学地理 16, no. 3 (2010): 32–41.

Jacka, Tamara. *Rural Women in Urban China: Gender, Migration, and Social Change.* Armonk, NY: M. E. Sharpe, 2006.
Jacobs, Harrison. "Inside 'iPhone City,' the Massive Chinese Factory Town Where Half the World's iPhones Are Produced." *Business Insider*, May 7, 2018.
Janku, Andrea. "From Natural to National Disaster: The Chinese Famine of 1928–1930." In *Historical Disasters in Context: Science, Religion and Politics*, edited by Andrea Janku, Gerrit Schenk, and Franz Mauelshagen, 227–60. New York: Routledge, 2012.
Jaros, Kyle. *China's Urban Champions: The Politics of Spatial Development.* Princeton, NJ: Princeton University Press, 2019.
Ji Fu. "Rijun Zhengzhou shucai zhushihuishe" 日军郑州蔬菜株式会社 [The Vegetable Corporation of the Japanese Army in Zhengzhou]. *Erqiqu wenshi ziliao* 二七区文史资料, no. 1 (2004): 82.
———. "Zhengzhou de zaoqi jichang" 郑州的早期机场 [Zhengzhou's early airfields]. *Erqiqu wenshi ziliao* 二七区文史资料, no. 1 (2004): 189–90.
Jia Zhiqiang. "Zhengzhou shi dushi cunzhuang 'liudong renkou' shequ rentonggan yanjiu" 郑州市都市村庄'流动人口'社区认同感研究 [A study of feeling of community identity among the "floating population" of Zhengzhou's urban villages]. MA thesis, Zhengzhou daxue, 2005.
Jiang Pei. "Kahoku ni okeru kindai kōtsū shisutemu no shohoteki keisei to toshika no shinten, 1881–1937" 華北における近代交通システムの初歩的形成と都市化の進展 1881–1937 [The initial formation of a modern transport system in North China and the development of urbanization, 1881–1937]. *Gendai Chūgoku kenkyū* 現代中国研究, no. 18 (2006): 2–19.
Jiang Xueqin. "Stealing the Land." *Far Eastern Economic Review*, February 7, 2002.

"Jianzhi yange he dili gaimao" 建置沿革和地理概貌 [Evolution of construction and survey of geography]. *Shangjie wenshi ziliao* 上街文史资料, no. 1 (2009): 1–3.

Jin Lingxia. "Zai Jing Jin Ji zhijian youdang de Hebei shenghui" 在京津冀之间游荡的河北省会 [Wandering between Beijing, Tianjin, and Hebei: The capital of Hebei]. *Hebei huabao* 河北画报, no. 4 (2015): 37–41.

"Kaifeng Zhengzhou liangshi caiche" 開封鄭州兩市裁撤 [Kaifeng and Zhengzhou: Two cities dissolved]. *Henan caizheng huikan*, no. 1 (1931): 511–13.

Kanbur, Ravi, and Anthony Venables. "Spatial Inequality and Development." In *Spatial Inequality and Development*, edited by Ravi Kanbur and Anthony Venables, 3–11. Oxford: Oxford University Press, 2005.

Kanbur, Ravi, Yue Wang, and Xiaobo Zhang. "The Great Chinese Inequality Turnaround." *Journal of Comparative Economics* 49, no. 2 (2021): 467–82.

Kearney, Michael. *Reconceptualizing the Peasantry: Anthropology in Global Perspective*. Boulder, CO: Westview Press, 1996.

Kelliher, Daniel. *Peasant Power in China: The Era of Rural Reform, 1979–1989*. New Haven, CT: Yale University Press, 1992.

Kent, Percy H. *Railway Enterprise in China: An Account of Its Origins and Development*. London: Edward Arnold, 1907.

Kimura Masutaro et al., eds. *Kiwai chitai no nōsakubutsu chōsa* 黄淮地帯の農作物調査 [A survey of agricultural crops in the Huang-Huai region]. Tokyo: East Asia Research Institute, 1940.

Kinzley, Judd. *Natural Resources and the New Frontier: Constructing Modern China's Borderlands*. Chicago: University of Chicago Press, 2018.

Kipnis, Andrew. *From Village to City: Social Transformation in a Chinese County Seat*. Oakland: University of California Press, 2016.

Knight, John, and Lina Song. *The Rural-Urban Divide: Economic Disparities and Interactions in China*. Oxford: Oxford University Press, 1999.

Köll, Elisabeth. *Railroads and the Transformation of China*. Cambridge, MA: Harvard University Press, 2019.

Kostof, Spiro. *The City Shaped: Urban Patterns and Meanings through History*. London: Thames and Hudson, 1991.

Kraus, Richard. *Cotton and Cotton Goods in China: The Impact of Modernization on the Traditional Sector*. New York: Garland, 1980.

Kwok, R. Yin-Wang. "Trends of Urban Planning and Development in China." In *Urban Development in Modern China*, edited by Laurence Ma and Edward Hanten, 147–93. Boulder, CO: Westview Press, 1981.

Laakkonen, Simo, J. R. McNeill, Richard Tucker, and Timo Vuorisalo. "Epilogue: What Makes a City Resilient?" In *The Resilient City in World War II: Urban Environmental Histories*, edited by Simo Laakkonen et al., 281–302. Cham, Switzerland: Palgrave Macmillan, 2019.

Labbé, Danielle. *Land Politics and Livelihoods on the Margins of Hanoi, 1920–2010*. Vancouver: University of British Columbia Press, 2014.

Lam, Tong. *A Passion for Facts: Social Surveys and the Construction of the Chinese Nation-State*. Berkeley: University of California Press, 2011.

Lamouroux, Christian. "From the Yellow River to the Huai: New Representations of a River Network and the Hydraulic Crisis of 1128." In *Sediments of Time: Environment and Society in Chinese History*, edited by Mark Elvin and Liu Ts'ui-jung, 545–84. Cambridge: Cambridge University Press, 1998.

Lander, Brian. *The King's Harvest: A Political Ecology of China from the First Farmers to the First Empire*. New Haven, CT: Yale University Press, 2021.

Lanza, Fabio. "A City of Workers, a City for Workers? Remaking Beijing Urban Space in the Early PRC." In *China: A Historical Geography of the Urban*, edited by Yannan Ding, Maurizio Marinelli, and Zhang Xiaohong, 41–65. Cham, Switzerland: Springer, 2018.

———. "The Search for a Socialist Everyday: The Urban Communes." In *Routledge Handbook of Revolutionary China*, edited by Alan Baumler, 74–88. London: Routledge, 2019.

Lary, Diana. *The Chinese People at War: Human Suffering and Social Transformation, 1937–1945*. Cambridge: Cambridge University Press, 2010.

———. "Drowned Earth: The Strategic Breaching of the Yellow River Dyke, 1938." *War in History* 8, no. 2 (2001): 191–207.

Lefebvre, Henri. *The Production of Space*. Translated by Donald Nicholson-Smith. Oxford: Blackwell, 1991 [orig. 1974].

Lei Yushe. "Zhengzhou jingshifang tudi jian bieshu diaocha: cunmin weiquan 2 nian weiguo" 郑州经适房土地建别墅调查: 村民维权2年未果 [An investigation into the building of villas on land designated for affordable housing in Zhengzhou: Villagers spend two years defending their rights without success]. *Zhongguo qingnianbao* 中国青年报, July 6, 2009.

"Lengyan wang Bian Zheng" 冷眼望汴郑 [A detached look at Kaifeng and Zhengzhou]. *Shibao* 時報 (Xi'an), July 27, 1948.

Li, Danke. *Echoes of Chongqing: Women in Wartime China*. Champaign: University of Illinois Press, 2010.

Li Duanxiang. *Chengshi renmin gongshe yundong yanjiu* 城市人民公社运动研究 [The urban people's communes movement]. Changsha: Hunan renmin chubanshe, 2006.

Li, Guannan. "Reviving China: Urban Reconstruction in Nanchang and the Guomindang National Revival Movement." *Frontiers of History in China* 7, no. 1 (2012): 106–35.

Li Hao (浩). *Ba da zhongdian chengshi guihua: xin Zhongguo chengli chuqi de chengshi guihua lishi yanjiu* 八大重点城市规划: 新中国成立初期的城市规划历史研究 [Planning in the eight key cities: A historical study of urban planning in the early period of New China]. Beijing: Zhongguo jianzhu gongye chubanshe, 2016.

——— "'Yi wu' shiqi de chengshi guihua shi zhaoban 'Sulian moshi' ma?" '一五' 时期的城市规划是照搬 '苏联模式' 吗? [Did urban planning in the First Five-Year Plan period imitate the "Soviet Model"?] *Chengshi fazhan yanjiu* 城市发展研究 22, no. 9 (2015): C1–C5.

Li Hao (昊). *Henan ren de shengcun zhi dao* 河南人的生存之道 [The road to survival of Henanese people]. Beijing: Zhongguo dianying chubanshe, 2006.

Li Hua. "Jintian de Zhengzhou yu Kaifeng" 今天的鄭州與開封 [Zhengzhou and Kaifeng today]. *Kangzhan wenyi* 抗戰文藝 1, no. 8 (1938): 87–88.

Li, Huaiyin. *The Making of the Modern Chinese State, 1600–1950*. London: Routledge, 2020.

Li Huishan. "Zhengzhou shi jiaoqu jianshe guocheng zhong nandian wenti yanjiu—yi chaiqian wei li" 郑州市郊区建设过程中难点问题研究———以拆迁为例 [A study into difficult problems in the process of construction in Zhengzhou's suburbs: Taking demolition and relocation as case study]. MA thesis, Henan nongye daxue, 2013.

Li, Lillian. *Fighting Famine in North China: State, Market, and Environmental Decline, 1690s–1990s*. Stanford, CA: Stanford University Press, 2007.

Li Rongjia. "Feng Yuxiang di'erci zhu Yu shi zai Zhengzhou de xinzheng he jianshe" 冯玉祥第二次主豫时在郑州的新政和建设 [New policies and construction in Zhengzhou during Feng Yuxiang's second period governing Henan]. *Zhengzhou wenshi ziliao* 郑州文史资料, no. 4 (1988): 6–71.

Li Runtian. *Henan sheng jingji dili* 河南省经济地理 [Economic geography of Henan Province]. Beijing: Xinhua chubanshe, 1987.

Liang Hong. *China in One Village: The Story of One Town and the Changing World*. Translated by Emily Goedde. London: Verso, 2021 [orig. *Zhongguo zai Liangzhuang* 中国在梁庄. Nanjing: Jiangsu renmin chubanshe, 2010].

Liang Liuke. *Kaifeng shi kechixu fazan yanjiu* 开封市可持续发展研究 [A study of sustainable development in Kaifeng City]. Beijing: Zhongguo shehui kexue chubanshe, 2007.

Liang Minling. "Jindai chengxiang guanxi de dazhi zouxiang—yi shiren suo lun suo xing wei zhongxin de shuli" 近代城乡关系的大致走向———以时人所论所行为中心的梳理 [The general direction of modern rural-urban relations—based on the thought and behavior of contemporaries]. *Sun Zhongshan daxue yanjiusheng xuekan* 中山大学研究生学刊 29, no. 2 (2008): 28–40.

Liang, Samuel Y. *Remaking China's Great Cities: Space and Culture in Urban Housing, Renewal and Expansion*. Abingdon, UK: Routledge, 2014.

Liang Xin. "Xiandai Zhongguo de 'dushi yanguang': 20 shiji zaoqi chengxiang guanxi de renzhi yu xiangxiang" 現代中國的 '都市眼光':20世紀早期城鄉關係的認知與想象 [Visions of the city in modern China: Early twentieth-century rural-urban relations in thought and imagination]. *Zhonghua wenshi luncong* 中華文史論叢, no. 114 (2014): 331–74.

Liao, Felix Haifeng, and Dennis Yehua Wei. "Regional Inequality in China: Trends, Scales and Mechanisms." RIMISP Working Paper Series, no. 202, Territorial Cohesion for Development Working Group, September 2016.

Liao Yongmin. "Feng Yuxiang yingjian Bishagang lingyuan" 冯玉祥营建碧沙岗陵园 [The Bishagang mausoleum park built by Feng Yuxiang]. *Zhengzhou wenshi ziliao* 郑州文史资料, no. 4 (1988): 1–8.

Lieberthal, Kenneth. *Revolution and Tradition in Tientsin, 1949–52.* Stanford, CA: Stanford University Press, 1980.

Lin Chuanjia. *Da Zhonghua Henan sheng dili zhi* 大中華河南省地理志 [Geographical gazetteer of China: Henan Province]. Shanghai: Shangwu yinshuguan, 1920.

Lincoln, Toby. "The Rural and Urban at War: Invasion and Reconstruction in China during the Anti-Japanese War of Resistance." *Journal of Urban History* 47, no. 3 (2012): 549–67.

———. *Urbanizing China in War and Peace: The Case of Wuxi County.* Honolulu: University of Hawai'i Press, 2015.

Ling, Minhua. *The Inconvenient Generation: Migrant Youth on Shanghai's Edge.* Stanford, CA: Stanford University Press, 2019.

Lipkin, Zwia. *Useless to the State: "Social Problems" and Social Engineering in Nationalist Nanjing, 1927–1937.* Cambridge, MA: Harvard University Asia Center, 2006.

Lipton, Michael. *Why Poor People Stay Poor: Urban Bias in World Development.* London: Temple Smith, 1977.

Liu Fenghan, ed. *Minguo jingji: qinlizhe koushu shilu* 民国经济:亲历者口述实录 [The Republican economy: Collected oral records of personal experience]. Beijing: Zhongguo dabaike quanshu chubanshe, 2010.

Liu Futan and Zhou Haichun. *Zhongyuan chengshiqun zhanlüe yu guihua* 中原城市群战略与规划 [Strategies and plans for the Central Plains City Cluster]. Beijing: Jingji kexue chubanshe, 2011.

Liu Guokai. *Renmin wenge lun* 人民文革論 [An essay on the People's Cultural Revolution]. Hong Kong: Boda chubanshe, 2006.

Liu Haiyan. "The Formation of the Marginal Area of Modern Tianjin." *Frontiers of History in China* 3, no. 3 (2008): 432–43.

———. "Jindai Huabei jiaotong de yanbian yu quyu chengshi chonggou (1860–1937)" 近代华北交通的演变与区域城市重构 (1860–1937) [The transformation of transportation and regional urban restructuring in modern North China (1860–1937)]. *Chengshi shi yanjiu* 城市史研究, no. 21 (special issue, 2002): 24–48.

Liu Hui. "Tielu yu jindai Zhengzhou chengshi de xingqi, 1905–1937" 铁路与近代郑州城市的兴起, 1905–1937 [The railway and the rise of modern Zhengzhou, 1905–1937]. *Osaka University Discussion Papers in Contemporary Chinese Studies*, no. 1 (2009): 1–11.

———. *Tielu yu Zhengzhou chengshihua jincheng yanjiu, 1905–1954* 铁路与郑州城市化进程研究, 1905–1954 [A study of the railroads and the process of Zhengzhou's urbanization, 1905–1954]. Beijing: Shangwu yinshuguan, 2018.

Liu Jingxiang. *Henan xinzhi* 河南新志 [New gazetteer of Henan]. Zhengzhou: Zhongzhou guji chubanshe, 1988 reprint [orig. 1929].

Liu, Li, and Xingcan Chen. *The Archaeology of China: From the Late Paleolithic to the Early Bronze Age.* Cambridge: Cambridge University Press, 2012.

Liu Ruilin. *Zheng xian zhi* 鄭縣志 [Gazetteer of Zheng County]. Zhengzhou, block-printed, 1916.

Liu Weide, Feng Yunhuai, and Chen Jie. "Zhengzhou shi beijiao tudi liyong bianhua de diaocha yu fenxi" 郑州市北郊土地利用变化的调查与分析 [Survey and analysis of land use changes in Zhengzhou's northern suburbs]. *Diyu yanjiu yu kaifa* 地域研究与开发 8, no. 5 (1989): 17–18.

Liu Yigao. "Chengshi jiaoqu tudi gaige zhong de jiexian huafen yu shehui geli—Beijing shi Haidianqu Bagoucun ji qi zhoubian cunzhuang yanjiu" 城市郊区土地改革中的界线划分与社会隔离——北京市海淀区巴沟村及其周边村庄研究 [Lines of division and social segregation in suburban land reform: A study of Bagou Village and surrounding villages in Haidian District, Beijing]. *Jindaishi yanjiu* 近代史研究, no. 3 (2013): 74–94.

Liu Yongli. "Minguo shiqi Zhengzhou chengshi renkou bianqian yanjiu" 民国时期郑州城市人口变迁研究 [Urban population changes in Zhengzhou during the Republican period]. MA thesis, Zhengzhou daxue, 2010.

Logan, Steven. *In the Suburbs of History: Modernist Visions of the Urban Periphery.* Toronto: University of Toronto Press, 2020.

Long–Hai tielu chewuchu shangwuke. "Long–Hai quanxian diaocha" 隴海全線調查 [A complete survey of the Long–Hai line]. 1933. Reproduced in *Minguo tielu yanxian jingji diaocha baogao* 民国铁路沿线经济调查报告, edited by Yin Mengjia and Li Qiang, vol. 7, 1–403. Beijing: Guojia tushuguan chubanshe, 2009.

Looney, Kristen. *Mobilizing for Development: The Modernization of Rural East Asia.* Ithaca, NY: Cornell University Press, 2020.

Lu, Duanfang. *Remaking Chinese Urban Form: Modernity, Scarcity and Space, 1949–2005.* Abingdon, UK: Routledge, 2006.

Lu, Hanchao. "Small-Town China: A Historical Perspective on Rural-Urban Relations." In *One Country, Two Societies: Rural-Urban Inequality in Contemporary China*, edited by Martin Whyte, 29–54. Cambridge, MA: Harvard University Press, 2010.

Lu Yinquan. "Anjing de Zhengzhou" 安靜的鄭州 [Peaceful Zhengzhou]. *Minzu shengming* 民族生命, no. 5 (1938): 8–10.

Lu Yunsheng. "Cheli Zhengzhou" 撤離鄭州 [Pulling out of Zhengzhou], *Xingzong kongyun dadui banyuekan* 行總空運大隊半月刊 1, no. 8 (1948): 6.

Luo Huiwu. "Wo de zhiqing shenghuo" 我的知青生活 [My life as an educated youth]. *Zhengzhou wenshi ziliao* 郑州文史资料, no. 28, part 1 (2007): 289–300.

Luo Jiurong. "Lishi qingjing yu kangzhan shiqi 'hanjian' de xingcheng: yi 1941 nian Zhengzhou weichihui wei zhuyao anli de tantao" 歷史情境與抗戰時期'漢奸'的形成——以 1941 年鄭州維持會為主要案例的探討 [Historical circumstances and the making of "traitors" during the war of resistance: An inquiry focused on Zhengzhou's 1941 Peace Preservation Committee]. *Jindaishi yanjiusuo jikan* 近代史研究所集刊, no. 24, part 2 (1995): 815–41.

Ma Junya. *Bei xisheng de "jubu": Huaibei shehui shengtai bianqian yanjiu* 被牺牲的"局部"——淮北社会生态变迁研究 [A "locality" that was sacrificed: Social and ecological change in the Huaibei region]. Beijing: Beijing daxue chubanshe, 2011.

Ma Yiping. "Jindai tielu yu Zhongyuan diqu nongye jingji fazhan tanjiu" 近代铁路与中原地区农业经济发展探究 [An investigation into modern railroads and the development of agriculture in the Central Plains region]. *Zhengzhou daxue xuebao* 郑州大学学报 43, no. 2 (2010): 132–38.

Ma, Zhao. "Individual Agency and Social Networking in Modern Chinese Cities." *Journal of Urban History* 36, no. 5 (2010): 729–41.

———. *Runaway Wives, Urban Crimes, and Survival Tactics in Wartime Beijing, 1937–1949.* Cambridge, MA: Harvard University Asia Center, 2015.

Ma Zimin. "Zhengzhou yiri youji" 鄭州一日遊記 [A travel account of a day in Zhengzhou]. *Shiye jikan* 實業季刊 2, no. 1 (1935): 10–12.

MacKinnon, Stephen. *Wuhan, 1938: War, Refugees, and the Making of Modern China.* Berkeley: University of California Press, 2008.

Mann, Susan. "Urbanization and Historical Change in China." *Modern China* 10, no. 1 (1984): 79–113.

Manning, Kimberley Ens, and Felix Wemheuer, eds. *Eating Bitterness: New Perspectives on China's Great Leap Forward and Famine.* Vancouver: University of British Columbia Press, 2011.

Massey, Doreen. "Politics and Space/Time." *New Left Review*, no. 196 (1992): 65–84.

Meek, James. "Somerdale to Skarbimierz." *London Review of Books* 39, no. 8 (2017): 3–15.

Meng, Xin, Nancy Qian, and Pierre Yared. "The Institutional Causes of China's Great Famine, 1959–1961." *Review of Economic Studies*, no. 82 (2015): 1568–1611.

Meng Yue, *Shanghai and the Edges of Empire.* Minneapolis: University of Minnesota Press, 2005.

Meng Ziming. "Feng Yuxiang zai wo cun de gushi" 冯玉祥在我村的故事 [Tales of Feng Yuxiang in my village]. *Zhengzhou wenshi ziliao* 郑州文史资料, no. 4 (1988): 171–72.

Merkel-Hess, Kate. "A New People: Rural Modernity in Republican China." Ph.D. diss., University of California, Irvine, 2009.

———. *The Rural Modern: Reconstructing the Self and State in Republican China.* Chicago: University of Chicago Press, 2016.

Merriman, John. *The Margins of City Life: Explorations on the French Urban Frontier, 1815–1851.* Oxford: Oxford University Press, 1991.

Mitter, Rana. *Forgotten Ally: China's World War II, 1937–1945.* Boston: Houghton Mifflin Harcourt, 2013.

Mostern, Ruth. *"Dividing the Realm in Order to Govern": The Spatial Organization of the Song State (960–1276 CE).* Cambridge, MA: Harvard University Asia Center, 2011.

Mote, Frederick. "The Transformation of Nanking, 1350–1400." In *The City in Late Imperial China,* edited by G. William Skinner, 101–53. Stanford, CA: Stanford University Press, 1977.

Mukherjee, Janam. *Hungry Bengal: War, Famine and the End of Empire.* London: Hurst, 2015.

Muscolino, Micah. *The Ecology of War in China: Henan Province, the Yellow River, and Beyond, 1938–1950.* Cambridge: Cambridge University Press, 2014.

Musgrove, Charles. *China's Contested Capital: Architecture, Ritual, and Response in Nanjing.* Honolulu: University of Hawai'i Press, 2013.

Nolan, Peter. *Growth Processes and Distributional Change in a South Chinese Province: The Case of Guangdong.* London: Contemporary China Institute, School of Oriental and African Studies, 1983.

Nolan, Peter, and Gordon White. "Urban Bias, Rural Bias or State Bias? Urban-Rural Relations in Post-Revolutionary China." *Journal of Development Studies* 20, no. 3 (1984): 52–81.

O'Donnell, Mary Ann, Winnie Wong, and Jonathan Bach, eds. *Learning from Shenzhen: China's Post-Mao Experiment from Special Zone to Model City.* Chicago: University of Chicago Press, 2017.

Oi, Jean. *State and Peasant in Contemporary China: The Political Economy of Village Government.* Berkeley: University of California Press, 1989.

Ong, Lynette H. "State-Led Urbanization in China: Skyscrapers, Land Revenue, and 'Concentrated Villages.'" *The China Quarterly* 217 (2014): 162–79.

Paltemaa, Lauri. *Managing Famine, Flood and Earthquake in Tianjin, 1958–1985.* Abingdon, UK: Routledge, 2016.

———. "Serve the City! Urban Disaster Governance in Tianjin City, 1958–1962." *Modern Asian Studies* 49, no. 4 (2015): 1143–76.

Pietz, David. *The Yellow River: The Problem of Water in Modern China.* Cambridge, MA: Harvard University Press, 2015.

Poling, Kristin. *Germany's Urban Frontiers: Nature and History on the Edge of the Nineteenth-Century City.* Pittsburgh: University of Pittsburgh Press, 2020.

Pomeranz, Kenneth. *Making of a Hinterland: State, Society, and Economy in Inland North China.* Berkeley: University of California Press, 1993.

Qi Chunfeng. *Zhong-Ri jingjizhan zhong de zousi huodong* 中日经济战中的走私活动 [Smuggling activity in the Sino-Japanese economic war]. Beijing: Renmin chubanshe, 2002.

"Quanguo ge xian xiangcun wujia zhishubiao: Henan sheng" 全國各縣鄉村物價指數表:河南省 [Tables for rural commodity price indexes for each county in China: Henan Province]. *Nongqing baogao* 農情報告 4, no. 10 (1936): 265–78.

Ramondetti, Leonardo. *The Enriched Field: Urbanizing the Central Plains of China.* Basel: Birkhäuser, 2022.

Ravallion, Martin, and Shaohua Chen. "Is That Really a Kuznets Curve? Turning Points for Income Inequality in China." *Journal of Economic Inequality* 20, no. 4 (2022): 749–76.

"Red Flag Commune Sets the Pace." *China Pictorial*, no. 1 (1961): 18–21.

Ren, Xuefei. *Governing the Urban in China and India: Land Grabs, Slum Clearance, and the War on Air Pollution.* Princeton, NJ: Princeton University Press, 2020.

———. "Lost in Translation: Names, Meanings, and Development Strategies of Beijing's Periphery." In *What's in a Name? Talking about Urban Peripheries*, edited by Richard Harris and Charlotte Vorms, 316–33. Toronto: University of Toronto Press, 2017.

Reynolds, Douglas. *China, 1898–1912: The Xinzheng Revolution and Japan.* Cambridge, MA: Harvard University Asia Center, 1993.

"Riqu fanrong zhi Zheng xian" 日趨繁榮之鄭縣 [Daily more prosperous Zheng County]. *Henan zhengzhi* 河南政治 2, no. 5 (1932): 7–11.

Robinson, Jennifer. *Ordinary Cities: Between Modernity and Development.* London: Routledge, 2006.

Rozelle, Scott, and Natalie Hell. *Invisible China: How the Urban-Rural Divide Threatens China's Rise.* Chicago: Chicago University Press, 2020.

Salaff, Janet. "The Urban Communes and Anti-City Experiment in Communist China." *The China Quarterly*, no. 29 (1967): 82–110.

Sawyer, Ralph. *Fire and Water: The Art of Incendiary and Aquatic Warfare in China.* Boulder, CO: Westview Press, 2004.

Sayre, Mary Geneva. *Missionary Triumphs in Occupied China*. Winona Lake, IN: Women's Missionary Society of the Free Methodist Church, 1945.

Schmalzer, Sigrid. *Red Revolution, Green Revolution: Scientific Farming in Socialist China*. Chicago: University of Chicago Press, 2016.

Schoppa, R. Keith. *In a Sea of Bitterness: Refugees during the Sino-Japanese War*. Cambridge, MA: Harvard University Press, 2011.

Scott, Munroe. *McClure: The China Years of Dr. Bob McClure*. Toronto: Canec Publishing and Supply House, 1977.

Sellew, Walter. *Clara Leffingwell: A Missionary*. Chicago: Free Methodist Publishing House, 1913.

Sewell, Bill. *Constructing Empire: The Japanese in Changchun*. Vancouver: University of British Columbia Press, 2019.

Shao, Qin. *Culturing Modernity: The Nantong Model, 1890–1930*. Stanford, CA: Stanford University Press, 2004.

Sheehan, Brett, and Wen-hsin Yeh, eds. *Living and Working in Wartime China*. Honolulu: University of Hawai'i Press, 2022.

Shen Songqiao. "Jingji zuowu yu jindai Henan nongcun jingji (1906–1937)—yi mianhua yu yancao wei zhongxin" 經濟作物與近代河南農村經濟 (1906–1937)——以棉花與菸草為中心 [Commercial crops and the modern Henan agricultural economy (1906–1937): A case study of cotton and tobacco]. In *Jindai Zhongguo nongcun jingji shilun wenji* 近代中國農村經濟史論文集, edited by Zhongyang yanjiuyuan jindaishi yanjiusuo, 327–78. Taipei: Zhongyang yanjiuyuan jindaishi yanjiusuo, 1989.

Shen, Tsung-han. "Food Production and Distribution for Civilian and Military Needs in Wartime China, 1937–1945." In *Nationalist China during the Sino-Japanese War, 1937–1945*, edited by Paul K. T. Sih, 167–94. Hicksville, NY: Exposition Press, 1977.

Sheng Fuyao and Chen Daiguang. "Yuejin zhong de Zhengzhou" 跃进中的郑州 [Zhengzhou in the midst of a leap forward]. *Dili zhishi* 地理知识, no. 5 (1976): 5–7.

Shepard, Wade. *Ghost Cities of China: The Story of Cities without People in the World's Most Populated Country*. London: Zed Books, 2015.

Sheridan, James. *Chinese Warlord: The Career of Feng Yü-hsiang*. Stanford, CA: Stanford University Press, 1966.

Shi Sutan. "Kangzhan qijian Rikou zai Kaifeng de qinlüe jiguan" 抗战期间日寇在开封的侵略机关 [Japanese-bandit organs of aggression in Kaifeng during the War of Resistance]. *Kaifeng wenshi ziliao* 开封文史资料, no. 19 (1999): 402–6.

Shiroyama, Tomoko. *China during the Great Depression: Market, State, and the World Economy, 1929–1937*. Cambridge, MA: Harvard University Asia Center, 2008.

Si Changyu. "Minguo shiqi Kaifeng chengshi jingji jindaihua zhuanxing yanjiu" 民国时期开封城市经济近代化转型研究 [The modernizing transformation of Kaifeng's urban economy during the Republican period]. MA thesis, Henan daxue, 2003.

Sikainga, Ahmad Alawad. *"City of Steel and Fire": A Social History of Atbara, Sudan's Railway Town.* Oxford: James Currey, 2002.

Skinner, G. William. "Introduction: Urban Development in Imperial China." In *The City in Late Imperial China,* edited by G. William Skinner, 3–31. Stanford, CA: Stanford University Press, 1977.

———. "Marketing and Social Structure in Rural China," parts 1, 2 and 3. *Journal of Asian Studies* 24, no. 1 (1964): 3–44; 2 (1965): 195–228; and 3 (1965): 363–99.

———. "Vegetable Supply and Marketing in Chinese Cities." *The China Quarterly,* no. 76 (1978): 733–93.

Smedley, Agnes. *Battle Hymn of China.* London: Victor Gollancz, 1943.

Smith, Nick. *The End of the Village: Planning the Urbanization of Rural China.* Minneapolis: University of Minnesota Press, 2021.

Snow, Edgar. *Red China Today: The Other Side of the River.* Harmondsworth: Penguin Books, 1970 [first ed. New York: Random House, 1962].

Soja, Edward. "The Socio-Spatial Dialectic." *Annals of the Association of American Geographers* 70, no. 2 (1980): 207–25.

Solinger, Dorothy. *Contesting Citizenship in Urban China: Peasant Migrants, the State, and the Logic of the Market.* Berkeley: University of California Press, 1999.

Song Zhixin. *1942: Henan dajihuang* 1942: 河南大饥荒 [1942: Henan's great famine]. Wuhan: Hubei renmin chubanshe, 2012 [revised and enlarged edition, first edition 2005].

Sorace, Christian. *Shaken Authority: China's Communist Party and the 2008 Sichuan Earthquake.* Ithaca, NY: Cornell University Press, 2010.

Stapleton, Kristin. *Civilizing Chengdu: Chinese Urban Reform, 1895–1937.* Cambridge, MA: Harvard University Asia Center, 2000.

———. *The Modern City in Asia.* Cambridge: Cambridge University Press, 2022.

———. "Outside the Gates: Chengdu's Suburbs during the Qing and Early Republic." In *Urban Morphology and the History of Civilization in East Asia,* edited by Senda Minoru, 191–210. Kyoto: Nichibunken, 2004.

———. "The Rise of Municipal Government in Early Twentieth-Century China: Local History, International Influence, and National Integration." *Twentieth-Century China* 47, no. 1 (2022): 11–19.

Steffen, Megan. "Fruits of Demolition: Generative Neglect in Zhengzhou's Urban Villages." *Positions: Asia Critique* 30, no. 3 (2022): 571–94.

———. "Unpredictability, Sociality, and Decision-Making in an Accelerating Chinese City." Ph.D. diss., Princeton University, 2016.

Strand, David. "New Chinese Cities." In *Remaking the Chinese City: Modernity and National Identity*, edited by Joseph Esherick, 211–24. Honolulu: University of Hawai'i Press, 1999.

Su Xinliu. *Minguo shiqi Henan shui han zaihai yu xiangcun shehui* 民国时期河南水旱灾害与乡村社会 [Rural society and Henan's flood and drought disasters during the Republican period]. Zhengzhou: Huanghe shuili chubanshe, 2004.

Sun Jianguo. *Xiandai Henan jingjishi* 现代河南经济史 [Economic history of contemporary Henan]. Zhengzhou: Henan daxue chubanshe, 2012.

Sun, Wanning. *Love Troubles: Inequality in China and Its Intimate Consequences*. London: Bloomsbury, 2023.

Sun Wenyu et al. *Yu E Wan Gan sisheng tudi fenlei zhi yanjiu* 豫鄂皖赣四省土地分類之研究 [A study of soil types in the four provinces of Henan, Hubei, Anhui, and Jiangxi]. Nanjing: Jinling daxue nongye jingjixi, 1936.

Sun Xiaoquan. "Zhengzhou xunri" 鄭州旬日 [Ten days in Zhengzhou]. *Lüxing zazhi* 旅行雜誌 5, no. 10 (1931): 61–64.

Tai, Jeremy. "Opening Up the Northwest: Reimagining Xi'an and the Modern Chinese Frontier." Ph.D. diss., University of California, Santa Cruz, 2015.

Tang Hao. "Tieqi maoyi, jiaotong biandong yu shizhen bianqian—yi Shanxi Yinchengzhen wei ge'an" 铁器贸易、交通变动与市镇变迁——以山西荫城镇为个案 [Ironware trade, transport changes, and the transformation of towns—taking Yinchengzhen in Shanxi as a case study]. *Chengshi shi yanjiu*, no. 44 (2021): 165–83.

Taylor, George. *The Struggle for North China*. New York: Institute of Pacific Relations, 1940.

"Te da chengshi fenfen fangkuan luohu, Wuhan Zhengzhou shei shi weilai zhongbu diyi cheng?" 特大城市纷纷放宽落户,武汉郑州谁是未来中部第一城 [Extra-large cities successively relax restrictions for settling in the city, Wuhan and Zhengzhou, which is the future no. 1 city of the Central Region?]. *Diyi caijing* 第一财经, December 13, 2019, available at https://www.yicai.com/news/100435368.html.

Thai, Philip. *China's War on Smuggling: Law, Economic Life, and the Making of the Modern State, 1842–1965*. New York: Columbia University Press, 2021.

Thaxton, Ralph. *Catastrophe and Contention in Rural China: Mao's Great Leap Famine and the Origins of Righteous Resistance in Da Fo Village*. Cambridge, UK: Cambridge University Press, 2008.

Tian Xiaofang. "Suiyue diandi" 岁月点滴 [Drips of time]. *Zhengzhou wenshi ziliao* 郑州文史资料, no. 28, part 1 (2007): 255–66.

Tilly, Charles. "Town and Country in Revolution." In *Peasant Rebellion and*

Communist Revolution in Asia, edited by John W. Lewis, 271–302. Stanford, CA: Stanford University Press, 1974.

Tōa dōbunkai, ed. *Shina shōbetsu zenshi, dai 8-kan: Kanan-shō* 支那省別全誌,第8卷:河南省 [Comprehensive gazetteer of the individual provinces of China, vol. 8: Henan Province]. Tokyo: Tōa dōbunkai, 1918.

Tōdaishi kenkyūkai, ed. *Chūgoku toshi no rekishiteki kenkyū* 中国都市の歴史的研究 [Studies of Chinese urban history]. Tokyo: Tōsui shobō, 1988.

Todd, O. J. "The Yellow River Reharnessed." *Geographical Review* 39, no. 1 (1949): 38–56.

Topik, Steven, and Allen Wells. "Commodity Chains in a Global Economy." In *A World Connecting, 1870–1945*, edited by Emily Rosenberg, 591–812. Cambridge, MA: Harvard University Press, 2012.

Tsang, Mun C., and Yanqing Ding. "Resource Utilization and Disparities in Compulsory Education in China." *China Review* 5, no. 1 (2005): 1–31.

Tsin, Michael. *Nation, Governance, and Modernity in China: Canton, 1900–1927*. Stanford, CA: Stanford University Press, 2002.

Tyner, James. *Genocide and the Geographical Imagination: Life and Death in Germany, China, and Cambodia*. Lanham, MD: Rowman and Littlefield, 2012.

Van Cleef, Eugene. "Hinterland and Umland." *Geographical Review* 31, no. 2 (1941): 308–11.

Van de Ven, Hans. *China at War: Triumph and Tragedy in the Emergence of the New China*. Cambridge, MA: Harvard University Press, 2018.

———. *War and Nationalism in China, 1925–1945*. New York: RoutledgeCurzon, 2003.

Van Duyn, Matthew. "Building Socialist Shanghai: Workers' New Villages and the Right to the City." Ph.D. diss., University of Washington, 2020.

Verdini, Giulio, Yiwen Wang, and Xiaonan Zhang, eds. *Urban China's Rural Fringe: Actors, Dimensions and Management Challenges*. Abingdon, UK: Routledge, 2016.

Wakeman, Frederic. "'Cleanup': The New Order in Shanghai." In *Dilemmas of Victory: The Early Years of the People's Republic of China*, edited by Jeremy Brown and Paul Pickowicz, 21–58. Cambridge, MA: Harvard University Press, 2007.

Walder, Andrew. "China's Extreme Inequality: The Structural Legacies of State Socialism." *The China Journal*, preprint online publication, May 12, 2023, available at https://www.journals.uchicago.edu/doi/10.1086/725576.

Walker, Kenneth. *Agricultural Development in China, 1949–1989: The Collected Papers of Kenneth R. Walker (1931–1989)*. Edited by Robert Ash. Oxford: Oxford University Press, 1998.

Wallace, Jeremy. *Cities and Stability: Urbanization, Redistribution, and Regime Survival in China*. Oxford: Oxford University Press, 2014.

Wampler, Ernest. *China Suffers; Or, My Six Years of Work during the Incident*. Elgin, IL: Brethren Publishing, 1945.

Wang, Di. *The Teahouse: Small Business, Everyday Culture, and Public Politics in Chengdu, 1900–1950*. Stanford, CA: Stanford University Press, 2008.

Wang Enxi. "Kaocha Dongnan daxue Zhengzhou mianzuo fenchang qingxing" 考察東南大學鄭州棉作分場情形 [An inspection of the situation at Southeast University's cotton branch farm in Zhengzhou]. *Nong shang gongbao* 農商公報 9, no. 3 (1922): 229–31.

Wang, Fei-ling. "Renovating the Great Floodgate: The Reform of China's Hukou System." In *One Country, Two Societies: Rural-Urban Inequality in Contemporary China*, edited by Martin Whyte, 335–64. Cambridge, MA: Harvard University Press, 2010.

Wang Guanglin. "Kangzhan shengli zai Zhengzhou shouxiang" 抗战胜利在郑州受降 [Victory in the War of Resistance—accepting the surrender at Zhengzhou]. *Erqiqu wenshi ziliao* 二七区文史资料, no. 1 (2004): 79–81.

Wang Jianguo. *Zhengzhou dadu shiqu jianshe yanjiu* 郑州大都市区建设研究 [A study of the construction of the Zhengzhou metropolitan area]. Beijing: Shehui kexue wenxian chubanshe, 2017.

Wang Jun. *Beijing Record: A Physical and Political History of Planning Modern Beijing*. Singapore: World Scientific, 2011.

Wang Junwei. "Dui chengshi renmin gongshe lishi de chubu kaocha" 对城市人民公社历史的初步考察 [A preliminary investigation into the history of urban communes]. *Dangdai Zhongguoshi yanjiu* 当代中国史研究, no. 2 (1997): 23–34.

Wang Junzhi. "Huashuo Jinshuihe" 话说金水河 [Recounting the Jinshui River]. *Zhengzhou wenshi ziliao* 郑州文史资料, no. 18 (1995): 96–102.

Wang, Liping. "Creating a National Symbol: The Sun Yatsen Memorial in Nanjing." *Republican China* 21, no. 2 (1996): 23–63.

———. "Tourism and Spatial Change in Hangzhou, 1911–1927." In *Remaking the Chinese City: Modernity and National Identity*, edited by Joseph Esherick, 65–89. Honolulu: University of Hawai'i Press, 1999.

Wang Liqi, ed. *Zhongyuan jiefangqu caizheng jingjishi ziliao xuanbian* 中原解放区财政经济史资料选编 [Selected materials on the history of government finance and the economy in the liberated districts of the Central Plains]. Beijing: Zhongguo caizheng jingji chubanshe, 1995.

Wang, Luman. *Chinese Hinterland Capitalism and Shanxi Pinghao: Banking, State, and Family, 1720–1910*. London: Routledge, 2020.

Wang Ruiming. "Zhengzhou zuizao de baihuo shangchang" 郑州最早的百货商场 [Zhengzhou's first department store] Zhengzhou wenshi ziliao 郑州文史资料, no. 15 (1994): 140.

Wang Tianjiang et al. *Henan jindai dashiji, 1840–1949 nian* 河南近代大事记, 1840–1949年 [A record of major events in modern Henan, 1840–1949]. Zhengzhou: Henan renmin chubanshe, 1990.

Wang, Wen, and Peter Moffat. "*Hukou* and Graduates' Job Search in China." *Asian Economic Journal* 22, no. 1 (2008): 1–23.

Wang, Xuefeng, and John Tomaney. "Zhengzhou—Political Economy of an Emerging Chinese Megacity." *Cities* 84 (2019): 104–11.

Wang Yan. "Guangyi chengxiang yitihua de neihan jieding yu pingjia fenxi—yi Zhengzhou wei li" 广义城乡一体化的内涵界定与评价分析——以郑州为例 [A broad definition of the content of rural-urban integration and critical evaluation: A case study of Zhengzhou]. *Quyu jingji* 区域经济 10, no. 1 (2011): 36–38.

Wang Yaowu and Zhang Yang. "Zhengzhou shi chengzhongcun diaocha yanjiu" 郑州市城中村调查研究 [Survey of Zhengzhou's villages-in-the-city]. *Wuhan zhiye jishu xueyuan xuebao* 武汉职业技术学院学报 10, no. 1 (2011): 19–22.

Wang Yongchuan. "1945 nian zhi 1948 nian Zhengzhou jianwen" 1945年至1948年郑州见闻 [Things seen and heard in Zhengzhou, 1945–1948]. *Henan wenshi ziliao* 河南文史资料, no. 32 (1989): 91–120.

Wang Youqiao. *Henan fang yu renwen zhilüe* 河南方舆人文志略 [A survey of geography and humanities in Henan]. Beijing: Xibei shuju, 1932.

Wang Yufeng and Cai Jiansheng, "Wang Hui jiangjun de Zhengzhou qingjie" 王辉将军的郑州情结 [General Wang Hui's Zhengzhou complex]. *Zhengzhou wenshi ziliao* 郑州文史资料, no. 28, part 1 (2007): 11–17.

Weber, Isabella. *How China Escaped Shock Therapy: The Market Reform Debate.* London: Routledge, 2021.

Webster, Douglas. "An Overdue Agenda: Systematizing East Asian Peri-Urban Research." *Pacific Affairs* 84, no. 4 (2011): 631–42.

Wegren, S. K. "The Rise, Fall and Transformation of the Rural Social Contract in Russia." *Communist and Post-Communist Studies* 36, no. 1 (2003): 1–27.

Wei Yingtao. *Jindai Changjiang shangyou chengxiang guanxi yanjiu* 近代长江上游城乡关系研究 [Urban-rural relations in the Upper Yangtze in the modern period]. Chengdu: Tiandi chubanshe, 2003.

Weil, Robert. "Conditions of the Working Classes in China." *Monthly Review* 58, no. 2 (2006): 25–48.

Wemheuer, Felix. *A Social History of Maoist China: Conflict and Change, 1949–1976.* Cambridge: Cambridge University Press, 2019.

———. *Steinnudeln: Ländliche Erinnerungen und staatliche Vergangenheitsbewältigung der "Großen-Sprung" Hungersnot in der chinesischen Provinz Henan* [Stone noodles: Rural memories and state dealing with the past of the "Great Leap" famine in the Chinese province of Henan]. Frankfurt: Peter Lang, 2007.

Westlund, Hans. "Urban-Rural Relations in the Post-Urban World." In *In the Post-Urban World: Emergent Transformation of Cities and Regions in the Innovative Global Economy*, edited by Tigran Haas and Hans Westlund, 70–81. London: Routledge, 2017.

White, Richard. *Railroaded: The Transcontinentals and the Making of Modern America*. New York: W. W. Norton, 2011.

White, Theodore, and Annalee Jacoby. *Thunder out of China*. London: Victor Gollancz, 1946.

Wilson, Scott. *Tigers without Teeth: The Pursuit of Justice in Contemporary China*. Lanham, MD: Rowman and Littlefield, 2015.

"Wo jiushi nimen kouzhong suoshuo de Zhengpiao" 我就是你们口中所说的郑漂 [I am what you call a *Zhengpiao*]. *Shijian* 世间, no. 2 (2018): 111–12.

Wou, Odoric Y. K. "The Chinese Communist Party and the Labor Movement: The May 30th Movement in Henan." *Chinese Studies in History* 23, no. 1 (1989): 70–104.

———. "Development, Underdevelopment and Degeneration: The Introduction of Rail Transport into Honan." *Asian Profile* 12, no. 3 (1984): 215–30.

———. *Mobilizing the Masses: Building Revolution in Henan*. Stanford, CA: Stanford University Press, 1994.

Wu Caixia. "Shixi Henan sheng wenge de jige tedian" 试析河南省文革的几个特点 [An experimental analysis of several features of the Cultural Revolution in Henan Province]. *Huaxia wenzhai* 华夏文摘, no. 335 (2003). Also available at http://www.cnd.org/HXWZ/ZK03/zk335.gb.html.

Wu Huimin. "Shengde Zhongxue zai Bishangang de shimo" 圣德中学在碧沙岗的始末 [The full story of Shengde Middle School at Bishangang]. *Zhengzhou wenshi ziliao* 郑州文史资料, no. 4 (1988): 20–21.

Wu Pengfei. "Kaifeng chengshi shengming zhouqi tanxi" 开封城市生命周期探析 [An inquiry and analysis of the life cycle of Kaifeng]. *Jianghan luntan* 江汉论坛, no. 1 (2013): 121–28.

Wu, Shellen Xiao. *Empires of Coal: Fueling China's Entry into the Modern World Order, 1860–1920*. Stanford, CA: Stanford University Press, 2015.

Wu Shixun. *Henan* 河南 [Henan]. Shanghai: Zhonghua shuju, 1936 [orig. 1927].

Wu Sizuo. *Zhongyuan chengshi shilüe* 中原城市史略 [An outline history of the cities of the Central Plains]. Wuhan: Hubei renmin chubanshe, 1980.

Xia Yuan et al. *Zhugan hepan zhiqing suiyue: jinian Henan sheng Zhengzhou shi laosanjie zhiqing fu Xinyang Luoshan xian Zhugan gongshe xiaxiang chadui wushi zhounian, 1968–2018* 竹竿河畔知青岁月——纪念河南省郑州市老三届知青赴信阳罗山县竹竿公社下乡插队五十周年 1968–2018 [Years of the educated youth on the banks of the Zhugan River: Commemorating fifty years since the Henan Zhengzhou "Three Old Classes" educated youth were sent down to join work teams in Zhugan Commune, Luoshan County, Xinyang, 1968–2018]. Self-published, 2019.

Xiao Feng and Wang Junzhi. "Wushi niandai qianqi Zhengzhou shi de chengshi guihua he shenghui qian Zheng" 五十年代前期郑州市的城市规划和省会迁郑 [City planning in Zhengzhou during the early 1950s and the move of the provincial capital to Zhengzhou]. *Henan wenshi ziliao* 河南文史资料, no. 73 (2000): 85–93.

Xiao Zhentao. "Zhengzhou shi chengzhongcun gaizao zhong liudong renkou wenti diaocha fenxi" 郑州市城中村改造中流动人口问题调查分析 [Survey and analysis of the issue of the floating population in Zhengzhou's villages-in-the-city redevelopment]. *Xue lilun* 学理论, no. 7 (2015): 122–23.

Xiao-Planes, Xiaohong. "Un contestataire de la politique agricole de Mao Zedong: Deng Zihui en 1953–1962" [A dissenter against the agricultural policy of Mao Zedong: Deng Zihui in 1953–1962]. *Études Chinoises* 34, no. 2 (2015): 121–61.

Xie Xiaopeng. *Jindai Zhengzhou chengshi bianqian yanjiu* 近代郑州城市变迁研究 [Urban changes in modern Zhengzhou]. Zhengzhou: Henan renmin chubanshe, 2016.

———. "Kangzhan shiqi Henan lunxianqu yanjiu de huigu yu zhanwang" 抗战时期河南沦陷区研究的回顾与展望 [Research on occupied Henan during the War of Resistance: Review and prospects]. *Henan daxue xuebao* 河南大学学报 56, no. 4 (2016): 139–44.

———. "1954 nian Henan shenghui you Bian qian Zheng de lishi kaolü" 1954年河南省会由汴迁郑的历史考虑 [A historical consideration of the 1954 move of the Henan provincial capital from Kaifeng to Zhengzhou]. *Dangdai Zhongguoshi yanjiu* 当代中国史研究 18, no. 6 (2011): 39–46.

Xie Yingjun, Geng Zhanjing, and Li Qiaosong. "Dui Zhengzhou shi shucai tizhi gaige de yijian" 对郑州市蔬菜体制改革的意见 [A view on reform in the Zhengzhou City vegetable system]. *Jingji tansuo* 经济探索, 1984 supplementary issue: 38–40.

Xigang cunzhi bianzuan weiyuanhui, ed. *Xigang cunzhi* 西岗村志 [Xigang Village gazetteer]. Zhengzhou: Self-published, 2014.

Xing, Guoxin. "Living with the Revolutionary Legacy: Communication, Culture and Workers' Radicalism in Post-Mao China." Ph.D. diss., Simon Fraser University, 2011.

Xing Hansan. *Riwei tongzhi Henan jianwenlu* 日伪统治河南见闻录 [A record of Japanese-puppet rule in Henan based on personal knowledge]. Kaifeng: Henan daxue chubanshe, 1986.

Xiong Yaping. "Du 'Zhonghua minguo zhuanti shi di jiu juan chengshihua jincheng yanjiu'—jian ji jindai huabei quyu chengshihua yanjiu de ruogan quxiang" 读《中华民国专题史第九卷城市化进程研究》——兼及近代华北区域城市史研究的若干趋向 [Review of *Thematic Histories of the Republican Period*, vol. 9: *The Process of Urbanization*, and some directions in the regional urban history of modern North China]. *Hebei guangbo dianshi daxue xuebao* 河北广播电视大学学报 21, no. 1 (2016): 9–12.

———. *Tielu yu Huabei xiangcun shehui de bianqian, 1880–1937* 铁路与华北乡村社会的变迁, 1880–1937 [Railways and the transformation of rural society in North China, 1880–1937]. Beijing: Renmin chubanshe, 2011.

Xu, Bin. *Chairman Mao's Children: Generation and the Politics of Memory in China*. Cambridge: Cambridge University Press, 2021.

Xu Daofu. *Zhongguo jindai nongye shengchan ji maoyi tongji ziliao* 中国近代农业生产及贸易统计资料 [Statistical materials on agricultural production and trade in modern China]. Shanghai: Shanghai renmin chubanshe, 1983.

Xu Lianshan and Wang Zongmin, eds. *Zhengzhou kangzhan jianshi* 郑州抗战简史 [A short history of the War of Resistance in Zhengzhou]. Zhengzhou: Zhonggong Zhengzhou shiwei dangshi yanjiushi, 2005.

Xu Xuelin. *Zhongguo lidai xingzheng quhua* 中国历代行政区划 [The administrative divisions of China through history]. Hefei: Anhui jiaoyu chubanshe, 1991.

Xu Youli. "Zhengzhou jian 'shi' de lishi kaolü" 郑州建'市'的历史考录 [A historical consideration of the establishment of Zhengzhou "City"]. *Huanghe jishu daxue xuebao* 黄河技术大学学报 14, no. 1 (2012): 20–24.

Xue, Charlie Q. L., Ying Wang, and Luther Tsai. "Building New Towns in China—A Case Study of Zhengdong New District." *Cities* 30 (2013): 223–32.

Yang Chunyu. "Zhengzhou fei gongyouzhi jingji yanjiu, 1980–2000" 郑州非公有制经济研究, 1980–2000 [Zhengzhou's non-state-owned economy, 1980–2000]. MA thesis, Xinjiang shifan daxue, 2022.

Yang Jianyun. "Zhengzhou huji jifen zhi gaige de silu" 郑州户籍积分制改革的思路 [Thoughts on the reform of Zhengzhou's household registration points system]. *Changjiang luntan* 长江论坛, no. 137 (2016): 67–71.

Yang Jisheng. *Tombstone: The Untold Story of Mao's Great Famine*. Abridged and translated by Stacy Mosher and Guo Jian. London: Allen Lane, 2012 [orig. 2008].

Yang Min. "Kaifeng, Kaifeng!" 开封, 开封! [Kaifeng, Kaifeng!]. *Juece* 决策, no. 7 (2008): 13–15.

Yang Zhenxing. "Zhengzhou tuoxian ji" 鄭州脫險記 [Record of an escape from Zhengzhou] *Pinghanlu kan* 平漢路刊, nos. 111–117 (December 5–23, 1948).

Yeh, Anthony Gar-On, and Zifeng Chen. "From Cities to Super Mega City Regions in China in a New Wave of Urbanisation and Economic Transition: Issues and Challenges." *Urban Studies* 57, no. 3 (2020): 636–54.

Yong Mu. "Gege cong Zhengzhou lai" 哥哥從鄭州來 [My older brother came from Zhengzhou]. *Daxue pinglun* 大學評論 2, no. 7 (1948): 10–11.

You He. "Zhengzhou Huijiao gaikuang" 鄭州回教概況 [A survey of Islam in

Zhengzhou]. *Chenxi xunkan* 晨喜旬刊 1, nos. 24–26 (combined issue, 1935): 31–33.

Young, Arthur. *China's Wartime Finance and Inflation*. Cambridge, MA: Harvard University Press, 1965.

Yue Guoding. "Houzhai zhiqing shiqilian" 侯寨知青十七连 [No. 17 Brigade of the Houzhai Educated Youth]. *Zhengzhou wenshi ziliao* 郑州文史资料, no. 28, part 2 (2007): 247–49.

"Yufeng jian ding" 豫豐減錠 [Yufeng mill cuts spindles]. *Fangzhi shibao* 紡織 時報, no. 816 (1931): 938.

Zanasi, Margherita. *Saving the Nation: Economic Modernity in Republican China*. Chicago: University of Chicago Press, 2006.

Zeng Qiji. "Ye Gong zhu Zheng banian" 叶公主郑八年 [Ye Gong's eight years governing Zhengzhou]. *Zhengzhou wenshi xiliao* 郑州文史资料, no. 3 (1987): 23–28.

Zhang Henshui. "Xiyou xiaoji" 西遊小記 [Jottings from a journey to the West]. *Lüxing zazhi* 旅行雜誌 8, no. 9 (1934): 7–10.

Zhang Jiangao. "Zhengzhou bu rang nongmin guache jincheng bushi ge xiao wenti" 郑州不让农民瓜车进城不是个小问题 [Zhengzhou not allowing peasant melon carts to enter the city is not a small issue]. *Xinhua meiri dianxun* 新华每日电讯, May 13, 2004.

Zhang Jingyu. "Henan jianshe zhi huigu yu qianzhan" 河南建設之回顧與前 瞻 [Henan construction: Reflections and outlook]. *Zhongguo jianshe* 中國建 設 13, nos. 1–2 (1936): 143–53 (part 1) and 45–94 (part 2).

Zhang, Li. *In Search of Paradise: Middle-Class Living in a Chinese Metropolis*. Ithaca, NY: Cornell University Press, 2010.

———. *Strangers in the City: Reconfigurations of Space, Power, and Social Networks within China's Floating Population*. Stanford, CA: Stanford University Press, 2002.

Zhang, Ling. *The River, the Plain, and the State: An Environmental Drama in Northern Song China, 1048–1128*. Cambridge: Cambridge University Press, 2016.

Zhang Nan. "1948–1953 nian Zhengzhou shi shehui gaizao yanjiu" 1948–1953年 郑州市社会改造研究 [Study of social transformation in Zhengzhou, 1948– 1953]. MA thesis, Zhengzhou daxue, 2012.

Zhang Qixian and Wu Xiaoya. *Dangdai Zhengzhou chengshi jianshe* 当代郑州 城市建设 [The urban construction of contemporary Zhengzhou]. Beijing: Zhongguo jianzhu gongye chubanshe, 1988.

Zhang Ruide. *Ping-Han tielu yu Huabei de jingji fazhan* 平漢鐵路與華北的 經濟發展 [The Beijing–Hankou Railroad and the economic development of North China]. Taipei: Zhongyang yanjiuyuan jindaishi yanjiusuo, 1987.

Zhang Weici. *Shizheng zhidu* 市政制度 [Systems of municipal administration]. Shanghai: Dongya tushuguan, 2007 reprint [orig. 1925].

Zhang Wensheng. "Chengzhenhua jincheng zhong de jiaoqu nongmin zhiye zhuanxing yanjiu: yi Zhengzhou shi Gouzhaocun wei li" 城镇化进程中的郊区农民职业转型研究——以郑州市沟赵村为例 [A study of the occcupational transformation of suburban peasants in the process of urbanization: Taking Gouzhao Village in Zhengzhou as case study]. MA thesis, Zhengzhou daxue, 2013.

Zhang, Xiaobo. "Fiscal Decentralization and Political Centralization in China: Implications for Growth and Inequality." *Journal of Comparative Economics* 34, no. 4 (2006): 713–26.

Zhang, Xiaobo, Yang Jin, and Wang Shenglin. "China Has Reached the Lewis Turning Point." *China Economic Review* 22, no. 4 (2011): 542–54.

Zhang Xichang. "Henan sheng nongcun diaocha 河南省農村調查 [A survey of the countryside in Henan Province]. *Zhongguo nongcun* 中國農村 1, no. 2 (1934): 47–63.

Zhang, Xin. *The Global in the Local: A Century of War, Commerce, and Technology in China*. Cambridge, MA: Harvard University Press, 2023.

———. *Social Transformation in Modern China: The State and Local Elites in Henan, 1900–1937*. Cambridge: Cambridge University Press, 2000.

Zhang Xingjun. "Zhengzhou: jinzhi nongyongche jincheng, guanong youxin" 郑州:禁止农用车进城, 瓜农忧心 [Zhengzhou: Farm vehicles barred from entering the city, melon farmers anxious]. *Xinhua meiri dianxun* 新华每日电讯, May 26, 2005.

Zhang Yanqing. "Zhengzhou mianhang jiuwen" 郑州棉行旧闻 [Old stories of the Zhengzhou cotton firms]. *Henan wenshi ziliao* 河南文史资料, no. 44 (1992 [orig. 1965]): 15–18.

Zhang Yiwen. "Kaifeng chengshi jianshe de fazhan" 开封城市建设的发展 [The development of urban construction in Kaifeng]. *Kaifeng wenshi ziliao* 开封文史资料, no. 11 (1991): 1–12.

Zhang, Yu. *Going to the Countryside: The Rural in the Modern Chinese Cultural Imagination, 1915–1965*. Ann Arbor: University of Michigan Press, 2020.

Zhang, Yuting. "Employment Policy and Sustainable Livelihoods of Landless Peasants in China: A Study in Zhengdong New Area." MS thesis, Columbia University, 2016.

Zhang Zhenzhi. "Bian Zheng Luo shengyou ji" 汴鄭洛勝遊記 [A pleasure trip to Kaifeng, Zhengzhou, and Luoyang]. *Jianguo yuekan* 建國月刊 2, no. 1 (1929): 78–87; and 2, no. 3 (1930): 105–12.

Zhang Zhonglu. "Guanyu yijiusi'er nian Henan dajihuang de jianwen" 关于一九四二年河南大饥荒的见闻 [Things seen and heard during the Henan famine of 1942]. *Kaifeng wenshi ziliao* 开封文史资料, no. 5 (1986): 294–99.

Zhao Fuhai. *Lao Zhengzhou: minsu shengdi Laofenggang* 老郑州:民俗圣地

老坟岗 [Old Zhengzhou: A sacred place for folk customs, Laofengang]. Zhengzhou: Henan renmin chubanshe, 2008.

———. *Lao Zhengzhou: Shangdu laozihao* 老郑州: 商都老字号 [Old Zhengzhou: The old businesses of the Shang capital]. Zhengzhou: Henan renmin chubanshe, 2009.

———. *Lao Zhengzhou: Shangdu yimeng* 老郑州: 商都遗梦 [Old Zhengzhou: Inherited dreams of the Shang capital]. Zhengzhou: Henan renmin chubanshe, 2004.

Zhao Guangyu. "Zhengzhou 'jiefang' hou de zhenxiang" 郑州"解放"後的真相 [The real situation in Zhengzhou after "liberation"]. *Zhongguo xinwen* 中國新聞 (Nanjing), December 16, 1948.

Zhao Jianhua. "Nongye duoyuan jiazhi daoxiang xia Zhengzhou chengjiao yinong shequ fazhan yanjiu" 农业多元价值导向下郑州城郊宜农社区发展研究 [A study of the development of agriculture-appropriate communities in Zhengzhou's urban fringe from the perspective of the multiple values of agriculture]. Ph.D. diss., Huanan ligong daxue, 2014.

Zhao Litao. "Chinese Society in 2019: Navigating Another Bumpy Year." *East Asian Policy* 12, no. 1 (2020): 32–44.

Zhao Shuling. "Zhengzhou chengshi kongjian kuozhan ji qi dui chengjiao jingji de yingxiang" 郑州城市空间扩展及其对城郊经济的影响 [The spatial expansion of Zhengzhou City and its effects on the economy of the city suburbs]. *Diyu yanjiu yu kaifa* 地域研究与开发 23, no. 3 (2004): 49–57.

Zhen Mou. "Huanghe xianshang de Zhengzhou" 黄河線上的鄭州 [Zhengzhou on the Yellow River front line]. *Guoxun* 國訊, nos. 245–46 (combined issue, 1940): 10.

Zheng Fazhan. "Jindai Henan renkou wenti yanjiu (1912–1953)" 近代河南人口問題研究 (1912–1953) [A study of population issues in modern Henan (1912–1953)]. Ph.D. diss., Fudan daxue, 2010.

Zheng Xiangqian. "Zhengzhou zuizao de gongyuan" 郑州最早的公园 [Zhengzhou's first park]. *Zhengzhou wenshi ziliao* 郑州文史资料, no. 15 (1994): 144–45.

Zhengxie Zhengzhou shi Erqiqu weiyuanhui, ed. *Yuanqu zhi jiyi: Erqiqu chengxiang jian zhi cun mu* 远去之记忆: 二七区城乡建置存目 [Distant memories: Surviving catalogues of the establishment of city and countryside in Erqi District]. Zhengzhou: Zhongzhou guji chubanshe, 2015.

"Zhengzhou de jingji gaikuang" 鄭州的經濟概況 [The economic situation in Zhengzhou]. *Yinhang tongxun* 銀行通訊 1, no. 4 (1940): 5a–6a.

"Zhengzhou ji qi linjing zhi diaocha" 鄭州及其鄰境之調查 [A survey of Zhengzhou and its neighboring places]. *Dalu yinhang yuekan* 大陸銀行月刊 2, no. 8 (1924): 59–61.

"Zhengzhou nongcun zuoheshe [sic] diaocha" 鄭州農村作合社調查 [A survey of cooperatives in rural Zhengzhou]. *Waibu zhoukan* 外部周刊, no. 37 (1934): 24–26.

"Zhengzhou nongmin weiji yanzhong" 鄭州農民危機嚴重 [Serious crisis for Zhengzhou's peasants]. *Tianjia banyuebao* 田家半月報 13, no. 15 (1947): 2.

"Zhengzhou shangbu zhi fada" 鄭州商埠之發達 [The development of Zhengzhou trading port]. *Nanyang shangwu bao* 南洋商務報, no. 28 (1907): 3.

"Zhengzhou shangye jinrong diaocha ji" 鄭州商業金融調查記 [Record of a survey of Zhengzhou's commerce and banking]. *Xinwenbao* 新聞報, April 13–17, 1922.

Zhengzhou shi chengshi guihua guanliju, ed. *Zhengzhou shi chengshi fenqu guihua tuji* 郑州市城市分区规划图集 [Planning atlas for Zhengzhou City subdistricts]. Zhengzhou: Zhengzhou shi renmin zhengfu, 1989.

Zhengzhou shi chengxiang guihuaju, ed. *Zhengzhou chengxiang guihua 2017* 郑州城乡规划 2017 [Urban-rural planning of Zhengzhou, 2017]. Zhengzhou: Chengxiang guihuaju, 2018.

Zhengzhou shi dang'anguan, ed. *Zhengzhou jiefang* 郑州解放 [The liberation of Zhengzhou]. Zhengzhou: Zhongguo dang'an chubanshe, 2009.

Zhengzhou shi difang shizhi bianzuan weiyuanhui, ed. *Zhengzhou shizhi* 郑州市志 [Zhengzhou City gazetteer]. 8 vols. Zhengzhou: Zhongzhou guji chubanshe, 1997–2000.

———. *Zhengzhou shizhi, 1991–2000* 郑州市志, 1991–2000 [Zhengzhou City gazetteer, 1991–2000]. 6 vols. Zhengzhou: Zhongzhou guji chubanshe, 2009.

Zhengzhou shi gongshangye lianhehui, ed. *Zhengzhou gongshangye xingshuai shi gaikuang, 1904–1948* 郑州工商业兴衰史概况, 1904–1948 (A survey history of the rise and fall of industry and commerce in Zhengzhou, 1904–1948). Zhengzhou: Zhengzhou shi gongshangye lianhehui, 1984.

Zhengzhou shi jianshe weiyuanhui, ed. *Zhengzhou shi chengshi jianshe guanli zanxing guize* 郑州市城市建设管理暂行规则 [Provisional regulations for administration of urban construction in Zhengzhou City]. Zhengzhou: n.p., May 7, 1959.

———. "Zhengzhou shi chengxiang jianshe zhi (songshen gao)" 郑州市城乡建设志 (送审稿) [Zhengzhou City rural and urban construction gazetteer (draft sent for approval)]. Unpublished manuscript, 1993.

———. *Zhengzhou shi jianshe zhi* 郑州市建设志 [Construction gazetteer of Zhengzhou City]. Zhengzhou: Zhongzhou guji chubanshe, 2005.

Zhengzhou shi jianwei guihua guanlichu. "Zhengzhou shi de chengshi guihua ji jianshe" 郑州市的城市规划及建设 [Urban planning and construction in Zhengzhou City]. *Jianzhu xuebao* 建筑学报, no. 11 (1959): 13–16.

Zhengzhou shi jiaoqu liangshiju, ed. *Zhengzhou shi jiaoqu zhi: liangshi zhi* 郑州市郊区志:粮食志 [Zhengzhou suburban gazetteer: Grain gazetteer]. Zhengzhou: Zhengzhou shi jiaoqu liangshiju, 1986.

Zhengzhou shi jiaoqu minzheng zhi bianxie zu, ed. "Zhengzhou shi jiaoqu minzheng zhi (zhengqiu yijian gao)" 郑州市郊区民政志(征求意见稿)

[Zhengzhou suburbs civil administration gazetteer (draft for seeking suggestions)]. Unpublished manuscript, 1985.

Zhengzhou shi jiaoqu zhi bianzuan weiyuanhui, ed. "Zhengzhou shi jiaoqu zhi (zhengqiu yijian gao), Baizhuang zhi" 郑州市郊区志(征求意见稿),白庄志 [Zhengzhou suburbs gazetteer (draft for seeking suggestions), Baizhuang gazetteer]. Unpublished manuscript, 1985.

———. "Zhengzhou shi jiaoqu zhi (zhengqiu yijian gao), nongye zhi" 郑州市郊区志(征求意见稿),农业志 [Zhengzhou suburbs gazetteer (draft for seeking suggestions), agriculture gazetteer]. Unpublished manuscript, 1986.

Zhengzhou shi shehui kexuejie lianhehui, ed. *Zhengzhou jingji shehui fazhan wenti yanjiu* 郑州经济社会发展问题研究 [A study of issues in the development of Zhengzhou's economy and society]. Zhengzhou: Henan renmin chubanshe, 2001.

Zhengzhou shi zenyang ban chengshi de renmin gongshe (wenda) 郑州市怎样办城市的人民公社(问答) [How does Zhengzhou run the city's communes: Questions and answers]. Beijing: Tongsu duwu chubanshe, 1958.

"Zhengzhou shi zhishi qingnian shangshan xiaxiang qingkuang zongshu" 郑州市知识青年上山下乡情况综述 [General narrative of the situation of Zhengzhou's sent-down educated youth]. *Zhengzhou wenshi ziliao* 郑州文史资料, no. 28, part 1 (2007): 1–10.

Zhengzhou tielu fenju shizhi bianzuan weiyuanhui, eds. *Zhengzhou tielu fenju zhi* 郑州铁路分局志 [Gazetteer of the Zhengzhou Railway Sub-bureau]. Beijing: Zhongguo tiedao chubanshe, 1997.

Zhiqing yinxiang: Zhengzhou jiaoqu Huayuankou Wuqi qingnian nongchang Yilian xiaxiang sishi zhounian jinian wenzhang xuanbian 知青印象:郑州郊区花园口五七青年农场一连下乡四十周年纪念文章选编 [Impressions of the educated youth: Selected articles commemorating the fortieth anniversary of the sending to the countryside of the First Brigade of the Seventh May Youth Farm at Huanyuankou in the Zhengzhou suburbs]. Self-published, 2012.

Zhonggong Henan shengwei dangshi yanjiushi, ed. *Henan sheng kangzhan sunshi diaocha* 河南省抗战损失调查 [A survey of losses in Henan Province during the War of Resistance against Japan]. 2 vols. Beijing: Zhonggong dangshi chubanshe, 2010.

———. *Henan sheng "yiwu" jihua he guojia zhongdian gongcheng jianshe* 河南省"一五"计划和国家重点工程建设 [The First Five-Year Plan in Henan Province and the key state construction projects]. Zhengzhou: Henan renmin chubanshe, 1999.

Zhonggong Henan shengwei ji Zhengzhou shiwei. *Zhengzhou shi gaikuang (neibu wenjian)* 郑州市概况(内部文件) [A survey of Zhengzhou city (internal document)]. Zhengzhou: Guoji huodong zhidao weiyuanhui bangongshi, June 1957.

Zhongguo di'er lishi dang'anguan, ed. *Zhonghua minguoshi dang'an ziliao huibian* 中华民国史档案资料汇编 [Compiled archival materials on Republican period history]. Nanjing: Jiangsu renmin chubanshe, 1994.

Zhou, Kate Xiao. *How the Farmers Changed China: Power of the People*. Boulder, CO: Westview Press, 1996.

Zhu Junxian. "Bianyuan yu zhongxin de huhuan: jindai Kaifeng yu Zhengzhou chengshi jiegou guanxi biandong yanjiu" 边缘与中心的互换:近代开封与郑州城市结构关系变动研究 [The exchange of periphery and center: Changes in the urban structural relations of Kaifeng and Zhengzhou]. *Shixue yuekan* 史学月刊, no. 6 (2012): 99–106.

———. "Wuxu shengcheng yu jindai Zhengzhou chengshi kongjian jiegou zhi biandong" 无序生成与近代郑州城市空间结构之变动 [Disorderly formation and changes in modern Zhengzhou City's spatial structure]. *Henan gongye daxue xuebao* 河南工业大学学报 7, no. 3 (2011): 84–90.

———. *Yin ge zhi bian: Zhongyuan quyu zhongxin chengshi de jindai bianqian* 因革之变:中原区域中心城市的近代变迁 [Transformations of inheritance and renovation: Modern change in the central cities of the Central Plains region]. Taiyuan: Shanxi renmin chubanshe, 2013.

———. "Zhengzhou chengshi guihua yu kongjian jiegou bianqian yanjiu" 郑州城市规划与空间结构变迁研究 [Zhengzhou urban planning and changes in spatial structure]. *Chengshi guihua* 城市规划 35, no. 8 (2011): 44–49.

Zhu, Pingchao. *Wartime Culture in Guilin, 1938–1944: A City at War*. Lanham, MD: Lexington Books, 2015.

Zhu Xiangwu. "Wo zai Zhengzhou shi congshi tongzhan gongzuo de jingli" 我在郑州市从事统战工作的经历 [My experience of united front work in Zhengzhou]. *Zhengzhou wenshi ziliao* 郑州文史资料, no. 23 (2002): 25–49.

Zhuang Xiao, ed. *Dangdai shiren song Zhengzhou* 当代诗人颂郑州 [Contemporary poets praise Zhengzhou]. Zhengzhou: Henan wenyu chubanshe, 1999.

"Zuijin Zhengzhou jinrong shang kuang diaocha lu" 最近郑州金融商况調查錄 [Record of a survey of Zhengzhou's recent financial trade]. *Yinhang zhoubao* 銀行週報 3, no. 14 (1919): 23.

Zung, G. S. "Marshall Feng and Rural Reconstruction." *The Chinese Recorder* 59, no. 8 (1928): 523–25.

Zuo Jinggang. "Dui chengshi jiaoqu shucai shengchan zhong de wenti yu jianyi" 对城市郊区蔬菜生产中的问题与建议 [Problems and proposals concerning the production of vegetables in the suburbs of cities]. *Henan jingji* 河南经济, no. 7 (1984): 68–70.

GLOSSARY-INDEX

Harvard East Asian Monographs
(most recent titles)